PENGUIN REFERENCE BOOKS

The Penguin Dictionary of Clichés

Julia Cresswell has written a number of other reference books, including the *Guinness Book of British Place Names* (with Fred McDonald) and the *Bloomsbury Dictionary of First Names*. She has also worked on several large reference works including the *Shorter Oxford English Dictionary* and the *Encarta World English Dictionary*.

Educated at Oxford and Reading universities, she holds degrees in Medieval Literature and the History of Language, and Medieval Studies, and has taught Medieval Literature and History of English at various Oxford colleges and at the English branches of major American universities. She is married with a son and lives in Oxford.

GW00507306

The Penguin Dictionary of

Clichés

Julia Cresswell

PENGUIN BOOKS

PENGUIN BOOKS

Published by the Penguin Group
Penguin Books Ltd, 27 Wrights Lane, London w8 5tz, England
Penguin Putnam Inc., 375 Hudson Street, New York, New York 10014, USA
Penguin Books Australia Ltd, Ringwood, Victoria, Australia
Penguin Books Canada Ltd, 10 Alcorn Avenue, Toronto, Ontario, Canada m4v 3b2
Penguin Books (NZ) Ltd, Private Bag 102902, NSMC, Auckland, New Zealand

Penguin Books Ltd, Registered Offices: Harmondsworth, Middlesex, England

First published 2000
10 9 8

Copyright © Julia Cresswell, 2000
All rights reserved

Set in 7.5/9.5pt ITC Stone
Typeset by Rowland Phototypesetting Ltd, Bury St Edmunds, Suffolk
Printed in England by Mackays of Chatham Ltd, Chatham, Kent

One of the most difficult aspects of writing this book was providing the definitions of some of the clichés. This is not because I did not know what they meant; but because, while 'everybody' may know what a given cliché means in a vague way, it may not actually have a precise meaning, more a mood or feeling that it evokes within a vague sense area. This nebulous quality, found in some but by no means all clichés, moves us towards a definition of what a cliché is. The difficulty of defining what a cliché is has in itself become a cliché of writing on clichés. When people refer to someone's style as being clichéd, or complain that an expression is a cliché, they usually mean that it irritates them; that they find the words trite, or that the phrasing grates on their ears. This is a highly subjective, personal reaction, and it is this very subjectivity that makes defining a cliché so difficult. While the subjective element is inescapable, it will obviously not do as a basis on which to compile a whole dictionary. The key element in what makes an expression a cliché must be over-use. This is one of the few things that everyone seems to agree on. However, that does not mean that everyone agrees which expressions are over-used. This is in part because many clichés are the result of fashion. 'Sick as a parrot' is an expression that people will often cite as a cliché. In fact, the excessive use of this was a passing fashion – footballers are now 'gutted' instead – and you will rarely find it used today except as what I have called a conscious cliché: an expression used deliberately as a cliché, as it were in invisible inverted commas, to create a special effect. I have called expressions which go in and out of fashion in this way vogue clichés; but even when clichés are more than passing fashions, there is still a gradual turnover of those in use. Eric Partridge compiled a dictionary of clichés in 1940, and while there is a core of clichés which have remained in use since it was published, there are also a large number which are now totally obsolete – such as 'leather and prunella' for 'something to which one is quite indifferent' – and many which seem old-fashioned poeticisms ('leonine locks', 'minion of fortune'); while many of the large number of Latin tags which he included would now seem hopelessly pretentious, rather than clichéd, if used today.

Despite the changes brought about by fashion, many of the expressions in this book are very old, although they may not have been clichés all their lives. Many are borrowed from Greek or Latin, and others have been in continuous use since the Middle Ages. 'Hither and thither', recorded from about 725 AD, has the longest continuous use in English of any phrase in the book, although a number of others are nearly as old. In many ways, despite the element of constant innovation, the English language is very conservative. Even if something has long been obsolete in everyday life, it can survive in the language once it has become established there.

Thus we still describe something as 'done to a turn' even though oven roasting has long replaced roasting meat on a spit in front of an open fire. Because of the enormous range in dates for these expressions and the variety of their sources, I have tried whenever possible to give some idea of when they are first recorded, when they became clichés and where they come from. Many of the older expressions are what I have called set phrases – words that have become fixed in the language as a group, often after they have become obsolete outside this group – so that 'yore' is only found in 'in days of yore', 'deserts' is rare unless coupled with 'just', and 'bounden' firmly linked to 'duty'. English is full of these set phrases, and I have only been able to include a small proportion. Many set phrases are what are known as 'doublets': expressions where two words of near or identical meaning are linked by 'and', as in 'dim and distant', 'fair and square'. Many of these come from disciplines such as law or theology, where the user wanted to be sure that he had covered all eventualities. Others are fixed in the language because they have survived from the fifteenth to the seventeenth century, a period when such doublets were very fashionable and using them was thought to add elegance to your style.

Some readers may feel that not all the set phrases I have listed here are clichés, which is one reason I have used the expression 'set phrase', as a way to fudge the issue. They may feel that some of the set phrases, and some other expressions, are idioms and not clichés. This is one of the more subjective areas of assessing clichédom. There is an area in which cliché and idiom overlap, but in general, if there is no other natural way of saying something in English, then an expression is probably an idiom rather than a cliché. But it is not possible to draw hard and fast lines between the two. During the writing of this book I asked my family if they thought a given expression counted as cliché or idiom so often that my young son took to wandering round singing the words 'Is that a cliché or an idiom?' to the tune of 'Down in Demerara'. Where a set phrase has become so well-established and so readily recognized that writers can play with it, substituting different words for effect, or where elements have always been variable, as in 'the x that ate y', which produces expressions such as the headline 'The mall that ate Manchester' to an article on the effects of an out-of-town shopping mall, I have called it a formula phrase. It is difficult to know where to place such formula phrases in a book presented in alphabetical order. Indeed, having looked at a wide range of books on English phrases, it has become clear that it is never easy to decide how they should be alphabetized. In this book I have listed the clichés by key word, based on the first invariable word in the expression, as there are so many variables in some of them, particularly formula phrases. I have tried to provide adequate cross-references. Where a pronoun is necessary but variable I have usually used 'you' or 'your'.

The final major category of clichés is quotations. Again, the lines that divide the types are hazy, for in the case of many of these the user has no idea that it is a quotation. Very few people, when using 'fast and furious' or 'kindred spirit' think of them as quotations from Burns and Gray. However, even unrecognized quotations are worth identifying, for sometimes the fact that a cliché is a quotation will explain odd grammar, or what, when you stop and think about it, is rather unusual usage in some other way. More importantly, the vast number of quotation clichés we use provides a fascinating historical record of what was read and familiar in the past; a sort of palimpsest of the works that have influenced our culture and, through the expressions they have left in our language, our ways of thought. The paramount importance of the Bible and Prayer Book, and of Shakespeare, becomes very clear from the sources of quotation clichés; but we can also see the influence that now unfashionable writers such as Sir Walter Scott and Henry Wadsworth Longfellow once had, while some of the earlier quotations are from writers who are otherwise totally unheard of today. Indeed, there are probably many expressions in the English language that have yet to be identified as quotations, and I would be pleased to hear from any reader who has spotted one. One further hazy category of quotation cliché is an expression, such as 'wait and see' or 'I'll be back', that was already established in the language, but was used in a new or memorable way either by an individual or, for example, in a song or film. This special use is often enough to reinforce or alter the public's consciousness of an expression, and may give it at least temporary cliché status.

Sorting clichés into types still leaves us with the question of what a cliché is and why people get so passionate about them. There are a number of sites on the world wide web dedicated to listing clichés, on one of which an anonymous contributor has defined a cliché as 'a grand truth that doesn't help anyone'. This is attractive, but not, I think, adequate. It would work better as a definition of a platitude, and while proverbs, platitudes and similes are very often hackneyed and over-used, I have tried to limit their inclusion in this book, for they are outside the area I wanted to examine, as well as being too numerous to be accommodated in a book of this size. A more useful definition of a cliché is that it is an expression that does your thinking for you: an expression so well established in the language that you know exactly how it is going to end once someone has started saying it, and which conveys instant meaning without your having to work out anything for yourself (despite the fact that the language of cliché is often highly figurative). This ability to do your thinking for you is both the attraction and the danger of clichés. It means that they can act as a sort of verbal shorthand, conveying something concisely and efficiently in a few words, without either the writer or the reader having to put too much effort into them. This is why they are so popular both with journalists and with the writers and readers of novels where the action is what counts, not motivation or deeper thoughts. Clichés are very useful in this sort of book, as they are for getting your ideas across in general conversation. Those who claim they never use clichés while chatting with friends are either deluding themselves or score very low on social skills. The negative side of this is that it is very easy to slip into the habit of using clichés. One can very easily lead to another, and it is possible to end up with a conversation or piece of writing that is without any true meaning, but is just a load of vague images, words put in to fill out the line – what Terry Pratchett in *Wings* has called 'The things humans say to each other to make sure they are still alive.' I have called these filler clichés. (As evidence for the addictive nature of clichés, the reader will find that I have deliberately used the same quotation to illustrate more than one cliché.) If you are exposed to this type of cliché-ridden language, not only can it be irritating; it can also be dangerous. Clichés can be put to highly manipulative use by politicians, publicists and those who want to get their own way, to manoeuvre their audience into thinking that more or less has been said or done than really is the case. The positive side of this is that clichés are very useful when you want to be tactful. Their power comes not so much from the users, but from the clichés themselves. As we have seen, many are quotations, which have got into the language because they say something more effectively than the speaker could in their own words. Many of the more powerful clichés work because they belong in a whole network of imagery and associations within the language, and unconsciously evoke other images and associations. I have tried to bring some of this richness out in the book through cross references (in SMALL CAPITALS) to other clichés, and by using associated words and phrases in the discussions of the clichés.

I am often asked where the information that goes into this sort of book comes from. It would be nice to be able to say that it all comes from first-hand research, but this is patently impossible. The foundation for anyone's work on the history of the English language must be the full-sized version of the *Oxford English Dictionary* (abbreviated in this book to *OED*). This is a magnificent work, which has given us a tool for a greater understanding of English than is available for any other language. Unfortunately for this book, the original remit for the dictionary was to look at single words, not words in groups, and although there is a mass of information on words in groups which can be extracted from it, particularly now the whole text is searchable on computer, many of our clichés are not covered in the work, or, even more infuriatingly, they are used in definitions but nowhere defined. Moreover, it must be remembered that the work is essentially based on nineteenth-century research. While most of *OED* was not published until the twentieth century, the bulk of the citations were collected by enthusiastic amateurs in the nineteenth century or the early years of the twentieth. Since its publication *OED* has been shamefully neglected. For although new material has been added, the so-called second edition only contained new material added on to the original text. There was no revision or correction of the old text, which means that while the history of some words, and a few phrases, may have been brought forward, the vast amount of scholarship on the early history of words and phrases that has appeared since the original publication has not been incorporated, although we are promised that this will be rectified when the third edition appears. This reliance on nineteenth-century scholarship inevitably distorts the accuracy of the dates that can be given for when clichés are first recorded, as does the way in which material for *OED* was collected. Different sorts of works were read for different periods. The original idea for *OED* was that it should cover only literary English, and for the earlier periods this is what was read. However, the people collecting material from the 1850s onwards were also reading newspapers and lighter writing and noting down anything of interest that they came across – exactly what I was doing as I collected material for this book. Because of this it is likely that the blossoming of the clichés that the dictionary implies happened in the nineteenth century is as much a result of the way citations were collected for the dictionary as of a real change in the language. However, it is the best record we have, and must be relied on, although I have tried to show through lavish use of qualifying terms such as 'in use by' that we must not think of dates as hard and fast.

Although it is the key text, *OED* is by no means the only resource available. There have been a number of earlier works on clichés. The most important of these is Eric Partridge's *Dictionary of Clichés* (Routledge 1940, and revisions), which has already been referred to. Partridge is the key twentieth-century figure in the field of writing on the history of the language for the general public. He was enormously learned, witty and prolific. By modern standards his work on clichés is terse, but it was the first work of its kind, and has been enormously influential, even if it is now somewhat dated. He makes an important distinction between first recorded uses of an expression and when it became a cliché. His dates for the latter are still standard. (It must, however, be noted that Partridge has a reputation for using best guesses where hard information is lacking – but he was so knowledgeable that his guesses are usually good and often confirmed by subsequent research.) I have also made use of two American works on clichés – *The Dictionary of Clichés* by James Rogers (Ballantine, 1985) and Christine Ammer's *Have a Nice Day – No Problem* (Plume, 1992) and of two recent British works, Betty Kirkpatrick's *Clichés* (Bloomsbury, 1996) and Nigel Rees's *Dictionary of Clichés* (Cassell, 1996) as well as a number of other books on language by Rees. Where these and a wide range of other works on the language have failed to supply dates for usage, I have turned to Project Gutenberg. This is a rather quirky project run by Illinois Benedictine College which uses volunteers (shades of *OED*) to transcribe a wide variety of non-copyright or out-of-copyright material into electronic form. The texts are accessible via the Internet, but for my purposes the important fact was that they are also available on CD-ROM, which meant that instead of searching several hundred texts individually hoping to find an early use of a cliché, I could let the computer quietly search through the whole disk in the background, while I got on with other things. The texts searched this way are a curious mixture, and they reflect the interests and enthusiasms of the volunteers. They can never be a substitute for something like *OED*, but they provide an enormous amount of material to sample and can at least indicate that a cliché was in use by a given date. Moreover, the works covered by Project Gutenberg do include popular writers such as Banjo Patterson or Edgar Rice Burroughs who are not normally the mainstay of lexicographers.

Most of the entries in this book are illustrated by citations from recent writings. I have not been fanatical about this. Where the entry is quite long enough without such illustrations, I have left them out. Where I have not been able to find good, clear usages, as is frequently the case in the more colloquial clichés, I have done without rather than use poor quality material. Some of the quotations are there to illustrate simple usage, some to illustrate bad usage, and some to amuse. I leave it to the reader to work out which is meant to be which. In a good number of cases these citations do not illustrate straightforward uses of the expression, but are plays on the expression. I have chosen them because the fact that a writer can play with an expression shows that he thinks that he need only allude to a part of the cliché and the whole of it will instantly spring to the reader's mind. An example of this sort of allusive use is a recent case when a businessman-politician retiring from office was described as going to 'spend more time with his money', playing on the standard 'spend more time with his family'. The citations are based on material I have collected from my own reading, heavily supplemented by material from the British National Corpus, a vast collection of modern English material in electronic form, compiled between 1991 and 1994 for research purposes by a number of major reference publishers (including Penguin). This invaluable resource is accessible via the Internet (http://info.ox.ac.uk/bnc/index.html) and can be searched on-line to give information on frequency of use, the forms that are found, and to provide illustrative citations. Its only drawback is that its texts, which are nearly all from the late 1980s and early 1990s, are not always dated, which is why the reader will find the occasional undated citation in this book.

Finally, I come to the individuals who have helped create this book. I must thank my editor, Martin Toseland, for his patience and support. Constance Fishwick and Anna Leinster have helped with suggestions and quotations. Fred McDonald has, as ever, proved a source of information, suggestion and enlightenment. An especial thank you is due to Irvin Mael for solving the long-standing mystery of 'Live fast, die young'. Above all I must thank my family. My son, Alexander, has been patient beyond all reasonable expectation while I have been distracted with this book, as well as contributing some really useful headwords; while my husband Philip has not only done all the things that writers' spouses are usually thanked for, but has provided invaluable computer support, has frequently come up with solutions to questions that have puzzled me for days, and has been a constant fount of unexpected information. The best lines in the book have been stolen from him.

Julia Cresswell

abilities see BEST OF MY ABILITIES

abject failure A popular cliché of sports writers and politicians, abject is used here in the sense of 'total' rather than its original sense of 'degrading'. The other companion of abject, abject apology, hovers between the sense 'total' and another original sense, 'self-abasing'. These uses probably developed from the third common pairing, abject poverty, which originally meant 'degrading' but can easily be understood as 'total'.

' "Having run out of excuses for the abject failure of your Government's economic policies," he said, "you are now trying to pin the blame on your predecessor, in whose Government you were responsible for economic policy." ' (*East Anglian Daily Times*, 1993)

'Vologsky kept his face grave, but the surging relief inside him made it impossible to inject quite the right note of abject apology into his voice.' (Peter Cave, *Foxbat*, 1979)

'That still leaves at least 250m Indians living in abject poverty, but at least life appears to be getting a little better for the rest.' (*The Economist*, 1991)

above board see OPEN AND ABOVE BOARD

accentuate the positive This is a quotation-cliché, from a 1944 song by Johnny Mercer, properly written 'Ac-cent-tchu-ate the Positive', the opening lines of which run, ignoring the phonetic spellings: 'You've got to accentuate the positive/Eliminate the negative/Latch on to the affirmative/Don't be Mister In-between.'

'Naturally with the adrenaline flowing freely on his sudden elevation, Wanless is anxious to accentuate the positive in NatWest's core retail and business banking.' (*Daily Telegraph*, 5 April 1992)

accident (or **tragedy** or **disaster**) **waiting to happen** These expressions have probably only become clichés since the 1980s, when they became popular with journalists benefiting from hindsight when reporting disasters. They are often used in combination with accusations about those who should have seen it coming.

'Bands like that are accidents waiting to happen in a world where 99 percent of groups are casualties of their own blatant ambition.' (*New Musical Express*, 1991)

'Ferraro demonstrated, they said, that women candidates are accidents waiting to happen because "they can't control the men in their lives".' (*Mail on Sunday*, 20 September 1998)

accidents do happen 'Accidents will occur in the best-regulated families' says

Charles Dickens in *David Copperfield* (1849–50), a variation on an expression that was becoming a cliché at the time, although it had been around for about 100 years beforehand. This acceptance of the inevitability of accidents is in marked contrast with the previous entry. The phrase can also be found as 'accidents will happen' and 'accidents can happen'.

'In a system that is lightly-stocked problems like these should not occur, but accidents will happen, and your system's ability to deal with them will be put to the test.' (*Practical Fishkeeping*, 1992)

acclaimed see HIGHLY ACCLAIMED

ace up your sleeve (or **in the hole**) Both of these expressions come from American poker. An ace up his sleeve is what the professional cardsharp would have to make sure he wins the vital hand, and is used to mean a surprise or a hidden weapon. An ace in the hole, used for a good move or something kept in reserve for when it is really needed, is a term used in stud poker for an ace that is face down on the table, its value known only to the person in whose hand it is.

'But in Foley, Spurs have an ace up their sleeve and the former Arsenal coach is orchestrating matters on the training pitch.' (*Evening Standard*, 10 September 1998)

'I wadded one into my shoulder holster as an ace in the hole, packing it down with the gun.' (Kim Newman, *The Night Mayor*, 1990)

acid test In the days when gold was a normal medium of exchange, people would use nitric acid as a diagnostic test to find out the proportion of gold present in a piece. This was the acid test, used, since the early twentieth century, to mean a test of the success or value of something.

'The acid test for art criticism is the solo exhibition.' (Joseph Darracott, *Art Criticism: A User's Guide*, 1991)

across the board At American racetracks you can find noticeboards showing the odds on a horse to come first, second or third. An across-the-board bet is one that places equal amounts of money on these three outcomes. From this the expression spread to more general use, and is particularly popular with writers on economics, especially with reference to wage negotiations. It became a cliché in the USA in the 1950s, and in England by the 1960s.

'The immediate effect of the revenue enhancement however, brought with it a more than proportionate increase in costs across the board and a surplus deflated by approximately £100,000.' (*The Cricketer*, 1992)

'In the health-conscious nineties, companies such as ICI, Shell, National Westminster Bank and Gestetner are closing down their in-house bars and applying a no-alcohol policy across the board, apparently with little resistance from staff.' (*Accountancy*, 1992)

act together see GET YOUR ACT TOGETHER

as the actress said to the bishop This is a cliché of innuendo, used to bring out the *double entendre*, whether initially deliberate or not, in a statement. It is also found as a formula phrase 'as the . . . said to the . . .', and sometimes the order of the bishop and the actress are reversed. The joke lies in the contrast between the assumed innocence or rectitude of the bishop and the old reputation of actresses for loose living – in the late nineteenth and early twentieth centuries the term could be a euphemism for prostitute. The expression was well established by the 1940s, and well used in radio comedy in the 1950s, but probably goes back at least to the beginning of the twentieth century. In the 1940s the comedienne Beryl Reid popularized the alternative 'as the art mistress said to the gardener', a catch-phrase used in her role as Monica in the popular radio comedy *Educating Archie*.

'Size, as the actress said to the Bishop, is part of the problem.' (*Esquire*, 1992)

add insult to injury This expression goes back to the Latin fables of Phaedrus, written in the first century AD, which includes the story of a bald man bothered by a fly, which bites him on the head. The man swats at the fly, and, of course, hits himself on the head, at which the fly comments 'You wished to kill me for a touch. What will you do to yourself since you have added insult to injury?' The actual wording first appears in the mid-eighteenth century in English.

'Apart from the fact that there was trouble with one of the other directors – apparently Jefferson was having a high old time with his wife and, to add insult to injury, charging the hotel rooms to expenses – you may recall that Downton lost two very valuable contracts with players in tennis and golf.' (Malcolm Hamer, *Sudden Death*, 1991)

'Losing was one thing but to lose as spinelessly as the Welsh XV did to Bridgend on Saturday was to add insult to severely injured pride.' (*Independent*, 2 October 1989)

afraid to ask See EVERYTHING YOU'VE ALWAYS WANTED TO KNOW ABOUT

after due consideration 'Due consideration' has a quasi-legal meaning, in that if you can be shown to have acted without the consideration due to something, then you may be liable to be prosecuted. In this sense, the wording has been around since the sixteenth century. From this has come a cliché, popular in business letters and formal pronouncements, which is meant to imply serious thought, but which in fact adds little or nothing to the statement.

'After due consideration, the Committee thought this remark "was not out of context in a programme well known for its fictional exposure of the more dubious side of the antiques trade".' (*New Statesman and Society*, 1992)

after your own heart See HEART

against the grain When working wood or any material with a natural grain, it is much easier to work with the grain, than against or across it – hence the development of 'against the grain' to mean much the same as to RUB THE WRONG WAY. The expression has been a common one since the seventeenth century.

'It was one of those pictures that went totally against the grain of everything that the movie industry believed it stood for.' (John Parker, *The Joker's Wild: The Biography of Jack Nicholson*, 1991)

'Although it goes against the grain to say this, the exercise is valuable, if indeed it has the effect of providing an accurate version of a distinguished person's world view.' (*New Scientist*, 1991)

age before beauty This expression started life in the late nineteenth century, probably as a graceful way for an older woman to acknowledge the courtesy of a younger one who stands aside to let her take precedence in entering a room. It soon came to be a gallantry of an older man to a girl, and to be used jocularly or maliciously between other pairs. Various ripostes developed: schoolchildren, for example, would retort 'dust (or dirt) before the broom'. But most famous is the exchange, variously attributed, but most often in the form of an anecdote that has Clare Booth Luce ushering Dorothy Parker through a door with 'age before beauty', only to have Dorothy Parker sweep past with 'pearls before swine'.

agenda A very active cliché, on its own or in combination, used loosely instead of 'plans', 'concerns' or 'intentions'. See also HIDDEN AGENDA.

'The change has been striking in two areas, with women's issues and environmental concerns thrust to the head of the party agenda.' (*Independent*, 3 October 1989)

'Harriet was weeping again, and he felt, knowing of course this was unfair, that she was breaking the rules of some contract between them: tears and misery had not ever been on their agenda!' (Doris Lessing, *The Fifth Child*, 1988)

the agony and the ecstasy The title of an Irving Stone novel (1961) made into a film in 1965, describing the life and works of Michelangelo, the agony and the ecstasy being particularly associated with the triumph and physical labour and the discomfort involved in painting the Sistine Chapel. It is a popular journalistic cliché, particularly of headline, for those wanting to convey a combination of joy and sorrow.

ain't broke why fix it see IF IT AIN'T BROKE

it (or **the opera**) **ain't over till the fat lady sings** This saying was created by the American sports commentator Dan Cook in 1975 (or, according to some authorities, 1976), while commenting on a basketball game, to mean that the result could change at any time right up to the end of the game, an elaboration on 'it ain't over till it's over'. The saying became popular in sporting circles, and gained wider currency in 1982 when it was used in an advertising campaign by the Baltimore Orioles baseball team, which showed a large aggressive-looking Valkyrie over the caption 'She ain't sung yet'. Although Cook is credited with the expression, similar expressions were already current, including 'Church ain't out till the fat lady sings', which would explain why it caught on so quickly.

'We're gathered here to test the hypothesis that it ain't over "till the fat lady sings," said Peggy Haine, of the Women of Substance Chorale.' (*Today*, 1992)

ain't seen (or **heard**) **nothing yet** A catch-phrase cliché, originally in the form 'you ain't heard nothing yet', strongly associated with Al Jolson, indicating that more is yet to come. These words were famously spoken by Jolson in the first ever talking film *The Jazz Singer* (1927), and the form with 'seen' was used the same year in a Broadway play called *The Barker* by Kenyon Nicholson. However, 'you ain't heard nothing yet' was already a Jolson catch-phrase before the film. Jolson acquired it in 1906 when he was singing in a San Francisco café and there was a burst of noise from a nearby building site. Yelling 'You ain't heard nothing yet', Jolson proceeded to sing at such a volume that he drowned out the building noises.

alive and kicking This expression, a cliché since the nineteenth century, comes from fishmongers who, to emphasize the freshness of their goods, would claim that they were so fresh they were not only alive, but alive and kicking.

'The horrific murder of a black man in Texas this week is a chilling reminder that racism is alive and kicking in America.' (*Independent*, 12 July 1998)

alive and well (and living in . . .) The expression 'alive and well' was well established by the middle of the nineteenth century, but was used mainly in a literal sense until the middle of the twentieth century. At about this time it took on a more ironic tone, and the addition 'and living in . . .' really took off. There was, in particular, a well known 1960s graffito 'God is alive and well and living in Argentina' (and variants), created in response to Nietzsche's statement, much debated at the time, that 'God is dead' and to various newspaper stories of Nazis still being alive and well and living in South America – in particular Adolf Eichmann, Nazi SS officer instrumental in running the death camps, who had been living under an assumed identity in Argentina, was kidnapped by the Israelis in 1960, taken to Israel, and tried and executed in 1961. A further boost was given to the expression by the musical *Jacques Brel is Alive and Well and Living in Paris* which ran in London from 1968–72.

'Australopithecus is alive and well and hanging round Pete's Cafe.' (Celia Brayfield, *The Prince*, 1990)

'Speaking of which, when one such status symbol ran dry here the other day, a child was lowered into a pit to clean out the drains, so the nineteenth-century tradition of infant chimney-sweeps is alive and well and living in Tuscany.' (J. Mortimer, *Summer's Lease*, 1988)

all ages see CHILDREN OF ALL AGES

all and sundry 'All and sundry' has been in use since the fourteenth century. Like so many doublet expressions, where each half means more or less the same as the other, it started life in legal language, the repetition used to cover the writer against loopholes. Nowadays it is simply used to mean 'everyone'.

'I guess you could call it "grace under pressure". All and sundry have been mightily impressed by my brave acceptance of the valetudinarian life.' (*Independent*, 5 September 1998)

all animals are equal but some are more equal than others see MORE EQUAL THAN OTHERS

all creatures great and small This is a quotation from the hymn 'All Things Bright and Beautiful', written by the Irish poet Mrs Cecil Alexander and published in 1848. She was also responsible for such well known hymns as 'There is a Green Hill Far Away' and the carol 'Once in Royal David's City'. 'All things bright and beautiful' itself ranks as a cliché, and the lines 'The rich man in his castle,/The poor man at his gate,/God made them, high or lowly,/And order'd their estate' are much-quoted as representative of VICTORIAN VALUES. In 1974 *All Creatures Great and Small* was used as the title of a film based on the autobiographical books of the vet James Herriot, and the success of this led to a television series with the same title which ran from 1978 to 1990. What has since come to be called 'Herriot Country' now has a take-away called 'All Pizzas Great and Small'. It was this media exposure which changed the expression from a popular quotation to a cliché.

'[Druidry's] central belief is the sacredness of the earth and nature of all living things – particularly all creatures great and small – and the relationship of the earth to the cosmos.' (*Independent*, 12 June 1998)

all cylinders see FIRING ON ALL CYLINDERS

all done in the best possible taste This cliché, typically used to justify such things as nudity in films, has never been the same since the English disc jockey and comedian Kenny Everett sent it up in his character of the buxom blonde movie star

Cupid Stunt, who did everything 'in the best possible taste, of course', usually said while crossing 'her' legs with maximum exposure. The character appeared in the television series *The Kenny Everett Explosion* which started in 1978. Since then, while the expression can be found used seriously, it is often ironic.

'Its spokeswoman said: "I haven't seen the Paul nude yet, but I'm told it's in the best possible taste." ' (*Daily Mirror*, 1992)

'We are now told that the statue in the Millennium Dome is to be of a man and woman embracing. All done in the best possible taste, I hope.' (*Today*, BBC Radio 4, June 1998)

all dressed up and nowhere (or **no place**) **to go** This comes from the title of a song, 'When You're All Dressed up and Nowhere to Go', written by B. H. Burt in 1916. It has been favourite of both caption writers and politicians ever since the American journalist William Allen White (1868–1944) described the Progressive Party as 'All dressed up with nowhere to go' when Theodore Roosevelt dropped out of the Presidential race in 1916.

all ears An expression used to indicate attention and willingness to listen, or to suggest an interest in gossip and desire to eavesdrop. It is found used poetically in John Milton's masque *Comus* (1634), 'I am all ear and took in strains that might create a soul under the ribs of death,' and since the form 'all ear' is still to be found in the eighteenth century, this may be the source of the expression.

'When we got back to our door Mrs Jonesy and Mrs Phipps were still loitering, all ears, so Frankie deliberately poured some of the icy water on Mrs Jonesy's feet.' (Kathleen Dayus, *Where There's Life*, 1991)

all for one (and) one for all This quotation expressing solidarity comes from Alexander Dumas's historical novel *The Three Musketeers* (1844).

'It was, said the prosecution, one for all and all for one, even when the gravity of the situation meant a murder charge could be considered.' (Central television news scripts, 1993)

all girls together see GIRL TALK

all Greek to me In Shakespeare's *Julius Caesar* (I.ii) Cicero, off-stage, makes a speech in Greek, but Casca, who is giving an account of events claims not to have understood what he said, because 'For mine own part, it was Greek to me.' From this, 'all Greek to me' has become a way of saying something is incomprehensible, usually with the implication that it is above your head.

'Steven's (groom's name) language is Greek and the Greek alphabet may be all Greek to you but it is surprising how much Greek we all use.' (A. Lansbury, *Wedding Speeches and Toasts*, 1992)

all in a day's work A twentieth-century cliché of unknown origin, used to indicate resigned acceptance of circumstances. IT GOES WITH THE TERRITORY is a companion cliché.

all in all Like ALL THINGS CONSIDERED, this is a cliché used for summing up, but which is often a mere filler or verbal tic.

'All in all, a good combination of relaxation and activity, good food and wine, in a beautiful location, Jandia Mar has to be the ideal answer to that often-heard question: "Where shall we go next summer?" ' (*HCI Club Holidays*, 1990)

to (or **for**) **all intents and purposes** This expression has been a cliché since the middle of the nineteenth century. Meaning 'effectively, virtually', the use of two words of such close meaning for emphasis is often used to try to hide the special pleading involved in the argument presented.

'Considering that this was a minor single on a label that, with respect, specialised in the production of minor singles, "Hand in Glove" was, for all intents and purposes, a hit record.' (Mick Middles, *The Smiths*, 1988)

all is said and done see WHEN ALL IS SAID AND DONE

all over bar the shouting Referring to something all but finished, or with a result that is a FOREGONE CONCLUSION, this expression comes from sport. It was in use by 1842, often in the form '. . . but the shouting', still the standard form in the USA.

'The buses were only just about running; she'd intended to go to the cathedral, but thought, at this rate, it would be all over bar the shouting by the time she arrived, so decided instead to make straight for the cemetery.' (Kathleen Conlon, *Distant Relations*, 1990)

all present and correct These are the normal words used by a sergeant-major to the officer in charge at a parade or inspection of troops. In general use they are a joking expansion of 'all present'.

'She looked as delightful as ever, trimly turned out in cream trousers and a bright red sweater and with the bumps all present and correct and in the right places.' (Malcolm Hamer, *Sudden Death*, 1991)

all seasons see FOR ALL SEASONS

all singing, all dancing This is used to mean flashy, full of BELLS AND WHISTLES, or at least with all the latest gimmicks, and is mainly used of financial services or computers. Its origin goes back to 1929 when sound was first coming into films, and the first ever musical, MGM's *Broadway Melody*, was advertised as 'The New Wonder of the Screen! All Talking, All Singing, All Dancing, Dramatic Sensation.'

'Whilst this little lot may cost you a packet, your PC will become the all singing all dancing box the salesman claimed it would be.' (*Practical PC*, 1992)

all systems go This cliché was adopted from the jargon used when launching rockets. In the 1960s and 1970s the launching of manned flights, particularly the flights to the moon, were prominently featured on radio and television, and the expression was picked up from these and had become a catch-phrase by the late 1960s.

'Belfast fight boss Eastwood revealed: "It's all systems go – I have faxed Frank Warren to say that Paul Hodkinson is prepared to fight Colin McMillan in November." ' (*Daily Mirror*, 1992)

all the fun of the fair see FUN OF THE FAIR

all the rage Surprisingly this expression goes back to at least 1785, when it was listed among other fashionable phrases, including 'the Thing', and 'Bore', used much as we use them today. We regularly use a whole range of expressions connected with insanity or extreme emotion for something that is fashionable; we have a craze for something (recorded 1813) or are crazy about it (1779), are mad for it (1670), or wild about it ('wild to' 1797, 'wild about' 1868).

'Who has the time anyway? That's why paying other people to do the boring stuff has become all the rage.' (*Stuff*, October 1998)

all things bright and beautiful see ALL CREATURES GREAT AND SMALL

all things considered This is a less formal equivalent of AFTER DUE CONSIDER-ATION. It too is often a filler rather than a true summing up, but it can also be used to DAMN WITH FAINT PRAISE, implying that something was not done well in absolute terms, but only in terms of what was expected.

'During our last home match of last season, I thought the team played exceedingly well all things considered.' (M. Gist, *Life at the Tip*, 1993)

all-time classic (or **great**) An expression used mainly by journalists writing on sport or media such as film or music, this came into use around the 1960s, picking up on the earlier uses of all-time high or low to describe stocks and shares.

'This will give me the pleasurable task of transcribing sections of two Zep tracks from the all-time classic album "Led Zeppelin II".' (*Guitarist*, 1992)

'Walker is more than just one of the all-time great middle distance runners, he was a pioneer, a barrier breaker who set new standards of performance and of attitude towards the art of miling.' (*Running*, 1991)

allegedly This is a knowing cliché, a shared joke. It is particularly associated with satirists, in the UK above all with the topical television show *Have I Got News For You*. It is used by people spinning a story, or commenting on the actions of people such as politicians, added at the end of some often outrageous statement in a heavily marked voice, so that, by qualifying the statement in this way, they may avoid possible prosecution for slander or libel.

all's fair in love and war This proverb has been in use since the mid-nineteenth century, although the sentiment has been around since at least the sixteenth century when John Lyly could write in *Euphues* (1578) 'Any impietie may lawfully be committed in love, which is lawless.' It is rarely used without a twist nowadays, and is often a formula phrase.

'He looked at it quite philosophically, seeing poaching as an irritant but also as an inevitable occurrence; in headhunting, all's fair in love and war.' (Stephanie Jones, *The Headhunting Business*, 1990)

'All is fair in love and golf.' (A. Lansbury, *Wedding Speeches and Toasts*, 1992)

all's well that ends well Versions of this proverb have been around since the fourteenth century, but it is nowadays identified as the title of a Shakespeare play rather than a proverb. Shakespeare's play, often classed as a tragi-comedy, is a story of bad behaviour and deceit which is finally resolved in harmony, the title implying that whatever may have gone before, the future will be calmer for those involved.

there is no alternative Although this is a common expression it was famously used by Margaret Thatcher on several occasions in the 1980s about her economic policies. As a result, when used in a way that marks it as a quotation, it has come to be used, both seriously and jokingly, to show firm conviction which is not open to argument.

'The right hon. Gentleman and all his colleagues have constantly reiterated the view that there is no need for a change of policy, that there is no alternative to present policies and that, if re-elected, the Government would pursue the same course.' (*Hansard Extracts 1991–1992*)

'There is no alternative. New Labour is the solution, not the problem.' (*Independent*, 26 September 1998)

always look on the bright side see LOOK ON THE BRIGHT SIDE

American as apple pie see APPLE PIE

American dream In use since at least 1835, this expression is used for the traditional values that the USA is held to stand for. However, as can be seen from the quotations, what exactly is meant can be rather vague, and the expression is often used emotively, rather than with any precise meaning.

'New York has been the scene for what might be termed a chessboard version of the American dream, that ability for a dispossessed citizen of a politically and economically bankrupt Eastern European state to come to Manhattan and not only make it, but make it big.' (Raymond Keene, *Battle of the Titans: Kasparov–Karpov*, 1991)

'There are, of course, several American dreams: one is the John Wayne tradition of the cowboy going out to the west and the whole notion of pioneering individualism; another is the immigrant American dream, this being the land of opportunity where the streets are made of gold.' (*New Statesman and Society*, 1992)

ample opportunity Ample, in modern speech, is nearly always used of the body – an ample figure, embrace, arms or bosom. The exceptions are usually ample opportunity, ample warning, ample means or ample accommodation. These are hangovers from the sense of 'generous, unlimited' that developed from the basic sense of 'large'. Ample accommodation is a cliché of estate agents and the like; the others tend to be rather formal, and usually have rather negative associations.

'I can give him the assurance that both he and the local authority in his constituency will have ample opportunity to express their views on how best to design the line to reduce the environmental impact.' (*Hansard Extracts 1991–1992*)

amused see WE ARE NOT AMUSED

and then some Meaning 'and more in addition', but now often used for nothing more than vague emphasis, this cliché developed in the USA at the very beginning of the twentieth century.

'The monster motor in this Italian beauty can rocket you from 0–60 mph in three seconds flat . . . bellowing as much as noise emissions allow (and then some, by the sound of it).' (*Stuff*, October 1998)

'I'll give them nice dry sense of humour, he thought savagely as he came out on to his floor and lumbered towards room 4038, I'll give them nice dry sense of humour and then some.' (Nigel Williams, *The Wimbledon Poisoner*, 1990)

angels fear to tread see FOOLS RUSH IN

angels with dirty faces An emotive description which comes from the title of a 1938 film, showing the battle for the hearts and minds of a group of slum kids between the gangster whom they admire and the priest determined to save them from going down the same path. In the end the tough gangster is persuaded to repel them by acting the coward when sent to the electric chair, and these innocents with the cards stacked against them are saved.

'Wearing his trademark Napoleonic hat and, possibly with the help of the Carlton make-up artiste, an air of raffish angels-with-dirty-faces innocence, he delivered his message.' (*Independent*, 5 September 1998)

another day see TOMORROW IS ANOTHER DAY

another nail in the coffin see NAIL IN THE COFFIN

any schoolboy or fool knows see AS ANY (OR EVERY) SCHOOLBOY KNOWS

anything goes Although this is best known as the title of a song written by Cole Porter in 1934, Porter was himself picking up an expression of disapproval that was already well established. In 1921 the *Ladies' Home Journal* could write, 'One of the few real "movie" fortunes has been made by a man who . . . has constantly exploited the vicious theory that "anything goes in fun".' Porter was thus mocking the strait-laced supporters of VICTORIAN VALUES when he wrote 'In olden days a glimpse of stocking/Was looked on as something shocking/Now, heaven knows,/Anything goes.' While 'anything goes' is still used in a disapproving way, it can also be used in a positive way, and this use probably owes much to Porter's jaunty, up-beat song.

'Thereafter, it's anything goes, really, and it's fun to experiment with this novel method of obtaining bass sounds.' (*Guitarist*, 1992)

apace see CONTINUE APACE

(**American as**) **apple pie** Apple pie, particularly Mom's apple pie, has come to represent all that is comforting and homely, and the domestic bliss that is part of the AMERICAN DREAM. As Joseph Heller wrote in his novel of American troops in World War II, *Catch-22* (1962) 'The hot dog, the Brooklyn Dodgers, Mom's apple pie. That's what everyone's fighting for.'

'Both senators, or at least both their press secretaries, claim their legislation protects children, Mom and apple pie, all worthy goals.' (*Independent*, 3 August 1998)

appliance of science A long-running advertising slogan used by Zanussi for their electrical goods which has become a catch-phrase cliché.

' "Could the appliance of science create a better bra?" ' asked the narrator on *Designs on Your Bra* (C4).' (*Independent*, 25 June 1998)

'Teachers are grappling with the appliance of science in the primary classroom.' (*Northern Echo*)

arm and a leg see COST AN ARM AND A LEG

armed to the teeth The image here is of someone so heavily armed that the only place left to carry a weapon is in their teeth, familiar today from pirate films, but one which has been around since the fourteenth century. It is still used literally, but is also now used metaphorically, often with the implication of being over-equipped.

'They were armed to the teeth with dagger, sword, dirk and a small array of throwing knives strapped in broad leather belts across their chests.' (Michael Clynes, *The White Rose Murder*, 1992)

'As for guitars, The Stairs travel armed to the teeth with a motley collection of Gibson semi-acoustics.' (*Guitarist*, 1992)

as a matter of fact see THE FACT OF THE MATTER

as any (or **every**) **schoolboy knows** (also **as any fule kno/as any skolboy**

kno) The use of this expression is particularly associated with Thomas Babington Macaulay, who used it on several occasions, and famously wrote, 'Every schoolboy knows who imprisoned Montezuma, and who strangled Atahualpa' in his 1840 essay *On Lord Clive*, a statement that may make us react as Lord Melbourne did, with 'I wish I was as cocksure of anything as Tom Macaulay is of everything.' 'As every schoolboy knows' became a cliché at about this time, although it had been used well before Macaulay. In recent years the statement has become mixed up with the language (and spelling) of Nigel Molesworth, Geoffrey Willans's great creation in a series of books telling of school life from a horrid boy's point of view (*Down with Skool*, *How to be Topp* and *Whizz for Atomms*) which appeared in the 1950s with illustrations by Ronald Searle. One of Molesworth's favourite expressions is 'as any fule kno', and this has, with wonderful inappropriateness, become blended with Macaulay's pronouncements.

'As every schoolboy knows, the steam locomotive was invented by Richard Trevithick in 1804, and so your story on George Stevenson's claim to fame . . . rather misses the point.' (*Independent*, 14 September 1998)

'Q. The capital of Morocco is . . . ? a) Paris b) New York c) Marrakesh. As any Eye reader kno, the capital of Morocco is New York. No prizes then, for anyone who puts "Rabat".' (*Private Eye*, 21 August 1998, quoting *Sunday Telegraph* competition)

as good as it gets A modern cliché used to express generalized approval and enthusiasm.

'I can't believe anyone else has been through an experience like the five years we had together at Blackburn . . . It was as good as it gets, we were the original adventure club.' (*Daily Mail*, 27 August 1998)

as it were This is little more than a verbal tic, a filler with virtually no meaning of its own, other than to show hesitation. It has been used in English since about 1300, but then was often used as a form of direct comparison. As a cliché it dates from at least the eighteenth century.

'Have you not been, as it were, hoist with your own petard, by Peter Mandelson's visit to Disneyland?' (*Today*, BBC Radio 4, 4 July 1998)

as the actress said to the bishop see ACTRESS SAID TO THE BISHOP

as the art mistress said to the gardener see AS THE ACTRESS SAID TO THE BISHOP

ashes see RISE FROM THE ASHES

ask not what . . . can do for you; ask what you can do for . . . A formula phrase, based on the 1961 Inaugural Address of the American President John F. Kennedy: 'And so my fellow Americans: ask not what your country can do for you – ask what you can do for your country.'

' "Ask not," Carnelian taunted, "what you can do for me, but what I can do for you." ' (Ian Watson, *Inquisitor*, 1993)

'Some might well say, "Ask not what Europe can do for the United Kingdom, but what the United Kingdom can do for Europe." ' (*Hansard Extracts 1991–1992*)

asphalt jungle see JUNGLE

at a stroke see STROKE

at dagger's drawn see DAGGERS DRAWN

at death's door see DEATH'S DOOR

at the crossroads Crossroads have been used since the late nineteenth century as a metaphor for a point in life where decisions have to be made about which path in life to choose. The expression is also used semi-literally of large geographical features.

'For musicians, the lure of the West must be strong . . . but as a result we stand at a crossroads: how can we possibly avoid the continuing standardisation of orchestral, instrumental and vocal production.' (*Gramophone*, 1992)

'The most prolific refining and distribution area is Ribat, which lies at the crossroads of three countries – Afghanistan, Pakistan and Iran.' (*Guardian*, 11 November 1989)

at the drop of a hat see DROP OF A HAT

at the end of the day This is a filler cliché, with little actual meaning, an alternative for WHEN ALL IS SAID AND DONE. It became very popular in the 1970s with politicians, trade unionists and allied trades.

'If one accepts the idea that there was a deal between MI6 and the KGB then at the end of the day everyone was satisfied.' (James Rusbridger, *The Intelligence Game*, 1991)

at this moment (or **point**) **in time** Both these expressions date from the 1970s, and like IN THIS DAY AND AGE are simply long-winded ways of saying 'now'. They are often used as mere fillers.

'Well, frankly, the problem as I see it at this moment in time is whether I should just lie down under all this hassle and let them walk all over me, or, whether I should just say: "OK, I get the message", and do myself in.' (*Guardian*, 20 December 1989)

'And André was in his element, enjoying the buzzing atmosphere around him the way she had used to at one point in time.' (Cathy Williams, *A French Encounter*, 1992)

at your earliest convenience see EARLIEST CONVENIENCE

the . . . that ate . . . A formula phrase, meant to be based on format titles of old horror films of the type spoofed in the first quotation. It is a development of the later twentieth century. There was a 1974 film called *The Cars That Ate Paris*, but this was probably itself derived from the format. There are certainly earlier films with titles starting 'The Monster that . . .', such as *The Monster that Challenged the World* (1957).

'It was a double bill at the Regal, a thriller called *Murder to Order* and an old horror film called *The Frog That Ate London*.' (Ann Pilling, *Henry's Leg*, 1987)

'The mall that ate Manchester.' (Headline, *Independent*, 2 September 1998)

avenue see EXPLORE EVERY AVENUE

avoid like the plague When clichés are mentioned, this seems to be one of the ones that most readily springs to people's minds. Certainly, anyone writing on clichés will lose count of the number of times people crack the joke about avoiding clichés like the plague. The expression goes back to at least the fourth century when St Jerome said, 'Avoid as you would the plague a clergyman who is also a man of business.'

'A gag currently doing the rounds is that the bumper cars in The Mall's leisure centre will be travelling faster than the traffic on the M60 and M63. The AA has already started issuing warnings to commuters and haulage companies: avoid the area like the plague – for ever.' (*Independent*, 2 September 1998)

axe to grind Although this expression for having a bias or your own purposes in doing something is usually attributed to Benjamin Franklin, it seems in fact to come from a column written by the American Charles Miner for the *Wilkes-Barre Gleaner* in 1811. In this he told the story of how, in his childhood a stranger asked to use the grindstone in his family backyard. With a mixture of charm and flattery the stranger got the young Miner to do all the work turning the grindstone, while he simply held the axe. Miner concludes, 'When I see a merchant over-polite to his customers, begging them to taste a little brandy and throwing half his goods on the counter – thinks I, that man has an axe to grind.' The attribution to Franklin may come from a passage in his autobiography, when he tells of his attempts to improve himself: 'I made so little progress in amendment, and had such frequent relapses, that I was almost ready to give up the attempt, and content myself with a faulty character in that respect, like the man who, in buying an ax of a smith, my neighbour, desired to have the whole of its surface as bright as the edge. The smith consented to grind it bright for him if he would turn the wheel; he turn'd, while the smith press'd the broad face of the ax hard and heavily on the stone, which made the turning of it very fatiguing. The man came every now and then from the wheel to see how the work went on, and at length would take his ax as it was, without farther grinding. "No," said the smith, "turn on, turn on; we shall have it bright by-and-by; as yet, it is only speckled." "Yes," said the man, "but I think I like a speckled ax best." '

'In addition, I have a particular axe to grind, as I have been a professional wood-carver for 25 years in both ornamental and sculptural disciplines so woodcarving tools hold a special interest.' (*Woodworker*, 1991)

baby with the bathwater see THROW OUT THE BABY WITH THE BATHWATER

on the back burner A ring or burner at the back of a stove is usually a smaller one, meant for simmering, so something that is on the back burner is left to simmer quietly, nothing being done to it for a while. The expression developed in the USA in the 1950s or 1960s.

'Ministers' committees are not always just a means of placing problems on the back burner. Their members, such as Professor Bernard Crick, can come up with good ideas too.' (*Independent*, 23 September 1998)

back from the brink The image behind 'back from the brink' is, as can be seen from the quotations, a dead metaphor, with no idea left of a retreat from the edge of something physically dangerous. In fact it seems to have become blended with the expressions 'on the brink of', a use of brink meaning 'on the verge of', found in English from the fourteenth century. Images associated with 'brink' were very much to the fore in 1956 during the Korean war, when John Foster Dulles, US Secretary of State, could say in splendidly mixed metaphors, 'Of course we were brought to the verge of war. The ability to get to the verge without getting into the war is the necessary art . . . If you try to run away from it, if you are scared to go to the brink, you are lost . . . We walked to the brink and we looked it in the face,' which led to accusations from Adlai Stevenson of 'boasting of his brinkmanship – the art of bringing us to the edge of the nuclear abyss'.

'The RFU last night attempted to pull the clubs back from the brink of those friendly fixtures. They announced the first five weeks of fixtures must take place without any Welsh teams playing English sides.' (*Evening Standard*, 28 August 1998)

back in the mists of time see MISTS OF TIME

back room The use of the term 'back room' to mean a place where support work, or sometimes secret work, is carried out dates from a speech made in March 1941 by Lord Beaverbrook who said, 'Now who is responsible for this work of development on which so much depends? To whom must the praise be given? To the boys in the back rooms. They do not sit in the limelight. But they are the men who do the work.' A few years earlier, using a catch-phrase invented by the cartoonist Tad Dorgan (1877–1929), Marlene Dietrich famously sang 'See what the boys in the back room will have', in the film *Destry Rides Again* (1939). In this song she is using back room in its literal sense. However, the film is known to have been a favourite of Beaverbrook, and one he had watched not long before he made his speech, and it has been suggested that it had an influence on his choice of words.

'It's stopped the bickering and forced 20 years' worth of planning out of the back room and on to the drawing-board.' (*Independent*, 2 September 1998)

back teeth see GIVE THE SHIRT OFF YOUR BACK

back to basics A political cliché, suggesting some nebulous, innocent golden age, before things were spoilt by theorists or over-complication. The expression had been used as a slogan by educational reformers in the USA in the mid-1970s, but became famous in 1993 when the Prime Minister, John Major, made a speech at the Conservative Party Conference, saying: 'The message from this Conference is clear and simple. We must go back to basics . . . The Conservative Party will lead the country back to these basics, right across the board: sound money, free trade, traditional teaching, respect for the family and the law.' Although Major was apparently going into detail, his speech was, in fact, little more than a string of clichés, leaving the listener no clearer as to what exactly 'basics' were. The slogan soon became discredited, in much the same way as VICTORIAN VALUES did, when the government was beset with a series of sexual scandals.

'I suspect what he means, although he daren't say it (remembering the "Back to Basics" and "Victorian Values" fiascos) is "less divorce" and "bring back the nuclear family".' (*Independent*, 17 September 1998)

'Graveney insists that Hick should go back to basics, and remain in that classic position he is in at the start of the bowler's run-up – to stand sideways-on, bat on the ground, knees slightly bent, feet about shoulder width apart, and head up and still with both eyes level.' (*The Cricketer*, 1992)

back to the (old) drawing board In 1941 a cartoon drawn by Peter Arno appeared in the *New Yorker*. It showed a badly crashed plane surrounded by frantic rescue workers, while in the foreground a little man, obviously the designer, is rolling up his blueprints, and with apparent unconcern is saying 'Well, back to the old drawing board'. Arno was probably using an expression that was already in use, but this much-reproduced cartoon certainly spread it. It reached an even wider audience when it was taken up by the makers of the Warner Brothers Loony Tunes animated cartoons, and used by characters such as Bugs Bunny and Wile E Coyote (when he was allowed to talk). It has now become a standard way of indicating, usually with resignation, that something must be rethought because it does not work.

'So it was back to the drawing board, undo the back and reknit it.' (*Machine Knitting Monthly*, 1992)

back to the wall The image of a fighter with his back to a wall to protect it while at bay will be familiar to anyone who has ever read adventure fiction or watched swashbuckling films. The expression has been in use since the sixteenth century, but reached cliché status in the First World War after General Haig sent out the following order on 12 April 1918, couched in resounding terms, but of small comfort to the cannon-fodder actually facing the enemy: 'Every position must be held to the last man: there must be no retirement. With our backs to the wall, and believing in the justice of our cause, each one of us might fight on to the end. The safety of our Homes and the Freedom of mankind alike depend upon the conduct of each one of us at this critical moment.'

'Never better than with their backs to the wall, or in this case fronts to the ball, the Gentlemen strode to their positions in the field as if in defence of Rorke's Drift.' (Amy Myers, *Murder at the Masque*, 1991)

back to your roots Coming from the same imagery as GRASS ROOTS, your roots are where, like a plant, you spring from. This use of 'roots' to mean your background, where you have ties, has only developed in the twentieth century, although expressions such as 'to put down roots', seem to be older. What exactly is meant by these roots has never been precisely defined, and 'back to your roots' is often used in an almost mystic sense, promising self-discovery or redemption.

'Next day I walked along the pier and suddenly this whole layer of memories came back. I realised it was because the place hadn't changed, it still felt the same. I thought, I have to get back to my roots!' (*You* magazine, 20 September 1998)

back yard see OWN BACKYARD

there is a bad (or **rotten**) **apple** (**in every barrel**) Surprisingly, this expression, seemingly so well established, has yet to be found in print before 1971. However, the sentiment is old. There is an old Latin proverb that says 'a rotten apple quickly infects its neighbours' and similar sayings have been found in English from the fourteenth century. Only the modern way of using it is new.

'With any breed, there's going to be a rotten apple in the barrel, but it's stupid of people not to think in the dog's best interest.' (*Dogs Today*, 1992)

'Leeds, having apparently got rid of their one bad apple in the week, now suspect the whole orchard might be contaminated.' (*Today*, 1992)

bad boy (**of**) A cliché much used by sports journalists in particular to label anyone, regardless of age, who has been in the news for his bad behaviour.

'United go cruising through but World Cup bad boy lands himself in trouble with ref for fierce challenge.' (Headline, *Daily Mail*, 27 August 1998)

'Coin-collecting seems an unlikely hobby for The Man in Black, but then the bad boy of country music has always confounded expectations.' (*Daily Telegraph*, 10 April 1992)

bad chemistry see CHEMISTRY

bad hair day A recent cliché from the United States, used to mean a day when everything goes wrong, starting with getting up in the morning and finding you can't do a thing with your hair.

'Perhaps Linda was going through some sort of existential crisis or she was having a bad hair day. Perhaps she just could not be bothered to get out of bed for Channel 4 and darling can you blame her?' (*Independent*, 18 September 1998)

'The Seventies. How come the joke decade of the century has been doing serious business in the Nineties . . . ? Because they were more than just bad flare days.' (*Independent*, 21 October 1998)

balance see HANG IN THE BALANCE, WEIGH IN THE BALANCE

ball is in your court Meaning the next move is up to you, this expression, adopted from tennis, came into use in the middle of the twentieth century. It belongs with a whole set of idioms from ball games – 'it's your ball', used as an alternative to 'the ball is in your court'; 'start the ball rolling'; 'you play ball with me and I'll play ball with you'; and so on.

'Given the amount of money it has already made . . . why can't Peel Holdings stump up? By the way, it owns the land through which the trams will travel, and will make even more money if it opens. The ball's in its court.' (*Independent*, 2 September 1998)

ballpark figure This American term for a rough estimate comes from the use of the term 'ballpark' (a baseball ground) to mean 'approximate, within the right range'. The idea behind this is the contrast between being at least in the ballpark, i.e. within the right area, and being so way out that it is outside the ballpark.

'The computer models, fed with cloud data and the assumption that the biggest climatic effect is produced when the cloud of sulphuric acid droplets is most widespread, all come up with figures in this ball park.' (*New Scientist*, 1991)

(jump) on the bandwagon A bandwagon is the sort of large wagon that would carry a band in a parade. Those caught up in the excitement of such a parade, might be tempted to join the performers by jumping or climbing on to the bandwagon. Hence the use of the expression, since the end of the nineteenth century, for joining something popular or fashionable.

'Armourers knew this and they, too, jumped on the funerary bandwagon, producing black-hilted and pommelled mourning swords with black scabbards.' (Julian Litten, *The English Way of Death*, 1991)

bang see NOT WITH A BANG BUT A WHIMPER

bang heads together The sight of someone subduing opponents by banging their heads together, used for either comic or dramatic effect, is a cliché of film, and it is not surprising that this has passed into speech as an expression meaning to reprimand severely or stop disagreement.

'Only someone with John Prescott's weight is going to be able to step into this impasse and bang some heads together.' (*Independent*, 2 September 1998)

bang on about This is a colloquialism that is fast becoming a cliché as it is used, in contexts where it would not previously have been expected, to mean to talk at (too great) length or tediously.

'He said the English were fine ones to bang on about cruelty when they sent little boys off to boarding school when they were eight.' (Jilly Cooper, *Polo*, 1991)

baptism of fire In the nineteenth century the expression 'baptism of fire', adopted from French, was used for the first time a soldier came under enemy fire. From that it came to be used in the twentieth century to mean any ordeal or difficult task, particularly a public one, faced for the first time. The expression, in a literal sense, can ultimately be traced back to the Bible.

'This week the hearing reached a milestone with the first session of full cross-examination – a baptism of fire for the Department of Energy, which surprised everyone by agreeing to be interrogated on the full gamut of Whitehall's current thinking on energy policy.' (*New Scientist*, 1991)

bar the shouting SEE ALL OVER BAR THE SHOUTING

bark worse than his bite The Latin version of this saying goes back to the first century AD, and the concept goes back to the seventeenth century in English, although the actual wording is not found until the nineteenth century. As might be expected from a saying that is inspired by the behaviour of a household pet, while it can be used to imply ineffectiveness, it is often used quite affectionately.

barrel SEE OVER A BARREL

bat SEE OFF YOUR OWN BAT

battle of the bulge The original Battle of the Bulge was fought in the Second World War in 1944, when the German forces broke through allied lines and advanced sixty miles into Belgium. The Allies were forced into a desperate action to contain this German breakthrough which formed a bulge in the lines of troops encircling German forces. The expression became popular after a successful film of the same name appeared 1965, but is now almost exclusively used to mean an attempt to lose weight and is particularly popular with headline and caption writers.

' "Slow down your eating" is excellent classic advice for those with a weight problem – and many of those who have struggled long in the battle of the bulge had probably read it before, and even tried to follow it.' (Audrey Eyton, *The Complete F Plan Diet*, 1987)

be all and end all A cliché meaning the most important thing, common since the nineteenth century, this is not often recognized nowadays as a quotation. Shakespeare uses it in *Macbeth* (I.vii) in a rather different way from its current sense. Macbeth is trying to steel himself to murder Duncan, and worries that the act will not be without knock-on effects. In a famous soliloquy he says 'If it were done when 'tis done, then 'twere well/It were done quickly. If th'assassination/Could trammel up the consequence, and catch,/With his surcease, success; that but this blow/Might be the be-all and the end-all.'

'Football isn't the be all and end all to me.' (Ernest Cashmore, *Black Sportsmen*, 1982)

be good – and if you can't be good, be careful SEE DON'T DO ANYTHING I WOULDN'T DO

'be it never so humble, there's no place like home' SEE HOME SWEET HOME

be that as it may A largely empty cliché of formal language, little more than a verbal tic. Its main virtue is to allow pedants to feel that they are using a subjunctive. It has been in use since the nineteenth century.

'Be that as it may, it may turn out that the preparedness not to acquiesce in any all-Ireland solution is decidedly stronger than most commentators until recently were prepared to accept, except for the work of Bew, Gibbon, and Patterson.' (John Fulton, *The Tragedy of Belief*, 1991)

beam me up, Scottie This expression is used as a catch-phrase and clichéd response to anything to do with science fiction or futuristic technology. Curiously, the expression was never used in the original *Star Trek* television series which ran from 1966, but it became common in popular speech with many users convinced that they had heard it used in the series. It was only after the expression was well established in the language that it was used in the *Star Trek* films.

beat a path to someone's door There has been much debate as to who actually coined the saying about a better mousetrap and the world beating a path to the maker's door. It has long been attributed to Ralph Waldo Emerson (1803–82), but Elbert Hubbard (1859–1915), coiner of 'Life is just one damn thing after another', claimed it for his own. It does not, in fact, appear in Emerson's published writings, but a Mrs Sarah Yule published a book called *Borrowings* in 1889, containing the following words, which she later claimed to have written down from a lecture given by Emerson: 'If a man write a better book, preach a better sermon, or make a better mouse-trap than his neighbour, tho' he build his house in the woods, the world will make a beaten path to his door,' and this is now generally accepted as the source.

'Environmental pollution, genetic engineering, pesticides and personal health, are just some of the reasons why consumers are beating a path to the organic door.' (*You* magazine, 20 September 1998)

if you can't beat them, join them This expression started life in the USA about 1940, probably in the cynical world of politics. Nowadays it is often used without any sense of working from the inside, but simply to express a willingness to go along with what others are doing.

' "Yes, who would have said that the ultimate triumph of Communism was to defeat capitalism from the inside? Who would have said that we would have joined you and then beaten you?" ' (*Independent*, 2 September 1998)

beautiful friendship see BEGINNING OF A BEAUTIFUL FRIENDSHIP

beauty see AGE BEFORE BEAUTY

beauty is only skin deep A proverb, warning against being taken in by appearances, this has been in use since the sixteenth century. Developments of it such as 'more than skin-deep' are quite common.

'When you think about it, the beauty of even the smartest kitchen is only skin deep.' (*Do It Yourself* magazine, 1991)

'Sometimes when you meet a beautiful woman, you know their beauty is more than skin deep, and so it was with Rachel.' (*Today*, 1992)

beauty secrets (or **tips**) A cliché of advertising and women's magazines, used to describe what in the past would have been described as 'hints and wrinkles', an expression no longer acceptable in the glamour industry now that all suggestions of wrinkles are taboo.

'Meanwhile, because what Ruby and Millie do best is girl talk, I asked them for their best-ever beauty secrets.' (*You* magazine, 20 September 1998)

'One of Roxanne's biggest beauty tips is available to everyone – a smile.' (*Today*, 1992)

bee in your bonnet The expression has been a cliché since the eighteenth century, and in use for even longer. The image behind it is that the ideas that obsess the person buzz round in their heads like a bee caught in headgear, and possibly make them behave as oddly as they would if a real bee were there.

'Mr Rodger Bell QC, for Mr Bewick, suggested that his client has a "bee in his bonnet" about surgeons being able to work anywhere at a drop of a hat.' (*Guardian*, 7 December 1989)

beer and skittles Beer and skittles have stood for the pleasures of life since the nineteenth century. Thomas Hughes in the novel *Tom Brown's Schooldays* (1857) famously wrote 'Life isn't all beer and skittles', and the expression is often used in this form. In earlier times the pleasure of drink and company was expressed by the term 'cakes and ale', hence Shakespeare's 'Dost thou think, because thou art virtuous, there shall be no more cakes and ale?' (*Twelfth Night*, II.iii), and Somerset Maugham's use of *Cakes and Ale* as the title of his 1930 novel.

before the dawn of time or history see DAWN OF TIME

beggars can't be choosers Once mainly used to indicate resignation about one's situation, nowadays this is often used more aggressively, of other people's situations, implying 'like it or lump it'. This expression was in use by 1546 when it appeared, in a book of proverbs compiled by John Heywood, in the form 'Folk say alway, beggers should be no choosers.' Another proverb, 'If wishes were horses, then beggars would ride', approaches the situation from a different angle; but this is more rarely used.

'But times change and beggars can't be choosers and bullets must be bitten, and now that Hilary Roberts finds herself in a superior position, who can blame her if she is inclined to condescend?' (Kathleen Conlon, *Distant Relations*, 1990)

it beggars description Meaning that something is all but indescribable, this expression has come a long way since 'to beggar' was first used by Shakespeare in this sense. In the wonderful passage in *Antony and Cleopatra* (II.ii) that describes Cleopatra's magnificent arrival in a gold-decorated boat with purple sails and surrounded by attendants, we are told 'For her own person,/It beggar'd all description.' 'Beggars description' had passed into general use by the end of the eighteenth century, and was also found in other set phrases such as 'beggars compare', but it is now quite unusual to find 'beggar' used as a verb outside 'beggars description', and the emphatic 'beggars belief'.

'In *Gravity's Rainbow*, conspiracies proliferate to such an extent that they beggar description.' (Edmund J. Smyth, *Postmodernism and Contemporary Fiction*, 1991)

this could be the beginning of a beautiful friendship A popular version of the final words of the film *Casablanca* (1942, script by J. J. Epstein, P. E. Epstein and Howard Koch, based on a play *Everybody Comes to Rick's* by Murray Burnett and Joan Alison). Rick (Humphrey Bogart) and Police Captain Louis Renaud (Claud Rains) have been in conflict throughout the film, united only in their apparent cynical self-interest, in their indifference to the morality of the Nazis and to the plight of those trying to escape them. By the end, Louis has lost his position and Rick his bar and Ilsa, the girl he loves, in order to help her and her Resistance hero husband escape to the USA. As they set out to join the Free French, Rick turns to Louis and says, 'Louis, I think this is the beginning of a beautiful friendship.' The film has been the source of a number of other popular sayings: 'Play it again, Sam' another misquotation; '(ROUND UP THE) USUAL SUSPECTS'; 'Of all the gin joints in all the towns in all the world, she walks into mine'; 'Here's looking at you, Kid' – as well as making the expression 'ain't worth a hill of beans' better known to English audiences.

'So I got up immediately and said it would be the end of a beautiful friendship if he accused me of necrophilia!' (Michael Aspel, *Michael Aspel: In Good Company*, 1989)

begins at home see CHARITY BEGINS AT HOME

believe it or not This cliché is often no more than a filler or verbal tic, rather than an offer of a genuine choice. In the USA the expression was made more current by the long-running syndicated newspaper column written and illustrated by Robert Ripley (1893–1949) and his successors, which dealt with STRANGE BUT TRUE information, while in London *Believe It or Not* was the title of a show that ran from 1939–40. The similar WOULD YOU BELIEVE IT?, used in much the same way, but now less common, seems to be the older of the two expressions, dating from at least 1776.

'The arguments of two common-as-muck tourists . . . are mirrored with tedious inevitability by an irritating posh couple (Lawrence and Bathhurst) in the adjacent hotel room. After the interval, believe it or not, things get worse.' (*Evening Standard*, 15 September 1998)

believed see SEEN TO BE BELIEVED

bells and whistles The image behind this cliché is of the multitude of bells, whistles and other noise-making devices found on old-fashioned fairground organs. Meaning much the same as ALL SINGING, ALL DANCING it was once mainly used of the trimmings and extras added on as gimmicks to computer software, but is now spreading to other areas.

'What might have been first visualised as a basic low cost word processor might have transformed into a full blown all bells and whistles application that has spreadsheets and databases built in, yet, if you're still using the first release, you could be losing out.' (*Practical PC*, 1992)

'It's more the "bells and whistles" of museum life which have grown so much in the last fifteen years, like restaurants, shops, publishing, which should be left to the private sector, and which generate important revenues for the museum.' (*The Art Newspaper*, 1993)

bells on see WITH KNOBS ON

bend over backwards Bending over backwards is a difficult and awkward action, so the phrase has come to mean putting yourself to considerable trouble to do something. It started life in the 1920s in the USA, and shows no sign of going out of fashion.

'You should bend over backwards to avoid bitter personal rows and the holding of grudges.' (Martin Edwards, *How to Get the Best Deal from Your Employer*, 1991)

(give someone) the benefit of the doubt In law you are innocent until proved guilty, and if there is any doubt about your guilt, you must be given the benefit of the doubt and considered innocent. 'Benefit of the doubt' began to be used figuratively in the nineteenth century, and had become a cliché by the end of that century.

'None of us yet knows whether Tony Blair and Gordon Brown . . . are really any better than their predecessors, but ever since they handed interest rate policy over to the Bank of England I have been prepared to give them the benefit of the doubt.' (*Mail on Sunday*, 20 September 1998)

bereft of life This euphemism-cliché meaning 'dead', or more correctly 'killed', has been in use since at least the beginning of the nineteenth century. However, the *Monty Python* Dead Parrot sketch of 1969 ('It's not pining – it's passed on! The parrot is no more! It has ceased to be! It's expired and gone to meet its maker! This is a late parrot! It's a stiff! Bereft of life, it rests in peace – if you hadn't nailed it to the perch it would be pushing up the daisies! It's rung down the curtain and joined the choir invisible! THIS IS AN EX-PARROT!') has been so influential and is so widely known that few people can now use 'bereft of life', or indeed any of the other clichés of death in that speech, without being aware of the comic implications.

'The World Wide Fund for Nature is to launch an extensive monitoring programme of the North Sea after video cameras supervising an underwater cable-laying operation from Germany to the Shetlands revealed that the sea bottom resembled "a lunar landscape" bereft of life.' (*The Environmental Digest*)

best efforts see DESPITE MY BEST EFFORTS

best . . . in the world A cliché of patriotic politicians, usually prefaced by the words 'we in Britain have . . .' and applied most frequently, without any substantiating evidence, to things like British television, inventiveness, the arts or higher education. Compare WORLD CLASS.

'Yes, after 25 years of successful development of the North Sea, our expertise is some of the best, if not the absolute best, in the world.' (*Hansard Extracts 1991– 1992*)

'It may well be that the Tories' most lasting and damaging contribution to the cultural life of the nation will have been their deliberate subjection of Britain's television companies to the crudest of market forces, which will almost certainly reduce the best programmes in the world to the shoddy idiocies everyone else in Europe and US is fed.' (*The Art Newspaper*, 1992)

to the best of my abilities This is a formal way of saying 'as well as I can', a qualification which tends to make one feel that an excuse (probably DESPITE MY BEST EFFORTS which goes naturally with it) is being prepared. It has been well used since the middle of the nineteenth century.

'Ensuring smooth and just running of the case by encouraging parties and witnesses to perform to the best of their abilities; and by checking unnecessary paperwork, disallowing repetition, speaking concisely, and always remaining aware of costs.' (*Law Society Publicity*)

'He said that he would devote his "best exertions and abilities" to the work, and concluded by asking for "proper time for a work of such importance".' (Ian Toplis, *The Foreign Office*, 1987)

best (or **pick**) **of the bunch** The attractively alliterative 'best of the bunch' is the more popular of these two, and also the older, having been in use since the later nineteenth century, while the form with 'pick' appears to be modern.

'With numbers [of pub chains] increasing at a rate of knots, *Stuff* assembled a team of pub testers, including food and drink expert Nigel Barden, and got on the road in search of the best of the bunch.' (*Stuff*, October 1998)

'The Peugeot/Citroen diesels, sharing similar engines, are generally regarded as the pick of the bunch for refined performance in the smaller cars.' (*Daily Telegraph*, 15 April 1992)

it was the best of times, it was the worst of times These are the opening words of Charles Dickens' 1859 novel of the French Revolution *A Tale of Two Cities*. Often used to describe a love–hate relationship, they can also be used to express the idea of something that was good in parts, but terrible in others (see CURATE'S EGG).

'It was indeed the best of times and the worst of times, as I have found most prolonged expeditions to be.' (*Photography*, 1990)

best possible taste see ALL DONE IN THE BEST POSSIBLE TASTE

best practice This description is what a usually unspecified authority, perhaps only the writer, thinks is the best way to tackle a particular problem. Although a useful expression in the right place, it is becoming increasingly, and increasingly loosely, used.

'Teachers, already overburdened, cannot be expected to clean up all our problems; but school is the only place where the mechanics of our collective life can be taught systematically. Best practice already incorporates current affairs discussions in the syllabus; for all our sakes, schools attended by the majority of our children should not lag too far behind.' (*Independent*, 23 September 1998)

(give your) best shot A modern cliché for to do your best, this comes from football, and is still particularly popular with sports journalists.

'Wycombe . . . expect to be backed by an army of 3,500-plus travelling fans and O'Neill promised: "We'll be giving it our best shot for them." ' (*Today*, 1992)

best (or greatest) thing since sliced bread This cliché started life in the USA in the 1950s as 'the greatest thing since sliced bread', the alternative 'best' being the British version. It is often used of a new invention, or else ironically.

'Organizations like this are not good at remembering the things you have done well and if, as most of us are, you are at the bottom of the pile, you will find that you are considered to be alternately either the best thing since sliced bread, or a liability to the organization.' (John Harvey-Jones, *Making It Happen*, 1988)

'What really attracted me to the whole idea was that June said: "Personally I think it is the greatest thing since sliced bread." ' (*Machine Knitting Monthly*, 1992)

best things in life are free Often used as a comfort for poverty or to assuage envy of the rich, or else ironically, this has strong musical connections. It started life as the title of a song written by Buddy de Sylva, Lew Brown and Ray Henderson for the 1927 Broadway musical (later filmed) *Good News*, which included such syrupy lyrics as 'The moon belongs to ev'ryone,/The best things in life are free,/The stars belong to ev'ryone,/They gleam for you and me.' The title of this song was then used in 1956 as the title of a musical film biography of its writers, following their lives from Broadway to Hollywood. The strongest modern musical association for most people is probably from the very different lyrics of the 1963 Janie Bradford/ Berry Gordy Jnr song, 'Money (That's What I Want)' made famous by the Beatles, with its opening lyrics 'The best things in life are free,/But you can keep it for the birds and bees,/Just give me money,/That's what I want.' The Beatles were later to popularize a similar sentiment, that money 'Can't Buy me Love'.

'If you've ever doubted that all the best things in life are free, book a Club Choice holiday and find out for yourself because in a selected range of our top hotels and apartments we can offer you some great FREE features to add even more value to your holiday.' (Club 18–30 Summer Holiday Brochure, 1990)

with the best will in the world Often a rather patronizing expression, suggesting that expectations have been unrealistic, this is a natural partner to DESPITE OUR BEST EFFORTS. It is a favourite expression of officialdom, and when not patronizing can sound querulous. It was well used by the middle of the nineteenth century.

'Of public concern in the past about football crowds he said: "With the best will in the world, the centre of the town was affected every time there was a major home game at Airdrie, attracting a large travelling support." ' (*Dogs Today*, 1992)

better late than never A proverb going back to at least the first-century BC writer Dionysius of Halicarnassus in the form, 'It is better to start doing what one has to late than not at all.' The snappier English version is found by the fifteenth century, although the idea was expressed earlier.

'He had promised, Mr Sands said, to bring some friends with him, but by four o'clock there had been no sign of them, until, suddenly, there was an immense bustle outside, and Mr Sands, rushing out, came back to announce triumphantly that Cousin James had arrived – "Better late than never" being his unoriginal version of the truth.' (Paula Marshall, *An American Princess*, 1993)

'But as the old saying goes, it's better late than never (and better never late! – Ed.).' (*Zzap 64!*, 1992)

for better or worse This cliché comes from the marriage service in the Book of Common Prayer (1546), 'for better, for worse, for richer, for poorer, in sickness and in health'. However, it was already well established in the language when the Book of Common Prayer was compiled. It is found in an earlier version of the marriage service from about *c.*1403 in the form 'to hald and to have at bed and at borde, for fayrer for layther [lit. 'lother' = 'more troublesome (circumstances)'], for better for wers . . . til ded us depart.' Something very similar is found in Old English, and Chaucer's friend, the poet John Gower used it in about 1390 in a form that suggests it was already a set phrase: 'For bet, for wers, for ought, for noght, Sche passeth nevere fro my thought.' ['For better, for worse, for anything, for nothing, She is never out of my thoughts.']

'For better or worse, with sincerity or mercenary attachment, the hip musical climate was heavily involved.' (Mick Middles, *The Smiths*, 1988)

better out than in This is a vulgarism, in use from about the 1920s as a comment on belching or farting. An American version is 'there's more room out there than in here', while a more elaborate alternative, in use since the nineteenth century, is 'better an empty house than a bad tenant'.

'I do rather object to the sort of chap who farts in public and then says "Better out than in." ' (Robert Barnard, *Little Victims*, 1993)

(gone to) a better place A cliché for heaven, in contrast to that worst of places, 'the other place', Hell. The expression is first recorded in this sense in Shakespeare (*Measure for Measure*, IV.ii), but there the speech puns on the sense of 'promotion' that 'better place' could have in his day. By the eighteenth century it was being used in sentimental poetry for heaven, and 'gone to a better place' has remained a stalwart of sentimental grief ever since.

'I'm sure Diana went to a better place. It would be wrong for any Christian not to remember what Christ said: "Though your sins be as scarlet, I will make them white as snow." ' (*Daily Mail*, 27 August 1998)

better than a slap in the face with a wet fish One of the most used of the 'better than . . .' formulas, indicating that something is better than nothing. Others include 'better than a dig in the eye with a blunt stick'; 'better than a KICK IN THE PANTS' (or, in Canada, '. . . in the ass with a frozen boot'). The wet fish version, at one time much used by low comedians, seems to come from the USA. These expressions have been common since the 1920s, but probably originated in the late nineteenth century.

better to have loved and lost see LOVED AND LOST

between a rock and a hard place see ROCK AND A HARD PLACE

between the devil and the deep blue sea see DEVIL AND THE DEEP BLUE SEA

between the sheets As a term for sexual activity, this has been in use since Shakespeare's day. In fact Shakespeare was rather fond of using 'sheets' in this way, doing so at least seven times, as, for example, when Iago expresses his suspicions that Othello has seduced his wife Emilia with the words 'And it is thought abroad that 'twixt my sheets/He has done my office' (I.iii).

'I'm convinced that Diana was behind it; that she wanted the story told from her standpoint before it broke in Morton's book or in some awful *News of the World* between-the-satin-sheets scandal.' (*You* magazine, 20 September 1998)

'He felt a tightness in his groin and muttered foul oaths: she was a fine lady with her laces and bows and arrogant looks but, between the sheets, a different matter, soft and pleading, turning and twisting beneath him.' (P. C. Doherty, *Crown in Darkness*, 1991)

between you and me; between you, me and the bedpost (lamppost or **gatepost)** The simple term 'between you and me' for 'in confidence' has been recorded since 1588, in the endearingly modern-sounding 'This I tell you between you and me, but I would have it go no further.' The more elaborate forms are nineteenth-century clichés. Dickens used 'Between you and me and the post' in *Nicholas Nickleby* (1838), and a Mrs Royal wrote in 1830 in *Letters from Alabama*, in a way that can still make purists wince, 'Between you and I and the bed post, I begin to think it all a plot of the priests.'

'And you know it is wrong to suggest that I've any motives in that quarter because, between you and me, I can't stand the man.' (Catherine Cookson, *The Wingless Bird*, 1990)

'Then, putting her knuckles to her head, indicating her brain, she added: "Between you, me and the gatepost, we used to think they had a screw loose." ' (Chris Kelly, *The Forest of the Night*, 1991)

beyond the dreams of avarice see DREAMS OF AVARICE

Big Brother (is watching you) In the bleak future society described by George Orwell in his 1948 novel *1984*, England is run by a sinister dictator known as Big Brother whose image is everywhere, often accompanied by the slogan 'Big Brother is watching you'. From this, 'Big Brother' has come to mean an over-restrictive or intrusive aspect of the POWERS THAT BE. Orwell chose to call his tyrant Big Brother because one of the themes of his book is the power of propaganda to twist things, and, at the time he was writing, 'big brother' was used as an image of care and protection. However, such was the power of his book that the term soon came to be used in his sinister way, and had become a cliché by the 1960s.

'Any public relations efforts to promote reading among young men are also a good idea . . . Tory objections to "Big Brother tactics" are frankly ludicrous.' (*Independent*, 17 September 1998)

big cheese (**big honcho, big shot**) Etymologists seem to have got themselves in a rather difficult position over the origin of 'big cheese'. There is an Urdu word *chiz*, meaning 'thing', which was adopted by the British in India by the beginning of the nineteenth century in the form 'cheese', as slang for anything particularly good. 'It's the cheese' was used as a term of great praise. The expression 'the big cheese' used initially to mean wealth and fame, then to mean an important person, is often linked to this, but is also recognized as an American usage. How then did it get from India to America? It seems likely that the development of the two terms was largely independent. Certainly the first recorded use of 'big cheese', in the American sense, is clearly using cheese in its usual sense. 'Del had crawled from some Tenth Avenue basement like a lean rat and had bitten his way into the Big Cheese . . . He had danced his way into . . . fame in sixteen minutes.' This comes from a short story by O. Henry, written in the first decade of the twentieth century. Since this author was a master of American low-life language, it seems best to look to New York slang for the origin of this. 'Big cheese' has been rather dated, but has recently been revived as City slang. 'Big shot' is again considered mainly American, although first recorded from England. It may have developed from the earlier expression BIG GUN used in the same way, both expressions indicating power. 'Big honcho' is by far the most recent of these American expressions, having come into use in the Second World War. Honcho is from *hancho*, a Japanese word for the leader of a small group or squad, and was adopted by American soldiers to mean 'boss'.

'This Christmas, I'll be surprised if there's enough in the coffers to pay for wrapping paper. Not that any of the big cheeses has said anything about how badly we've been hit by problems in Moscow.' (*Independent*, 9 September 1998)

'In Cheltenham, he goes unnoticed; untouched by the glare of publicity and yet abroad, where powerboating can match motor racing for fans and followers, he's a big shot.' (Central television news scripts, 1993)

big gun 'Big gun' is used in two ways. The first is as an alternative to 'big shot' (see BIG CHEESE above), for an important person. The second uses the idea of bringing up the heavy artillery to bully someone into doing what you want, or to solve your problems. The first sense has been in use since the beginning of the nineteenth century, initially in the alliterative form 'great gun', while the second is more recent.

'The names of Jason Ratcliffe, Nadeem Shahid, Ian Ward and Joey Benjamin do not exactly get autograph hunters salivating and licking their pencils, but what they have achieved in the absence of the big guns is quite something.' (*Independent*, 1 September 1998)

'The reason the Government seems to be directing its big guns at unpasteurised milk producers has more to do with the big dairy industry's concerns at the erosion of their share of the market.' (*Guardian*, 31 December 1989)

big headed see TOO BIG FOR HIS BOOTS

big honcho see BIG CHEESE

big picture To see the big picture is to have the ability to take an overview and to see everything in its place. It is the opposite of 'can't see the wood for the trees' (an expression in use since the sixteenth century). This use of 'big picture' is a recent one, the expression having previously been used of the main feature in the days when more than one film was shown in a programme at the cinema.

'For more senior positions there are more subtle attributes such as self-knowledge and the ability to see "the big picture" which increase with age, these are the reasons why most institutions and societies rely on older leaders.' (W. T. Singleton, *The Mind at Work*, 1989)

big shot see BIG CHEESE

big stick This is originally an American expression, meaning a display of force or power. 'Speak softly [sometimes found as "talk softly"] and carry a big stick' is a saying associated with President Theodore Roosevelt (1858–1919) who used it several times. In a letter of 1900 he wrote, 'I have always been fond of the West African proverb: "Speak softly and carry a big stick; you will go far." ' By 1917 Kipling could write 'The secret of power . . . is not the big stick. It's the liftable stick' (*A Diversity of Creatures*). At first the expression was used mainly of international power (hence the expression 'big stick diplomacy'), but nowadays it is used more generally.

'No one expected to reverse the pull of 14 years of refugee resettlement overnight, and there is little doubt that voluntary repatriation would pick up speed if the Hong Kong authorities used quiet persuasion instead of the big stick.' (*Guardian*, 13 December 1989)

bigger and better An automatic coupling of words which developed in the twentieth century. It is particularly associated with advertising, but is found in a wide range of contexts.

'It was one of the biggest sporting success stories of last year and now it is back – bigger and better than ever before.' (*Evening Standard*, 1 September 1998)

'Pineapple and gin have a truly spectacular affinity, combining to make something bigger and better than either.' (*Daily Telegraph*, 5 April 1992)

the bigger they come (or **are**), **the harder they fall** This is a nineteenth-century catch-phrase from the world of boxing, a useful sentiment for the underdog. It is often attributed to the boxer 'Ruby' Robert Fitzsimmons (1862–1917), but what he actually said, when faced with a match against James J. Jeffries in 1900, was 'You know the old saying, "The bigger they are, the further they have to fall" ', so he was not claiming to have invented the expression. The saying was particularly appropriate in this context, for Fitzsimmons, who had already lost his world heavyweight championship to Jeffries the previous year and was to lose to him again, was light enough to have boxed and won the world championship at both middleweight and light-heavyweight, and weighed only 170 pounds. Jeffries, nicknamed 'The Boilermaker' and later known as the 'GREAT WHITE HOPE', was 6 foot 2½ tall and weighed 220 pounds. It was a real DAVID AND GOLIATH match, but this time Goliath won. Fitzsimmons was British-born, but spent much of his fighting life in the USA, and the saying still has strong American associations. As a catch-phrase, the expression was particularly popular among troops in the First World War.

bike see ON YOUR BIKE

bird see LITTLE BIRD TOLD ME

birds of a feather The proverb 'birds of a feather flock together', meaning that people of a similar type will be drawn together, has been in use since the sixteenth century in English, although similar sentiments are found as far back as Homer. The shortened form, 'birds of a feather', has only been really popular since the nineteenth century. 'Of a feather' here means 'of the same species'. The expression is nearly always used disapprovingly, suggesting that it is bad qualities the people have in common. It is still too soon to tell if the highly successful television comedy of clashing aspirations called *Birds of a Feather* will significantly affect the way people use the expression, but it can be found used with reference to the series.

'Novice anthropologists are not all birds of a feather but most readers of this book are likely to have grown up in a modern industrialised society of the sort which presupposes a particular type of major distinction between private affairs and public affairs.' (Edmund Leach, *Social Anthropology*, 1986)

bishop said to the actress see AS THE ACTRESS SAID TO THE BISHOP

bite off more than you can chew We have all seen a child struggling to chew an over-large mouthful, even if we have not had first-hand experience of the sensation. The figurative use of the expression developed in the USA, the first recorded use of it being in 1878, in the very American-sounding 'You've bit off more'n you can chaw' (J. Beadle, *Western Wilds*), but it was fully naturalized in the UK by the early twentieth century.

'Skil has also used an antistall mechanism, which is claimed to prevent motor burn-out when the machine attempts to "bite off more than it can chew".' (*Do It Yourself*, 1992)

bite the bullet In the days before anaesthetics, a man wounded in battle might be given one of the large, lead rifle-bullets to bite on to help him stop himself screaming while being operated on. It would also prevent him swallowing his own tongue. Early uses of 'bite the bullet' – such as Kipling's in 1891 in *The Light That Failed*: 'Bite on the bullet, old man, and don't let them think you're afraid' – retain an idea of using the bullet to control fear, but nowadays it is simply used to indicate doing something unpleasant or difficult.

'In the February issue I warned you that I was going to bite the bullet and buy a real computer.' (*What Personal Computer*, 1993)

bite the dust So strongly is this associated with old cowboy and Indian films – and this is probably where its modern use as a cliché comes from – that it can come as quite a shock to discover that the expression goes back to some of the earliest literature we have. The expression is used by Homer in the *Iliad* – 'May his fellow warriors . . . fall round him to the earth and bite the dust' – and was copied by Virgil. The origins of the expression in English can be seen in translations of these two. Dryden, translating the *Aeneid* in 1697 has 'So many Valiant Heros bite the Ground', and Pope, translating the *Iliad* in 1718, has 'First Odius falls, and bites the bloody sand'; but the first recorded use of 'dust' comes from another translation – that by Smollett of Lesage's *Gil Blas* of 1749.

'Many experts in the auction rooms make it their business to hang out with aristos waiting for the time Uncle Marmaduke's Van Dyck has to bite the dust.' (*Harpers & Queen*, 1989)

bite the hand that feeds you This expression, meaning to act ungratefully or against someone who has been helping you, comes from feeding domestic animals such as dogs. It is found from the beginning of the eighteenth century.

'Philosophical reflexivity is not high on the agenda and in an organisation which makes much of the concept of loyalty but really means subservience, the insider can find it hard to bite the hand that feeds and reveal any unhealthy aspect in the agenda.' (Malcolm Young, *An Inside Job*, 1991)

bitter end, bitter experience Bitter experience – usually 'from bitter experience' – has been in use since the beginning of the nineteenth century, and by 1858 *The Times* blended two clichés by writing, 'Bitter experience has taught us not to cook our hare before we have caught it' (see also FIRST CATCH YOUR HARE). But there is much debate about the origin of 'bitter end'. In the Bible (Proverbs 4) we find the words, 'But her end is bitter as wormwood, sharp as a two-edged sword.' Normally, this would be a perfectly acceptable source, and no one would think about it further. However, there is also a nautical term, 'bitter-end', recorded in English from 1627. A bit on a ship is something that you can wind a rope round; the loops of the rope are bitters, and the bitter end is the end of this rope. As Admiral W. H. Smyth says in his *Sailor's Word-book* of 1867, 'A ship is "brought up to a bitter" when the cable is allowed to run out to that stop ... When a chain or rope is paid out to the bitter-end, no more remains to be let go.' In other words, you are literally at the END OF YOUR TETHER. Whichever of these is the true source of the expression, it was well established by the middle of the nineteenth century.

'Charlotte had just begun to take stock of what needed to be removed from Jackdaw College when Mrs Mentiply arrived, intent on discharging her housekeeping duties to the bitter end.' (Robert Goddard, *Hand in Glove*, 1993)

'Jane knew from bitter experience that love is a rare thing, so she felt very strongly that nothing should be allowed to come in its way.' (Jean Bow, *Jane's Journey*, 1991)

black hole The term black hole for a collapsed star with gravity so strong that everything, even light, is sucked into it, was only coined in 1968, yet by 1980 was being used metaphorically to replace other terms which conjured up images of limitless capacity and no hope of return, such as the biblical bottomless pit or abyss.

'It will be hard if not impossible for the [Russian] government to borrow from its own citizens, let alone from abroad. Only the International Monetary Fund looks a possible lender but it must fear more loans simply disappearing into a black hole.' (*Daily Mail*, 27 August 1998)

blackboard jungle see JUNGLE

blaze of glory This is generally used as 'to go out in a blaze of glory', like a fire giving a final burst of flames before being extinguished. However, this is a fairly recent development, for in the past the expression was usually used of such things as sunsets. The first recorded use of the phrase, perhaps the source of it, is in the poem *The Hind and the Panther* (1686) by Dryden (a poet once much more widely read than he is today), where he writes, 'Thy throne is darkness in the abyss of light,/ A blaze of glory that forbids the sight.'

'McRae, who landed the double for St Helens in his first season in 1996, is bidding to go out in a blaze of glory after being told last month that his contract would not be renewed.' (*Daily Mail*, 27 August 1998)

blessing in disguise This expression for an apparent misfortune that turns out to be beneficial dates from the mid-eighteenth century, and was a cliché by the late nineteenth century.

'She failed her eleven-plus and ended up at a local secondary modern school, which turned out to be a blessing in disguise.' (David Oates and Derek Ezra, *Advice from the Top*, 1989)

blissfully ignorant; blissful ignorance see IGNORANCE IS BLISS

blonde bombshell Coined by Hollywood publicity people in the 1930s this was used by them mainly of the blatantly sexy Jean Harlow (it was the title of a film she made in 1933), but also of Betty Hutton. It is now applied, as the *Oxford English Dictionary* rather coyly puts it, to 'a fair-haired person, esp. a woman, of startling vitality or physique'. Further evidence for the media's fixation with BOTTLE BLONDES can be found in the expression GENTLEMEN PREFER BLONDES.

'When we see pictures in the colour supps of some half-dead, prunelike Hollywood mogul escorting a twenty-year-old blonde bombshell about the place, we do not say, "Oh I thought he would have gone for somebody more half-dead and prunelike." ' (Ben Elton, *Gridlock*, 1992)

blood see COLD BLOOD

blood on the streets (or **your hands**) Blood on the streets was originally a cliché of war and slaughter, but has become diluted to mean people in trouble, a mess, in much the same way as CRUCIFIED has come to be used in everyday speech. In the same way to have blood on your hands, which once meant that someone was a murderer, now means nothing more than the person who did something or the guilty party.

'There's a lot of blood on the streets out there.' Comment from a dealer in Japanese currency, on the fall of the yen. (*News at Ten*, ITV, 18 June 1998)

'Castro described the action of his former communist allies as "repugnant", saying that they would have blood on their hands in the event of US invasion.' (*Keesing's Contemporary Archives*, 1990)

bloody but unbowed This cliché comes from an 1888 poem called *Invictus* ('Undefeated') by W. E. Henley, which contains the lines 'Under the bludgeonings of fate/ My head is bloody, but unbowed.' It is used to describe someone who has taken a battering, but who has not given up.

'The last thing they all want is a Saddam bloody but unbowed (President Bush, for the first time, last week urged the Iraqis to take matters into their own hands and force Saddam to "step aside").' (*The Economist*, 1991)

blow by blow A phrase that comes from descriptions of the fight in the world of boxing. As an early example of the expression has it, 'Radio announcers . . . describe the struggle as they see it, give the blow by blow account of its progress' (*American Speech*, 1933).

'Few Americans were so sanctimonious or unimaginative as to imagine that their own sex acts would sound dignified if exposed by a blow by blow analysis.' (*Independent*, 22 September 1998)

blow the whistle In sport, when the referee blows his whistle everything stops. From this, two senses of 'blow the whistle' have developed. Firstly it is used simply to mean bring to a halt. Secondly, from the stopping of play after a foul, it is used to mean the reporting of crime or misconduct to the authorities or making unacceptable behaviour public, particularly that of one's employers.

'Having parted company with intended launch editor John Mulholland . . . many expected Mirror Group to blow the whistle on its plans for Britain's daily sports newspaper.' (*Independent*, 22 September 1998)

' "He was shot in cold blood because he knew too much and was about to blow the whistle," a detective said.' (*Today*, 1992)

be blown away It has been suggested that the expression 'blown away' for 'dead' comes from a New Orleans tradition of marching a coffin through the streets to the accompaniment of a jazz band, and that this was known locally as 'blowing a friend away'. However, this theory has little evidence to support it, and is unnecessarily complicated. A much simpler explanation is that it comes from soldiers' slang, perhaps of the Second World War, describing the effects of heavy gunfire. The expression comes from America, and by the 1950s had expanded, at least in Black dialect, to include the sense 'impress very much', a transition from killing to an expression of appreciation also made by the word 'slay'.

'Tell Luke I'm blown away by the new poem.' (*Esquire*, 1992)

' "I shot him in the back." Bailie asked Larkins to hide the gun and warned him that if anything happened to it, he'd be the next to be "blown away".' (*Central News* autocue data)

'Who would have thought that the Oakland As, celebrated by Mr Will and thought to be a collection of giants, would have been blown away in the World Series by a bunch of journeymen from Cincinnati?' (*The Economist*, 1991)

blushing bride The term 'blushing bride' dates back to at least the eighteenth century, and reflects the modesty and purity expected in an innocent bride, for she is blushing not only because she is the centre of attention, but because marriage inevitably leads to bed. Modern mores being what they are, it is not surprising that this cliché is in decline.

'A picture of Augusta in *The Queen*: "a blushing rosebud, soon to be a blushing bride".' (Pamela Haines, *The Diamond Waterfall*, 1984)

board see ACROSS THE BOARD

to boldly go where no man has gone before These words have been used in the voice-over to every episode of *Star Trek* since it was first broadcast in 1966. In the even more successful *Star Trek, the Next Generation*, made eighteen years after the first series, 'no man' was changed to the more POLITICALLY CORRECT 'no one'. As well as becoming the most famous split infinitive in the English language, these words have become a cliché of headline writers and journalists.

'The SOG Gold Power Plier is for those who search for the front line in experimental design . . . you can go where no one has gone before.' (*Stuff*, October 1998)

'While we've all been quick to condemn guitar manufacturers for being too timid to boldly go where no other has gone before design-wise, I found myself unwilling to applaud the Valley Arts Carlton for its daring to be different. (*Guitarist*, 1992)

bollocks see DOG'S BOLLOCKS

bolt from the blue If you have DARK CLOUDS HANGING OVER YOU, you are not too surprised to find lightning, or, in more old-fashioned terms, a thunderbolt. But if there is a clear blue sky above you, then a bolt from the blue comes as a real surprise. 'The blue' has been used to signify the sky since at least the eighteenth century – John Wesley, in one of his translations of the psalms writes of 'the etherial blue' – and 'a bolt from the blue' has been in use since the first part of the nineteenth century. 'Out of the blue' is a shorter version which does not seem to have come into use until the twentieth century.

'Defender Gary Pallister said: "It's a bolt from the blue. I'd never have guessed we were signing him if you gave me 300 goes." ' (*Today*, 1992)

'Gordon Brown was cheerfully forecasting 2 percent growth . . . Now he is halving the figure, as if foreign events had come out of the blue just yesterday to change his plans.' (*Independent*, 8 October 1998)

bolt the stable door see LOCK THE STABLE DOOR

bombshell see BLONDE BOMBSHELL

bonnet see BEE IN YOUR BONNET

book see THROW THE BOOK AT

boots on see DIE WITH YOUR BOOTS ON; TOO BIG FOR HIS BOOTS

born and bred This alliterative expression has been in use since the fourteenth century, and by 1542 Nicholas Udall, headmaster of Eton, could use the elaboration 'In the same Isle born, bred and brought up'. In modern times the expression is often used as a way of marking yourself as a member of a particular group.

'He set himself to heal the rifts in the party, and apparently succeeded, not only because Labour politicians are hungry for office but also because of his position of centrality, born and bred in the Labour movement.' (*Daily Telegraph*, 11 April 1992)

'No one but an old Londoner who has been born and bred and has lived for 50 to 60 years in London can have any idea of the extent of the change.' (Ben Pimlott and Susanne MacGregor, *Tackling the Inner Cities*, 1991)

some are born great . . . In Shakespeare's *Twelfth Night*, when the roistering Sir Toby Belch, Sir Andrew Aguecheek and the maid Maria want to get their own back on the Puritan Malvolio, who has tried to put a stop to their enjoyment of the good things of life, they decide to trick him into thinking his employer, Olivia, is in love with him. They leave a letter for him to find, apparently from her, in which he is told, 'Be not afraid of greatness: some men are born great, some achieve greatness, and some have greatness thrust upon them' (II.v). This quotation has now become a formula phrase.

'On her tombstone should be written this: Some are born great. Some achieve greatness. And some hire great PR companies.' (*Evening Standard*, 28 August 1998)

both ways see CUT BOTH WAYS; HAVE IT BOTH WAYS

bottle blonde A media cliché, used, despite the fact that, it is said, GENTLEMEN PREFER BLONDES, to disparage a woman who bleaches her hair, as opposed to the more approving BLONDE BOMBSHELL.

'She bustled through from the lounge when I pressed a bell on the bar and pushed a strand of bottle blonde hair from her forehead.' (Val McDermid, *Dead Beat*, 1992)

bottom line In accounting, the bottom line is the one that shows the profit or loss on the balance sheet. Thus the bottom line came to be an indicator of success or failure. This became a cliché in the middle of the twentieth century, but by the 1970s it was beginning to spread its range to mean the ultimate criterion, the most important thing, or even the equivalent of the FINAL STRAW.

'In the end, if a paper is to be judged on its bottom line like a widget factory, the seven-day *Express* can be arguably judged as "success".' (*Independent*, 22 September 1998)

'Pinning the responsibility on one individual is most unfair, he says – and Mr Hutton, above all, has been a very positive force for the paper. The bottom line is that Mr Hutton stays as editor-in-chief but must feel somewhat uncomfortable . . . knowing that the staff resent his presence.' (*Independent*, 29 September 1998)

bottomless pit see BLACK HOLE

bound hand and foot see HANDS ARE TIED

bounden duty Few people today are ever going to use the word 'bounden' – an old past participle of the verb 'to bind' – outside this set phrase. A bounden duty is literally one you are kept to by legal or moral ties. The expression dates from the sixteenth century, and has probably been kept alive by its use in the Book of Common Prayer, where the Communion Service has both 'It is very meet, right and our bounden duty, that we should at all times, and in all places, give thanks unto thee O Lord,' and 'We beseech thee to accept this our bounden duty and service.'

'Notwithstanding the plant's poor track record, Tom O'Reilly considered it to be his bounden duty to respond to the call for help from his compatriot, the Irish Prime Minister.' (M. Kilby, *Man at the Sharp End*, 1991)

boys in the back room see BACK ROOM

boys will be boys The idea behind this proverb, usually an expression of exasperation or resignation, goes back at least as far as a Latin proverb that said 'Boys will be boys and do boyish things.' It was in use in English by the sixteenth century, and a cliché by the nineteenth. While 'girls will be girls' was also in use in the nineteenth century, perhaps in these days of sexual equality we need to revive Thomas Deloney's 1597 comment that 'Youth will be youth'.

'In particular, many deviant and indeed criminal male roles either receive public approval – "boys will be boys" – or are at least positively portrayed.' (F. Heidensohn, *Women and Crime*, 1985)

brand image As the public has become more and more aware of what is involved in marketing and advertising, so the term 'brand image' has become more and more common. It is now being used figuratively to refer to public images in general or as an alternative to 'identifying characteristics'.

'Given the importance, in this sound-bite age, of being seen to have a clear brand image, it's become all the more important to have people to help develop that image.' (*Independent*, 23 July 1998)

brave face see PUT A BRAVE FACE ON

brave new world This is a double quotation: in *The Tempest*, Shakespeare has the naïve Miranda, brought up on an island with only her father for human company, respond to seeing a group of shipwrecked men, who mostly turn out to be corrupt, with the words 'Oh brave new world,/That has such people in it' ('brave' here meaning 'fine, handsome'). When Aldous Huxley wrote his novel of a future world in which babies were reared in bottles, and sex was encouraged, but love and affection, and especially individuality, were taboo, he borrowed Shakespeare's words, and called it *Brave New World* (1932), and it is from this that we take the phrase for a nightmare society. The irony of both Shakespeare's and Huxley's use is now often missing.

'Hong Kong Special Report: A brave new world tumbles down: Hong Kong tries to be optimistic about Chinese rule.' (*Independent*, 13 October 1989)

'It was mysterious, powerful, expensive – to an eight-year-old like myself, all part of the optimistic brave new world of big science.' (*New Scientist*, 1991)

breach see ONCE MORE INTO THE BREACH; STEP INTO THE BREACH

bread and circuses The Roman poet Juvenal (AD 60–130) in his tenth *Satire* complained '[The Roman people] long for two things only; bread and circuses.' Both of these were provided for Roman citizens for free or at subsidized prices, so what Juvenal was saying was that as long as the people had their food and entertainment, they didn't much care what happened. At a much later date the same idea was expressed as the OPIUM OF THE MASSES.

'Whatever you do, don't mention the *Titanic*. Iraqi state television has shown James Cameron's film three times (he can forget about the royalties) as a balm for hardship, the Baghdad equivalent of bread and circuses.' (*Independent*, 19 October 1998)

breeches see TOO BIG FOR HIS BOOTS

breeds contempt see FAMILIARITY BREEDS CONTEMPT

one (or **two**) **bricks short of a load** (or **wall**) To describe someone in this way is to imply that their ideas are wrong, not because they are 'thick as two short planks', but because they are 'not all there'. The expression 'one (or two) cards short of a deck' is equally well used. The formula has been a popular one, seized on as a chance to show off one's wit, and giving rise to similar expressions such as the not-uncommon 'one (or several) sandwiches short of a picnic' or one-off coinages such as the description of a political party in a recent election as being 'several policies short of a manifesto'.

'For others it is sufficient to look or act like a gouger by being rough-looking and dirty or disrespectful to and disliking the police, "giving lip" and swearing, coming from "a problem family" and being of low intelligence ("not all there", "air getting in", "not right", "a few bricks short of a full load").' (John Brewer and Kathleen Magee, *Inside the RUC*, 1991)

'I knew lots of males who were two bricks short of a wall who enjoyed making spectacles of themselves, and I'd certainly never trust them to mind kids.' (Mike Ripley, *Angel Hunt*, 1991)

bridge too far This cliché, for BITING OFF MORE THAN YOU CAN CHEW, developed after the publication of Cornelius Ryan's 1974 book *A Bridge Too Far*, made into a highly successful film in 1977. The book was an account of the Allied operation of 1944 which parachuted troops into Holland to capture eleven bridges needed to secure the approach to Germany. Lieutenant-General Sir Frederick Browning is supposed to have protested to Field-Marshal Montgomery at the time that eleven might be 'a bridge too far', but this is probably spurious. The expression rapidly degenerated into a formula phrase, much used in headlines.

'We didn't want the Sunday game which was foisted upon us in Edinburgh last year and we felt that the Irish match would be a Sunday match too far for our supporters.' (*Daily Mail*, 27 August 1998)

'As always, however, these are nicely balanced by examples of people who have gone "a bridge too far", stuck with totally unobtainable ambitions and allowed the whole company to be pushed into the pursuit, usually, of a product dream which the market has quite clearly rejected and which cannot be made to fly.' (John Harvey-Jones, *Making It Happen*, 1988)

brief encounter In 1945 a film called *Brief Encounter* was made from Noel Coward's play *Still Life*. It starred Celia Johnson and Trevor Howard as the lovers who put duty before feelings. Helped by the lush Rachmaninov music, it became the ultimate weepy of its day. Ever since, 'encounter' rather than the more common 'meeting' has been the chosen pairing with 'brief'.

'Nor is there any real evolution, only the inevitable modifications of time, in his personal feelings, the loyal determined affection for his drab wife Mana, his jealous longing for Lady Barbara Wellesley and his brief encounter with Mane de Graçay during his escape from France.' (Margery Fisher, *The Bright Face of Danger*, 1986)

bright side see LOOK ON THE BRIGHT SIDE

bring on board This is a modern business cliché, used to mean to employ, give a position to. The image is from shipping, and of making someone a member of the crew. The equally popular 'take on board' – for 'accept', 'grasp', 'understand', comes from a similar image, that of provisioning a ship.

'The new voice of the man in the street is David Mellor . . . He has been brought on board after initial contractual problems meant Wallis had to beg Petrie to stay after his official leaving date.' (*Private Eye*, 4 September 1998)

brink see BACK FROM THE BRINK

broken why fix it see IF IT AIN'T BROKE

broken-hearted see EAT YOUR HEART OUT

win (or **earn**) **brownie points** Some say that this expression, for gaining credit for your behaviour, particularly by flattery or sucking up to someone, comes from the junior branch of the Girl Guides, the Brownies, and their totting-up points for their good deeds for the day. More cynical people derive it from the American expression to 'brown-nose' someone, to flatter or curry favour, itself a euphemism, which translates into more vigorous English as being an 'arse-licker'. In all probability, both concepts are at work; the brown-nosing being the basic idea, but the association with those cute little Brownies making it possible for the expression, introduced in the 1950s or 1960s, to spread into respectable use.

'He was a particular influence on the great German Panzer commanders, Guderian and Nanstein, and lost a lot of brownie points with the British Establishment for championing them after 1945, on the dubious grounds that they were merely professional soldiers.' (*Independent*, 14 September 1998)

brute force 'Brute force', like its near synonym 'mindless violence', suggests lack of thought or intelligence behind an action, but very often the 'brute' part of this coupling is purely automatic and adds nothing to the sense. This cliché is the product of the Enlightenment, setting reason against the animal side of nature. A sermon of 1726 laments, 'Some kind of brute Force within, prevails over the Principle of Rationality.'

'Add the fact that the dominating sport, American football, venerates the combination of meticulous planning with the sudden application of brute force, and you may have an explanation for the macho tone of much of American policy-making.' (*The Economist*, 1991)

bubble SEE BURST SOMEONE'S BUBBLE

the buck stops here In nineteenth-century America poker players would put some small object, such as a pencil stub, on the table in front of the person dealing. When the deal passed to another player, the previous dealer would have to 'pass the buck' to them. Why the word 'buck' was used is obscure, but perhaps a piece of buckshot was sometimes used. From this custom the expression 'to pass the buck', meaning to pass responsibility to, or put the blame on someone else came into use, and became common from the early part of the twentieth century. The American President Harry S Truman (1884–1972) had on the presidential desk a sign which read 'The buck stops here', indicating that he took ultimate responsibility and it was this that popularized the term.

'The Chief Inspector is, of course, responsible for everything AIB does – the buck stops with him as far as aircraft accident investigation in the UK is concerned.' (William Tench, *Safety is No Accident*, 1985)

buck the trend The association between the idea of a horse bucking to unseat its rider and stubbornness and a refusal to conform is American in origin. What exactly 'the trend' is, is often unclear.

'The recession may still be biting, but video games company Nintendo continues to buck the trend.' (*Liverpool Daily Post and Echo*, 1993)

build a decent life SEE DECENT LIFE

Bulge SEE BATTLE OF THE BULGE

bullet SEE BITE THE BULLET

bumpy ride This image, from driving along a bumpy road, means having a difficult time. In popular speech it is sometimes a misquote of Bette Davis's remark in the 1950 film *All About Eve*, by Joseph L. Mankiewicz, 'Fasten your seat-belts, it's going to be a bumpy night' – meaning 'look out, here comes trouble' – and this sometimes gives it an extra spin.

'American experts think the drug might impede the absorption of vitamins . . . [but] it isn't every day that the dowdy and the middle-aged get a chance for a second adolescence. So we might as well get ready for the bumpy ride that is ahead.' (*Independent*, 22 September 1998)

bums on seats A media cliché, used to mean the members of an audience – particularly their numbers, and the revenue they bring in.

'He only knows about money, Arts Council grants, stuffy councillors going on about "bums on seats".' (Alison Leonard, *Gate-Crashing the Dream Party*, 1990)

'If he has the secret of putting bums back on pews – as his detractors certainly have not – then tomorrow's C of E may well belong to him.' (*Independent*, 17 September 1998)

bunch see BEST OF THE BUNCH

buried see DEAD AND BURIED

burning desire This set phrase, common since the eighteenth century, belongs to a group of expressions for strong feeling which contain words meaning 'burning' or 'hot', such as CONSUMING PASSION, and the old-fashioned ardent or fervent wish.

'Young hopefuls in dead-end jobs with a burning desire to make a quick buck were seen, along with unworldly yet ambitious and arrogant graduates.' (Alexander Davidson, *The City Share Pushers*, 1989)

burst someone's bubble If someone is elated or uplifted, we can describe them as 'bubbling over with happiness', or with similar images. If you destroy their happiness or shatter their illusions, you burst their bubble, and they become deflated.

'Hopefully we can go out and beat them; it'd be great to burst their bubble. (*Daily Mirror*, 1992)

'When he arrived back last night he was so happy about his love and wanting to marry Maria Luisa I couldn't burst his bubble so soon.' (Natalie Fox, *Love or Nothing*, 1993)

Burton see GONE FOR A BURTON

but not as we know it see LIFE, JIM, BUT NOT AS WE KNOW IT

(looks as if) butter wouldn't melt in his/her mouth This has been an English proverb since at least the sixteenth century, implying a gentle or innocent appearance, when the reality is usually the opposite. Thackeray sums up the type in *Pendennis* (1849) when he writes, 'When a visitor comes in, she smiles and languishes, you'd think that butter wouldn't melt in her mouth', while Swift produces a more elaborate version of the saying with 'She looks as if butter would not melt in her mouth, but I'll warrant cheese won't choke her' (*Polite Conversation*, 1738). The idea behind the expression is probably that reserved innocence is cool, against the fiery passion of the forward or experienced. The idea of coldness was certainly picked up on by the English actress Elsa Lanchester who is reputed to have said of the Irish actress Maureen O'Hara, 'She looked as though butter wouldn't melt in her mouth. Or anywhere else.'

by and large In the days of square-rigged ships, 'by' meant to sail within six points of the wind, and 'large' to sail with the wind pretty much at right angles to the course of the ship. An order to the steersman to sail 'by and large', therefore, was a vague one, indicating a range of possible directions – the sort of order that is difficult to understand without first-hand knowledge of square-riggers. From being a nautical term, 'by and large' was adopted in the eighteenth century to mean 'all ways' and from that to mean 'on the whole'. It has now lost all connection with sailing, and is usually merely a filler.

'Journalism is, by and large, a game where familiarity and advancing age often breed unemployment.' (*Mail on Sunday*, 20 September 1998)

(go or **do) by the book** Meaning to follow the rules, this has been recorded from the middle of the nineteenth century. It is frequently an alternative for keeping to

the letter of the law (in use from the first half of the seventeenth century). Compare
THROW THE BOOK AT.

'Or the jurors could have taken the path they did in fact elect, . . . and conclude
that these officers were only doing what they have been trained to do and that all
the famous video footage demonstrated was that they had indeed gone by the book.'
(*New Statesman and Society*, 1992)

Caesar's Gaul see DIVIDED INTO THREE PARTS

call see CLOSE CALL; YOUR CALL; DON'T CALL US

call a spade a spade In Greece and Rome, rhetoric – the art of choosing your
words carefully and persuasively – was highly admired, not just for its own sake, but
because much of politics and the law was run by people standing up in the open
market place and persuading others to think their way. The study of rhetoric sometimes encouraged the use of over-elaborate language, and both Greek and Roman
writers describe as preferable the simple language of calling a spade a spade. That
paragon of public speakers, Cicero, said, 'A wise man will call a spade a spade.' This
idea was picked up by English writers of the sixteenth century, and it is easy to see
how the idea of choosing plain words could drift into the idea of plain speaking, or
not mincing matters. The expression was very common in the nineteenth century,
and Oscar Wilde uses a variant of it when, in *The Importance of Being Earnest* (1895),
he has Cecily say 'When I see a spade I call it a spade', to which the refined Gwendolen
replies, 'I am glad to say that I have never seen a spade.' By the early nineteenth
century, someone who spoke with unnecessary bluntness could be described as one
who 'calls a spade a bloody shovel'.

'There are many people around who call a spade a spade, but who do so in such
a rude, offensive way, that this kind of plain-speaking becomes something to be
avoided.' (Michael Lawson, *Facing Conflict*, 1991)

call in(to) question In the days when lawyers all had fluent Latin, they would be
familiar with the Latin legal term *in dubium vocare*, meaning 'to call in question, or
doubt'. This literal translation appeared in English by the late sixteenth century,
and from the start, although it was also used in the legal sense of to summon for
trial, was used in contexts where a simple 'question' would do just as well. 'Call
into . . .' was an alternative form of the expression from the first, and this is now
the commoner form in the UK, although 'in' was the norm until this century, and
is still well-used in the States.

'The findings again call into question the Government's attempt to privatise
nuclear power despite constant warnings over the costs. The shadow Energy Secretary, Mr Frank Dobson, claimed yesterday that the CEGB's accounts had been
"massaged and adjusted to suit the Government's privatisation policies".' (*Guardian*,
22 December 1989)

calling unto deep see DEEP CALLING UNTO DEEP

came to pass see COME TO PASS

can of worms This is an American expression from the mid-twentieth century.
The image comes from a container of fishing bait. It is used to mean something
complicated, but is coming more and more to mean something unpleasant that
someone wants to keep hidden because it might cause problems. The expression is

most commonly used with 'to open', for when you open a can of worms, there is always the worry about what might get out.

'The prosecution could open a can of worms, since Mr Shalabai who has denied any wrongdoing had connections at every level.' (*Independent*, 13 October 1989)

can't be doing with A dialect term for finding something unacceptable, this expression has recently become more and more common in standard prose. Interestingly, the *OED* marks the construction 'to be doing with' as obsolete, recording it only between the years 1601 and 1724.

'All his performances are much more like Karajan than the composer he's playing of course. I can't be doing with any of his recordings of twentieth-century music, which emasculate anything remotely troubling and awkward.' (*Evening Standard*, 1 September 1998)

can't hide see RUN BUT CAN'T HIDE

can't hold a candle to; **not fit to hold a candle to** In the days before electric or gas light, servants might hold a candle to help someone to see. Thus Jessica, running away from her father Shylock in *The Merchant of Venice*, says that she is glad that it is night, so that her lover Lorenzo cannot see her disguised as a boy. Lorenzo replies that she must act as his torch-bearer, and Jessica replies with 'What! Must I hold a candle to my shames?' (II.vi). The term came to be used to mean a lowly status, so that someone who is not fit to hold a candle to someone else is, to use Laurence Hope's more extreme expression, 'Less than the dust, beneath thy Chariot wheel' (*The Garden of Kama*, 1901).

'There are players now valued in the £2m bracket who can't hold a candle to Ian in terms of ability and George Graham must be thinking he has bought himself a star on the cheap.' (*Today*, 1992)

can't see the wood for the trees see BIG PICTURE

can't teach an old dog new tricks see LIFE IN THE OLD DOG YET

cap fits see IF THE CAP FITS

captain of industry This expression was coined by Thomas Carlyle, who used 'Captains of Industry' as a chapter heading for his book *Past and Present* in 1843. It became a popular expression, particularly in newspapers, to describe the leaders of big business, but now has a slightly old-fashioned ring to it. Such people are nowadays more likely to be called the much less respectful FAT CATS.

'Vadinamia doesn't care if you're a criminal or a captain of industry (not that there's much difference).' (Douglas Hill, *The Fraxilly Fracas*, 1989)

cards short of a deck see BRICKS SHORT OF A LOAD

caring (and) sharing A cliché from the 1970s, reflecting the vast expansion in the use and meaning of 'caring' in modern social and political use. The expression is now being overtaken in some areas by TOUCHY-FEELY.

'People will be amazed in the next few months at the change in her image, but they should realise that first and foremost she is a caring, sharing woman.' (*She* magazine, 1989)

carrot and stick This image of persuading a donkey to move either by dangling a carrot in front of it or by hitting it with a stick is not recorded until 1895, but may well be older.

'The carrot and stick approach is to do with reward and punishment, incentives and pressures.' (Philippa Davies, *Status: What it Is and How to Achieve it*, 1991)

carte blanche The French for a blank piece of paper, the underlying idea behind this expression is of handing someone a blank sheet on which they can write their own terms. From this has developed the idea of giving someone a free hand to do what they want. The term first came into use in the eighteenth century in this sense, although it had been used since the mid-seventeenth century in the special sense of a hand containing no court cards in the card game piquet.

'She had carte blanche to bring home as many friends as she liked.' (Mary Gervaise, *The Distance Enchanted*, 1983)

case see ON THE CASE

cash cow A recent cliché of the business world, a cash cow is a business or product you can milk for a steady income. Although the expression is recent, the idea is old. 'Milk' has been used in this sense since the early sixteenth century.

'Clive Hollick saw *The Express* as a cash cow which could make money, not by increasing circulation but by cutting costs.' (*Independent*, 22 September 1998)

'A chocolate and wafer combination, it strikes directly at arch-rival Rowntree's £130m cash cow Kit Kat.' (*Marketing Week*, 17 January 1992)

cast into outer darkness see OUTER DARKNESS

cast pearls before swine see PEARLS BEFORE SWINE

cast the first stone In the biblical story of the woman taken in adultery, Jesus is asked what should be done with the woman, since the law of Moses says that she should be stoned. He replies, 'He that is without sin among you, let him first cast a stone at her' (St John 8:7). Since none of her accusers could claim to be without sin, they slink away, leaving her unharmed. 'To cast the first stone' therefore means to make accusations, particularly when the accusers are not in too strong a moral position themselves.

'There is no point in arguing who cast the first stone or threw the first bomb, destroying a church hall or a GAA club.' (*Belfast Telegraph*)

'Let him who has never lifted the seam of a cricket ball cast the first stone.' (*Daily Mirror*, 1992)

cat among the pigeons Although to put or set the cat among the pigeons, with its imagery of farmyard domesticity, sounds old, it has not been recorded before the middle of the twentieth century, and its history is largely unknown.

'If it is your intention to set a cat among the pigeons or let loose an eagle in the dovecote, you don't send a postcard in advance announcing your intentions.' (Alistair MacLean, *Santorini*, 1987)

cat's paw see HOT POTATO

catch-22 'There was only one catch and that was Catch-22, which specified that a concern for one's own safety in the face of dangers that were real and immediate was the process of a rational mind.' This definition comes from the 1961 novel by Joseph Heller, *Catch-22*, which created the expression. In the novel, Yossarion, flying combat missions in the chaos of the Second World War, tries to feign madness to avoid getting himself shot down and killed, but finds that he can only be reassigned from duties if he applies for a medical certificate, but that the very act of applying for such a certificate is taken as evidence that he is in his right mind. It did not take long for this handy term for a NO-WIN SITUATION to catch on as a term for something so often met with in modern life.

'What Havel wittily shows is the kind of Catch-22 situation faced by a dissident in a despotism: whether to cling fiercely to your own moral integrity (thereby landing others in the shit) or whether to conform and perpetuate a corrupt system.' (*Guardian*, 31 December 1989)

catch with your pants (or **trousers**) **down; catch napping** Both these expressions mean to be caught unawares, although being caught with your pants down is usually the more embarrassing. 'To catch napping' is an old expression – in use by Shakespeare's day – and is self-explanatory. Someone who is asleep can be approached without being seen – particularly dangerous for a soldier, probably the original context of the phrase. To be caught with your pants down – sometimes anglicized to 'with your trousers down' – may also be military, the fate of a soldier caught by the enemy while relieving himself. However, it has also been suggested that it derives from a man caught in an adulterous situation, and it is certainly found used in a sexual sense as a cliché.

'But one thing for certain, as far as the tour was concerned, French was not going to be caught with his pants down.' (*Rugby World and Post*, 1992)

'When Graham arrived, Constable Jamieson was almost caught napping, and just had time to get himself in position behind the door.' (C. F. Roe, *The Lumsden Baby*, 1990)

catch your hare SEE FIRST CATCH YOUR HARE

categorical denial A set phrase, popular with politicians and similar, the first recorded use of which goes back to before 1619. 'Categorical', in origin a philosophical term meaning 'unqualified', rarely means anything more than 'complete' when used in this phrase, and the hearer's reaction is likely to be that the speaker is blustering, or that he PROTESTS TOO MUCH.

'They have called on the Northern Regional Health Authority to issue a categorical denial that it has any plans to merge 15 health care districts into six super districts.' (*Northern Echo*)

(different as) chalk and cheese To understand this comparison you need to think of a white, young cheese rather than a mature yellow one, and freshly gathered chalk, rather than something prepared for the blackboard. They can look very similar, but their taste and value are very different. The image is an old one. In his *Confessio Amantis* of about 1383 John Gower criticizes the Church for teaching one thing and doing another, saying, 'Lo, how they feignen chalk for chese' ('pretend that chalk is cheese'), and again, several thousand lines on in this lengthy book, he shows us the origin of the expression when he writes of the greedy man who does not care what he sells as long as he makes money: 'And thus fulofte chalk for cheese He changeth with ful little cost' ('Thus he frequently swaps chalk for cheese at very little cost'). This sense of comparative worth has of course now been lost, but the phrase lives on, no doubt kept in use by English speakers' love of alliteration.

'The partnership between the two was never a comfortable one – as personalities they were chalk and cheese – but politically it was immensely successful and entirely crucial to the Government up to 1983.' (Norman Fowler, *Ministers Decide*, 1991)

champagne corks will be popping see DANCING IN THE STREETS

chance of a lifetime An advertising cliché, now also used outside advertising and common since the 1930s, but dulled by over-use to promote 'one-off' offers. Both this and the related, earlier, 'once in a lifetime' were clichés by the mid-twentieth century.

'For the chance of a lifetime, simply fill in the coupon and send it to the address below, together with your photographs, no later than Monday March 4, 1991.' (*Clothes Show*, 1991)

'Celebrating the start of our once in a lifetime holiday in style by sipping rum punches on the open deck we watched the sun beginning to set before being escorted to our cabin.' (*Wedding and Home*, 1992)

change from a sixpence see STILL HAVE CHANGE FROM A SIXPENCE

change into something more comfortable see SOMETHING MORE COMFORT-ABLE

charity begins at home Charity is a difficult word. While most modern users limit it to the idea of giving money to help the needy, the Latin word it is based on had a far different meaning. *Caritas* meant 'dearness, love based on respect (as opposed to sexual attraction)', as well as 'expensiveness', much in the way that we use 'dear' for both senses in English. Charity was thus the word chosen in the King James Bible for 'Christian love', and many of our sayings containing the word charity originally used it in this sense, including 'charity begins at home'. Since one aspect of Christian love is giving alms to the poor, the two senses 'love' and 'giving' have always existed alongside each other, and it is not surprising that the two have become confused. Both these ideas are found in the Epistle to Timothy, in the instruction, 'But if any provide not for his own, and specially for those of his own house, he hath denied the faith, and is worse than an infidel,' and in the instruction that children should 'learn first to shew piety at home'. Forms of the saying are found from the fourteenth century, and by the early seventeenth were well-enough known for Beaumont and Fletcher to write, 'Charity and beating begins at home' (*Wit without Money*, 1616).

charmed life This is a quotation-cliché, from Shakespeare's *Macbeth*. Deluded as in so many things by the witches, Macbeth believes himself invulnerable in battle, for, as he tells Macduff, 'I bear a charmed life, which must not yield to one of woman born' (V.vii). However, Macduff answers him, 'Despair thy charm . . . Macduff was from his mother's womb/Untimely ripp'd', thereby winning a psychological victory which is soon followed by a physical one. By the nineteenth century charmed life had become a cliché to describe anyone who had DICED WITH DEATH and survived, and in the twentieth century expanded to include the inanimate.

'Totten pounced on Dermot McCaul's poor overhead clearance to crash the ball home off a post and lift the siege on his own goal which had led a charmed life.' (*The Belfast Telegraph*)

'What I'm not prepared to accept is that he's entitled to lead a charmed life while others struggle and falter and fail.' (Robert Goddard, *Into the Blue*, 1990)

a . . .'s charter The use of 'charter' to mean a licence to do something that the speaker objects to, is a recent, but popular one. Early uses usually refer to legislation, hence the choice of the word charter with its legal associations, but now it is used of almost any thing or action someone wants to protest against.

'A guide on how to avoid traffic jams on some of the most congested motorways in Britain will be launched next week amid claims by motoring organisations it was a "rat runners charter".' (*Independent*, 8 August 1998)

'Without public debate or scrutiny by Parliament, the police are likely to gain, as Liz Parratt from the organisation Liberty puts it, "a snoopers' charter for the Internet".' (*Independent*, 7 September 1998)

cheap at the price Originally a huckster's cry of good value, this expression still carries with it a certain feeling of suspicion that all is not as it should be. The object for sale may not be 'cheap and nasty' (cliché from the early nineteenth century) or 'cheap and cheerful' (a modern cliché), but is, the seller would argue, good value for money. Ironically, this was the original meaning of the word 'cheap', which, as a noun, meant the act of buying or barter, and hence the price of something. We only got our adjective 'cheap' in the sixteenth century, when the expression 'good cheap' meaning 'a good price', 'a bargain' was shortened just to 'cheap'. The ironic elaboration 'cheap at half the price' probably goes back to the nineteenth century.

'The total cost of repairing the medieval fabric of All Saints' and making it suitable for the next millennium was a mere £1.7m – cheap at the price.' (*Private Eye*, 18 September 1998)

cheer to the echo This is an adaptation of Shakespeare's 'I would applaud thee to the very echo/That should applaud again', from *Macbeth*. This obscure quotation is explained by the *OED* as 'so vociferously as to produce echoes'. It has been a cliché from at least the nineteenth century, and now has a rather literary, old-fashioned feel to it, although it was used by Tony Blair at the 1997 Labour Party Conference, celebrating his party's recent victory.

good (or **bad**, or **the right**) **chemistry** The use of the word 'chemistry' to describe the reaction between people or their personal characteristics actually goes back to the sixteenth century, Queen Elizabeth I being the first recorded user. However, as a cliché, used with terms such as 'good' or 'bad', it belongs to the twentieth century. This use probably grew up with the spread of knowledge of human physiology, particularly the bio-chemical processes involved in attraction between people, as shown in the expression 'sexual chemistry' for physical attraction. An early use of this is found in George Bernard Shaw's *You Never Can Tell* (1898): 'No, no, no. Not love: we know better than that. Let's call it chemistry . . . Well. You're attracting me irresistibly – chemically.' From the idea of sexual attraction, 'chemistry' spread to cover other areas of getting on together.

'We seem to have the right chemistry. It must be a quirk of nature because we are from totally different ends of the game but what we share is a sense of family and a real hunger.' (*Daily Mail*, 27 August 1998)

cheque in the post A conscious cliché of the business world, representing a standard excuse for non-payment of a debt.

'Yesterday the [Russian] government was reported to have missed a £55m interest payment on some slightly longer-term debt. Officials later insisted that the payment was being made. A cheque was in the post, perhaps?' (*Daily Mail*, 27 August 1998)

chickens come home to roost see COME HOME TO ROOST

children of all ages A cliché of advertisers since the middle of the twentieth century, this represents an unconvincing attempt to imply that something will be fun for everyone. Even worse are variants such as 'children from seven to seventy'.
'A world of verse for children of all ages.' (*Daily Mail*, 27 August 1998)

chinless wonder 'Chinless' was used in the nineteenth century to imply a lack of character, a firm chin being felt to indicate firm resolve. While this idea still lurks behind 'chinless wonder', the expression, in use since the 1960s, is mainly used of those who are both dim and privileged, who could also be classified as 'upper-class twits', or, more generally, just the aristocracy.
'The chinless wonders themselves are bashful about defending their anomalous hereditary rights.' (*Guardian*, 17 October 1998)

chip off the old block When this expression first appeared in the sixteenth century, it was 'a chip of the old block' or 'of the same block'. The change from 'of' to 'off' only seems to have happened in the twentieth century. Whichever form is used, the idea is that a chip from a block of wood is a smaller version of the original, but made up of exactly the same material. This basic idea goes back much further than the sixteenth century, for the Greek poet Theocritus, in his *Idylls*, written about 270 BC, uses the expression 'a chip of the old flint'.
'His grandfather, who taught him songs and ballads and regaled him with tales of his own "merry" youth when he fought with gamekeepers, clearly saw the young poacher as a chip off the old block.' (Michele Abendstern *et al.*, *I Don't Feel Old*, 1990)

chip on your shoulder Originally a chip on your shoulder meant you were spoiling for a fight, but is now likely to imply a grievance or inferiority complex about something, or even a BEE IN YOUR BONNET. It comes from an early nineteenth-century American way of proving your machismo. As the *Long Island Telegraph* of 1830 put it: 'When two churlish boys were *determined* to fight, a *chip* would be placed on the shoulder of one, and the other demanded to knock it off at his peril.'
'Raving Red Sam Sylvester had a bit of a chip on his shoulder about the status of the Hawkwood Comprehensive . . . compared with the elite Greycoats Independent down the road.' (K. M. Peyton, *Who, Sir? Me, Sir?*, 1988)

chips are down The term 'chip' has been used for a gamblers' token since at least the 1840s, and has been a slang term for money for almost as long. Once all the chips are down you find out if your gamble has paid off. Thus, 'when the chips are down' comes to mean a time of decision, or more generally the MOMENT OF TRUTH when PUSH COMES TO SHOVE.
'They have now got superior 4 × 4 transmissions, diff locks and the rest, and doubtless would leave the Trooper literally standing when the chips were down off-road.' (*Farmers' Weekly*, 1991)
'The happiest humans seem to be those who believe in themselves, who have confidence in their ability to deal with problems and hardship, and have faith in the resilience of their minds and bodies when the chips are down.' (Simon Romain, *How to Live Safely in a Dangerous World*, 1989)

the . . . of choice This way of saying 'preferred', 'chosen' seems to have developed in the world of science, particularly medicine. The earliest quote found, from the

British Journal of Urology (1938), is fairly typical of the sort of linguistic environment it comes from. 'Epididymectomy is the operation of choice in tuberculous emididymitis.' It passed into general speech, perhaps via the common 'drug of choice', and the fact that the construction is not a normal English one does not seem to be stopping its spread.

'Organic bread, carrots and potatoes are becoming the food of choice.' (*You* magazine, 20 September 1998)

choirboy see VICARAGE TEA PARTY

choosers see BEGGARS CAN'T BE CHOOSERS

circumstances (or **forces**) **beyond my control** These are the natural companions to bureaucratic excuses such as TO THE BEST OF MY ABILITIES and DESPITE MY BEST EFFORTS. They date from the nineteenth century.

'Due to forces beyond my control, I missed that 21st anniversary of the sad day when Elvis passed from one Graceland to another.' (*Independent*, 5 September 1998)

'You long to get away and enjoy some freedom, but circumstances beyond your control dictate otherwise.' (*Best*, 1991)

classic see ALL-TIME CLASSIC

clean breast see MAKE A CLEAN BREAST

cleaners see TAKE TO THE CLEANERS

clear the decks On a sailing ship going into battle, the first thing to be done is to clear the decks of anything that might get in the way. Anyone who has visited one of the old ships of the line that have survived will know in what cramped conditions sailors worked, and how easily the everyday things they were surrounded by could become lethal in a battle. The expression is used in two senses – to tidy up or make everything shipshape, and to get ready for action. The literal use is found from the middle of the eighteenth century, but the figurative is a nineteenth-century cliché.

'Former Saint Wallace, 28, is being made available by United as they clear the decks before moving into the transfer market to solve their own goal drought.' (*Today*, 1992)

'Some people like to remote all the petals to "clear the decks"; others will remove just enough from the centre to give enough space to work.' (Bill Swain, *Roses: Questions and Answers*, 1990)

cling on for dear life see DEAR LIFE

clock see TURN THE CLOCK BACK

clockwork see LIKE CLOCKWORK

close shave (**call**, or **thing**) These expressions all mean a narrow escape, often from death, but have come to be used more generally. A close call and a close thing come from sport, a close call referring to an umpire's decision, a close thing to a race result – hence the description of the Battle of Waterloo attributed to (but never actually said by) the Duke of Wellington as 'a damn close-run thing'. A close shave come from the days of cut-throat razors, the world of Sweeney Todd the demon barber, when a clumsy movement while shaving could result in injury, and be literally a close shave with death. All these expressions, like many others referring to life and death, are popular with sports writers, particularly when describing football results.

'That calm, matter-of-fact voice belonged to Jack Swigert, the command module pilot, who survived that close call but died of cancer a few weeks ago.' (*New Scientist*, 1991)

'When I was much younger I did take chances from time to time and can recall more than one close shave.' (Bob Smithson, *Rabbiting*, 1988)

'We were all roped together, so we got him out, but it was a close thing.' (Caroline Anderson, *The Spice of Life*, 1993)

closet see SKELETON IN THE CUPBOARD

cloud cuckoo land This is the nineteenth-century translation of the Greek name, *Nephelococcygia*, coined from the words for 'cloud' and 'cuckoo' by the Greek dramatist Aristophanes for his play *The Birds*, first performed in 414 BC. He gave the name to a city built by the birds in the clouds which he used to satirize Athens and the Athenians. Often used in the form 'living in cloud cuckoo land', the expression means living in a state of fantasy.

'In short, I entered complementary medicine's cloud cuckoo land where the sun shone everlastingly and love oozed from every portal.' (Raymond Hitchcock, *Fighting Cancer: A Personal Story*, 1989)

clouds hang over see DARK CLOUDS HANG OVER

coach and horses see DRIVE A COACH AND HORSES THROUGH

cock of the school, cock of the walk see RULE THE ROOST

cockles of the heart see WARM THE COCKLES OF YOUR HEART

cold see LEAVE OUT IN THE COLD

cold blood, cold-blooded A cold-blooded human has nothing to do with reptiles and similar animals. Instead it goes back to the ancient theory of the four humours, and their qualities of hot and cold, dry and wet. If your physiology was out of balance and you were too hot, you acted rashly, in the HEAT OF THE MOMENT. If it was too cold, you were over-calm and rational. Emotions heated the blood, which cooled down with calmness. As a writer of 1619 put it: 'When the heate of that lust and lustinesse is past . . . they come againe unto their cold blood.' The same idea is found in French, in the expression *sang-froid*, which literally means 'cold blood'. The expressions go back to Shakespeare's day.

'Yet soon after his enthronement, Romero's close friend Fr Grande and two parishioners were callously shot in cold blood by security forces.' (George Carey, *I Believe*, 1991)

'Millwall's chagrin was heightened by the knowledge that their redoubt had been stormed by a full-back, Bowen's 60th minute winner being a cold blooded execution from Robert Fleck's spear of a short through-ball.' (*Independent*, 2 October 1989)

cold comfort The earliest example of this term for inadequate consolation comes from the late fourteenth-century poem *Patience*, in which the anonymous author says of Jonah in the whale's belly, 'Lord, cold was his comfort, and his care huge.' Contemporary use of the expression is affected by the enormous success of Stella

Gibbons's 1932 novel *Cold Comfort Farm* which satirized the craze for novels of grim country life, such as those of Mary Webb.

'Another drop in the inflation rate was cold comfort yesterday for the 2.74 million jobless.' (*Daily Mirror*, 1992)

(to get) cold feet There are various views about the origin of the expression 'cold feet' for a loss of nerve. However, there is probably no need to look for an elaborate story to explain its origin. It first occurs in this sense in the USA at the end of the nineteenth century, and is most likely to be no more than a reflection of the way the extreme discomfort of cold feet can make even the keenest give up an enterprise.

'By then, however, Norway, with the weakest and least industrialised economy of the three major states, was beginning to get cold feet and insisted upon appending a minority report saying that it could not, given its current economic situation, contemplate joining a customs union.' (Derek Urwin, *The Community of Europe*, 1991)

cold heart(ed) A cold heart, or to be cold-hearted, are companion ideas to COLD BLOOD(ED), all from the association of emotion with heat and lack of emotion with cold. The similar 'cold fish' is an extension to the literally 'cold blooded', a fish being both cold and unable to express emotion. This is an expression which dates only from the 1940s, while both 'cold heart' and 'cold hearted' are first recorded in Shakespeare.

'In areas of declining population the designation of key villages has become an emotionally charged issue with allegations of villages being "left to die" by cold-hearted and remote planners.' (H. Newby, *Green and Pleasant Land*, 1985)

'He said: "If Charles is a cold fish and Diana needs someone warm they'd probably be better off apart." ' (*Daily Mirror*, 1992)

cold shoulder see WARM WELCOME

collapse of stout party A catch-phrase cliché, used as the punch-line in many a mid-nineteenth-century cartoon of the type that used to appear in *Punch* magazine. These were usually drawn in great detail with heavily etched lines, showed two people, and had a long piece of dialogue underneath. One of the characters would usually be blustering or pompous, and a deflating remark by the other would lead to the collapse of this stout party.

'He was showing off, as is the way with adolescent boys in the first flush of manhood (let he who has not sinned throw the first stone), and, as is the way with adolescent boys in the first flush of manhood, he slipped and fell in the pool – collapse of stout party etc.' (Mike Harding, *Walking the Dales*, 1989)

(chickens) come home to roost This is an allusion to the proverb that curses, like chickens, come home to roost. Chaucer used it of birds in general, but the form with chickens is not found until Southey used it in 1810: 'Curses are like young chickens, they always come home to roost.' It is also sometimes used of other birds.

'He [Michael Howard] must reckon that he will be rewarded by not being returned to the Home Office to see his pigeons come home to roost.' (*Independent*, 24 April 1996)

come of age, come into your own To come of age, reach the age of majority, is a sign of maturity, and in recent years 'come of age' has increasingly been used figuratively to mean 'matured'. To 'come into your own' is from the same idea, that of taking control of your own affairs when you reach the necessary legal age.

'With stock markets faltering across the world, hedge funds now have the chance to prove that they have come of age.' (*Evening Standard*, 7 October 1998)

come thick and fast see THICK AND FAST

come to grief This expression for meeting with disaster or mishap, or failing, has been a cliché since the mid-nineteenth century. The construction is rather odd, and presumably indicates 'to arrive at a state of grief'.

'Numberless are the ministers who have come to grief at the height of their peroration as a child has let out a deep sigh, articulating the inner feelings of some and distracting into amusement the rest of the congregation who were listening.' (Stewart Lamont, *In Good Faith*, 1989)

'It is not unknown for so-called "unspinnable" aircraft to come to grief by getting into a stable spin.' (Derek Piggott, *Gliding Safety*, 1991)

come to pass This expression, used frequently in the Bible, and a staple of mock sermons, is perhaps best known from Luke 2:1, the opening of the Christmas story: 'And it came to pass in those days, and there went out a decree from Caesar Augustus, that all the world should be taxed.' It was well established in the language by the sixteenth century, and a cliché by the eighteenth. Modern users are probably rarely aware of the biblical connection.

' "Don't laugh," he shouted and launched into the expletive-spattered story of how this rum situation had come to pass.' (*Mail on Sunday*, 20 September 1998)

come up and see my etchings A conscious sexual cliché, used as a humorous invitation to join one in one's flat or bedroom. The origin is that of the caddish seducer of the innocent maiden using an apparently innocent stratagem to get her in his clutches. The expression may well have been used seriously in an early talking film, but if so, no one has yet spotted which one. The great Eric Partridge, in his *Catch Phrases* (1977) suggests that it is American in origin, and quotes a correspondent who says he knew it by the 1920s, and suspected it was earlier. Partridge also points out that there is a play of 1710 which uses a collection of prints in much the same way. In fact the motif goes back even further, to Wycherley's 1675 play *The Country Wife*, where both pictures and a collection of porcelain are used as an excuse for a couple to be alone together, and it may be even older.

come (or **turn**) **up trumps** This cliché comes from card games such as whist or bridge, in which trumps are the winning suit. The phrase means to do well or better than expected. In the nineteenth century the more logical 'turn up trumps' was the usual expression, but as it got more divorced from its origin and card-playing has become less central to social life, 'come up trumps' has come to replace it.

'So here we see again that whilst most diets are ineffective in reducing inches and cellulite, my new diet again came up trumps.' (Rosemary Conley, *Rosemary Conley's Hip and Thigh Diet*, 1989)

'How interesting it was, thought Dyson, how extraordinarily intriguing, to find that out of the whole team the only one who was actually turning up trumps was himself.' (Michael Frayn, *Towards the End of the Morning*, 1969)

in the comfort of your own home An advertising cliché, used to create an atmosphere that the copywriters do not feel is found in a simple 'at home' or 'by post'.

'If you would like to view a videogram of Colwyn in the comfort of your own home for 7 days FREE LOAN, forward your cheque in the sum of £10 payable to Colwyn Borough Council with your Name, Address and Postcode to: . . .' (Leaflet on tourism in Wales)

coming or going Usually found in a form such as 'I don't know if I'm coming or going', this expression for being confused or in a whirl is not well attested before the twentieth century, but that it was established by the late nineteenth is suggested by the names of Mr Cummings and Mr Gowing, friends of the immortal Charles Pooter in George and Weedon Grossmith's *Diary of a Nobody* (1892).

'I'd been left out at the start of the season, brought back for the game at Birmingham, and then left out again. I didn't know if I was coming or going.' (*Daily Mail*, 27 August 1998)

coming out of your ears People have been described as being 'up to their ears' in something since Nicholas Udall wrote, sometime before 1553, 'If a woman smile, up he is to the hard ears in love.' The more emphatic 'coming out of your ears', with its implication of not just being full of something, but so full of it that it is leaking out of the highest orifice, is, however, so recent that it does not even make it into the biggest dictionaries. It can be a dangerous expression to use, leading to incongruities, as can be seen from the quotations below. 'Up to your ears' has itself developed the more emphatic (or vulgar) variant 'up to your arse', as in the business proverb 'When you're up to your arse in alligators, it's hard to remember that you set out to drain the swamp.'

'By this time the team had propellers coming out of their ears.' (*Scrapheap*, Channel 5 TV, 11 October 1998)

'This must be the first year when new rock boot models haven't been coming out of everyone's ears.' (*Climber and Hill Walker*, 1991)

coming up roses see EVERYTHING'S COMING UP ROSES

comparisons are odious (or **invidious**) 'Comparisons are odious' is an old proverb, well known in the Middle Ages, and enough of a cliché by Shakespeare's day for him to have made a joke of Dogberry's malapropism 'Comparisons are odorous' in *Much Ado About Nothing* (III.v). 'Comparisons are invidious' is a recent development.

'Curiously, what really irks about this immensely tedious and overwrought book is the revelation that no-nonsense Ms Campbell is a visiting professor of women's studies at the University of Newcastle-upon-Tyne. That's right. Someone somewhere is laying out public money on the incubation of these groovy thoughts. Needless to say comparisons are invidious, but at least Julie Burchill's book has pictures.' (*Private Eye*, 26 June 1998)

concrete jungle see JUNGLE

condemn without reservation A political cliché, particularly as used by those suspected of perpetrating some outrage or knowing more about it than they should. It is a formula phrase, and various other high-sounding but vague terms may be substituted at will.

'Mr Kinnock said: "I condemn without reservation whoever gave this little girl's name to the newspapers." ' (*Northern Echo*)

consideration see AFTER DUE CONSIDERATION

considered see ALL THINGS CONSIDERED

considered opinion A term much used in reports and bureaucratic language as a way of implying both detailed work and a lack of personal responsibility. 'AFTER DUE CONSIDERATION' is an alternative.

' "It is the considered opinion of the board of governors," he said, "that in the interests of the good name of the medical profession, and" – he gave a diplomatic cough – "of St Andrew's, it would be much easier for all concerned if you were to resign.' (Noel Barber, *The Other Side of Paradise*, 1992)

consign to the history books (**scrap heap** or **scrapyard**) A cliché of the mid-twentieth century, 'the history books' is a cliché of politics, 'the scrap yard' popular with journalists writing about redundancies, but not exclusive to them.

'Tinker Dill, the sidekick on TV of wheeler-dealer Lovejoy, helped British Rail consign some of its antique trains to the history books.' (*The East Anglian*, 1993)

'Economists have told me this could be the final push that will consign up to 250,000 people to the scrap heap.' (*Independent*, 6 October 1989)

conspicuous consumption This is a quotation cliché, derived from Thorstein Veblen's statement that 'Conspicuous consumption of valuable goods is a means of reputability to the gentleman of leisure' in *The Theory of the Leisure Class* (1899).

'Even so, a significant number of takeover bids were probably no more than a form of corporate conspicuous consumption.' (*British Economic Performance 1945– 1975*, 1993)

conspiracy of silence So over-used has this expression been, that simply to use this cliché risks making you sound as if you have a persecution complex or at the very least a BEE IN YOUR BONNET, however true the accusation may be. It probably came into the language from French, as the earliest known use of it is in J. S. Mill's 1865 book on the French philosopher Auguste Comte (1798–1857): 'M. Comte used to reproach his early English admirers with maintaining the "conspiracy of silence" concerning his later performance.' By the late nineteenth century it was so well established that when Sir Lewis Morris asked Oscar Wilde what he should do about the conspiracy of silence among reviewers who were ignoring his publications, Wilde could curtly respond 'Join it.'

'There has been a conspiracy of silence between the nuclear industry and the Government on providing information about the contracts that Dounreay has signed and about the discussions and negotiations that have taken place or are taking place with foreign reactors.' (*Hansard Extracts 1991–1992*)

consuming passion This term for an all-absorbing interest is a companion piece to BURNING DESIRE, and links up with all the images of hot and cold representing strong or controlled emotions. It does not seem to have come into common use until the late nineteenth or early twentieth century, but it was a cliché by the second decade of the twentieth century – a great favourite with Edgar Rice Burroughs, for example. 'Time and again did Numa charge – sudden, vicious charges – but the lithe, active tormentor always managed to elude him and with such insolent ease that the lion forgot even his great hunger in the consuming passion of his rage, leaving his meat for considerable spaces of time in vain efforts to catch his enemy' (*Jungle Tales of Tarzan*, 1919). Nowadays 'consuming passion' is often used by journalists with a pun on 'consumerism'.

'*Stuff* assembled a motley crew of former CD buyers and prescribed a radical course of music therapy to see if their consuming passion in [*sic*] music could be revived.' (*Stuff*, October 1998)

consumption see CONSPICUOUS CONSUMPTION

continue apace This set phrase is the only time most people will ever use the word 'apace'. It comes from the Old French 'à pas', literally 'at pace' understood as 'at a considerable pace, quickly'. The expression has been ignored by the philologists, and little is known of its history, but it does not seem to have become a cliché until the twentieth century.

'News and rumours of Western brewers interested in acquiring stakes in Eastern plants continue apace.' (*What's Brewing*, 1991)

'Technical advances in fleece continue apace such as with the stretch version which gives improved insulation and greater mobility through a closer fit.' (*Outdoor Action*, 1992)

control see CIRCUMSTANCES BEYOND MY CONTROL

cooking the books see CREATIVE ACCOUNTING

Cool Britannia When this expression was used by the Labour Party it acquired instant cliché status and instant inbuilt redundancy. However, the expression has a far longer history than just as a political slogan. The politicians picked it up from the name of a strawberry and chocolate flavoured ice cream produced by the firm of Ben and Jerry in 1996, who stopped manufacturing it in June 1998 after the expression became politicized, not wanting to get involved in controversy. But the expression goes back still further, to the last time that Britain was the place for cool youngsters, in the 1960s. Then, Vivian Stanshall wrote the following lyrics for the Bonzo Dog Doo Dah Band, recorded in 1968, 'Cool Britannia, Britannia take a trip, Britons ever, ever, ever, shall be hip.'

'In the shallow days of Cool Britannia, in which our past is seemingly dismissed as so much rubbish, here is a book which reminds us of one of the things that makes us Great Britain.' (*Mail on Sunday*, 20 September 1998)

'Cool Britannia may well be dying of hypothermia.' (Quotes of the Week, *Mail on Sunday*, 20 September 1998)

it's cool; **I'm cool**; **cool as a cucumber**; **cool, calm and collected** To be cool, like many of the expressions using 'cold', has long indicated a lack of heated emotions. As early as 1615 Beaumont and Fletcher wrote of 'young maids as cold as cucumbers'. 'Cool, calm and collected' seems to date from the nineteenth century. From the idea of cool as 'not heated emotionally', found in English even in the Anglo-Saxon poem *Beowulf*, comes that of cool as undisturbed, calm, and hence relaxed. In this sense it was used, particularly of a type of jazz, from the 1940s, although it may well have been used earlier, for its genesis was in Black American English, and that is not well recorded. Since this sort of jazz was fashionable, cool added 'fashionable' to its list of meanings. Nowadays young Americans and British will use 'Cool', 'It's cool' or 'I'm cool' to mean little more than 'OK', 'Fine by me' or 'Nice'.

corks will be popping see DANCING IN THE STREETS

corner see TURN THE CORNER

corridors of power This expression for the senior levels of government, where influence is more important than the rule book, was coined by the novelist and scientist C. P. Snow. He first used it in his 1956 novel *Homecomings*, then as the title of a novel published in 1963. Snow also coined *The Two Cultures*, the title of a lecture series on the conflicting cultures of the arts and sciences he gave in 1959.

'With the party having re-entered the corridors of power through a side door, and with the Liberals beginning to divide over the conduct of the war, the Conservatives' prewar fears had been dissipated.' (*Twentieth Century British History*, 1991)

cost an arm and a leg An alternative to 'cost the earth', this expression started life in the USA in middle of the twentieth century.

'All round, an interesting tool, that sits comfortably in the hand, is kind to the elbow, and doesn't cost an arm and a leg.' (*Woodworker*, 1991)

'Just because very few hotels have that many single rooms it doesn't mean you should pay an arm and a leg for the privilege of being alone.' (Club 18–30 Summer Holiday Brochure, 1990)

could do better A conscious cliché, imitating the typical damning comment from a school report, now used as an ironic comment on someone's level of achievement.

'Perhaps "end of term" reports on individual authorities and schools after their first two and a half years or so of implementing the 1981 Act (when the research data were finally gathered) would range from commenting, "Encouraging progress has been made", through the ubiquitous "Could do better" to "Disappointing work".' (*Special Educational Needs*, 1989)

'Six out of ten to the Oxford Stage Company; could do better.' (*Guardian*, 11 November 1989)

counted see STAND UP AND BE COUNTED

counted them all out ... counted them all back (or **in**) 'I'm not allowed to say how many planes joined the raid but I counted them all out and I counted them all back', was said in a radio report by the journalist Brian Hanrahan during the 1982 Falklands War, when information was being heavily censored by the military. Public opinion was not in favour of the censorship, and this quickly became a catch-phrase cliché.

'He [Michael Howard] must reckon that he will be rewarded by not being returned to the Home Office to see his pigeons come home to roost. He counted them out, but let some other guy count them in again.' (Polly Toynbee, *Independent*, 24 April 1996)

courage of your convictions This expression seems to have come into English from the French expression (recorded in the mid-nineteenth century) *'le courage de son opinion'*. For a while it could appear as either the courage of your convictions or of your opinions, but as so often in English, the alliterative version won in the end. Nowadays it is more often used to point to someone lacking the necessary courage, rather than having it.

'This is really the key to getting the economy stabilised but the Chancellor didn't have the courage of his convictions to do it.' (*Today*, 1992)

court see LAUGH OUT OF COURT

crack a nut see SLEDGEHAMMER TO CRACK A NUT

(from) cradle to grave In the eighteenth and nineteenth centuries this expression was simply a more poetic way of saying the whole of a lifetime – Bulwer Lytton in *Maltravers* (1837), has 'What else have we to do with our mornings, we women? . . . Our life is a lounge from the cradle to the grave' – but in the twentieth century the expression has taken on extra resonances. Shortened from 'from the cradle to the grave' to 'from cradle to grave' it became strongly associated with politics and the sort of state welfare that looks to the well-being of its people from birth to death, a policy esteemed at times in the twentieth century, and denigrated at others. More recently it has come to be used by environmentalists to represent the environmental effect of the whole cycle of production, use and disposal of an object.

'The cradle to grave provision of welfare, implicit in the Beveridge proposals, has proved to be too expensive and . . . the demand for welfare has grown faster than has the national income to pay for adequate comprehensive services and benefits.' (Dennis Kavanagh, *Thatcherism and British Politics*, 1990)

'They should also inform shoppers as to the product's environmental friendliness from cradle to grave – evaluated according to standardized criteria.' (*New Internationalist*)

crawl back into the woodwork see WOODWORK

crazy about see ALL THE RAGE

creative accounting A term in use since the 1970s for presenting financial information in a way that hides the real situation, now often used as a euphemism for outright fraud, for 'cooking the books' (an expression for falsifying accounts that has been used since the seventeenth century).

'The black economy is spreading up the social scale into traditionally white-collar areas . . . [with] company directors using creative accounting.' (*Guardian*, 8 August 1992)

creatures great and small see ALL CREATURES GREAT AND SMALL

crème de la crème This expression, literally 'the cream of the cream', is the French equivalent of the 'pick of the crop' (in the US the 'cream of the crop'), the very best. The phrase has been in use in English since the middle of the nineteenth century, but received an added boost, and ironic resonance, when used repeatedly in Muriel Spark's novel *The Prime of Miss Jean Brodie* (1961, filmed 1969).

'We've had more than 600 entries for the awards . . . collectively representing the crème de la crème of the new food revolution which is sweeping the country.' (*You* magazine, 20 September 1998)

cried all the way to the bank see LAUGHED ALL THE WAY TO THE BANK

critical acclaim A set phrase, saying little more than 'praise'. 'Acclaim' itself is rarely seen outside publicity for a performance.

'As a result, the homes at West Moor are among the first in the country to be awarded the critical acclaim of a Gas Warm Award from British Gas.' (*Wimpey Newsletter*)

cross the Rubicon see DIE IS CAST

crossroads see AT THE CROSSROADS

crowning glory 'Crowning', in the sense of 'completing, most perfect' is recorded from the mid-seventeenth century when Oliver Cromwell wrote of 'crowning mercy', but the history of 'crowning glory' is obscure. The *OED* does not record it until the beginning of the twentieth century (and its first citation as a description of a woman's hair is from 1922, in James Joyce's *Ulysses*), but it is probably much older. It is used twice in John Muir's *Steep Tracks*, which, although it was not published until 1918, four years after Muir's death, was written up from diaries kept on his exploratory trip to the American West in 1864. 'Descending the mountain, I followed the windings of the main central glen on the north, gathering specimens of the cones and sprays of the evergreens, and most of the other new plants I had met; but the lilies formed the crowning glory of my bouquet – the grandest I had carried in many a day.'

'The first purpose-built department store in the country (1909), the crowning glory of Oxford Street, Selfridges is a British institution.' (*Evening Standard*, 1 September 1998)

(to be) crucified The slang term 'crucified', meaning 'criticized' or 'caused anguish', sounds very modern, but in fact as early as 1621 we can find it used in the sense of tormented mentally, in Robert Burton's *Anatomy of Melancholy*: 'As great trouble as to perfect the motion of Mars and Mercury, which so crucifies our astronomers.' However, it has only reached cliché status since the middle of the twentieth century.

'We've been crucified several times in my lifetime.' (Welsh sheep farmer on business conditions, *Today*, BBC Radio 4, 14 August 1998)

cruel to be kind This is a quotation cliché from Shakespeare. In *Hamlet* (III.iv), Hamlet upbraids his mother for her incest in marrying her dead husband's brother, (banned by the church, see further at FLESH AND BLOOD) and makes her realize the difference in quality between his father and his murderous uncle. He leaves Gertrude with the words, 'I must be cruel, only to be kind', which involves a play upon the many meanings of 'kind' then current, which included our modern meaning; 'relating to proper behaviour'; 'natural'; and 'relating to family, kin'. However, modern use of the expression simply means to act in a way that seems harsh but is for someone's ultimate good. The phrase is used as an alternative to the more recent TOUGH LOVE.

'You will have to be a little cruel to be kind or she'll never regain her stability or independence.' (*She* magazine, 1989)

crushing blow This expression usually, but not invariably, starts with the old-fashioned 'deal' instead of 'give', which suggests the language of knighthood and links it to the original image of a hand-to-hand fighter bringing a weapon down in a blow that will literally crush. However, the earliest example I have been able to locate is in Stephen Crane's *Red Badge of Courage* (1895): 'As he ran, a thought of the shock of contact gleamed in his mind. He expected a great concussion when the two bodies of troops crashed together. This became a part of his wild battle madness. He could feel the onward swing of the regiment about him and he conceived of a thunderous, crushing blow that would prostrate the resistance and spread consternation and amazement for miles.' The style of writing here does not suggest that 'crushing blow' was anything but a set phrase at the time.

'Grandma Williams was hit most seriously of all by it; the death of her first-born was a crushing blow and she died herself soon afterwards.' (Michael Freeland, *Kenneth Williams: A Biography*, 1990)

cuckoo see CLOUD CUCKOO LAND; FIRST CUCKOO

I have a cunning plan This was a long-established cliché of popular literature, when it was deliberately used as such by the creators (Rowan Atkinson, Richard Curtis) of the *Blackadder* television series which ran from 1983. The favourite phrase of the oafish servant Baldrick, used to introduce some fantastic idea that would either get a withering response from Edmund Blackadder or else land him in the most excruciatingly embarrassing or dangerous situation, it soon became a catch-phrase cliché. Earlier instances are found in *The Book of Mormon*, which was introduced to the world as the work of an ancient prophet by Joseph Smith in 1827: 'O that cunning plan of the evil one! O the vainness, and the frailties, and the foolishness of men!' (2 Nephi 9:28).

cupboard was bare While this image is taken from an everyday phenomenon, the use of 'the cupboard was bare' is no doubt influenced by the nursery rhyme, 'Old Mother Hubbard'.

'While Campbell and Anderton would tempt clubs both at home and abroad, the Spurs cupboard would have a decidedly bare look if they were taken out.' (*Daily Mail*, 27 August 1998)

cups see IN YOUR CUPS

curate's egg This is the title of a cartoon which appeared in volume 109 of *Punch* in 1895, showing a formidable bishop and a timid curate having breakfast. The caption read, 'I'm afraid you've got a bad egg, Mr Jones.' 'Oh no, my Lord, I assure you! Parts of it are excellent!' Hence, 'like the curate's egg – good in parts'.

'The Escort has been one of Britain's top-sellers for many years and having tested various examples of the latest in the range I have to give a curate's egg verdict.' (*Country Living*, 1991)

curiouser and curiouser A quotation cliché from Lewis Carroll's *Alice in Wonderland* (1865). As befits a saying from this source, it is often used to suggest something rather surreal.

'Curiouser and curiouser, on the other side of the Pyrenees in Spain, in the high escarpment near the attractive village of Ager, north of Lerida, is yet a third lithographic limestone, again restricted to a very small area and exactly like the other two in lithology, fauna, flora and age (and even yielding a feather).' (Derek V. Ager, *The Nature of the Stratigraphical Record*, 1984)

current see SWIM AGAINST THE TIDE OR CURRENT

the customer is always right In about 1909 H. Gordon Selfridge adopted the slogan 'the customer is always right' for his Oxford Street department store, and it rapidly spread through the business world.

'In education no single customer is always right; people aren't all looking for the same things.' (Mike Sullivan, *Marketing your Primary School*, 1991)

cut a swathe Both the area of grass cut by the swing of a scythe, and the cut grass itself are called a swathe, so this image is an economical way of saying 'to bowl them over', 'cut a dash', or to swagger through life making a great impression. It developed in the mid-nineteenth century in the USA, but is now firmly established on both sides of the Atlantic.

'I've always envied the profligate, the improvident – those financial reprobates who cut a swathe through life and never seem to worry about the strong arm of American Express.' (*Mail on Sunday*, 20 September 1998)

a cut above This rather odd expression, notoriously popular as a name for hair-dressers, has been in use since the end of the eighteenth century. The word 'cut' seems to have become an expression of superiority via the use of 'cut' for the way clothes or hair are shaped. From being something fashionably cut, it came to mean 'fashion, style' – as in the now dated 'I don't like the cut of his jib', and from there developed into an assessment of worth.

'The end result was definitely a cut above the average village manor, with its pediment thrusting forward, its roof line to match, and the strong outline of the window casing, all echoing baroque.' (Candida Lycett Green, *The Perfect English Country House*, 1991)

cut both ways Arguments have long been described in terms such as 'sharp' or 'cutting'. The origin of this expression can be seen in the literal use in the 1809 description of some sabres by Viscount Valentia: 'They were all Persian, but had been lengthened in Egypt at both ends, so as to give the Mameluke point, which cuts both ways,' and the transition to figurative use in J. Martineau's *Essays* (1866): 'The charge . . . is double edged, and cuts both ways.'

'Such a tax is often claimed to encourage saving but the argument can cut both ways.' (Philip Jones and John Cullis, *Public Finance and Public Choice*, 1992)

cut off in the springtime of life see SPRINGTIME OF LIFE

cut out for you see WORK CUT OUT FOR YOU

cut the mustard In the early years of the twentieth century 'to be the mustard' was a term of approval, meaning to be the best of anything, something hot, something that adds zing to life, just as mustard perks up dull food. Quite where the cut part comes from is not clear; a range of explanations has been offered, but none of them convinces.

'Ideally you will: Have at least 3 years experience within performance measurements. Be of graduate calibre. If you feel you can cut the mustard and help this company retain its position at the top of the pile, call us now!' (*Evening Standard*, 7 September 1998)

cut through the Gordian knot see GORDIAN KNOT

cutting edge Cutting edge began to be used in the middle of the twentieth century by the scientific community to mean research which was in the forefront of the field, breaking new ground. By the 1970s it was passing into general use, and had become a cliché by the 1980s. An alternative expression is LEADING EDGE.

'Yet it is easy for pioneer users and IT investors to remain with the tried and tested applications and miss out on the cutting edge opportunities just around the corner.' (*Caterer & Hotelkeeper*, 1991)

'Hall was apt to be described as "a tough-as-nails reporter with a marshmallow centre", though in her "Dear Unity" role, the emphasis was rather on the concoction of sympathy than on the cutting edge of insight.' (*Daily Telegraph*, 13 April 1992)

Daddy of all . . . see MOTHER OF ALL . . .

at daggers drawn Any image of people quarrelling so violently it could lead to the use of daggers, is self-evidently an old one. The phrase is first found in the sixteenth century, in the form 'at daggers drawing', which explains the rather odd 'at', used originally to signify 'at the point of '. It appears in its modern form by 1668, but became a cliché only in the nineteenth century. A similar idea is found in the expression 'at each other's throats', but this has not lost its sense of physical violence in the same way that 'daggers drawn' has.

'Mr MacSharry and Commission President Jacques Delors have been at daggers drawn for weeks over tactics in the GATT talks with the Americans with Mr Delors accused of favouring the powerful French farm lobby.' (*Liverpool Daily Post and Echo*, 1993)

(earn or **win your) daily bread** This expression for earning a living or your food is from the Lord's Prayer: 'Give us this day our daily bread.' It was already in general use by the seventeenth century, but really took off as a cliché in the nineteenth century.

'And Douglas had sounded really upset himself, although murders, if not quite his daily bread, were certainly common enough in his line of work.' (C. F. Roe, *Deadly Partnership*, 1992)

'Once, in the closing years of the last century, a poor woman earned her daily bread by working long hours at her treadle sewing machine.' (Penelope Fitzgerald, *Offshore*, 1988)

what's the damage? Used as a jocular way of asking how much you owe, particularly in places like pubs, and often in the deliberately old-fashioned form, 'What's the damage, Squire?' This expression, although rather dated now, has a long history. 'What is the damage?' dates back to at least the early nineteenth century, while 'damage' by itself, as a slang word for 'cost', was in use by the mid-eighteenth century, and, since slang is often slow to get into the written record, may well be earlier. The slang expression, in turn, probably developed from the legal use of the word (now always used in the plural, 'damages') for the estimated value of something lost or money to be paid in compensation.

' "Now then, Taylor, what's the damage this time?" the Duke would ask and on being told he would briskly reply "Cheque in post tomorrow." ' (Richard Holt, *Sport and the British*, 1989)

damn see FRANKLY, MY DEAR, I DON'T GIVE A DAMN

damn with faint praise The concept of 'faint praise' has been around since at least 1633, when Phineas Fletcher wrote in *The Purple Island*, 'When needs he must, yet faintly then he praises.' The expression we use today comes from 1733, when Alexander Pope published a poem called *Epistle to Dr Arbuthnot* in which he advised the literary critic to 'Damn with faint praise, assent with civil leer, and, without sneering, teach the rest to sneer.' In these lines he used 'damn' in a special sense, which had been around for about a century, for 'to publicly condemn a work of art as a failure'. The expression 'damn with faint praise' summed up the ability of critics to condemn by condescending or hesitant praise so well that it soon passed into the general language.

'The great comic who retired from the business 11 years ago has delivered his verdict on the current crop of comedians; some are damned with faint praise, others are just damned.' (*Evening Standard*, 17 September 1998)

damp squib If the type of firework known as a squib gets wet, then all you get is a splutter or nothing at all – hence 'damp squib', in use since the middle of the nineteenth century, for something that doesn't meet expectations, that fails to develop. Before damp was used to mean slightly wet, it was used to mean 'depressed' or 'choked', so it is not surprising to find a number of expressions in English suggesting failure or suppression involving the word – we 'damp down high spirits', we 'put a damper on things', while 'soggy' and 'wet', as in 'wet blanket', have the same ring to them.

'The traditional Easter turkey boom – the second biggest after Christmas – was a damp squib because hard-up families bought cheaper chickens.' (*Daily Mirror*, 1992)

dance attendance To dance attendance means to pay obsequious attention to someone, to be ready to carry out their least whim. It has been in use since the middle of the sixteenth century, was well-used in the later sixteenth and seventeenth centuries, and has always carried a suggestion of sarcasm or contempt, an image of the over-eager courtier. Since we nowadays have little or no use for 'attendance' to mean 'paying attention' outside this expression, it probably owes its survival as a set phrase in English, to Shakespeare who used 'To dance attendance on their lordship's pleasures' in *Henry VIII* (V.ii).

'The last occasion on which the monarch was required to make a real choice occurred when the Queen was obliged to dance attendance on a sick Harold Macmillan in October 1963.' (Jeremy Paxman, *Friends in High Places*, 1990)

dance to a different beat (or **tune**, or **drummer**) see DIFFERENT TUNE

dancing in the streets Usually in the form 'they'll (or there'll) be dancing in the streets tonight', this cliché is a favourite of journalists, particularly sports journalists, to indicate celebration. It is often found in conjunction with, or as an alternative to, '(champagne) corks will be popping'. Both clichés date from the middle of the twentieth century. 'Dancing in the streets' had its position in the language reinforced by the success of the 1964 song with that title, written by William Stevenson and Marvin Gaye, although it had already been used as a song title by George Gershwin in 1932.

'What I do know is that people like Havel have been getting a little impatient with those relishing pieces appearing lately in the American press that say, roughly: "Right, you guys over there have had your romantic Ruritanian fun and games with revolution and dancing in the streets." ' (*Guardian*, 31 December 1989)

Daniel come to judgement 'A Daniel come to judgement! Yea, a Daniel! O wise young judge, how I do honour thee!' are the words spoken in Shakespeare's *The Merchant of Venice* (IV.i) in praise of Portia's legal wisdom in agreeing with his case, by Shylock the moneylender, referring to the biblical prophet Daniel's status as a judge. Thus the expression is used, usually in rather literary contexts, to hail an opinion that one agrees with. However, there is often an ironic twist to its use, for while Portia agrees that Shylock is entitled to his POUND OF FLESH according to the agreement he has made with Antonio, Shylock soon finds that he ceases to admire Portia's judgement. For she tells him he can only have it if he takes no blood with it.

'This wild and wayward child of the Prophets – "a Daniel come to Judgement" – needed the thick padded hide of the antediluvian monster, whose maw he had so precipitately fled from.' (Donald Davie, *Studies in Ezra Pound*, 1991)

dare not speak its name see LOVE THAT DARE NOT SPEAK ITS NAME

it was a dark and stormy night This is a conscious cliché, best known from children's jokes such as the one that runs, 'It was a dark and stormy night, and the Bo'sun said, "Captain, tell us a story" and this is the story he told: "It was a dark and stormy night . . ." ', and so on *ad infinitum*. Its origins have been traced to Bulwer-Lytton's novel *Paul Clifford*, published in 1830, and it has long been a stock scene-setting phrase. There is an annual Bulwer-Lytton Fiction Contest for composing bad opening sentences of imaginary novels. The 1998 winner, Bob Perry, came up with 'The corpse exuded the irresistible aroma of a piquant, ancho chilli glaze enticingly enhanced with a hint of fresh cilantro as it lay before him, coyly garnished by a garland of variegated radicchio and caramelised onions, and impishly drizzled with glistening rivulets of vintage balsamic vinegar and roasted garlic oil; yes, as he surveyed the body of the slain food critic slumped on the floor of the cozy [*sic*], but nearly empty bistro, a quick inventory of his senses told corpulent Inspector Moreau that this was, in all likelihood, an inside job.'

dark clouds hanging over you This image of someone threatened as if by lowering thunderclouds has been in use from at least the 1730s. An earlier associated expression which either lies behind it, or at least reinforces the imagery, is UNDER A CLOUD, recorded from the fifteenth century, while threat from the sky is also found in a BOLT FROM THE BLUE, not recorded before the 1830s.

'While much of the UK is looking gloomily at the dark clouds of a major recession, it seems poetic justice that for at least some of Belfast's population, the future looks better than it has for many years.' (*Management Today*, 1991)

dark horse This cliché, used of someone or something with hidden qualities, comes from horse racing, where it has been used, since the first part of the nineteenth century, to describe a horse about which little is known. In the political context, for someone who is unexpectedly elected, it is also used in the USA for someone who is not an official candidate, but who is chosen as a compromise.

'Jerry Brown, the Democrats' dark horse in the presidential primaries, is settled in a worn armchair, cradling a 10-month-old baby called Peter.' (*Daily Telegraph*, 6 April 1992)

'Leicester continue to blow hot and cold, although one of the reasons they looked a little below par in their first game was because they were playing a Gloucester side that could be a dark horse for the title.' (*Rugby World and Post*, 1992)

dark night (of the soul) Although not widely recognized as such, this is a quotation. The Spanish Christian mystic, St John of the Cross (1542–91) used the expression, *'La noche oscura del alma'* as the title of one of his books. He used it in a technical sense, to describe a period of spiritual aridity suffered by a mystic. It does not seem to have become a cliché until the twentieth century. Its popularity was probably helped by F. Scott Fitzgerald's comment, 'In a real dark night of the soul it is always three o'clock in the morning, day after day' ('Handle with Care', *Esquire*, March 1936). The shorter form, 'dark night', seems to be used increasingly to mean just a 'difficult time', rather than a period of mental or spiritual depression.

' "We should tell him," Clinton said at Martha's Vineyard last Friday, "that if they'll be strong and do the disciplined, hard things they have to do to reform the country and the economy and get through this dark night, we'll stick with them." ' (*Evening Standard*, 1 September 1998)

'His dark night of the soul came in the Chinama Motel in faraway Lusaka, after his escape from South Africa, as he lay listening to the foreign service of Radio South Africa describing him as a liar, a crook and a psychopath.' (*Esquire*, 1992)

darken my door see NEVER DARKEN MY DOOR AGAIN

darkest hour This is based on the proverbial saying, in use since the mid-seventeenth century, 'The darkest hour is just before dawn', meaning that things seem worst just before they start to get better. The illustrations suggest a certain self-consciousness in its use, an awareness of its cliché status.

'He doesn't actually use the words but his philosophy is clearly that the New Zealand sojourn may have been the darkest hour but that the darkest hours comes [*sic*] before the dawning of a new day.' (*Rugby World and Post*, 1991)

'The darkest hour may be just before the dawn but it is no time to go to sleep on the job.' (*IBOA Newssheet*)

'Mr Shevardnadze chose the moment of his return well, arriving at Georgia's darkest hour: the whole country periodically blacked out by power cuts, hot water and central heating a dim memory, public transport ground to a halt, and even bread rarely to be seen.' (*Daily Telegraph*, 4 April 1992)

(the forces or **powers of) darkness** This cliché for the devil, the Prince of Darkness, or evil in general, echoes biblical expressions, such as Colossians 1:13 where thanks are given to God 'who hath delivered us from the power of darkness'. 'Powers of darkness' is first recorded in the fourteenth century, was a commonplace of religious writings from the seventeenth century, and reached cliché status by at least the nineteenth. The use of 'forces' rather than 'powers' seems to have come from the common expression 'forces of evil', which was in use by 1862.

dash someone's hopes Hopes have been being dashed since the sixteenth century, keeping alive a sense of 'to dash' for 'to confound' which has otherwise long been obsolete.

'Interest rate setters left base rates unchanged at 7.5% today, dashing faint hopes that the crises in Russia and the Far East . . . might have led to an early British cut.' (*Evening Standard*, 10 September 1998).

David and Goliath The story in the Bible (I Samuel 17) tells how the shepherd boy David, using simply his sling and a pebble he picked up, killed the gigantic warrior-champion of the Philistines, Goliath, who until then had terrorized the kingdom. From this came the idea of the underdog, David, winning against a powerful opponent. The history of this cliché is obscure, but it only seems to have come into regular use in the twentieth century. It is very popular with sports journalists when a minor team has unexpectedly beaten a better known one, but is also well used in other contexts.

'It's a head-to-head affair of David and Goliath proportions – and David, it seems, has misplaced his sling.' (*Independent*, 2 September 1998)

'Once more, it was David against Goliath: on the one hand, as Reaganite statistics liked it, 65,000 well-drilled troops, the largest army ever amassed on the soil of Central America; on the other . . . about 12,000 simple folk, determined to stop Communism as it seeped outwards towards Honduras, El Salvador and Costa Rica.' (Ann Wroe, *Lives, Lies and the Iran–Contra Affair*, 1991)

(before) the dawn of time (or **history**) These expressions have been clichés of popular history since the later nineteenth century, and have been well used in book titles. Both can be used as alternatives to DIM AND DISTANT PAST. 'Dawn of history' seems to have been more frequently used in the past than 'dawn of time', but 'time' is now the more common.

' "What is true," writes mason investigator Stephen Knight, "is that the philosophic, religious and ritualistic concoction that makes up the speculative element in freemasonry is drawn from many sources – some of them, like the Isis–Osiris myth, dating back to the dawn of history.' (Kevin Logan, *Paganism and the Occult*, 1988)

'Personal transport had since the dawn of time been limited to footslogging or a horse not too exhausted by its labour in the fields.' (Hannah Hauxwell and Barry Cockcroft, *Daughter of the Dales*, 1991)

Day see AT THE END OF THE DAY

in this day and age At best this filler means little more than 'now, nowadays'. It is generally used to try to give dignity to a statement. The expression has probably been around for some time, and has been widely condemned since the 1970s.

'Events have also shown that in this day and age the exercise of a right to silence affords protection for the guilty and is unnecessary to safeguard the innocent.' (*Weekly Law Reports*, 1992, Volume 3)

day of destiny A favourite cliché of sports journalists when describing an important match, this is also used by politicians, as is 'rendezvous with destiny'. This latter comes from a speech made by Franklin D. Roosevelt in 1936 when he claimed, 'This generation of Americans has a rendezvous with destiny.'

'Strangely, for a man fighting for sport's most brutal crown, Bowe finds himself apologising for his obvious lack of aggression in the countdown to his day of destiny.' (*Today*, 1992)

day of reckoning 'To reckon' originally meant 'to count', and very early on in its history 'reckoning' came to mean an account or bill. The day of reckoning is therefore the day you have to settle your account, and the expression soon came to take on a religious sense, to mean judgement day. This spread to more general use in the nineteenth century, and in modern journalese often means no more than 'the crunch'.

'The fight against relegation from League Two remains close and Bedford's win seems to have postponed the day of reckoning until their game at Morley on April 25.' (*Daily Telegraph*, 13 April 1992)

days are numbered This is a nineteenth-century cliché, but echoes the language of the Bible which has both 'the number of thy days' (Exodus 23:26) and 'God has numbered thy kingdom, and finished it' (Daniel 5:26).

'And he called on Mr Mellor to resign as Heritage Secretary, saying: "His days are numbered." ' (*Daily Mirror*, 1992)

in days of yore Yore ('a long time ago', 'in times past') survived as an archaism until the nineteenth century, but now survives only in this set phrase. It is recorded from the seventeenth century, but only came to be used frequently and loosely in the nineteenth, often as a less emphatic version of 'the MISTS OF TIME' or instead of the formal story-telling setting, 'long ago and far away'. Nowadays it is nearly always used jocularly.

'In days of yore I worked on a gossip column. Back then there was no worthier day's toil than "linking" some B-list celeb with another of the same ilk.' (*Evening Standard*, 1 September 1998)

day's work see ALL IN A DAY'S WORK

D-Day In army jargon, in use since the First World War, D-Day and H-Hour mean the designated day and hour that an operation is due to begin. For most people, however, D-Day means 6 June 1944, when Allied forces landed in Normandy and started an operation that was to lead to the end of the Second World War. Nowadays its meaning has been diluted, and it is often interchangeable with DAY OF RECKONING.

'The government's official line is that it is aiming for an agreement with East Germany on monetary matters by the end of next month; it does not deny reports that D-Day for GEMU could be July 1st.' (*The Economist*, 1990)

'Earlier in the week US President George Bush had emphasised that the expiry of the UN deadline would not signify "D-Day" in the sense of imminent military action.' (*Keesing's Contemporary Archives*, 1991)

de gustibus non est disputandum see TAKES ALL SORTS

de rigueur Literally 'in strictness', this was adopted from French in the nineteenth century to describe 'things' that were demanded by etiquette or fashion. It can now sound rather pompous, although it can also be found used loosely to mean 'compulsory' or 'obligatory'. It belongs more, perhaps, in the world of P. G. Wodehouse's toff, Bertie Wooster, as in 'Here was Jeeves making heavy weather about me wearing a perfectly ordinary white mess jacket, a garment not only *tout ce qu'il y a de chic*, but absolutely *de rigueur*, and in the same breath, as you might say, inciting Gussie Fink-Nottle to be a blot on the London scene in scarlet tights.' (P. G. Wodehouse, *Right Ho, Jeeves*, 1934)

'. . . unlike the smug bunch on last night's *Teen Spirit* (ITV), who were all so busy having sex, getting drunk and going clubbing that their lives had little room for profound ontological reflection. Still too young to go on an 18–30 package holiday to Ibiza (where such behaviour is positively de rigueur) . . .' (*Evening Standard*, 21 October 1998)

dead and done with; dead and buried These are nineteenth-century emphatic clichés. 'Dead and done with' was the more common in the nineteenth century, with the balance tipped in favour of 'dead and buried' in the twentieth. Both have obvious connections with the next entry.

'Gregory converted it too and Northampton knew they were dead and buried.' (*Daily Telegraph*, 12 April 1992)

dead and gone 'Dead and gone' as a formal description of the finality of death goes back to the Middle Ages. When Ophelia runs mad in Shakespeare's *Hamlet* she sings a song with the lines 'He is dead and gone Lady, he is dead and gone' which suggests that the phrase had already lost much of its power by Shakespeare's day. Nowadays, 'dead and gone' used of the dead tends to sound over-sententious, like 'not lost but gone before'. Instead it is used in a general sense for 'finished', in the same way as DEAD AND DONE WITH.

'There would be tales of family heroes, dead and gone, and there would be the quiet looking round the room wondering who would be the next to go.' (Geoffrey Howard, *Wheelbarrow across the Sahara*, 1990)

'But as the priest stood at his study window, fingers joined in thanksgiving to the night sky for his release from the bitter-sweet torture of reliving what was dead and gone, his mind quailed before his new dilemma.' (David Marcus, *A Land Not Theirs*, 1993)

dead as a dodo Surprisingly, the *OED* has only one citation for this expression, and that as recently as 1960. This suggests that it took the twentieth century's concern over extinction before it replaced the earlier 'dead as a doornail'. This goes back to the fourteenth century, and uses the alliterating doornail (the sort of big-headed nail used to stud old doors) as the type of thing that is totally lifeless. America also has 'dead as a mackerel' and the earlier 'dead as a herring'.

'In the second half, Oxford brought on winger, Chrissy Allen in the hope of livening things up, but the game was as dead as a dodo.' (Central Television news scripts, 1993)

dead but won't lie down Someone who is dead but won't lie down, is someone who will not recognize the fact of their defeat, but keeps struggling, regardless. It is generally used when such behaviour is not felt to be heroic, but going beyond what is reasonable. At best it is an acknowledgement of doggedness. It has been in use since the beginning of the twentieth century.

dead duck The cliché 'dead duck' comes from an old saying, 'never waste powder on a dead duck' – that is, do not waste effort on a hopeless case (presumably, one saves the gunpowder for shooting a SITTING DUCK). The expression, which originated in the USA, has been in use since the early nineteenth century.

'It was bad enough having to admit that the APT train project was a dead duck, but BR shot itself in the foot and provided the cynical national media with a field day by selling off some of the vehicles to a Sheffield scrapyard.' (David St John Thomas and Patrick Whitehouse, *BR in the Eighties*, 1990)

dead from the neck up This expression for stupidity, more forceful than 'not much up top', probably originated in the USA in the 1920s.

'Ol' Turry's back and this time there'll be trouble, 'coz he's what's known in the trade as a fruit-and-nut case (he needs a check-up from the neck up).' (*Zzap 64!*, 1992)

dead in the water A sailing ship that is dead in the water is stationary, with no wind in its sails to make it come alive. Transferring this to everyday life, to mean 'not going anywhere, brought to a halt' was only a small step, although, as the first quotation shows, it can be rather confusing if not used carefully.

'One second I had been speeding at fifty miles an hour along a ribbon of uninterrupted concrete; the next ... there was a loud crunch, every shock absorber on the Nissan thudded home to its end-stops and I found myself dead in the water by a pothole large enough to accommodate half Balboa's army.' (Simon Winchester, *The Pacific*, 1992)

'The Japanese were never willing to relinquish real power to their British or American employees. As a result, these firms were dead in the water before they even started to compete in the City.' (*Evening Standard*, 10 September 1998)

dead men's shoes A cliché from the nineteenth century, this comes from the expression 'to wait for dead men's shoes'. This originally meant to wait for an inheritance, but now tends to be used of promotion, particularly due to retirement.

dead of night The dead of night is 'dead' because it is the stillest, darkest period. It has been in use since the sixteenth century, and was popular in Shakespeare's day (he used it several times). Nowadays it means no more than 'in the middle of the night, late'.

' "The days must go when they can wake up a judge at dead of night, give him a drop of brandy, show him a deadline from *The Sun* and get him to sign an injunction," Mr Todd said.' (*Independent*, 5 October 1989)

dead to the world The proper meaning of 'dead to the world' is a religious one, describing the state of someone who has left worldly things to dedicate him or herself to God. As Wordsworth put it, 'A few Monks, a stern society, Dead to the world and scoring earth-born joys' (*Cuckoo at Laverna*, 1837). It can still be found in modern English used in this way: 'Henceforth, like St Paul, she was dead to the world and alive only to God' (*The English Mystics of the 14th Century*, 1991). However, by the late nineteenth century the expression was also being used to mean 'unconscious' and from there it was but a short step to the commonest modern sense of 'deeply asleep'.

'He was dead to the world, so deeply asleep that she wondered what on earth he could have been doing half the night.' (Kristy McCallum, *Driven by Love*, 1993)

deadly earnest There is nothing truly deadly about this expression which has been in use since the nineteenth century. 'Deadly' has travelled from its associations with death along much the same route as 'terribly' and 'awfully' have from 'terror' and 'awe'. As early as 1660 Samuel Pepys was writing in his Diary: 'A deadly drinker he is, and grown exceedingly fat.'

'When the various occult organisations get wind of the non-existent secret's existence, of course, they take it in deadly earnest and will stop at nothing to discover it and so make themselves Masters of the World.' (*Independent*, 14 October 1989)

deaf as a post It is not clear why a post was chosen to represent deafness. Presumably it was because a post is an inanimate, unresponsive object in the same way that the doornail is in DEAD AS A DOORNAIL, a view reinforced by the fact that in the past someone could also be 'stupid as a post'. The expression became a cliché in the nineteenth century.

deaf ears see FALL ON DEAF EARS

deafening silence When this was first introduced sometime in the 1960s, it must have seemed a striking paradox, but it rapidly degenerated into a cliché. In the past the expression 'eloquent silence' would have been used in the same way, but 'deafening' is now more often found.

'Tsarmina prowled silently out of the main door onto the sunlit parade ground. An immediate deafening silence fell over all.' (Brian Jacques, *Mossflower*, 1988)

deal see DONE DEAL

dear departed Dear departed belongs with other Victorian pieties such as NOT LOST BUT GONE BEFORE, LATE LAMENTED, and GONE BUT NOT FORGOTTEN. Once used in all seriousness, it is rarely used without irony today.

'Clad head-to-toe in black, she could be a mourner at a wake, but from her body language one cannot quite make out her precise attitude towards the dear departed.' (*Esquire*, 1991)

'Still, this orgy of food and sex would have suited the dear departed Peter Langan (with whom I worked for four years) very nicely.' (*Independent*, 12 October 1989)

for dear life The 'dear' in 'for dear life' means 'dear to you'. It came into use in the nineteenth century, where 'to ride for dear life' was common, but now it is most frequently used with 'run', 'cling on' or 'hold on'.

'It must have been within inches of the goal because when Swift collected the deflection, he was running along his own goal-line for dear life.' (*Daily Telegraph*, 4 April 1992)

'Hold on to that for dear life, because once you've lost it, you've lost everything.' (Mary Gervaise, *The Distance Enchanted*, 1983)

death by a thousand cuts The death by a thousand cuts was a particularly unpleasant Chinese method of making sure that your victim died very painfully. In *Quotations of Chairman Mao* (*The Little Red Book*) Mao wrote, ' "He who is not afraid of death by a thousand cuts dares to unhorse the emperor" – this is the indomitable spirit needed in our struggle to build socialism and communism.' Since the English version of the book is the first recorded use of the expression in our language, it is likely that this statement, in a book that was all but obligatory reading for the young at the time (1966), was responsible for introducing the term into the language. It has become a cliché, particularly of commentators on financial cuts and cuts to public services and is showing signs of becoming a formula phrase.

'I wondered yet again whether the people who queue up eagerly to bask in the cathode rays on such shows realise that they'll be stitched up a treat afterwards in the editing suite, and suffer death by a thousand cuts.' (*Evening Standard*, 6 October 1998)

'While the religious police of Saudi Arabia and Iran will arrest a Western woman in the streets for showing a leg, remarking on the oddity of the legions of black-clad Muslim women in our cities will result in death by a thousand accusations of religious bigotry.' (*Mail on Sunday*, 20 September 1998)

death trap When journalists report an ACCIDENT WAITING TO HAPPEN the place where the tragedy occurred is frequently described as a 'death trap'. At other times a death trap may be nothing more than something that trips you up or causes some minor accident. The phrase has been used from the mid-twentieth century.

'The EC is today expected to announce the release of funds to repair a North Wales road bridge branded a potential death trap for children.' (*Liverpool Daily Post and Echo*, 1993)

'Fire broke out in an old, litter-strewn stand which soon became a death trap in which fifty-six people perished.' (D. Waddington, *Contemporary Issues in Public Disorder*, 1992)

(like) death warmed up This expression for feeling or looking ill dates only from the middle of the twentieth century, probably as forces slang. It is usually used humorously.

deathless prose The classic description of deathless prose in English literature is to be found in Shakespeare's *Sonnet 18*, when he says of his 'eternal lines', 'So long as men can breathe, or eyes can see,/So long lives this, and this gives life to thee.' Nowadays, however, you would be hard put to it to find anyone using 'deathless prose' in any way but ironically.

'You can't write all day long, and in intervals of composing deathless prose you could help us in our schemes – and we've got lots, seething in our brains.' (Mary Gervaise, *The Distance Enchanted*, 1983)

at death's door The image here is of a door through which a person passes from life to death, an image linked to the idea of heaven and hell having gates through which the soul passes. It has been in use since the sixteenth century, and has been a cliché since the nineteenth.

(build or **make a) decent life** A cliché of modern journalism. It is often used with other emotive terms such as SUFFERED ENOUGH to create a vaguely uplifting atmosphere. More cynical readers may, however, be inclined to ponder the nature of the opposite of a 'decent' life.

'In a way that is what he had been doing – leaving the rumours and the gossip and the conspiracy theories to others, while he set about building a decent life for himself, as far removed from his father's as it was possible.' (*Daily Mail*, 10 August 1998)

'But from the moment she was lucky enough to secure a factory job when she left school at fourteen, she was determined to make a decent life for herself.' (Mary Jane Staples, *The Pearly Queen*, 1992)

like moving (or **rearranging**) **the deckchairs on the *Titanic*** This clichéd simile for futile activity dates from the 1970s, possibly inspired by a comment recorded in the *Washington Post* on 16 May 1976: 'After losing five of the last six primaries, President Ford's campaign manager, Rogers Morton, was asked if he plans any change in strategy. Said Morton: "I'm not going to rearrange the furniture on the deck of the *Titanic*."'

'Mr Maud went on to condemn Mr Brown for borrowing for social security payments. "You're moving the deckchairs around on the *Titanic*."' (*Independent*, 4 November 1998)

deep calling unto deep A quotation-cliché for recognizing hidden depths which derives from Psalm 42, verse 7: 'Deep calleth unto deep'. It has been in use since the middle of the nineteenth century, and was regarded as pompous even then, but is now rare.

to deep six Originally an American expression meaning to kill or dispose of someone or something. Its origin, in the USA in the 1920s, has been traced to the practice of burial at sea in six fathoms of water. The term attracted particular attention in 1973 when it was claimed at the Watergate hearings that someone had been instructed to deep six vital incriminating documents, which had been thrown into the Potomac river.

deep(ly) regret A standard form of apology from the 1980s, this phrase avoids the word 'sorry' and keeps an emotional distance.

'"Ben has apologised to me, to Alec and to his team-mates," said Graveney. "He feels he has let everyone down. He deeply regrets his actions and has been very apologetic."' (*Daily Mail*, 27 August 1998)

defining moment A cliché since the 1980s. An article published in the *Independent* on 5 August 1998 catalogued the rise of the term 'defining moment' as represented on the newspaper's database from 62 examples in 1993, to 411 in 1997, and 302 in the first five months of 1997, making it one of the clichés of the moment. The same article also pointed out that WATERSHED was an even more popular term. Sometimes one is lucky enough to find a blend of the two:

'It is difficult to pinpoint the exact moment at which British education went into decline, so lengthy and inexorable has the process been. But the replacement of O-levels by GCSE in 1988 was a defining watershed.' (*Daily Mail*, 27 August 1998)

deliberate falsehood In use since the nineteenth century, this is an accusation of premeditated deceit. The speaker avoids using the word 'lie', but gives the accused no chance of claiming that the misinformation they gave was a slip of the tongue, and as such is popular with politicians.

deliver an ultimatum This expression, adopted from the world of diplomacy, has become a much-used substitute for 'threaten'.

'Next they deliver this ultimatum: "Unless you get at least X clients in and on the market over the next week, you're history."' (Alexander Davidson, *The City Share Pushers*, 1989)

deliver the goods This cliché has its origins in legal language, meaning to supply the goods or services contracted for. The term has been in use from the eighteenth century. Its modern use, to perform as expected, does not seem to have evolved until the middle of the twentieth century.

'Rugby has been rushing to follow football's lead, sacking anyone who is perceived to have failed to deliver the goods.' (*Evening Standard*, 1 September 1998)

demon drink One of the ringing phrases of the nineteenth-century campaign for the abolition of drink, this expression has survived as a set phrase long after most people have stopped talking of demons in any other context. The expression 'demon rum' (for alcoholic drinks in general) seems to have been in use in the United States twenty to thirty years earlier than 'demon drink'.

'There's a belief that alcohol feeds productivity, when it does the exact opposite. I'm so proud that she has overcome the demon drink and is back to being the best she always was [*sic*].' (*Independent*, 3 August 1998)

'Totally miserable, he had a long, serious chat with Mike Turner of Cambridge about his training and demon drink problems and went home with much to think about.' (*Running Magazine*, 1991)

denial see CATEGORICAL DENIAL

depart this life Like REST IN PEACE and DEAR DEPARTED, this is a cliché of bereavement, which has been in the language since the sixteenth century, and a cliché since the nineteenth. Partridge, in his *Dictionary of Clichés*, says of it, 'It began as a euphemism, became a genteelism, and is now a stupidity.'

deserving poor see POOR BUT HONEST

despite my (our) best efforts This cliché is used as an excuse for failure. It is usually used in pompous self-justification rather than in apology, with the implication that if the speaker could not do it, it could not be done. The speaker is quite likely to go on to mention having worked 'to the BEST OF MY ABILITIES'. As a result it is often used ironically.

'However, despite the best efforts of the BBC and other giant mass publishing houses to clog the best-seller lists with the epitome of semi-literate publishing, literacy keeps breaking through in the most unlikely places, and nearly always from American rather than British programmes.' (W. J. West, *The Strange Rise of Semi-Literate England*, 1992)

destiny see DAY OF DESTINY

between the devil and the deep blue sea This expression for being caught between two evils has been in use since the seventeenth century, although 'blue' is a twentieth-century addition. Literary types might describe the situation as being caught 'between Scylla and Charybdis', from the monster and the whirlpool that made the strait between mainland Italy and Sicily so dangerous according to ancient stories (most notably Homer's *Odyssey*). A more colloquial alternative is BETWEEN A ROCK AND A HARD PLACE.

'If the government had executed the plans it came up with in 1856, peasants would have been justified in thinking that the devil of serfdom was preferable to the deep blue sea of reform.' (David Saunders, *Russia in the Age of Reaction and Reform 1801–1881*, 1994)

devil incarnate The devil incarnate is the devil made flesh, the opposite of Christ, who is God made flesh. The first recorded use of 'incarnate' is in the insult 'A son of perdition, and a devil incarnat' in 1395, and the term has been used as a general insult ever since.

'Arthur Scargill is just as much the devil incarnate to the true blue supporter now as he was in the front line at Orgreave Colliery.' (Crispin Aubrey, *Melt Down: Collapse of a Nuclear Dream*, 1991)

devil-may-care Care, in this description, meaning light-hearted, reckless, has the sense 'look after' still found in 'take care'. The expression comes from an old exclamation meaning 'the devil can see to it!', which came into use in the eighteenth century.

'Not that Sri Lanka, the dashing devil-may-care team of one-day cricket, made life easy for any batsman.' (*Evening Standard*, 28 August 1998)

dial-a- . . . A modern cliché, reflecting the growth of businesses which provide services or goods which can be ordered over the telephone, and often, in cases such as dial-a-pizza companies, delivered to your door. Because such services require little or no effort on the part of the customer, dial-a . . . has come to mean something equally easily or undeservedly obtained. An earlier cliché from a similar source was RENT-A-MOB.

'Dial a Saint equals cheap man-made grace, say the objectors.' (Stewart Lamont, *In Good Faith*, 1989)

diametrically opposed to Diametrically means across a diameter, hence, opposite, the antithesis of to 'come full circle'. It was already in use by the seventeenth century, but was not in common use in the sense 'very opposed' until the later nineteenth century. Use of the phrase has been growing since then. This probably reflects the spread of education, particularly in science, introducing a wider audience to the literal sense of the words. 'Diametrically opposite' is also common, and it is sometimes used in ways that show that awareness of its original sense has been lost.

'He used the columns of the *Irish Times* to inform Roman Catholic consciences of permitted interpretations of state divorce on the grounds of religious liberty, interpretations which were diametrically opposed to that of the Irish bishops.' (John Fulton, *The Tragedy of Belief*, 1991)

'A youth tried to sell me a Socialist Worker and seemed confused when I told him that in my experience the words were diametrically opposed.' (*Daily Telegraph*, 11 April 1992)

a diamond is for ever see GIRL'S BEST FRIEND

dice with death The image of Death playing a game for the life of a living person is an ancient one, although perhaps most vividly realized in Ingmar Bergman's 1956 film *The Seventh Seal*, in which a knight plays chess with Death. Surprisingly, the expression 'to dice with death' has not been recorded before the middle of the twentieth century. Where, then, apart from the attraction of the alliteration, does it come from? There are other 'dice' images in the language, the idea of staking your all on the fall or roll of a dice which goes back to the Middle Ages, and the DIE IS CAST which is even older. Most significantly, the image of death combined with dice is found in that mainstay of school poetry classes, Coleridge's *The Ancient Mariner*, where the Mariner witnesses Death and Life-in-Death playing dice for the lives of the crew of his ship, with the result that all of them die except him. The expression is a mainstay of journalists, and is often associated with driving. Indeed, the first recorded use in the *OED*, in 1941, describes 'the journalists' former habit of writing about their being "speed demons dicing with death".'

'Many of today's smokers . . . tend to think of themselves as dicing, romantically, with death and adventure, or leading a late-middle-aged charge against conformism.' (*Independent*, 8 October 1998)

did you feel the earth move? or **did the earth move for you?** see EARTH MOVE

to die for This is a recent cliché, of American origin, meaning 'extremely good'. It comes from the idea of a cause or belief that is worth dying for (Jimmy Porter, in John Osborne's 1956 play *Look Back in Anger* famously complained that there were no causes left to die for). 'To die for' should therefore be seen as a shortening of an expression such as 'good enough to die for'.

'As for the building itself, it's snazzy, but nothing to die for.' (*Independent*, 5 September 1998)

'There are women who have silver hair to die for, great metallic masses of it.' (*She* magazine, 1989)

die in harness This means to die when still employed, usually with the implication that the job was one held for a long time, or particularly liked. 'In harness', an image taken from working animals such as horses, was common in the later nineteenth century to mean 'in work', and the expression developed from this. Claims that Shakespeare uses it in this sense when Macbeth says 'At least we'll die with harness on our back' come from a misunderstanding, for Shakespeare is here using 'harness' in an old sense, to mean 'armour'. In fact, Macbeth is using an expression closer to DIE WITH YOUR BOOTS ON.

'Although he was sacked he was taken back a fourth time and he did indeed die in harness.' (Group Captain T. G. Mahaddie, *Hamish: The Story of a Pathfinder*, 1989)

the die is cast This is an ancient expression, going back to 49 BC when Julius Caesar is supposed to have said it as he took his troop south towards Rome across the river Rubicon, a minor river just north of Rimini. The significance of this action was that the Rubicon marked the border between what the Romans regarded as Italy proper, and the province of Gaul. Caesar was governor of Gaul, and had used his troops to conquer vast tracts of land there (see DIVIDED INTO THREE PARTS), but no general was allowed to bring active troops into Italy. So when Caesar decided to cross the Rubicon, it was as if he was staking everything on the fall of a dice, DICING WITH DEATH, for his actions were a declaration of civil war, and if he failed he would literally die. He did succeed at this point, only to fall to his assassins' knives on the Ides of March.

die the death This phrase has three different meanings. It was originally used as a solemn phrase to mean 'suffer death', or, in legal contexts, 'be put to death' (in use since the sixteenth century). A little later, in the 1611 translation of the Bible (Numbers 23:10) are the lines 'Let me die the death of the righteous, and let my last end be like his', and the term is still used in this sense: 'James gave to Mr Gilton some pleasing indication of a change of feeling, and he prayed earnestly that he might die the Death of the Righteous' (Robert Cecil, *The Masks of Death*, 1991). From these 'to die the death' developed, by the late nineteenth century, a further sense, as a grandiose way of saying 'to die', and again, this can still be found: 'If you intend to fight a missile duel, the chances are that most of your highly mobile force will attract a disproportionate amount of your enemy's firepower and will die the death' (Bill King and Andy Chambers, *High Elves*, 1993). Finally, the nineteenth-century meaning was transferred from a literal sense, to mean 'fail, flop', particularly of a play or other performance, an extended form of the theatrical use of 'to die' in this sense. 'The last tour I had the whole thing note-for-note worked out and it got a bit boring after a while; this way it stays exciting and sometimes I pull it off and sometimes I die the death' (*Guitarist*, 1992).

die with your boots on Originally this expression, also found as 'to die with your shoes on', and dating from the late seventeenth century, meant to be hanged. Grose's *Dictionary of the Vulgar Tongue* of 1785, a wonderful book and our main source of early slang, has the entry: 'You will die the death of a trooper's horse, that is with your shoes on, a jocular method of telling any one he will be hanged.' The expression could also be used to mean to die suddenly and unexpectedly. The opposite of this sense would be to die in your bed, or die with your boots off. It then came to mean to die in battle, and is now used as a conscious cliché of the Wild West, an association established early on, for we find, in 1873, 'If you keep on slinging your six-shooter around loose . . . you will . . . die with your boots on' (J. Miller, *Life amongst Modocs*). From this developed the sense of to die while actively occupied, a sense which coincided with to DIE IN HARNESS, a connection latent in the quotation from Grose.

different as chalk and cheese see CHALK AND CHEESE

different tune (or **song**) Sorting out the set of clichés that cluster round 'different tune' or 'different song' is no easy matter. To 'sing another song' or 'sing a different tune', meaning to speak or act in a different (probably improved) way is very old, going back to at least the fourteenth century. As can be seen from the quotes below, the 'different tune' has begun to drift away from the act of singing. In the twentieth century one can also dance or march to a different tune or a different beat or even a different drummer. This last has its source in H. D. Thoreau's *Walden* (1854), where he writes, 'If a man does not keep pace with his companions, perhaps it is because he hears a different drummer.'

'You're singing a different tune now from the one you sang after you'd left her behind and got yourself arrested.' (E. V. Thompson, *Wychwood*, 1992)

'But shadow spending ministers pander to health workers, teachers and the low-paid with a different tune.' (*Hansard Extracts 1991–1992*)

'Clough has always marched to a different tune, but this time his perversity may finally be his undoing.' (*Today*, 1992)

'On the surface all is well; but the steps taken are danced to a different tune.' (Edward de Bono, *Atlas of Management Thinking*, 1988)

different wavelength see WAVELENGTH

dig a hole for yourself Meaning to get yourself into trouble, this is a development of DIG YOUR OWN GRAVE. It is also found as 'dig yourself into (or out of) a hole' and leads to the advice, 'when in a hole stop digging'.

'It's a charming effort to dig all three of us out of a hole. Charming but ultimately insincere, of course.' (*Evening Standard*, 24 September 1998)

dig in the eye with a blunt stick see BETTER THAN A SLAP IN THE FACE WITH A WET FISH

dig your own grave This is a twentieth-century cliché meaning to get yourself into difficulties through your own actions.

'Too often the role is left to a houseproud male or to the women who dig their own grave when entrapping themselves into a traditional duty, by doing it themselves out of resignation.' (Sander Meredeen, *Study for Survival and Success*, 1988)

dim and distant past The association of 'dim' and 'distant' is an obvious one when describing views, and is used by Shelley in his 1818 poem *Lines Written among the Euganean Hills*: 'The dim low line before/Of a dark and distant shore/Still recedes.' 'Dim and distant past' was in use by the 1870s, but when writing of the difficulties of seeing into poorly recorded eras of history. Its looser sense, as an alternative for the old-fashioned 'long ago and far away' or a more general sense of before the DAWN OF HISTORY, seem to be twentieth-century developments.

'In the dim and distant past, say 1992, there were probably no more than 200,000 Internet users in the entire world.' (*Independent*, 7 September 1998)

dinosaur This term, for someone or something that has failed to adapt, or is thoroughly out of date, is very much a cliché of the moment. The usage dates only from the middle of the twentieth century, and has been steadily growing ever since. At one time it was most often found in the term 'dinosaur of rock' in the musical press, but now it can be found in almost any paper, used of almost anything.

'We are assured by government spokesmen and examination board PR men that GCSE standards have never been more rigorous and that anyone who claims otherwise is by implication an education dinosaur.' (*Daily Mail*, 27 August 1998)

'Most of us are content to answer the question by beading together words such as "irrelevant", "outdated" and, of course, "dinosaur".' (*Independent*, 17 September 1998)

dire emergency 'Dire' in general has become a popular word, generally diluted from its original sense of extremely serious. 'Dire emergency', and the 'dire conse-quences' of nothing being done are its most common set phrases.

'England can argue that they have an obvious replacement opener in Alec Stewart. Yet only the direst emergency should force him back up to No. 1 while he is both captaining the team and keeping wicket.' (*Evening Standard*, 28 August 1998)

dire straits This is even more common than DIRE EMERGENCY, but its use is distorted by the fame of the musical group that has that name. In fact, a search of the British National Corpus shows that the bulk of citations for 'dire straits' there are references to the group. They had their first hit records in the late 1970s, and the growth in the use of the expression coincided with the growth in their popularity. Few people use the word 'straits', in the sense of 'difficulties', other than coupled with the word 'dire'.

'But if members tell us they are in dire straits, without a job, gone bankrupt, and the wife's run off with the milkman, then we will move heaven and earth to help them.' (*Accountancy*, 1993)

dirty see DO THE DIRTY ON

dirty mac brigade; dirty old man Dirty old men (DOMs) – those who enjoy pornography or chasing younger women – are traditionally thought of as wearing dirty mackintoshes. There is a basis of truth in this, for accounts by comedians who worked at places such as the Windmill Theatre, famous for its nude shows in the Second World War, describe the way in which the DOMs who used to sit through show after show, gradually moving forward until they reached the front row, always wore a long coat of some kind, or at least kept a newspaper on their laps, so no one could see what they were doing with their hands. From this tradition 'dirty mac' has come to be an alternative for dirty old man, and hence has come to represent something that is seedy or degrading.

'I asked Toby to do me a favour and tell the Fleet Street "dirty mac brigade", who covered crime and other seedy activities, that I had given him an exclusive.' (Malcolm Hamer, *Sudden Death*, 1991)

dirty tricks While the simple expression 'dirty tricks' for a dishonest action has been around since the later part of the nineteenth century, the special sense of underhand activity designed to discredit someone dates only from the mid-twentieth century, when it was CIA slang for covert intelligence operations, the CIA itself getting the nickname 'The Department of Dirty Tricks'. Both uses are common.

'Jones, reeling from a £20,000 fine and suspended six-month ban imposed by the FA for his part in a video nasty about soccer dirty tricks, has to pick himself up at Middlesbrough.' (*Today*, 1992)

'Town halls should not use dirty tricks, harassment or intimidation to stop schools opting out of local council control, Education Secretary John Patten warned yester-day.' (*Liverpool Daily Post and Echo*, 1993)

dirty work Two expressions have fallen together here. Firstly there is the simple idea that work that involves getting dirty is unpleasant, so that 'dirty work' comes to mean anything that is unpleasant to do, as in the catch-phrase 'It's dirty work (or "a dirty job") but somebody has to do it.' Secondly, there is a shortening of the nineteenth-century expression 'dirty work at the crossroads', meaning foul play.

The source of this expression is rather obscure but probably comes from the idea of crossroads being an ideal place for highwaymen and robbers to hang out. Its history is further complicated by the fact that at the time of the First World War, when the full expression was in vogue, it was also used as an expression for sexual activity. The full form is rarely heard in any sense today.

'He likes to get other people – usually me, of course – to do the dirty work: make the awkward telephone call, tell the gardener who comes for four hours a week that he has ruined the asparagus bed, speak to Tom's teacher about his appalling arithmetic.' (Nina Bawden, *A Woman of my Age*, 1991)

'At first, economic pressures pushed clients to a grudging, reluctant use of search consultants, and a realisation that they were acceptable and tolerable on the grounds that they could save time and hassle and ultimately even money, and could carry out confidential corporate dirty work in tight spots.' (Stephanie Jones, *The Headhunting Business*, 1990)

disaster waiting to happen see ACCIDENT WAITING TO HAPPEN

distance lends enchantment This is a quotation cliché, from Thomas Campbell's poem *Pleasures of Hopes* (1799). When the Queen made her famous *annus horribilis* speech in 1992, she said, 'Distance is well-known to lend enchantment, even to the less attractive views.'

divided into three parts (**like Caesar's Gaul**) When Julius Caesar became governor of Gaul he made up his mind to make a political name for himself, and started a campaign of conquest that turned what had been a small province into one of the largest then under Roman rule. The legality of this was dubious, so, being a master of propaganda, he sent home a brilliantly written series of dispatches justifying his actions. These were then collected into a book, *De Bello Gallico* (*The Gallic Wars*), later studied by generations of schoolchildren, the opening words of which are, '*Gallia est omnis divisa in partes tres*' ('All Gaul is divided into three parts'). By 1892 it was a well-enough established cliché for a writer to be able to play on it, saying 'All golf . . . is divided into three parts – driving, iron play, and putting.' The decline in Latin in schools does not seem to have stopped its use, although it now has a decidedly old-fashioned ring to it.

'Gaul might be divided into three parts, but this film, imperfectly cobbled together from two separate stories, displays no such narrative neatness.' (*Independent*, 12 October 1989)

'Diesel Cars: Escalating the Gallic wars Diesel-wise, Gaul is divided into three parts – Renault, Peugeot and Citroen.' (*Daily Telegraph*, 15 April 1992)

dizzy heights Used both literally and figuratively this has been a cliché since the middle of the twentieth century, either referring to things truly high enough to make you dizzy, or to a position of importance. It is often used ironically.

'And descending from the dizzy heights of Labour's megalithic conference platform, he was as caustic as ever of the slick political selling job it symbolized.' (*Independent*, 10 May 1989)

'This week, they play three nights at London's Town & Country Club, which isn't bad, but it's a high step down from the dizzy heights of packing out Wembley for several shows on the trot as they did five years ago when they were one of the biggest bands in Europe.' (*Punch*, 1992)

do and/or die see THEIRS NOT TO REASON WHY

do as you would be done by This warning against selfishness has been endured by generations of children, since Charles Kingsley used this ancient proverb in *The Water Babies*, published in 1863. There Tom, the ignorant and abused chimney sweep, is taught how to behave with consideration to others by Mrs Doasyouwouldbe-doneby, and taught the consequences of not doing so by Mrs Bedonebyasyoudid. George Bernard Shaw in his *Maxims for Revolutionists* (1907) cast a new light on the maxim: 'Do not do unto others as you would they should do unto you. Their tastes may not be the same.'

' "If you had to sum up our philosophy in a few words, it would be: 'Do as you would be done by' ", says Margaret.' (*East Anglian Daily Times*, 1993)

do by the book see BY THE BOOK

(let's) do lunch A vogue expression starting life on Madison Avenue as an alternative to 'Let's have lunch', this reached Britain in a big way in the 1980s, although few outside the media and advertising dared use it in cold blood.

do not pass GO; do not collect £200 (or **$200**) see GO DIRECTLY TO JAIL

do or die Used in its literal sense, to persist at something vital, even if death is the result, this expression is so clichéd that it is often used with irony. In more informal contexts, it is used simply to mean 'earnest, over eager'.

'It had looked like a melodrama – a little group in a candle-lit attic, holding up their arms with fists clenched and swearing to do or die.' (David Craig, *King Cameron*, 1991)

'What appeals to people is the normality of the show; there is nothing do or die about it which makes it very easy to relate to it.' (Sasha Stone, *Kylie Minogue: the Superstar Next Door*, 1989)

do the dirty on This expression for to cheat or betray came into use about the same time as DIRTY WORK at the crossroads became popular. It obviously derives from expressions such as dirty work and DIRTY TRICKS.

'It's almost as though he's afraid they are going to cheat him out of something, or do the dirty on him.' (Michael Lawson, *Facing Conflict*, 1991)

do the honours Meaning to act as host, or hand round food or drink, this dates from the sixteenth century, and was a cliché by the eighteenth.

'Actually, the former Soviet Union had been invited to do the honours but declined, not being up to it organisationally nor economically at present.' (*The Art Newspaper*, 1992)

' "You keep 'em coming," he said, "and I'll do the honours." ' (Chris Kelly, *The Forest of the Night*, 1991)

do the world of good see WORLD OF GOOD

do you come here often? This is a conscious cliché, imitating the desperate, embarrassed attempt of a tongue-tied youth to find some way of opening a conversation with a girl. It also became a catch-phrase after being used on *The Goon Show* in the 1950s, in which case the correct response is 'only in the mating season'. This exchange can still be heard.

' "Do you come here often?" piped the lead singer after uneasily beginning with "Having No Money".' (*Hot Press*, 1991)

do your own thing This slogan of the hippy revolt of the 1960s has now settled down into meaning little more than 'do whatever it is that you would like to do' (a sentiment echoing Rabelais' *'Fay ce que vouldras'* ('do what you like') written above the entrance to the Abbey of Thélème in his *Gargantua* (1534)). It is particularly popular with writers of travel brochures where its attempt to evoke total relaxation and a lack of stress and worry still carries some of the original hippy associations.

'Here at Club M'Diq, you can either do your own thing or involve yourself in the daily and evening activities and events available for free; you can lazy [*sic*] on the spacious sandy beach, or go off on the optional excursions to see something of what this colourful Moslem country has to offer.' (*HCI Club Holidays*, 1990)

dodo see DEAD AS A DODO

the dog ate my homework A conscious cliché, the sort of desperate excuse the class slacker might make, now used for comic effect.

'Following the pioneering work by British Rail (remember the wrong kind of snow) some of our most prominent captains of industry are churning out world-beating [excuses] faster than you can say: "The dog ate my homework, Sir." (*Independent*, 27 July 1998)

'He came across as having all the *joie de vivre* of a man whose winning lottery ticket has just been eaten by the dog.' (*Daily Mail*, 27 August 1998)

dog eat dog This term for ruthless competition seems to come from a proverb, found in the first century BC in Latin, and in English from the sixteenth century, that 'dog does not eat dog'. Dog eat dog is not found until the twentieth century, and presumably represents a situation where the LAW OF THE JUNGLE has taken over, and dog does now eat dog. The expression is very often found in the form 'It's dog eat dog out there.'

'A negative view of marketing is the "dog eat dog" view where the school can only gain by putting another school at a disadvantage or loss.' (Mike Sullivan, *Marketing Your Primary School*, 1991)

dog has his day see EVERY DOG HAS HIS DAY

dog in the manger In one of Aesop's fables a dog, lying comfortably in a manger full of hay, refuses to let an ox come and eat the hay, even though the ox is hungry and, as the ox mildly points out, the dog cannot eat the hay itself. From this the dog in the manger has come to represent selfishly hanging on to something you cannot use yourself. It has been firmly fixed in the language since the seventeenth century.

dogged determination One thing a dog is good at is holding on once it has got its teeth into something. So 'dogged determination' is found in someone who won't let go of their aim, very often someone who is DEAD BUT WON'T LIE DOWN. 'Dogged', an old adjective, in the past meant 'dog-like', both in the sense of 'faithful hound' and 'cur', but is now obsolete in these senses.

'It was a long game, and despite his dogged determination not to be shuffled to the sidelines Edward, naturally, was not privy to all the machinations.' (Frank Kippax, *The Butcher's Bill*, 1992)

the dog's bollocks A British cliché of the late 1990s for 'the best, excellent'. The expression originated in the early twentieth century in the north of England to mean 'outstanding', because that is what a dog's bollocks are (presumably there was originally some expression, now lost, such as 'stands out like a dog's bollocks'). It started to come into fashion as youth slang about 1990, and was made known to a wider audience in 1993, when the Wychwood Brewery (whose Managing Director I have to thank for the above information) produced an outstanding real ale called 'The Dog's Bollocks'. The expression grew steadily in use, being used even in advertising, but looks to be falling out of fashion as rapidly as it came in. One problem with the expression is that it is often shortened to 'the bollocks', leading to confusion between 'It's the bollocks' (good), and 'It's bollocks' (bad). 'Puppy's privates' has been recorded as a politer variant.

dog's chance 'He hasn't got a dog's chance' has been a cliché since the nineteenth century. Its history is obscure, but 'dog' has long been used for something that is poor quality or subordinate, the source of such plant names as the dog rose and of the current use of describing an unattractive person or no-hope situation as 'a dog'. It is tempting to link the expression to the term 'dog-chance' found in the seventeenth century, meaning the worst or losing throw at dice, which goes back to the Latin words, *canis* or *canicula* ('dog' or 'little dog') used in the same way, but there is no evidence to link them. (See also below.)

it's a dog's life 'Dog' has been used in numerous phrases which reflect the hard life of dogs in the past. We get 'dog tired', 'go to the dogs', we say something 'isn't fit for a dog', describe something messy as 'a dog's breakfast', while someone overdressed 'looks like a dog's dinner', and we 'give a dog a bad name and hang him'. The use of dog in this way is very ancient – the ancient Greeks called one school of philosophers 'cynics', from the Greek word *kynikos* for dog-like, because they rejected the trappings of civilization, and, allegedly, lived like dogs. 'A dog's life' has been used in England for a hard life since the sixteenth century, although it does not seem to have become a cliché until the nineteenth. However, dogs' lives have become so much better in the late twentieth century that the term is now often used ironically, to describe a life of comfort.

dogs of war This cliché comes initially from Shakespeare's *Julius Caesar* in which Mark Antony, standing over Caesar's body, prophesies the civil war that will split Rome and says, 'Caesar's spirit, ranging for revenge . . . shall . . . Cry "Havoc!" and let slip the dogs of war;/That this foul deed shall smell above the earth/With carrion men, groaning for burial' (III.i). The term 'dogs of war' was familiar enough in the nineteenth century that a writer in 1842 could play on it in a popular novel with the threat to 'let slip the dogs of law on him'. It took off as a term for mercenaries after the success of Frederick Forsyth's novel *The Dogs of War* (book, 1974; film, 1980) about a mercenary's attempt to take over an African country.

'Journalists blame this on the fact that Mr Heseltine, David Mellor and the other "dogs of war" who make for the best viewing concentrated on attacking Labour.' (*Daily Telegraph*, 12 April 1992)

done and dusted Like SORTED, this cliché based on housework is used to suggest a business-like efficiency. It is used to mean completely finished or ready, and is a fairly recent introduction.

'Lo and behold, you have the full twelve-month series from Jan. to Dec. done and dusted, in the format you typed the first one.' (*Practical PC*, 1992)

' "I'll do all the places along the Shambles and you do Chittling Street and then we can push off back to the Yard, job done and dusted. Okay?" ' (Terry Pratchett, *Feet of Clay*, 1996)

done deal This business cliché started life comparatively recently in the USA. It is used to mean that a deal has been finalized.

'Meantime, the agreement under which Encore Computer Corp may switch to the Alpha from the Motorola Inc 88000 that it presently uses is apparently not a done deal yet.' (*Unigram x*, 1993)

done to a turn This cliché for 'perfectly cooked', in use since the eighteenth century, reflects the days when roasting was done on a spit, turned constantly before an open fire. When the roast was perfectly cooked it was 'done to a turn', neither turned too long in front of the fire, nor too little. The tenacity of some phrases in English is well illustrated by this one, used without a second thought well after the oven had replaced the spit in general use.

'So everything from a 25lb turkey to a full complement of 50 fairy cakes will be done to a turn.' (Advertising leaflet)

done with see DEAD AND DONE WITH

don't call us, we'll call you This is a cliché of the performing arts, which spread first to cover a wider job market, and then into general colloquial use where it has come to mean that the speaker is not impressed by something someone has just done or suggested. It had its origins in the American theatre, where it was used as a euphemistic way of telling an actor he or she had not got the part.

don't do anything I wouldn't do A colloquial cliché, in use from the beginning of the twentieth century, used as a jocular comment to anyone going somewhere to enjoy themselves, particularly if there is a possibility of sex being involved. An alternative is 'be good – and if you can't be good, be careful', which dates from about the same time and which was taken from the title of an American popular song of 1907.

don't give a damn see FRANKLY, MY DEAR, I DON'T GIVE A DAMN

don't know if I'm coming or going see COMING OR GOING

don't know what hit you see KNOW WHAT HIT YOU

don't try this at home A conscious cliché, used in imitation of television presenters about to try something potentially dangerous, or more often used to warn children of something it would be stupid to do.

doom and gloom; doom merchants The set phrase 'doom and gloom' has been in use since at least the middle of the twentieth century, and was given greater currency by its use by the pessimistic leprechaun played by Tommy Steele in the film version of *Finian's Rainbow* (1968). The phrase was also in the original production of 1947. At the same time there was another catch-phrase in use from the radio comedy series *Round the Horne* (1965–7) in which the character of Spasm, butler to Lady Counterblast, played by Kenneth Williams, would go round saying 'we be doomed . . . doomed', which became 'we're doomed' in popular speech. This may have had some influence on the development of 'doom merchants'.

'The constant exposure to doom and gloom that most of us take for granted can be a source of hidden stress – if you have real problems to contend with you do not need this extra mental burden.' (Linda Gamlin and Jonathan Brostoff, *The Complete Guide to Food Allergy and Intolerance*, 1989)

'Crying Scotsman and former police officer Rod Mackay, 67, has out-grumped dozens of doom merchants to take our coveted title.' (*Liverpool Daily Post and Echo*)

double whammy An expression meaning a two-fold problem or setback, taken from the American cartoon strip 'Li'l Abner' created by Al Capp (1909–79). There, a character called Evil-Eye Fleegle claims to be able to put a hex, or as he calls it, 'shoot a whammy' on people by pointing a finger towards them with one eye open. If necessary, he can put in a double whammy, with both eyes open. The expression was not introduced to the British public until the Conservatives' general election campaign of 1992. It became very popular for a short time after this, but has now faded somewhat.

'Of course, one can't help wondering where Chris Patten would be if, in 1992, he had not pulled off that extraordinary double whammy – as chairman of the Conservatives, he saw electoral victory of the party, but lost his own seat in Bath by 3,000 votes.' (*Independent*, 14 September 1998)

down on the farm For journalists, particularly headline writers, events hardly ever take place 'on a farm', but nearly always 'down on the farm'. The source of this peculiar construction is probably the 1919 American hit song 'How 'ya Gonna Keep 'em down on the Farm (After They've seen Paree)' (words by Sam M. Lewis and Joe Young). The song refers to the US soldiers who had been to Europe in the First World War.

'Fur flies down on the farm,' (Headline, *Independent*, 26 September 1998)

down the line SEE FEW YEARS DOWN THE LINE

Draconian powers (**measures** or **punishment**) In the seventh century BC the city of Athens appointed a man called Draco to reform its laws, taking punishment for crimes out of the private sphere and handing it over to the state. Traditionally – although modern scholars doubt this – Draco's laws were very severe. When he was asked why most crimes were punished with death he is said to have replied that small offences deserved death and he knew of no severer penalty for great ones. Someone else remarked that he wrote his laws in blood not ink. Most of these laws were repealed a century later, but their reputation lived on. However, the word 'Draconian' only appeared in the nineteenth century (although 'draconical' was used in the seventeenth), and set phrases such as 'Draconian powers' only became clichés of journalism in the middle of the twentieth century. The fact that it is now often written with a small 'd' shows how thoroughly it has been absorbed into the language.

'In the most draconian punishment ever handed out to Scottish internationalists, Billy Bremner, Joe Harper, Pat McCluskey, Willie Young and Arthur Graham were told they would never play for their country again.' (Stuart Cosgrove, *Hampden Babylon*, 1991)

'Malaysia can pass as many draconian laws as it wants, and still enjoy royal visits and British arms export guarantees.' (*Independent*, 23 September 1998)

drag kicking and screaming see KICKING AND SCREAMING

(make a) drama out of a crisis 'We won't make a drama out of a crisis' was a heavily advertised slogan for an insurance company in the 1980s. It quickly caught on, particularly with headline writers, often as a formula phrase.

drastic action (or **measures**, or **powers**) Drastic was originally a medical word, meaning powerful or vigorous, and a drastic purge, would, for instance, be a strong laxative. The use of 'drastic' to mean something approaching 'desperate' as well as 'strong' is a mid-twentieth-century development.

'The situation called for some drastic action and so I laid it on the line; either they won this game or I would resign.' (M. Gist, *Life at the Tip*, 1993)

'Sir Robin Day, realising that drastic measures were called for, started to make funny faces.' (*Daily Telegraph*, 6 April 1992)

draw the line at This cliché, meaning to set a limit, developed in the nineteenth century. It comes from the idea of drawing a line on the ground as a boundary, over which a person may not step.

'The Gulf war will revive a debate about where to draw the line between commercial sense and military prudence.' (*The Economist*, 1991)

draw your own conclusions The use of 'draw' in this common idiom, in use since the sixteenth century, seems to come from the falling together of two different senses of this very complex verb. Firstly, there is the sense 'extract', as to draw a cork from a bottle; secondly, 'compile, put together', as in to draw up a will.

'She could not – or would not – be more specific, but had suggested that he should speak further with Quex and draw his own conclusions.' (Robert Richardson, *The Lazarus Tree*, 1992)

drawing board see BACK TO THE OLD DRAWING BOARD

the dread hand of ... The history of this expression is undocumented, but it would appear to stem from William Blake's poem *The Tiger* (1794) in which he writes: 'And what shoulder, and what art,/Could twist the sinews of thy heart?/And when thy heart began to beat,/What dread hand? And what dread feet?' I have been unable to trace any further use of the expression until modern times, although William Morris does use 'dreaded hand' in his *Earthly Paradise* (1868–70). If Blake is the source, the construction 'the dread hand of . . .' has drifted a long way from its original sense. It is usually used today not just to mean something that is to be feared, but something that will blight what it touches.

'Hopefully, there will be enough superb BBC journalists left to fight off the dread hand of the Beeb's executives.' (*Evening Standard*, 7 October 1998)

dream come true (or **turned to a nightmare**) Both these are journalistic clichés of the middle twentieth century. 'Dream' in the sense of 'aspiration' is largely a twentieth-century development, with terms such as the AMERICAN DREAM dating from the 1930s, 'dreamboat', for someone attractive, from the 1940s, and DREAM TICKET from 1960 – although the much earlier DREAMS OF AVARICE can come close to this sense. By the 1960s, 'dream come true' was well-enough established as a cliché for 'dream turned to a nightmare' to develop from it.

'It was a fan's dream come true to watch it and a commentator's dream to be part of it.' (*Daily Mirror*, 1992)

dream team (or **ticket**) 'Dream ticket' is an expression which was coined in 1960 to describe the candidacy of Richard Nixon and Nelson Rockefeller for President and Vice-President of the United States, the idea being that they represented the perfect team to appeal to the electorate. From then it was applied to other such political teams. More recently the idea of 'ticket' has developed beyond the use of 'list of candidates' in the original coinage, to the more general sense of an opportunity to do something or go somewhere. 'Dream team' seems to have developed out of 'dream ticket', the attraction being the rhyme, while the sense is not greatly changed.

'Is this the dream ticket America has been waiting for – presidential hopeful Bill Clinton and superstar Barbra Streisand?' (*Daily Mirror*, 1992)

'Like the Beatles, Keegan was a legend in Liverpool and he has given United a dream ticket to ride all the way back to the Premier League.' (*Daily Mirror*, 1992)

'The National's production of Shakespeare's *Antony and Cleopatra* had casting to die for: a dream team of Alan Rickman and Helen Mirren – probably the two sexiest 50-plusses in the country.' (*Independent*, 24 October 1998)

dreaming spires SEE IVORY TOWER

(rich) beyond the dreams of avarice 'I am rich beyond the dreams of avarice' is a quotation from an obscure play called *The Gamester* written by Edward Moore in 1753, although the term 'dreams of avarice' in the sense of 'illusions' was already well established at this date. Moore's line, which has been used steadily since the eighteenth century, must have passed into the language quickly for it is used by Boswell in his *Life of Samuel Johnson* of 1781. It sometimes occurs in the form 'wealth beyond the dreams of avarice'.

'The hon. Member for Oldham West may giggle, but £30,000 is riches beyond the dreams of avarice to many of the people whom he claims to represent.' (*Hansard Extracts 1991–1992*)

'I'm not poor by any means, but he was wealthy beyond even Sybil's dreams of avarice.' (Annabel Murray, *Only Two can Share*, 1993)

dressed to kill This is a surprisingly old cliché, 'kill' in the sense of 'make a conquest' being well established by the early eighteenth century, and the full 'dressed to kill' by the early nineteenth. Modern journalists like to pun on the literal and figurative uses of the expression.

'Both sported a magnificent moustache, both wore a ten-gallon hat and both were dressed to kill at the Golden Boot Awards for Westerns in Beverly Hills last night.' (*Daily Mirror*, 1992)

drink like a fish Fish do not, of course, drink very much. However, they do appear to be gulping liquid down as they open and close their mouths to pass water over their gills, and this, combined with their liquid environment, means that they have been associated with excessive drinking since the seventeenth century.

'Then he started to pull himself together, returned to Hollywood and stayed sober – except for Sundays, when he would lock himself away and drink like a fish.' (Michael Munn, *Hollywood Rogues*, 1991)

I'll drink to that The idea of drinking to someone or something in the sense of making a toast has been around since at least the sixteenth century. By the early twentieth century 'I'll drink to that' had become a stock expression for agreeing to have a drink, and by the middle of the century it had taken the small step to being used as a catch-phrase for general assent or agreement. This development took place in the USA, and spread gradually to the UK. A big boost to the currency of the expression was given, on both sides of the Atlantic, by its use as a catch-phrase in the highly successful television comedy *Rowan and Martin's Laugh In* (1968–71).

'I don't know who wrote Ainsley's voiceovers, but lines like "A lot of the wine here is available in the UK, but at twice the price – I'll drink to that!" just won't do.' (*Independent*, 23 September 1998)

drive a coach and horses through The early forms of this expression usually involve 'a coach and six', one of the largest kinds of coach. To be able to drive such a coach through something it has to have a very big hole in it. In the early sixteenth century Thomas Otway, in his play *The Atheist* wrote: 'Is there not a hole in my belly, that you may turn a coach-and-six in?' 'Big enough to turn a coach and six in', survived in dialect until at least the late nineteenth century. The expression we use stems from a comment made about 1672 by Sir Stephen Rice (1637–1715), Chief Baron of the Exchequer. We are told: 'This man was often heard to say, before he came to be a judge, That he would drive a Coach and Six horses through the Act of Settlement.' Thereafter, 'drive a coach and horses through' seems to have been restricted to destroying laws or parliamentary bills until it gained a more general use in the twentieth century.

'If you cannot agree on matters of discipline, your child will soon spot the differences in outlook and drive a coach and horses through your serenity.' (Martin Herbert, *Discipline: a Positive Guide for Parents*, 1989)

drop anchor This nautical term is used as a jocular way of saying 'stop'. As can be seen from the quotation, thought has to be given to whether or not it is appropriate for the context.

'All that technology is going to have you hacking down the trails faster than you've ever experienced, so you'd better get some good brakes for when it's time to drop anchor.' (*Stuff*, October 1998)

drop-dead gorgeous A colloquialism currently making the transition to cliché through over-use. The use of 'drop dead' to emphasize 'gorgeous' is related to the use of TO DIE FOR.

'Pretty Polly legs are drop dead gorgeous.' (Advertisement, September 1998)

'Drop dead, gorgeous.' (Headline to article on models, *Independent*, 21 September 1998)

drop in the bucket (or **the ocean**) 'Drop in the bucket' for a small quantity, usually of a larger whole, comes from the Bible (Isaiah 40:12–15) where we are told God 'hath measured the waters in the hollows of his hand . . . and weighed the mountains in scales, and the hills in a balance . . . Behold, the nations are as a drop of a bucket, and are counted as the small dust of the balance.' 'A drop in the ocean' is a more emphatic version of 'drop in the bucket', and seems not to have developed until the mid-twentieth century.

'Sales in the product's first year of deliveries amounted to only $1m, a drop in the bucket for a firm that's been through two rounds of venture capital totalling $7.5m.' (*Unigram x*, 1993)

'Teams of security staff police the laboratory, guarding the precious property, protecting what potentially could lead to the greatest fortune ever; the combined wealth of Rockefeller, Vanderbilt and Onassis is a mere drop in the ocean compared to the promise of test-tube fusion.' (Frank Close, *Too Hot to Handle*, 1992)

at the drop of a hat This cliché, which developed in America in the middle of the nineteenth century, refers to the habit of sweeping off a hat or dropping a handkerchief to mark the start of a race or contest. Since the contestants would spring into action as soon as the signal was given, it came to mean 'immediately, instantly'.

'The ability to produce flowers at the drop of a hat or a cake to celebrate a customer's birthday should all be at his or her fingertips.' (*Caterer & Hotelkeeper*, 1991)

'Mr Rodger Bell QC, for Mr Bewick, suggested that his client had a "bee in his bonnet" about surgeons being able to work anywhere at a drop of a hat.' (*Guardian*, 7 December 1989)

drop the pilot A rather dated cliché which comes from a *Punch* cartoon drawn by Sir John Tenniel (illustrator of Lewis Carroll's *Alice* books) in 1890. It was inspired by events in Germany, where the Kaiser forced Bismarck to resign as Chancellor, after he had piloted his country through political difficulties for many years. The cartoon showed Bismarck dressed in the uniform of a pilot who guided big ships through difficult waters, leaving a ship, and had the caption 'Dropping the Pilot' (an expression used for the point at which the pilot disembarked and the ship was left to make its own way). Although not met with regularly, this expression is still used when some prominent leader is sacked, and was very much in evidence when Mrs Thatcher was ousted from power, and again when Helmut Kohl lost his post as Chancellor of Germany in 1998.

drown your sorrows Drown your sorrows is a twentieth-century version of expressions such as 'drown yourself in drink' and 'drown yourself in wine' which have been around since the Middle Ages. It presumably is a shortening of 'drown your sorrows in drink'.

'He went to a local pub in the mining village where he was staying to drown his sorrows and found himself sitting next to a stranger who remarked on his dejected demeanour.' (David Oates and Derek Ezra, *Advice from the Top*, 1989)

drunken stupor A cliché from the middle of the twentieth century. Since 'stupor' technically means a state of unconsciousness or near-unconsciousness, it is interesting to note that the quotations below describe activity while in a drunken stupor. This reflects a growing trend to use the expression for a state of extreme drunkenness, rather than in its original meaning of passed out from drink.

'About the only way a current computer program could ever win a single game against a master player would be for the master, perhaps in a drunken stupor while playing 50 games simultaneously, to commit some once-in-a-year blunder.' (*New Scientist*, 1991)

'Maybe she thought he would get up in some drunken stupor and ravish her.' (Iain Banks, *The Crow Road*, 1993)

dry as a bone Although this simile is recorded only from 1806, its imagery is very ancient, going back at least to the Book of Isaiah and the vision of the valley of dry bones.

'If a piece of glass is dipped in water, the drops of liquid stay on the surface for several seconds; with a diamond they run off instantly, leaving the stone dry as a bone.' (Frederick Forsyth, *The Negotiator*, 1989)

dubious charms Dubious charms is a standard way of implying that others may find a person or thing attractive, but the speaker cannot tell why. It has been a cliché since the mid-twentieth century.

'Anatomy of a truly disastrous love affair . . . or just what happened when a golf widow from Guildford fell helplessly for the dubious charms of a proletarian conceptual artist from Notting Hill.' (*Daily Mail*, 27 August 1998)

ducking and diving The most usual sense of ducking and diving is to be evasive, difficult to pin down. However, if you are good at ducking and diving to avoid being caught, you are quick on your feet, and so it has come to share this expression's meaning of fast thinking or skilful behaviour. Both uses are quite recent.

'Considerable credit must go to the superb Gary Moore and his band for under-pinning the whole evening with some musically adept ducking and diving, particularly during the unpredictable Buddy Guy's set.' (*Guitarist*, 1992)

'Drugs in rugby will become a much more widespread problem if the sort of ducking and diving that took place when Messrs. Swart, Du Preeze and van den Bergh tested positive is the only form of official discouragement on offer.' (*Rugby World and Post*, 1991)

due consideration SEE AFTER DUE CONSIDERATION

dulcet tones Dulcet is a poetic word for 'sweet', rarely found nowadays unless linked to 'tones'. Although the phrase can be found used straight, it is most often ironic, to suggest the exact opposite.

'It is always a pleasure to reply to the beguiling and dulcet tones of the hon. Member for Bradford, South (Mr. Cryer).' (*Hansard Extracts 1991–1992*)

dumbing down At the time of writing this is one of the most frequently used clichés in British newspapers. It is a recent import from the USA, using the American sense of 'dumb' to mean stupid. Used to lament a perceived lowering of standards, it is, in effect, the modern equivalent of the old codger's lament 'things aren't what they used to be'.

'The whole philosophy of the GCSE exam is based on twin untruths. Firstly, that everyone is deserving of a prize . . . and secondly that educational standards can best be measured by "units" of coursework. The first premise was patently absurd, and is part of the general "dumbing down" that is affecting British society at all levels.' (*Daily Mail*, 27 August 1998)

dunghill cock SEE RULE THE ROOST

dust SEE BITE THE DUST

dust from your feet SEE SHAKE THE DUST FROM YOUR FEET

dust to dust One of those clichéd phrases used vaguely by those who want to avoid talking directly about death and the DEAR DEPARTED, this is taken from the words said at the interment in the Burial of the Dead from the Book of Common Prayer: 'Earth to earth, ashes to ashes, dust to dust.' It has been a cliché since the mid-nineteenth century.

'In the end, Clara, exasperated beyond endurance, brought up once more the possibility of cremation . . . and Mrs Maugham, square, immutable, said quite astonishingly for her, and invoking sanctions she had been deriding for thirty years, that ashes must go to ashes and dust to dust.' (Margaret Drabble, *Jerusalem the Golden*, 1988)

dusted see DONE AND DUSTED

dyed-in-the-wool Often used of political parties or beliefs, this cliché comes from America and dates from the very beginning of the twentieth century. Wool can be dyed at four different stages of manufacture: in the wool, before it is spun; in the yarn, before it is woven; in the piece, when it is a length of cloth; and once it has been made up. The earlier in the process it is dyed, the more thoroughly the colour is incorporated into the final garment. Hence the use of 'dyed-in-the-wool' to mean thoroughgoing, unchanging.

'Nick Drake has had a genuine re-discovery amongst a far wider constituency of music lovers than just retro-fiends and dyed-in-the-wool folkies.' (*Independent*, 14 September 1998)

dynamite Dynamite is an explosive mixture, itself a cliché since the 1970s, capable of creating a major impression, so it is no surprise to find that it is used to mean something unsettling or dangerous. It took about fifty years from the invention of dynamite for it to become a cliché used in this way. 'Political dynamite' is a particularly common combination.

'On the polo field they had been dynamite and almost telepathic in anticipating each other's moves.' (Jilly Cooper, *Polo*, 1991)

'Claims such as Professor Brenner's can be political dynamite.' (*New Scientist*, 1991)

each and every This has been in use since the middle of the seventeenth century. At first it was mainly used in legal and similar expressions as part of the legal tendency to make sure that the writer has covered every eventuality. By the middle of the nineteenth century the expression was often little more than a filler. The modern 'each and every one of you' is a particularly empty phrase.

'As proud as each and every one of their internationals must have felt as they have waltzed off to represent their country, there is no doubt that they will have cast more than one anxious glance over their shoulder wondering whether Surrey can manage without them.' (*Independent*, 1 September 1998)

eager beaver This is an American cliché which reached the UK about the middle of the twentieth century. The beaver has been held up since the eighteenth century as an example of hard work and industry as it builds its dams and lodges, but the rhyming 'eager' only seems to have been attached to it in the twentieth century.

'He also gives us a measured degree of self doubt mixed with evasiveness and a realistic progression from a young, ambitious eager beaver on the music hall circuit to a very old man languishing with his memories in Switzerland.' (*Today*, 1992)

eagle eye Legend has it that the eagle has the sharpest eyesight of all birds. When its sight grows dull with age it flies up towards the sun, and, by staring at the sun which only it can do, it burns away all the cloudiness of age. This story has been known and referred to for as long as we have written records of English, having been introduced to the Anglo-Saxons by Christian missionaries. However, 'eagle eye' or 'eagle eyed', used without reference to the legend, to mean (keeping) a sharp watch on something has only been a cliché since the early nineteenth century.

'Prisons and young offenders' institutions come under the eagle eye of Chris Woodhead, the Chief Inspector of Schools.' (*Independent*, 24 September 1998)

the eagle has landed These were the words of Neil Armstrong as he landed the lunar module 'Eagle', the first manned craft to reach the moon, in 1969. It became a catch-phrase, used when putting something tricky in place, or as a cry of achievement. The expression was further popularized when it was used, for a totally unrelated reason, as the title of a 1975 novel by Jack Higgins (filmed in 1976), after which it became a formula phrase, used by headline writers. It should not be confused with 'where eagles dare', also used as a formula phrase, the title of a 1967 novel by Alistair Maclean.

ear to the ground Old Westerns would often show a character jumping off his horse, lying down and placing an ear to the ground. If he was a really good tracker or scout, he would then tell his companions exactly how many horses were following and how far away they were. The character doing this was often a Native American, for it is a technique they were credited with having developed. It is from this that the expression 'to have (or keep) an ear to the ground', for monitoring what is going on around you, developed in the nineteenth century.

'His parting advice to those interested in taking the challenge was "keep an ear to the ground, your back to the wheel and get your foot in the door".' (*The Bookseller*, 1993)

(at your) earliest convenience A cliché of formal writing, most often found in business letters, where it has been used since the early part of the nineteenth century as an elaborate way of saying 'as soon as possible'.

'I also enclose a Medical Assessment Card which you should complete and return at your earliest convenience.' (*Lothian Regional Council*)

early bath see TAKE AN EARLY BATH

early bird From the saying 'the early bird catches the worm', in use since the seventeenth century. The proverb is used to mean that the person who gets there first will have an advantage, but 'early bird' by itself now often means simply an early riser. The fact that Early Bird was the name given to the first commercial communications satellite (launched 6 April 1965) may have led to a growth in use.

' "It seems General Wolf is an early bird," he said; "you have a meeting with him in his office at six." ' (Frederick Forsyth, *The Deceiver*, 1992)

'We are pleased to be able to offer an early bird festival saver for those wishing to attend all events within this year's YEMF (except Event 16).' (Tourist information, York)

early days This expression is used as a catch-all to explain why something has not worked. It is often used as an excuse or in expressions such as 'Oh well, it's early days yet', to reassure.

'At a recent VR lecture tour in Amsterdam, Leary, the founder of multi-media software company Knoware, acknowledged that these are early days for VR (most of the audience were disappointed by what they saw but impressed by what they heard).' (*Wave Magazine*, 1990)

'Striker Atkinson said: "These are early days and I still don't believe I have hit top form." ' (*Today*, 1992)

earn brownie points see BROWNIE POINTS

earn your daily bread see DAILY BREAD

earner see NICE LITTLE EARNER

ears see COMING OUT OF YOUR EARS

up to your ears (or **arse**) see COMING OUT OF YOUR EARS

did you feel the earth move? (or **did the earth move for you?**) Ernest Hemingway used the words 'But did thee feel the earth move?' for the big sex scene in his 1940 novel of the Spanish civil war, *For Whom the Bell Tolls* (filmed 1943), and this rather pretentious expression soon became a humorous way of referring to the intensity of sexual reaction.

'Sex does, of course, have a place in marriage. It's just that for a great many women it's somewhere behind mortgage payments, . . . cleaning and gardening (the only area in which the earth regularly moves).' (*Mail on Sunday*, 20 September 1998)

earth shattering An exaggerated way of saying 'very important', often used ironically. It was a cliché by the mid-twentieth century.

'So let me turn to an issue, less Earth shattering, but no less vexatious – the keeping of mink in Shetland.' (*New Scientist*, 1991)

'While this does not appear to be such an earth shattering decision, it is one of the few occasions when a coroner's action has been criticised.' (William Tenet, *Safety is No Accident*, 1985)

easy come, easy go A nineteenth-century cliché, usually used of money or possessions. It can be approving or disapproving, depending on the speaker's point of view.

'Well it's "easy come, easy go" in those places, you should put it behind you and carry on with life, that's the best thing.' (Michael Falk, *Part of the Furniture*, 1991)

eat your heart out The ancients believed that sorrow or envy were bad for the heart, and would eat away at it, each sigh draining blood from the organ. This idea made its way to England and became well established – Shakespeare often refers to it, as in, 'Might liquid tears, or heart-offending groans,/Or blood-consuming sighs recall his life,/I would be blind with weeping, sick with groans,/Look pale as primrose with blood-drinking sighs' (*Henry VI*, part 2, III.ii). We still describe someone as broken-hearted by grief. By the beginning of the twentieth century, 'to eat your heart out' was well-established as a term for pining; but more recently it has also been used as a cry of triumph when someone else has cause to envy the speaker.

'If you had any sense you'd forget him, but eat your heart out if you want to.' (Pamela Bennetts, *Topaz*, 1988)

'For HP 9000 Unix workstations and business servers . . . customers can increase processing power without incurring software-upgrade fees – eat your heart out, IBM AS/400 users.' (*Unigram x*, 1993)

echo see CHEER TO THE ECHO

economical with the truth The current fashion for using this expression for being evasive, or, more frequently, simply lying, derives from a statement made by Sir Robert Armstrong in the Supreme Court, New South Wales, during the 'Spycatcher' case, when the government was trying to stop the publication of a book by a former member of MI5. '[The letter] contains a misleading impression, not a lie. It was being economical with the truth.' However, Sir Robert was not being original in his use of this phrase. Edmund Burke in *Two Letters on Proposals for Peace* (1796) has 'Falsehoods and delusion are allowed in no case whatsoever: But, as in the exercise of all the virtues, there is economy of truth.' And the expression is used by Samuel Pepys and Mark Twain, among others. In fact, 'economy of truth' is an old theological term which originally meant presenting doctrine in a way that suits the hearer, but which in the nineteenth century was nearly as much of a cliché, and used in the same way, as 'economical with the truth' is today.

'Were they economical with the truth? Would you blame them if they were? They have a right to their secrets, and doubtless their accounting to their friends is rather different from their accounting to the *Independent*.' (*Independent*, 5 September 1998)

egg on your face This expression for seeming foolish or ridiculous developed in the mid-twentieth century in the USA. The idea of poor performers having eggs thrown at them may lie behind it.

'The marketmeisters of New York and the economic overlords of Washington alike have been left with plenty of egg on their faces.' (*Independent*, 15 October 1998)

eggs in one basket SEE PUT ALL YOUR EGGS IN ONE BASKET

'Elementary, my dear Watson' Although this is one of the quotations that 'everybody knows' is from the Sherlock Holmes stories, it has not, in fact, been found in Conan Doyle's writings. But it *was* used in some sequels written by his son Adrian with John Dickson, and, most importantly, in the 1930s Basil Rathbone films based on the Sherlock Holmes books.

'Perhaps we'll find Burrows' fingerprints at the scene, then it'll be "Elementary, my dear Watson".' (Stella Shepherd, *Black Justice*, 1988)

eleventh hour In the Bible, Matthew (20:1–16) tells a parable in which the doctrine of grace is explained in a story of the labourers in the lord's vineyard who were all paid the same for their work whether they had been working all day, or had only started in the eleventh hour – the last hour of the Roman working day. This biblical use means the expression has been in the language from the earliest records. It was given further resonance in the twentieth century when at the end of the First World War the Armistice was signed on the eleventh hour of the eleventh day in the eleventh month of 1918. Nowadays it is generally used without reference to these, but simply as an alternative to 'last minute' or 'LAST DITCH'.

'It remains to be seen whether at this eleventh hour for the English countryside, those other giants, the forestry and the agriculture industries, are also prepared to take seriously a wider frame of reference.' (J. Purseglove, *Taming the Flood*, 1989)

eloquent silence SEE DEAFENING SILENCE

empty nest A term used to describe the feelings of parents, particularly mothers, whose children have all left home, which seems to have been coined in the 1970s. It is not surprising it is so recent, as it is not long since it was quite usual for children to live at home until they got married. The image of the home and family as a nest is an old one. We are quite likely to say of the children who have left that the 'birds have flown the nest', quite possibly to set up in their own homes with the help of money from their parents' 'nest egg'.

'Writers about midlife are fond of referring to the empty nest syndrome, much to the annoyance of feminists, who deplore the notion that women need children to bolster their sense of self-worth.' (Mary Batchelor, *Forty Plus*, 1988)

encounter see BRIEF ENCOUNTER

to encourage the others Voltaire, in his satirical novel *Candide* (1759) wrote: 'In [England] it is considered good to kill an admiral from time to time to encourage the others', and this ironic use caught on. It is often used in the original French '*pour encourager les autres*'.

'It suggests to me either an act of personal revenge or, alternatively, a demonstration to encourage the others, as the French say.' (Colin Forbes, *Whirlpool*, 1991)

end all see BE ALL AND END ALL

(it will all) end in tears A warning endured, and ignored, by generations of children, this has now become a way of predicting something unpleasant, often with a strong hint of 'I told you so.'

'There was a tension about Holmes' race over a mile which had to do with the fear – hers, and the spectators' – that her first serious competition after a 13-month absence with injury might end in tears.' (*Independent*, 1 September 1998)

end of an era A popular cliché with journalists and speechmakers, this expression is useful if the writer really is speaking of an era, but is often used to speak of the end of a sports career, or simply for someone leaving a particular job or place.

'Furthermore this match marked the end of an era in English rugby for a record-breaking team which will never play together again.' (*Rugby World and Post*, 1992)

the end of ... as we know it 'The end of civilization as we know it' was a Hollywood cliché for a great disaster, in use from the 1930s. Most notably, in Orson Welles' and Joseph Mankiewicz' great film *Citizen Kane* (1941) a possible World War was described as 'A project which would mean the end of civilization as we now know it.' This set phrase has now developed into a formula, so that any change can be seen as the end of something as we know it.

'If football is a business, bought for purely business reasons, then by the same token, it will be sold for business reasons ... This might not necessarily be bad or good for football. Just the end of football, as we know it.' (*Independent*, 7 September 1998)

end of the day see AT THE END OF THE DAY

end of the road (or **line**) The imagery of these two expressions both come from transport, and both mean little more than 'the end'. The use of 'end of the road' as a cliché seems to owe something to the 1924 song 'Keep right on to the End of the Road', by Harry Lauder and William Dillon, for the expression is not recorded before then. 'End of the line' is not found until nearly twenty-five years later.

'For some members of the Church of England it'll be the fulfilment of years of campaigning, for others it's the end of the road.' (Central Television news scripts, 1993)

'At the end of the line, the local authority careers service is called in to rescue what remains of this shambles.' (*Hansard Extracts 1991–1992*)

end of the tunnel see LIGHT AT THE END OF THE TUNNEL

end of your tether The imagery of 'at the end of your tether' (or 'rope' in North

America) comes from a tethered animal, which can go so far, but no further. 'Tether' had come to mean the limit of what you are able to do by 1579, when we are told, 'Men must not pass their tedder', but 'end of your tether' is not recorded until 1809.

'I've spoken with the daughter on the telephone within the last couple of months, and each time our telephone conversations are exactly the same – the daughter's at the end of her tether; she doesn't know what to do.' (Janet Askham and Catherine Thompson, *Dementia and Home Care*, 1990)

ends of the earth A cliché from the nineteenth century, this expression for the furthest limits of the world comes from Psalm 65, 'O God of our salvation: who art the confidence of all the ends of the earth.' The similar 'four corners of the earth' is also found in the Bible (Isaiah 11:12 and Revelations 7:1). The persistence of an expression once it has become fixed is evident in the way that no one is uncomfortable with these phrases, despite the fact that flat-earthers are now few and far between.

'If he put up a scheme, you would be willing to follow him to the ends of the earth to ensure its fulfilment.' (Stephen Studd, *Herbert Chapman. Football Emperor*, 1981)

'The salons were filled with honours, medals, awards, degrees from all corners of the earth, set out in cabinets according to the continent of origin.' (Mark Almond, *The Rise and Fall of Nicolae and Elena Ceausescu*, 1992)

English rose The rose is, of course, the symbol of England, so that it is not surprising that the pale rosy complexion typically found in our northern climes should be dubbed 'English rose'. However, it did not become a cliché until the middle of the twentieth century.

'Instead of the Duchess of York's trademark red hair and freckles, [her half-sister] Alice has the fresh-faced looks of an archetypal English rose.' (*Daily Mail*, 27 August 1998)

'The jobs of more than 400 production staff and a brand name known worldwide for its 'English Rose' image are in jeopardy.' (*Daily Mail*, 27 August 1998)

enough said see NUF SAID

envy of the world A companion cliché to the BEST . . . IN THE WORLD, this is used by politicians, journalists and the like to boast and try to stir up national pride, often on questionable evidence.

'Christmas cards, chocolate boxes and tourist literature, proclaiming a timeless tradition that is supposed to be the envy of the world.' (R. Holder *et al.*, *Trouble Brewing*, 1991)

'Labour's greatest ever achievement, without fear of any contradiction, the greatest achievement of the Labour movement was the introduction of the NHS which still remains, to a large extent, the envy of the world.' (Labour Club public meeting, recorded on 3 July 1993)

equal but different see MORE EQUAL THAN OTHERS

to err is human This comes from the line, 'To err is human, to forgive divine', in Alexander Pope's *Essay on Criticism* (1709), although Pope himself was merely adapting an ancient Latin proverb.

etchings see COME UP AND SEE MY ETCHINGS

even a worm turns see WORM TURNS

every dog has his day A popular proverb since the sixteenth century, this is used as a rather depressing form of encouragement, or claim that something will go right at least once.

'Davies, once described fondly by a former captain of Wasps, Alan Black, as the clown prince of rugby, said enigmatically afterwards that every dog had his day.' (*Daily Telegraph*, 13 April 1992)

'Every druid has his day.' (Headline, *Independent*, 12 June 1998)

every last one The 'last' here is used for emphasis, is entirely redundant, and no difference is made if it is removed. It has been a cliché since at least the 1930s.

'They took out large orders of tea and coffee on cardboard trays, and after wondering for a while if they were anything to do with the film business, Lucy finally decided that every last one of them was probably either a builder or a shopfitter.' (Stephen Gallagher, *Rain*, 1990)

every little helps Usually a feebly encouraging expression, this has been a cliché since the nineteenth century. Those irritated by it might like to take comfort in the fact that the user is probably unaware that it is a shortening of a proverb found from the sixteenth century: 'Every little helps as the ant said as it pissed in the sea at midday', or of its variant which replaces the ant with a wren.

'As with so many of the environmental issues that face us now, every little helps.' (Health promotion and education leaflet)

every schoolboy or fool knows see AS EVERY SCHOOLBOY KNOWS

everything to play for A sporting cliché, particularly favoured by football commentators, this is used most often when a football team has scored against the leading side, and now has a chance to avoid defeat. It is now being extended to non-sporting use.

'In theory the teams started equal, with everything to play for – but the tide was now running West Indies' way.' (Gerry Cotter, *England versus West Indies*, 1991)

everything you've always wanted to know about . . . but were afraid to ask This formula phrase comes from the title of a book *Everything You Always Wanted to Know about Sex, but Were Afraid to Ask*, written in 1969 by David Reuben. In 1972 Woody Allen used it for the title of one of his films. He had purchased the right to use the title from Reuben, but the film and book have nothing else in common. For another sex manual that has become a formula phrase see THE JOY OF . . . .

'Everything you didn't need to know about sex . . . but the media insisted on telling you.' (Headline, *Evening Standard*, 15 September 1998)

everything's coming up roses An expression coined by Stephen Sondheim for his 1958 musical *Gypsy*, which became firmly fixed in the language within ten years – so much so that the *OED* has yet to recognize its origin. Sondheim's own definition of the meaning is 'things are going to get better than ever'. Its rapid acceptance may owe something to the fact that 'everything in the garden is lovely', used to much the same effect, was already established as a cliché. This came from a song popularized by the music hall singer Marie Lloyd in the first decades of the twentieth century. 'Everything's coming up roses' is sometimes found as a formula phrase, and sometimes shortened to 'everything's roses'.

'She's been missing for a week, was going to marry a rising Minister, successful career, everything coming up roses.' (Janet Neel, *Death of a Partner*, 1991)

evils see LESSER OF TWO EVILS

it's the exception that proves the rule The original meaning of the proverb 'the exception proves the rule' (in use in English in 1640, but based on a Latin saying) was that the fact that there can be an exception proves that there is a rule. Nowadays it is often used simply as a comment on something that does not fit an expected pattern, or which has gone wrong.

'The event was meant to have been a demonstration of the balloonist's art and the accident was dismissed by the organisers as the exception which proves the rule.' (Central Television news scripts, 1993)

'Great books seldom make great movies but John Ford's film of *The Grapes of Wrath* . . . is an exception that proves the rule.' (*Daily Telegraph*, 5 April 1992)

expletive deleted When transcripts of the Watergate tapes, the secret recordings made of conversations by US President Nixon, were published in 1973, the exceedingly salty language used by the President and his associates was bowdlerized, '[expletive deleted]' replacing the words it was felt would shock the general public. The expression immediately caught on as an alternative for an asterisk, or a euphemism (see further under – GATE).

'They hate the press because you're capitalist [expletive deleted], we like you because we're class collaborationists.' (*Independent*, 17 September 1998)

'President Nixon, whose grasp of such matters was immortalised on tape in "Well, I don't give a [expletive deleted] about the lira" . . . responded on 15 August 1971 by suspending indefinitely the convertibility of the dollar into gold.' (John Harrison *et al.*, *Capitalism since 1945*, 1991)

explore every avenue The word 'avenue' derives from the Latin for 'to come towards, approach', and its original meaning in English (from about 1600) was an approach. This became a standard military term for a way of access, a passage, the sort of place a wise commander would make sure was thoroughly explored before he took his troops through it. However, 'to explore every avenue', an alternative to 'LEAVE NO STONE UNTURNED', did not become a cliché until the twentieth century. According to an article in the *London Morning Post* in 1936, quoted in James Rogers' *Dictionary of Clichés*, it was 'invented by the Marquis of Landsdowne when he was Foreign Secretary at the turn of the century' and has 'exercised a mortal fascination over politicians . . . The exploring of avenues has become one of the main preoccupations of political life.'

'They failed to break the deadlock from two well hit out short corners but East Antrim strikers Colin Black and Gary Hamilton explored every avenue in search of gold which never came.' (*Belfast Telegraph*, c.1990)

explosive mixture see DYNAMITE

(go the) extra mile Used to mean make an extra effort or do the job properly, this expression is based on the passage from the Bible (Matthew 5:41): 'And whosoever shall compel thee to go a mile, go with him twain' – one of the precepts for Christian conduct that goes with 'turn the other cheek'. It derives from the power of officials in the Roman Empire to make inhabitants of occupied territories do forced labour, such as acting as porters, at little or no notice.

'The key elements are: imagination, planning, foresight, thoroughness and a never-ending willingness to go that "extra mile" in dealing with people and details.' (Harvey Thomas and Liz Gill, *Making an Impact*, 1989)

with extreme prejudice To 'terminate with extreme prejudice' is reputedly CIA slang for 'to assassinate', although it is now found used more loosely to indicate general violence. This blackly humorous expression came into use in the 1970s.

'My contract was promptly terminated with extreme prejudice.' (Michael Dibdin, *Dirty Tricks*, 1991)

an eye for an eye A code of vengeance advocated in the Bible (Exodus 21). In full, the passage runs: 'And if any mischief follow, then thou shalt give life for life, eye for eye, tooth for tooth, hand for hand, foot for foot, burning for burning, wound for wound, stripe for stripe.' The form 'an eye for an eye', used to indicate retaliation in kind, sits more comfortably than the original on the English tongue, and became a cliché in the second half of the nineteenth century.

'The reciprocity usually takes the form of direct equivalence: an eye for an eye, a glass of beer for a glass of beer.' (Edmund Leach, *Social Anthropology*, 1986)

eye of newt This quotation from the witches' scene in Shakespeare's *Macbeth*, while a borderline cliché, has become standard shorthand for indicating the contents of a witch's brew, either directly, or as a formula phrase.

'Lambs' brains, fishes' eggs and raw scallops, reminiscent of "eye of newt, and toe of frog", are redeemed only by plenty of garlic to keep the devil away.' (*Harpers & Queen*, 1990)

face (the) facts This is a cliché with a sting in its tail, for it is rarely used without the implication that while the speaker can see the reality of the situation, and is prepared to deal with it, the person being spoken to or of is either incapable of understanding the reality, or too emotionally involved to do so.

'Nobody's interest is served by the suppression of the truth; least of all when it is undertaken in a spirit of cowardice and a refusal to face facts.' (*Daily Telegraph*, 10 April 1992)

'I fully sympathise with the hon. Lady's constituents, but one must face the facts of life: in a recession, and coming out of a recession, jobs are always being lost.' (*Hansard Extracts 1991–1992*)

the fact of the matter When they started life in the seventeenth century, expressions such as 'the fact of the matter' or 'as a matter of fact', had a legal or semi-legal sense, but since at least the middle of the nineteenth century they have been mere fillers, rarely adding anything to what is said. Of 'as a matter of fact', Partridge, in his *Dictionary of Clichés*, says, 'Usually the prelude to a lie – or, at best, an evasion.' The same can often be said of the related 'and that's a fact'.

'The fact of the matter is that we, as a country, desperately need to catch up with our counterparts in Europe, in the USA and in Japan, when it comes to the level of qualification held by the workforce.' (*New Musical Express*, 1991)

'As a matter o' fact we sat on this very seat, an' if I remember rightly, I stole a kiss.' (Harry Bowling, *The Girl from Cotton Lane*, 1992)

'I'll not be wanting to live with a man what's too proud to take a helping hand from someone as was like our own son, and that's a fact.' (C. Lorrimer, *The Spinning Wheel*, 1993)

fail to impress This is a sporting cliché, used by journalists to DAMN WITH FAINT PRAISE.

'The Second Division club opened the season with two victories but have failed to impress in their last two games.' (*Evening Standard*, 1 September 1998)

faint praise see DAMN WITH FAINT PRAISE

fair and square The 'fair' part of this cliché is self-evident; and 'square' is still used in expressions such as 'square dealing' to mean honest and straightforward. It comes from the idea that something that is truly square, each angle right, each side lined up with a carpenter's square, is the opposite of crooked or twisted. 'Square' is first recorded in this sense at the end of the sixteenth century, and only a few years later, in 1604, we find the first use of the rhyming doublet 'fair and square'.

'An ally is a nation which you beat fair and square in a war some time ago and which is now on your side.' (*Independent*, 5 October 1989)

fair game Fair game, meaning a legitimate target, has been a cliché for about 200 years. The imagery comes from hunting, where game is either forbidden, because it is out of season or because you have no right to hunt for it, or it is 'fair' game. 'Game' in a metaphorical sense, for something that may be pursued or attacked, has been in use since the sixteenth century, and 'forbidden game' for something you must not attack, is first recorded in 1780, before 'fair game' is found. Nowadays, 'fair game' can also have strong sexual connotations – not surprising when you consider the other sexual associations of the word 'game'.

'Also, the salesmen distinguished between those on their rounds who should not be fiddled (such as disabled people, ex-salesmen) and those who qualified as "fair game".' (Ian Marsh, *Crime*, 1992)

fair in love and war see ALL'S FAIR IN LOVE AND WAR

fair sex In use since the seventeenth century, this cliché, originally meant as a compliment, is now not only hopelessly old-fashioned, but usually downright offensive, particularly when used in combination with, or with the implication of, the 'weaker sex'. This latter dates back to the same period, while the even more offensive, but obsolescent, 'weaker vessel' goes back to the Bible.

'And they had to admit that what the "fair sex" lacked in muscle they made up for in guile as the ladies took a mid-game lead with a well-converted try.' (*Alton Herald*, 1992)

'Women are bracketed with minors and the code is basically concerned with the protection of women as the "weaker sex".' (Marilyn Thomson, *Women of El Salvador*, 1986)

fall of a dice see DICE WITH DEATH

fall on deaf ears The Bible is full of images of deafness representing a refusal to hear. One of the most delightful, from Psalm 58, describes the wicked, who, compared with the righteous, 'are like the deaf adder that stoppeth her ear; Which will not hearken to the voice of charmers, charming never so wisely.' This became a standard image of the benighted for medieval moralists, and so entered the English language. The expression 'deaf ears' has been in use since the fifteenth century, and 'fall on deaf ears' a cliché since the nineteenth. More common still at that date was the more active 'turn a deaf ear', made famous in the eighteenth century by Swift's lines,

'They never would hear,/But turn the deaf ear,/As a matter they had no concern in' (*Dingley and Brent*, 1724).

'After months of turning deaf ears to warnings by the City and industry, the Department of Energy has at last conceded that nuclear plant cannot be included in the share float without state support.' (*Guardian*, 11 August 1989)

'As this book demonstrates, shortage of manpower (as women also discovered) will work wonders where political agitation falls on deaf ears.' (*New Statesman*, 1992)

fall on your sword This expression comes from the Old Testament, 1 Samuel 31:4–5 (the story is repeated in very similar words at 1 Chronicles 10). King Saul has been defeated by the Philistines and wounded: 'Then said Saul unto his armourbearer, Draw thy sword, and thrust me through therewith; lest these uncircumcised come and thrust me through, and abuse me. But his armourbearer would not; for he was sore afraid. Therefore Saul took a sword, and fell upon it. And where his armourbearer saw that Saul was dead, he fell likewise upon his sword, and died with him.' The same action occurs in Homer, and defeated Roman generals would behave in the same way (indeed Shakespeare has plainly used the biblical passage as a source for the conspirators' suicide at the end of *Julius Caesar*) which may have helped spread the expression.

'Predictions made in good times, many of them backed by large amounts of hard cash, have turned sour. Senior executives at UBS and IMG Barings have fallen on their swords.' (*Independent*, 15 October 1998)

false dawn In some areas of the world there is a brief lightening of the dark about an hour before dawn, known as the false dawn or sunrise, a translation of an Arabic phrase. This has only come to be used to mean a cause of hope that comes to nothing in the second half of the twentieth century.

'Mr Burns, of the Central Rail Users Consultative Committee, said that signs of improvement shortly after the privatisation of the train operating companies began at the start of 1996 had proved to be a false dawn.' (*Daily Mail*, 27 August 1998)

familiarity breeds contempt A proverb that has been used in various forms since at least the time of Chaucer, but which goes back in Latin to Roman times. It is found not only as a frequently used proverb, but also as a formula phrase.

'As far as sexual intercourse is concerned, it is axiomatic that familiarity breeds contempt.' (W. Self, *My Idea of Fun*, 1993)

'Journalism is, by and large, a game where familiarity and advancing age often bring unemployment.' (*Mail on Sunday*, 20 September 1998)

family see SPEND MORE TIME WITH YOUR FAMILY

(selling off) the family silver In 1985 Harold Macmillan, former British Prime Minister now elevated to Lord Stockton, made a speech in the House of Lords criticizing the government's policy of privatization. He described the government as like a profligate heir, saying, 'First all the Georgian silver goes, and then all that nice furniture that used to be in the salon. Then the Canalettos go.' This was summarized by the newspapers as 'selling off the family silver' and immediately became popular journalistic shorthand for the privatization of state-owned assets.

'Brown sells state silver for £12bn.' (Headline, *Independent*, 12 June 1998)

'The Post Office is the largest commercial enterprise left in the public sector, the sole significant survivor of the family silver.' (*Independent*, 18 September 1998)

family values Like VICTORIAN VALUES, this is one of those expressions much loved by modern politicians and moralists, although few venture to define this vague but emotive concept.

'A disgusted Torie Clarke, spokeswoman for the Bush re-election campaign, told *The Sunday Telegraph*: "We will put George and Barbara Bush's marriage, and their family and their commitment to family values, up against anybody's in this country, including the Clintons." ' (*Daily Telegraph*, 5 April 1992)

'The magazine exploited popular Catholic themes, such as anti-abortion campaigning and family values, to channel middle-class resentment into a political movement.' (*Independent*, 2 October 1989)

fancy free see FOOTLOOSE AND FANCY FREE

far and away This is a doublet-cliché, each half meaning more or less the same as the other, and used only for emphasis. It has been common since the nineteenth century.

'And believe me, being young, say between 18 and 30, is far and away the best time to travel.' (Club 18–30 Summer Holiday Brochure, 1990)

far and wide This is another doublet-cliché, found very early on in English. It is used to mean 'widely, extensively', both literally and figuratively.

'Both optimism and pessimism are highly infectious so it is possible to affect the mood of an entire group – just as throwing a stone into the water causes ripples to spread far and wide.' (Ursula Markham, *Your Four Point Plan for Life*, 1991)

'They were both Swiss, both Reformed (i.e. Calvinist), both theologians rather than historians or biblical specialists, and both men of immense intellectual power and energy, capable of ranging far and wide over the whole spread of Christian thought.' (Alasdair Heron, *A Century of Protestant Theology*, 1993)

far be it from me This expression has been in use since the fourteenth century and a cliché since the eighteenth. It is a fine example of weasel words, for the user is nearly always about to do the very thing he protests he should not.

'Far be it from me to give Mr Major advice, but I would suggest that insults towards any of these people, such as his recent attacks on "froth and bubble" Lord Tebbit, will backfire.' (*Daily Mirror*, 1992)

far between see FEW AND FAR BETWEEN

a far cry (from) The expression 'within cry of', meaning near enough for a shout to be heard, is found in English from the mid-seventeenth century, but a 'far cry', meaning 'a long way', is not found until 1819, when Sir Walter Scott, that great reviver of rustic phrases and inventor of new ones, wrote in his *Legend of Montrose*, 'One of the Campbells replied, "It is a far cry to Lochow", a proverbial expression of the tribe, meaning that their ancient hereditary domains lay beyond the reach of an invading army.' There is further evidence to link early uses of the expression in its literal sense to Scotland, but by the later nineteenth century its figurative use had become a cliché in general English.

'The market is now expecting pre-tax profits to emerge at about £70m this year, a far cry from the £138m taxable profits reported in 1988.' (*Independent*, 13 October 1989)

far from the madding crowd see MADDING CROWD

farm see DOWN ON THE FARM

fast and furious This cliché, popular with journalists since the late nineteenth century, is actually a quotation from Robert Burns's 1793 poem *Tam O'Shanter*: 'As Tammie glow'red, amazed, and curious,/The mirth and fun grew fast and furious.' THICK AND FAST is an alternative.

'A fast and furious encounter between Aldenham and King Edward School, Witley, had yielded no goals when, with just minutes to go, Aldenham's Jason Clemow tried a long-range shot, the goalkeeper parried, and Kazeem Abimbola poked in the rebound.' (*Independent*, 11 October 1989)

fast as lightning see LIGHTNING

(in the) fast lane The term 'fast lane', in its literal sense, is only recorded in English from 1966, yet by 1978 an American magazine was writing of 'the image usually associated with the superjet, "fast lane" set', showing how quickly a descriptive phrase can move from its introduction to figurative use to cliché. Those who 'live life in the fast lane', must, of course, accept the risk that they will LIVE FAST, DIE YOUNG.

'Not surprisingly, people in the north-east of the country, where the work ethic and the climate push the pace of life ever upward, reside permanently in the fast lane.' (*Independent*, 5 October 1989)

fat cats This expression developed about 1920, according to that great commentator on the American language, H. L. Mencken, who says it originally meant 'a rich man willing to make a heavy contribution to a party campaign fund', although Clarence Major, in his *Juba to Jive, a Dictionary of African-American Slang*, simply lists it as in use from about 1900 for a wealthy, impressive person, although he does not list 'cat' being used of a male until the 1940s. Whatever its origins, it is currently a very popular cliché, used until recently mainly of wealthy City businessmen, but in the last few years particularly applied to directors of such things as privatized utilities whose income has increased enormously. The expression contains an implication that the vast sums of money paid to the fat cats have not been earned by exceptionally hard work.

'Camelot fat cats have cashed in after persuading lottery watchdogs to drop a limit on profits.' (*Daily Mirror*, 21 July 1998)

'The plunge in the stock exchange during the election campaign is not just a case of City fat cats worrying about their wallets.' (*Daily Telegraph*, 5 April 1992)

fat chance In societies where food supplies are not reliable but depend on luck and weather, fatness is a sign of richness and prosperity. Thus in the Bible (Psalm 92:14) we are told that the righteous 'shall be fat and flourishing'. From this idea there developed a wide range of uses of 'fat' to mean great, rich, abundant, and the 'fat' chance belongs with this sense, although its use has always been ironical, implying the opposite. The expression seems to have developed in the USA in the early part of the twentieth century, and to have crossed the Atlantic soon after.

'Right now, though, these fine sentiments have got a fat chance of being put into practice where I'm standing, boiling the milk for yet more midnight cocoa: with a baby of six weeks in the family, the philosophy of parental detachment is a far cry from reality.' (*Daily Telegraph*, 4 April 1992)

fat cheque A set phrase for a cheque for a large amount of money. 'Fat' carries with it images of large size and abundance. It has been used to refer to a good source of income such as a job, or particularly a church benefice, since the fourteenth century; and Milton, in 1642 uses it in *Apology . . . against Smectymnuus*: 'I would wish him the biggest and the fattest Bishoprick.' The linking of this use of 'fat' with 'cheque' is probably twentieth century.

'Fat black lacquer pens . . . are used by fat chairmen of companies to sign even fatter cheques from the company to themselves.' (*Guardian*, 26 August 1998)

fat lady sings SEE AIN'T OVER TILL THE FAT LADY SINGS

the fat of the land This cliché for 'the best of everything' is another biblical quotation: 'Ye shall eat the fat of the land' (Genesis 45:18). As a cliché it dates from the nineteenth century.

'He'd never had a good word to say for them before, a bunch o' thieving magpies, he always said, living off the fat of the land while he had to pay taxes to keep 'em.' (Bette Howell, *Dandelion Days*, 1991)

fate worse than death This cliché-euphemism for rape or a fall from sexual grace dates from the early nineteenth century and grew in use with that century's obsession with female 'purity': but with the more balanced views of the twentieth century it became more and more difficult to use it seriously. It is now often used in non-sexual contexts.

'The only way to save lamb-eaters from a fate worse than death, a "government scientist" was allowed to intone on the BBC, would be to destroy every sheep in the country. More than 40 million of them.' (*Private Eye*, 18 September 1998)

'He dominated the conversation, holding the Hackett and Townshend women spellbound as he told of how he had broken up a white-slave ring in Dublin, and how he had rescued an innocent young girl from a fate worse than death.' (Thomas Hayden, *The Killing Frost*, 1991)

fear of contradiction SEE WITHOUT FEAR OF CONTRADICTION

fear of God SEE PUT THE FEAR OF GOD INTO

feeding frenzy Animals such as sharks may be attracted to a food source in large numbers, and become so aggressive that they attack each other. The expression only came into English in the early 1970s, and has recently been transferred to the behaviour of people competing frantically for something, particularly in the media.

'Her office had been inundated with phone calls from just about every major publishing house in New York, not to mention a dozen or so Hollywood studios. "It's a real feeding frenzy," she said. "Congratulations, you're hot." ' (*Mail on Sunday*, 20 September 1998)

feel-good factor A cliché from the 1980s, with a strong whiff of psychobabble about it, this was at first used to explain political and economic phenomena of the times, but now is generally used to suggest added satisfaction or simply as a general term of approval.

' "Basically I buy what I like myself," says Noel. "I like well-made, functional pieces that also make me smile. It's the feel-good factor of modern furniture that I want to endorse." ' (*Evening Standard*, 28 August 1998)

'Silvana is one of many who knows that organic food offers that added feel-good factor.' (*You* magazine, 20 September 1998)

feel the earth move SEE EARTH MOVE

feet of clay In the biblical book of Daniel (2:31–5), King Nebuchadnezzar has dreamed a disturbing dream which, come the morning, he can no longer remember. Rather unreasonably, he insists that his magicians and astrologers not only interpret the dream, but tell him what it was in the first place. Only Daniel can perform this task, and he tells the king: 'Thou, O king, sawest, and behold a great image . . . This image's head was of fine gold, his breast and his arms of silver, his belly and his thighs of brass, his legs of iron, his feet part of iron and part of clay. Thou sawest till that a stone was cut out without hands, which smote the image upon his feet that were of iron and clay, and brake them to pieces. Then was the iron, the clay, the brass, the silver, and the gold, broken to pieces together, and became like the chaff of the summer threshingfloors.' Daniel interprets this dream to represent a decline in the quality of kings, until the dynasty is swept away. In the nineteenth century this image came to be used of a fatal flaw or weakness that would bring down any enterprise or person, no matter what other qualities they had.

'Now that the truth of Iraq's defeat is sinking in, and their former hero is seen to have feet of clay, some Maghrebis are turning their frustration not against him but against the West.' (*The Economist*, 1991)

'After all, audiences want to be entertained, not see their idols with feet of clay.' (*The Face*, 1992)

feller me lad SEE YOUNG FELLER ME LAD

festive season (occasion, etc.) It is very rare, nowadays, for the word 'festive' to signify anything other than 'Christmas'. This restriction seems to have had its birth in the eighteenth century, but not to have become dominant until the twentieth. Almost anything can become 'festive' – decorations, spirit, food. The old cliché 'festive board' for a richly laden table seems to be rare now outside this same context.

'Will your cooker stand the strain of the festive season and all the extra entertaining that comes with it?' (*Ideal Home*, 1991)

few and far between Although the expression 'few and far between' has been in the language since the mid-seventeenth century, it probably owes its elevation to cliché status to the poetry of the now little-read Thomas Campbell, who wrote, in 1799, 'What though my wingèd hours of bliss have been,/Like angel-visits, few and far between' (*Pleasures of Hope*). Certainly the expression grew in use throughout the nineteenth century.

'The times were few and far between when she could look at him and not be reminded of his many faults and shortcomings.' (Domini Highsmith, *Frankie*, 1990)

a few years down the line This is a recent cliché, a more elaborate way of saying 'later', the image being that of a series of years, months, or whatever.

'However, a few years down the line, a heavily discounted car might not look quite such a good bargain.' (*Good Housekeeping*, 1992)

'If scientists had any sense, they'd stop passing on information like this, since it will only put us all off reproducing, and there'll be no one to fund their pensions 30 years down the line.' (*Evening Standard*, 30 September 1998)

fiddle while Rome burns According to legend, the music-mad Emperor Nero fiddled while a devastating fire swept through Rome, a fire he is also supposed to have started himself in order to be able to rebuild the city on the scale he wanted.

He blamed the arson on the Christians and they were persecuted. In fact, Nero could not have fiddled, since the violin had not been invented at the time – Nero's instrument of choice was the lyre. However, he did do nothing much to stop the fire, and Roman historians do claim that he sang while the fire was burning. Whatever the truth, 'to fiddle while Rome burns' has been, since the nineteenth century, a cliché for doing nothing at a time when action is demanded. Presumably, the choice of 'fiddle' was to pun on the sense of 'fiddle' meaning time-wasting behaviour.

'So America fiddled while the world burned. Demonstrations were broken up on the skyscraper-lined streets of Kuala Lumpur, as President Clinton's taped evidence on the Lewinsky affair was played on American TV.' (*Independent*, 23 September 1998)

fight a losing battle see LOSING BATTLE

fight the good fight This is a quotation cliché, best known from the hymn, sung in countless schools and Sunday gatherings, 'Fight the good fight with all thy might', written by the Irish cleric John Monsell in 1863. Monsell was himself quoting the Bible: 'Fight the good fight of faith, lay hold on eternal life' (I Timothy 6:12), followed in the Second Epistle (4:2) by 'I have fought a good fight, I have finished my course, I have kept the faith.' That the expression had reached clichéhood by the nineteenth century can be seen from Oscar Wilde's description of W. E. Henley: 'He has fought a good fight and has had to face every difficulty except popularity.'

'She championed women playwrights at the Royal Court and co-founded the brilliant Joint Stock company . . . She has consistently "fought the good fight", as she says.' (*You* magazine, 20 September 1998)

fight to the finish The original sense here is a fight until someone is dead, or thoroughly defeated. As the *Westminster Gazette* of 1902 put it: 'Not a peace by interruption of hostilities; but a simple, unconditioned, termless peace supplied by a "fight to the finish".' Journalists, however, tend to use this of someone or something, such as a football team, that keeps on fighting until the end of a given time.

'But if the polls are wrong and it's a fight to the finish, the verdict may not be known until the West Coast results are in.' (*Today*, 1992)

fighting chance This cliché, popular with sports journalists, from the world of boxing and other combative sports, indicating that great effort could lead to success, has been in use since the nineteenth century.

'Alan Davies has done a very good job in a short space of time and if he remains as coach for three seasons or more Wales will be in with a fighting chance for the future – and certainly in the next World Cup.' (*Rugby World and Post*, 1991)

fighting fit A cliché which has an almost identical origin and history to FIGHTING CHANCE, but is used both in a literal sense and to mean 'as fit as can be'.

'Consequently, it hosts an excellent wild brown trout population and fish are pink-fleshed and fighting fit, averaging 10oz in weight.' (Bruce Sandison, *Tales of the Loch*, 1990)

'During my annual medical check-up in 1987, Dr Dingle discovered a blood irregularity, but as I was fighting fit he said it was probably just a virus.' (Marti Caine, *A Coward's Chronicles*, 1990)

figment of the imagination This expression, in use since the mid-nineteenth century, can take on a wide range of meanings. While it is often little more than an emphatic way of saying 'imaginary', it can also be used to convey ideas such as 'wishful thinking', or be a polite way of calling something a lie. The latter connects with the earliest uses of 'figment', from the Latin for 'to feign, fashion'. It first appeared in English in the fifteenth century to mean something designed to deceive.

'However, his stated grounds for that opinion were a figment of his imagination: his misdescriptions of the performance were so fundamental as to vitiate any factual basis for his criticism.' (Geoffrey Robertson, *Media Law*, 1990)

'Or is it all an illusion, a phantasm derived from mere figures, a figment of journalistic imagination, an evanescent creature of dream and the wishful thinking of those for whom history is proceeding too slowly?' (Simon Winchester, *The Pacific*, 1992)

filthy lucre This expression for tainted money, a cliché since the mid-nineteenth century, has a biblical source, I Timothy 3, where the personal qualities desirable in the leaders of the new religion are set out: 'A bishop then must be blameless, the husband of one wife, vigilant, sober, of good behaviour, given to hospitality, apt to teach. Not given to wine, no striker, not greedy of filthy lucre; but patient, not a brawler, not covetous.' It is found again at Titus 1:11. The original Greek of these passages uses words that would now be translated as 'shameful gain', but the early translators of the Bible chose the word 'lucre' because it not only carried the meaning 'profit' from its Latin source, but also a secondary sense of 'avarice'.

'Finally, the sweet exchange of personnel from agency to corporation (and vice versa) and the extent to which some agency officials are amenable to getting their hands grubby with filthy lucre again make the executive suite a relatively safe place for planning illegal behaviour.' (Steven Box, *Power, Crime, and Mystification*, 1992)

in the final analysis This expression, used as a grandiose alternative for 'to sum up', or instead of WHEN ALL IS SAID AND DONE, is often a mere filler. The expression, adopted from the French '*en dernière analyse*' in the nineteenth century, was originally used by philosophers, usually in the form 'last analysis', and only became a cliché in the mid-twentieth century.

'As Jock Young suggests, "it is not the criminal nor even the administration of crime, but, in the final analysis, the system itself that must be investigated".' (Ian Marsh, *Crime*, 1992)

final frontier In the past 'the final frontier' was used of places such as the Wild West, but nowadays it is associated in most people's minds with Gene Roddenberry's *Star Trek* and *The Next Generation*, every episode of which opens with the words 'Space, the final frontier . . . These are the voyages of the starship *Enterprise*.' See further TO BOLDLY GO.

'As a result they talk a lot of bullshit about how this is their generation's answer to LSD (It's our "final frontier") and also call up the memories of past sins and traumas – playground racism, the suicide of a Viet vet father, some modish videotape voyeurism, bullying and murder even – which then return to haunt them in the real world.' (*The Face*, 1990)

final nail in the coffin see NAIL IN THE COFFIN

final straw see LAST STRAW

fine tuning The image here is of someone delicately adjusting the tuning on a radio set to get perfect reception. The expression began to be used of things like the economy in the 1960s and from there passed into more general use. Nowadays it is often used as a euphemism for what is really tinkering, and often making things worse (as no doubt the original fine tuning of a radio did).

'The Tories were heading for disaster if they continued to delude themselves that only a little fine tuning of presentation was required to secure a fourth consecutive general election victory.' (*Independent*, 14 October 1989)

their finest hour On 18 June 1940 Winston Churchill made a speech in which he said that the Battle of Britain was about to begin and that the fate of Western civilization hung on the result. He concluded 'Let us therefore brace ourselves to do our duty, and so bear ourselves that, if the British Commonwealth and its Empire lasts for a thousand years, men will say, "This was their finest hour".' Although Churchill's words were unlikely to have been original to him, their fame led to their adoption as a cliché. Initially their significance was too well remembered for them to be used lightly, but today they are often used ironically, while the meaning has changed from 'time of great heroism' to 'moment of triumph'.

'My finest hour of the campaign came on the night the Conservatives broadcast Labour HQ's phone number.' (*New Statesman and Society*, 1992)

'Webb's finest hour came in 1984 when, with Derby just days away from going out of business with debts of £1.5 million, he promoted himself from managing director to chairman.' (*Daily Mirror*, 1992)

have a finger in . . . pies This image of someone going round a kitchen prodding and poking every pie, has been around since at least the 1600s. Shakespeare obviously knew it, for in *Henry VIII* he has an irritated Duke of Buckingham say of Cardinal Wolsey, 'The devil speed him! No man's pie is freed/From this ambitious finger.' The implication that the owner of the finger is interfering is inherent in the image. There is now sometimes an added implication that to have a finger in too many pies is not necessarily right or honest.

'The RA licenses the airwaves, and has a finger in several pies, from digital and satellite TV to taxi radios, police radio, defence, and commercial broadcasting.' (*Evening Standard*, 10 September 1998)

finishing touches This image originally came from the completion of a work of art, such as adding the final brush-strokes to a painting, and was well-established in this sense in the eighteenth century. The expression still has artistic connotations, even if they are now more often the applied or domestic arts.

'While the officials, commentators and chess groupies then lingered over an enjoyable buffet, the players and their seconds rushed off to put the finishing touches to six months of preparations.' (*Independent*, 2 October 1989)

fire see BAPTISM OF FIRE

fire fighting This is a modern business cliché, now spreading to other areas, used to mean to take emergency or temporary action, rather than to work in some planned way.

'In recent years the Employment Department and the Department of Trade and Industry have been responsible for appropriate interventions but they have been more of a fire fighting nature than a sustained development of policy and role.' (Elizabeth Clough and Bob Gibbs (eds), *The Reality of Partnership*, 1991)

'His team has manfully cleared blocked gutters, downpipes . . . they have been "fire fighting" the leaks in the sanctuary roof to limit deterioration of the fabric.' (Queen's Park Baptist Church Magazine)

firing on all cylinders A cliché from the early days of motoring, when vehicles may not have been firing on all cylinders, and were therefore seriously under-powered. It is used to mean working at full strength or full speed, and is popular with sports journalists.

first and foremost This doublet, each half meaning the same as the other, has been around since the later fifteenth century, but only became a cliché in the mid-nineteenth century.

'Conran is first and foremost an entrepreneur, who lives up magnificently to his own definition of what such a person should be: someone who takes risks after carefully assessing the opportunities available to him.' (David Oates and Derek Ezra, *Advice from the Top*, 1989)

first catch your hare This is a mid-nineteenth-century cliché. At that time it was said to be the opening instructions for cooking a hare in Hannah Glasse's 1747 cookbook. Nowadays it is often attributed to Mrs Beeton, but it is in neither. In the past it was used in the sense of FIRST THINGS FIRST, but now it is most often found as a formula phrase.

'First catch your caterpillar: a guide to good butterfly breeding.' (*Country Living*, 1991)

'Division is all very well, but you must first catch your plant, and in order to do this, it means applying to nurseries or garden centres.' (Ann Bonar, *Herbs*, 1989)

first cuckoo of spring This is a conscious cliché, used either to represent the first signs of spring or the sort of journalism that concentrates on such things. At one time *The Times* regularly printed letters reporting the first hearing of the cuckoo. The cuckoo itself has been a symbol of the coming of warmer weather since the beginnings of English literature, found, for example in the thirteenth-century lyric, 'Summer is icumen in. Lhude sing cuccu' ['Summer has come in. Loudly sings the cuckoo'].

'He felt disappointed because writing "Voice of Vangmoor" was the only money-making activity he did that he enjoyed, and this would have been more enjoyable than usual, a piece of real journalism as against the usual pedestrian stuff about the view from the top of Big Allen or hearing the first cuckoo.' (Ruth Rendell, *Master of the Moor*, 1988)

first past (or **last to**) **the tape** An image taken from the tape that marks the finish of a race, it probably owes its popularity to the expression being heard so often on television and radio sports commentaries.

'Channel 5 was first to the tape with an autopsy on Fashanu.' (*Independent*, 4 September 1998)

first stone see CAST THE FIRST STONE

first things first A nineteenth-century cliché, often indicative of a plodding attitude, or of stating the obvious..

'Thorstvedt said last night: "First things first, I'll take the Crystal Palace game and then decide what to do." ' (*Daily Mirror*, 1992)

'Treatment centres focus on first things first: alcohol and drugs may cause immediate threat to life itself in some sufferers, as can anorexia or bulimia or other forms of addiction in others.' (Robert Lefever, *How to Combat Alcoholism and Addiction*, 1988)

fish see DRINK LIKE A FISH

fits and starts A set phrase, both words here being used for a sudden state of activity, in regular use since the early seventeenth century.

'The Italian Government has taken an extremely sporadic interest ever since, and research continues only in fits and starts, though over two million people a year to visit the site.' (*Daily Telegraph*, 8 April 1992)

'This means the machine tends to go forward in fits and starts, sometimes quite quickly but at other times embarrassingly slowly.' (*Warhammer Armies: Orcs and Goblins*, Games Workshop, 1993)

flagpole see RUN IT UP THE FLAGPOLE

flash in the pan This cliché, meaning a brief spurt of success, came into use in this sense in the 1920s, although it was used in the previous century to mean an abortive effort. The origin of the expression goes back much further, to early firearms. These would have a pan of priming gunpowder designed to ignite the charge in the barrel. Sometimes, however, the gunpowder in the pan would ignite with a flash, but the combustion would not be carried through to the charge. Then you were left waiting to see what was going to happen, knowing, as with a faulty firework, that if you interfered your risked finding it was working after all. This fault was known as a flash in the pan.

'One of our Committee members, the Rev. Ray Arnold, gave a short address and dedication, saying that enterprises like this one can so easily be a flash in the pan, but this one has surmounted its problems so far and achieved much.' (Keith Lucas *et al.*, *Bishop's Castle Railway Society Journal*, 1990)

flaunt it see IF YOU'VE GOT IT, FLAUNT IT

flavour of the month This cliché, for something briefly fashionable, began life in the USA in the middle of the twentieth century, when ice-cream parlours started promoting a different 'flavor of the month' to attract customers. It did not reach the UK until the 1980s.

'I've never been a flavour of the month. Five or six years ago it would be, "why aren't I Juliet Stevenson? I wish I could do this or that." ' (*Evening Standard*, 28 August 1998)

'This week's campaign could be a flavour of the church to come.' (*Independent*, 17 September 1998)

with a flea in your ear This expression, which originated in French, has been in steady use since about 1430. The imagery is that of the words of a stinging reproof hurting the ears as the biting of a flea would.

' "That was your Dr Stigmore. Not a loveable man, not at all." "Jess and I call him the creep." "Very apt. He was insisting Maggie would like him to talk to you, so I sent him away with a flea in his ear." ' (Susan Cooper, *The Boggart*, 1993)

fleet of foot This poeticism for quick on your feet has been a cliché from at least the nineteenth century. It has the feel of a quotation cliché, but if so it has yet to be traced.

'I did love hockey – I was fleet of foot and played on the wing.' (*Independent*, 23 July 1998)

flesh and blood This is a cliché with two meanings. It can mean 'human', a use that goes back to the Bible, or it can mean 'blood relative'. They have both been used since earliest times. The latter sense comes from the theories of the nature of sexual intercourse current in the ancient world, which, it was believed, involved an exchange of blood between the two people involved, so that they literally became of the same blood. This also explains why the Christian Church still bans marriage to any close relative of a deceased spouse, regarding it as incest, a ban enshrined in English law until the end of the nineteenth century.

'The reason is, of course, that a few computers will be able to cope with the task of detecting the lies, evasions, inconsistencies, and omissions in our tax returns more surely, and much more rapidly, than the flesh and blood calculators whom they are about to replace.' (*New Scientist*, 1991)

flock together see BIRDS OF A FEATHER

flotsam and jetsam This expression comes from ancient maritime law, where flotsam, from the French *floter*, to float, is salvage found floating on the waves, and jetsam, a shortening of jettison, that which has been deliberately thrown overboard. By the nineteenth century this had come to be a cliché for odds and ends, with terms such as 'human flotsam', a popular term to describe the outcasts of society in modern times.

'Better-heeled passengers penned a succession of sad descriptions of the flotsam and jetsam of Europe they encountered beached on many an American station.' (Jeffrey Richards and John M. Mackenzie, *The Railway Station: a Social History*, 1988)

'It wasn't that he was afraid of the human flotsam outside his window, he simply didn't understand them and the lack of understanding made him uneasy.' (M. Dobbs, *Last Man to Die*, 1991)

flowers see SAY IT WITH FLOWERS

a fools' paradise This cliché, for an illusory state of happiness, has been in the language since the fifteenth century and has been used steadily ever since.

'One rationalist had hardly done calling Christianity a nightmare before another began to call it a fool's paradise.' (G. K. Chesterton, *Orthodoxy*, 1909)

fools rush in where angels fear to tread A quotation-cliché which, like TO ERR IS HUMAN, comes from Alexander Pope's *An Essay on Criticism* (1711). It is often used in the shortened form 'fools rush in', while the second half, 'where angels fear to tread', is widely familiar as the title of an E. M. Forster novel published in 1905.

'The handling of the "Fools rush in where angels fear to tread" theme, though not wholly elegant, showed ambition, and the assumption that Clara was responsible for the dismissal of Higginbotham showed courtesy, though she would have preferred his name to be left out of it altogether.' (Margaret Drabble, *Jerusalem the Golden*, 1988)

footloose and fancy free This cliché for being without ties or emotional commitments combines an American nineteenth-century coinage 'footloose' – the opposite of hobbled, tied down – with 'fancy', in use to mean 'love, amorous inclination', since 1559, and, although marked as obsolete in the dictionaries, surely still surviving as a verb in the sense of 'sexually attracted'.

'Men propping up the bar over lunch will bewail the loss of earlier freedoms when they were footloose and fancy free.' (Janet Mattinson and Christopher Clulow, *Marriage Inside Out*, 1989)

a ... for all seasons A formula phrase, based on the title of Robert Bolt's 1960 play about Sir Thomas More, *A Man for All Seasons*, which was made into a highly successful film in 1966. Bolt in turn took the title from a contemporary description of More as, 'As time requireth, a man of marvellous mirth and pastimes, and sometime of as sad gravity, as who say: a man for all seasons', which in *its* turn echoed Erasmus's description of More as 'a man for all hours'. 'A man for all seasons' is nowadays used to describe someone of outstanding abilities, while the formula is popular with headline writers.

'If there ever was a man for all seasons it is the redoubtable John Jackson, whose posts include a board seat at electronics group Philips and the vice chairmanship of Ladbroke.' (*Daily Telegraph*, 5 April 1992)

'A poet for all seasons.' (Headline, *Independent*, 5 September 1998)

for better or worse see BETTER OR WORSE

for dear life see DEAR LIFE

for my sins This suggests modesty, though in fact often a false modesty to disguise a boast. 'For my sins' started to be used in a jocular way in the eighteenth century, but the deprecating element seems to be a relatively modern introduction.

'Anyway, we have to wrap up now. Richard has "to do a book show on Sky, for my sins".' (*Independent*, 21 September 1998)

forces beyond my control see CIRCUMSTANCES BEYOND MY CONTROL

forces of darkness (or **evil**) see DARKNESS

foregone conclusion These words come from Shakespeare's *Othello*, when Othello responds to Iago's account of Cassio's behaviour in his sleep as 'evidence' of Desdemona's infidelity with the line, 'But this denoted a foregone conclusion' (III.iii). It is not clear what Shakespeare meant by these words, but they are used today to mean something that was inevitable, sometimes with the idea that the inevitability was because of prejudice or interference. The expression has been a cliché since the mid-nineteenth century.

'It was perhaps a foregone conclusion that he would go into the family firm founded by his great-grandfather, John Cadbury, in 1824, although he had two tempting offers from outside industry when he had completed his degree.' (David Oates and Derek Ezra, *Advice from the Top*, 1989)

'John Blake, the advocate for the Town and Country Planning Association, which had played a prominent role at the Sizewell public inquiry, described the outcome as a "foregone conclusion" and largely withdrew to the sidelines.' (Crispin Aubrey, *Melt Down: Collapse of a Nuclear Dream*, 1991)

foreign field These words come from Rupert Brooke's rousingly patriotic poem *The Soldier* (1915): 'If I should die, think only this of me:/That there's some corner of a foreign field/That is for ever England.'

'In what corner of what foreign field did he still keep the faith, further the revolution, wake up his current lover at three in the morning to discuss the delicate interweavings of class and race.' (Sara Maitland, *Three Times Table*, 1990)

foremost see FIRST AND FOREMOST

forlorn hope When this expression was first introduced into English in the late sixteenth century it was as a translation of the Dutch *verloren hoop* meaning 'lost troop', used of the soldiers who led an attack and were most likely to be killed, or of a skirmishing party. However, instead of choosing 'heap', the nearest English equivalent to the Dutch *hoop*, it was anglicized as 'hope', which almost immediately started to affect the meaning, and change it to the modern sense of a faint or desperate hope.

' "Anyway, the prospect of making a large profit is little more than a forlorn hope," says Philip Telford, of the Consumer's Association. "You may have £10,000 more, but after 25 years think how much that would be worth." ' (*Independent*, 9 September 1998)

fort see HOLD THE FORT

foul your (own) nest This expression for polluting or destroying your own environment is a very early image in English. In *The Owl and the Nightingale*, one of the first poems to have survived from the period in which English literature re-emerged after the Norman Conquest, one of the insults hurled at the owl by the nightingale is that it literally lets its young foul their own nest. The obsolete proverb 'It is an ill bird that fouls its own nest' is also medieval.

'We all want basic comforts, but there are intelligent ways of producing these comforts and intelligent limits to impose on oneself in order not to foul the nest for everybody else.' (Fox FM News)

four corners of the earth see ENDS OF THE EARTH

Frankenstein Baron Frankenstein was, of course, the name of the scientist who created the monster in Mary Shelley's 1818 novel, but 'Frankenstein' has long been used as a shortening of the more correct 'Frankenstein's monster'. It has now become an adjective, used to describe the creations of modern science, with particular reference to genetically modified foods.

'In a discovery which undermines repeated assurances from manufacturers and the Government that so-called 'Frankenstein foods' pose no risk, researchers at the prestigious Rowett Institute in Aberdeen found they could in fact damage the immune system of rats.' (*Daily Mail*, 10 July 1998)

frankly, my dear, I don't give a damn These are the famous words said by Rhett Butler (Clark Gable) to Scarlett O'Hara (Vivien Leigh) in the 1939 film *Gone with the Wind*. They were, in turn, an adaptation of the original words in Margaret Mitchell's 1936 novel on which the film was based: 'Scarlett . . . I wish I could care what you do or where you go but I can't . . . My dear, I don't give a damn.' In both film and book, Scarlett's ultimate response is TOMORROW IS ANOTHER DAY. Rhett Butler's words caused a considerable stir as they represented strong language for films at that more innocent time, and they rapidly passed into the language.

'Nigel Lawson enrolled in the Clark Gable "Frankly, I don't give a damn" school when he fell foul of his own party over a rise in interest rates just before the Tory conference.' (*Independent*, 7 October 1989)

free . . . with every . . . This cliché of modern advertising and promotion has become a standard ploy to attract more custom, to the extent that it is now found used as a formula phrase as an ironic put-down. It has also become blended with political slogans, so that, for instance, jokes were made about the Free Nelson Mandela campaign getting phone calls from people wanting to know where they could get their free Nelson Mandela.

'Filling stations on the mainland are all offering free travel with every 12 litres of petrol, but the company is not running the offer in Northern Ireland because they say people are not interested.' (*Belfast Telegraph*)

fresh fields and pastures new This is the usual misquotation of the line 'Tomorrow to fresh Woods and Pastures new' from John Milton's poem *Lycidas* (1638). It is, however, occasionally found in its correct form, and is often shortened to just 'fresh fields' or 'pastures new'.

'Or do they just move on, looking for fresh fields and pastures new to flood?' (Bruce Sandison, *Tales of the Loch 1990*)

'Remembering my conversations with him at the end of 1975 and the beginning of 1976, it was clear that he wanted fresh fields to conquer, that he thought he had more than proved himself as a racing driver and that he thought he could, with no great difficulty, follow a Bruce McLaren, for instance, and make his own way in cars of his own.' (Keith Botsford, *The Champions of Formula One*, 1988)

'Countless independent "free house" owners have copied brewers' fashions and wrought untold havoc with unassuming old country pubs before moving on to pastures new.' (R. Holder *et al.*, *Trouble Brewing*, 1991)

friend in need From the proverb, 'A friend in need is a friend indeed', this sentiment goes back to at least the third century BC, when Ennius wrote that 'a sure friend is known in unsure times'. Another form of the proverb (which translates as 'a friend shall be known in time of need') was used by the Anglo-Saxons. The use of 'a friend in need' for 'a dependable friend' goes back to the nineteenth century.

'He also saw that by inviting Nixon when he was out of office with few prospects of getting back into it, Ceausescu struck a chord with the future US President, who would remain loyal to his friend in need.' (Mark Almond, *The Rise and Fall of Nicolae and Elena Ceausescu*, 1992)

-friendly see USER-FRIENDLY

'Friends, Romans, countrymen' see LEND AN EAR

frighten the horses In the days when horses were the main source of transport, frightened horses were a real source of physical danger in the streets, and everyone would have been brought up to take care not to frighten the horses. A hangover from this can still be seen today in the exaggerated care some drivers take to slow down when overtaking riders. The famous actress Mrs Patrick Campbell (1865–1940) is supposed to have said: 'It doesn't matter what you do in the bedroom as long as you don't do it in the street and frighten the horses', and the fame of this quotation has no doubt added to the associations the expression has.

'I can't be doing with any of his recordings of twentieth-century music, which emasculate anything remotely troubling and awkward and turn everything into a smooth sort of Berlin Philharmonic noise, guaranteed not to frighten the horses.' (*Evening Standard*, 1 September 1998)

from cradle to grave see CRADLE TO GRAVE

the . . . from hell A formula phrase which is currently ubiquitous, used to describe a range of objectionable things. While often used in a straightforward way, it is also used as an opportunity to exercise the wit or imagination.

'Mr Elliott dubbed her "the wife from hell" and her third husband, John Stuart, said: "I have never met anyone as able to come on as charming as her and then to change so instantly." ' (*Mail on Sunday*, 20 September 1998)

'The yellow nylon shirt with the frothy frill amounts to an offence against taste bordering on the criminal, yet it somehow works to offset his complexion (pale blue) and the ensemble enables him to come on like a chat-show host from Hell.' (*Independent*, 6 October 1989)

from pillar to post This cliché, for being driven from place to place, physically or metaphorically, dates from the fifteenth century, and has been a cliché since the eighteenth. There is disagreement about its origin. Some claim it refers to the pillory and whipping post of earlier punishment, but it is more likely to refer to parts of a real-tennis court, and presumably reflects the fate of the weaker player or of the ball, as early uses are often 'tossed from pillar to post'.

'There were not enough teachers, those there were harassed almost beyond bearing and driven from pillar to post, and no one ever seemed to know who Jasper was, still less remember his name.' (Barbara Vine, *King Solomon's Carpet*, 1992)

from the neck up see DEAD FROM THE NECK UP

from the sublime to the ridiculous see SUBLIME TO THE RIDICULOUS

full monty Used to mean something thorough or complete or the full amount, this expression has been around as a colloquialism for a while, but only became a cliché with the success of the 1997 film *The Full Monty*, as a result of which it has also developed the sense of 'naked'. There are two theories about its origin. One is that it refers to the former chain of Montague Burton tailor shops, so that the full monty would be a smart three-piece suit and tie outfit, suitable for SUNDAY BEST. The alternative links the expression to the nickname of Field Marshal Montgomery, who, it is said, insisted on a full English cooked breakfast, even in the heat of Egypt.

'His best novels (*A History of the World*, *Flaubert's Parrot*) are essentially essays pretending to be fiction. But literary history and convention are goading him to show that he can do the full monty as a novelist: characters, plot, twisty narrative.' (*Private Eye*, 4 September 1998)

'Admittedly, Bicknell began the current campaign sluggishly as he experimented with an abbreviated approach, then reverted to the full Monty in the B&H quarter-final against Lancashire to help set up a notable victory.' (*Wisden Cricket Monthly*, 1992)

full story A cliché taken from modern journalism, used either for a story that will never be wholly known, or for one that can be told for the first time because the speaker holds the key.

'The full story of what happened has never been reported, but it seems that Kambona had lost in a power struggle with other key figures in the Cabinet and TANU.' (Graham Mytton, *Mass Communication in Africa*, 1983)

'They claim Granada Television has been advertising the two-hour film *Hostages* as the "full story for the first time".' (*Daily Mirror*, 1992)

full to the gills see UP TO THE GILLS

fun and games This expression for exciting goings-on dates from the early twentieth century. It is often used in an ironic or disparaging sense, and also functions as a sexual euphemism.

'What I do know is that people like Havel have been getting a little impatient with those relishing pieces appearing lately in the American press that say, roughly: "Right, you guys over there have had your romantic Ruritarian fun and games with revolution and dancing in the streets."' (*Guardian*, 31 December 1989)

'Alone together they fell to tender embraces that rapidly shifted up a gear to heavy petting, and before long they had retired to the girl's bedroom for more adventurous fun and games.' (Robin Smith, *The Encyclopaedia of Sexual Trivia*, 1990)

(all) the fun of the fair A term taken from the cries of the fairground huckster which is usually used ironically, or as a largely meaningless scene-setter.

'Before I leave, I stop by Contracts to sprinkle a little salt in the wounds of the deskbound by describing (almost) all the fun of the Fair.' (Nick Thumb, *The Dyke and the Dybbuk*, 1993)

'Roll up, roll up, for all the fun of the fair – the All Formats Computer Fair, that is!' (*Zzap 64!*, 1993)

further ado see WITHOUT MORE ADO

gainful employment An expression used in legal documents to avoid arguments about what the definition of a job is – 'gainful employment' meaning work that is paid and recognized as such. Used to just mean 'work, a job', it is unnecessarily pompous.

'The person covered by the Plan is the person named on the Midland FlexiLoan Agreement Form who on the date of the Agreement must be: aged 18 or over but less than 65, actively in permanent and gainful employment (including self-employment) of not less than 16 hours a week, and not absent due to sickness or injury.' (Financial leaflet from Midland Bank)

'Many students can tell of months of frustration and many dozens of letters written in search of gainful employment.' (*New Scientist*, 1991)

gala occasion Originally 'gala' by itself was enough, having been used to mean 'a FESTIVE OCCASION' since about 1700. However, nowadays it is used to mean 'special, elaborate, memorable', or just to indicate some vague air of distinction.

'Leonard Bernstein once said that every Koussevitsky concert was "a gala occasion".' (Richard Osborne, *Conversations with Karajan*, 1991)

'In aid of the Flax Trust, the formal event at the Europa Hotel on March 23 promises to be a gala occasion.' (*Belfast Telegraph*)

galaxy of stars Surely the coinage of some Hollywood publicity master, as indeed the whole concept of 'stars' was, this cliché is now used as much of the football world as it is of film actors.

'We have a galaxy of stars and a wide range of talent. All we are doing is making sure we have got them in the right places and the right time.' (*Evening Standard*, 7 October 1998)

game for a laugh 'Game' here is used to mean 'eager, willing'. The expression's history is obscure, but it seems to have started off as a colloquialism that has gradually established itself in more serious language.

'Alan Clark used to be game for a laugh ... Of late, though, there have been worrying signs that the Conservative MP for Kensington and Chelsea is losing his legendary sense of humour.' (*Independent*, 1 September 1998)

the game is not worth the candle This was originally a French expression *'Le jeu ne vaut pas la chandelle'*, applied literally to card games where the money changing hands did not cover the cost of the candles used to illuminate it. It was well-established in English by the later seventeenth century, and the advent of other forms of lighting does not seem to have dimmed its use.

'It was a dismal prospect, what with the strikes and inflation, the endless chores, the daily boredom and the uphill struggle to make ends meet; the whole effort was of doubtful benefit and hardly worth the candle.' (Rosemary McCall, *Hearing Loss? A Guide to Self-help*, 1992)

a game of two halves A cliché of sports writers and managers, used to suggest that a losing team may well make a comeback in the second half of the match. Often no more than a filler of the 'you never can tell' type.

'It was a classic case of "a game of two halves" when Warrington Town's eight-match unbeaten record came to an end in a 3-2 defeat at Great Harwood Town on Wednesday.' (*Liverpool Echo & Daily Post*, 1993)

game plan This expression originated in American football, used to describe a strategy for winning, worked out in advance. It dates from at least the 1940s, and by chance is actually recorded slightly earlier in a figurative use – for a plan of campaign in a non-sporting context – than in a literal one.

'The customers' experience is the ball; the sales targets, monthly accounting reports are the scoreboard. Our game plan has to be to keep our eyes on the ball and direct it to where it will count for us and against a competitor.' (*Around Resources* magazine, quoted in *Private Eye*, 24 July 1998)

'For that reason alone, according to sources here, Mr Ortega's summit game plan could come to naught, leaving the Sandinistas to fight an election and a war, and the peace process close to collapse.' (*Guardian*, 10 December 1989)

game, set and match This is the umpire's announcement at the end of a tennis match, familiar to countless watchers of Wimbledon, used as an alternative to TO WIN HANDS DOWN. It has been a cliché since at least the 1960s.

'Now SCO suspends MIPS/ACE development: game set and match against the initiative?' (*Unigram x*, 1993)

–gate On 17 June 1972 burglars broke into the national headquarters of the Demo-cratic party in the Watergate building in Washington DC, looking for material that could be used by the Committee for the Re-election of the President to smear the Democratic Party and their candidate. This bungled break-in and attempt to tap telephones led to the Watergate hearings (see EXPLETIVE DELETED) and the resignation of President Nixon in 1974. By August 1973 –gate was already established as a journalistic suffix, used to indicate a scandal or a secret that needs to be revealed, and the use has not died down with time, as is shown by such recent coinages as Whitewatergate, Nannygate, Camillagate and Zippergate. Another 'contribution' to the English language from the affair was the extraordinary use of the word 'inoperat-ive' when White House press secretary Ronald L. Ziegler said on 17 April 1973 that all previous statements issued by the White House about events surrounding Watergate were 'inoperative', that is, lies.

'Yesterday afternoon the journalist Greg Pallas, who broke the Cronygate story in *The Observer* a few months back, was stunned to be refused entry to the conference hall.' (*Independent*, 29 September 1998)

Gaul, divided into three parts SEE DIVIDED INTO THREE PARTS

gauntlet SEE PICK UP THE GAUNTLET or RUN THE GAUNTLET

gentle giant A journalistic cliché that is likely to be used of anyone of above average size who does not actually project menace. It has been in use since the nineteenth century.

'The life of this normally gentle giant of a man was also punctuated from time to time by acts of sudden, often inexplicable, violence, usually associated with an over-generous intake of alcohol.' (*The Dictionary of National Biography: Missing Persons*, 1993)

'Only minutes earlier, the gentle giant was in the bar chatting with friends and fans, the next he's on stage and screaming himself raw as the tortured madman at the wheel of the flaming incandescence that is Into Paradise live.' (*New Musical Express*, 1991)

gentlemen prefer blondes A companion cliché to BLONDE BOMBSHELL, this was the title of a 1925 novel by Anita Loos, the sequel to which was called *But Gentlemen Marry Brunettes*.

'Edinburgh Filmhouse is now offering a chance to examine the flipside of the gender coin with Gentlemen Prefer Bonds?, a ten-week course analysing celluloid representations of masculinity, using examples of different film genres.' (*Scotsman*)

'Men do prefer blondes, she thought, and unconsciously pushed back a strand of her own urchin-cut black hair.' (Alice Grey, *Hearts in Hiding*, 1993)

get a life A slang expression moving more and more into the mainstream. From a way of saying that a life lacks the qualities to be worth living this has developed into a general insult. Use is generally restricted to younger people.

'Of course, they are being treated with the contempt they deserve and you have to wonder why they don't just get a life.' (*New Musical Express*, 1992)

'I've just one more thing to say – Simon, get a life and some new clichés!!' (*Hot Press*, 1991)

get away from it all A cliché of the holiday brochure and journalist; even action-packed adventure holidays are advertised as away from it all, although what 'it' may be is never specified. The phrase is recorded by the mid-nineteenth century, but it is a cliché only from the mid-twentieth. Compare 'let me TAKE YOU AWAY FROM ALL THIS'.

get into bed with As a cliché this originally belonged in a business context, but is now spreading to other areas. It means to merge or establish a close working relationship with someone else or another organization. It has been well used since the 1970s.

'People in the party want to increase tax, spend more on the welfare state and want interest rates to come down and don't want to get into bed with Paddy Ashdown.' (*Independent*, 29 September 1998)

'Little more than a year ago you couldn't give away shares in the small computer company sector – so friendless were they that Star Computer Group Plc found it necessary to get into bed with a purveyor of pizzas to improve its visibility and rating.' (*Computergram International*)

get it together see GET YOUR ACT TOGETHER

get out of line see OUT OF LINE

get out of the kitchen see STAND THE HEAT

get real A slang alternative for 'be realistic', this is a young person's cliché, often used to express incredulity or contempt.

'There was quite a bit of hurt pride and some back-stabbing but a sense of failure amongst all those pin-striped suits and highly polished black Oxfords? Get real.' (*Independent*, 15 October 1998)

get the lowdown see LOWDOWN

get up and go An expression for energy or drive originating in the USA in the form 'get up and get' or 'get up and git', which is found as early as 1864. The joke 'my get up and go got up and went' almost qualifies as a cliché in its own right.

'She knew Eva's worth, and her own brand of quiet determination was the perfect foil to Eva's "get up and go" philosophy.' (Wendy Green, *Getting Things Done: Eva Burrows – A Biography*, 1988)

get your act together; get it together Fashionable expressions from the late 1960s, originally very much part of the hippy scene. They may possibly have started as theatrical expressions, but since words like 'scene' for 'where you were at' were very much in vogue at the time, this is not necessarily the case. Also found as 'get your head [i.e. what is going on in your mind] together'.

'Yes, the market is tiny. But if British farmers get their act together, the potential is enormous.' (*Independent*, 10 September 1998)

'It has taken some time but it is beginning to look as if Surrey have finally got it together in the truest sense of the word.' (*Independent*, 1 September 1998)

get your head (a)round This belongs very much with the language and era of the previous entry. 'Head' here means 'mind, understanding' and the expression is linked with such expressions as 'get it into your head' and to 'grasp an idea'.

'It is the squad ethic – something that the English, and possibly even the British, find hard to get their heads around.' (*Independent*, 1 September 1998)

' "People can't get their head around a bunch of miners doing something like this," says Stan. "They forget that mining is about problem-solving, engineering." ' (*Big Issue*, 24–30 August 1998)

gild the lily The original form of this expression was 'to gild refined gold, to paint the lily', which comes from Shakespeare's *King John* (IV.ii) and is part of a list of things that it would be superfluous to do, which includes 'To smooth the ice, or to add another hue/Unto the rainbow' all of which 'Is wasteful and ridiculous excess'. The spoiling of the point by compressing the quote to 'gild the lily' seems to be comparatively recent. Byron in *Don Juan* (1819–24) wrote, 'But Shakespeare also says, 'tis very silly/"To gild refined gold, or paint the lily"' (canto 3 stanza 76), and 'paint the lily' can still be found in the early years of the twentieth century. However, nowadays the correct quotation is only used by pedants.

'The better the jam the better the rolypoly, and I like to gild the lily by lacing the dough with almonds and orange zest, too.' (*Country Living*, 1991)

gills see UP TO THE GILLS

gird up your loins This expression occurs a number of times in the Old Testament, most notably in the form 'Gird up now thy loins like a man' (Job 38:3). The expression reflects the simply cut, loose and flowing long garments of the time, when to do anything physically demanding involved using a girdle or belt to keep your clothes from tripping you up. The expression was already being used figuratively when St Paul wrote 'Gird up the loins of thy mind' (I Peter 1:13).

'If (and hopefully when) you do finally quit, it may create more of a problem than if you gird your mental loins at the outset and make up your mind to do it first and foremost.' (Lizzie Webb, *Total Health and Fitness*, 1989)

girl power A very recent cliché, closely associated with the Spice Girls group. Quite what girl power is seems to be a pretty flexible concept, ranging from the right to follow the course in life you want, to the right to behave as badly as some young men.

'Why does the Government assume [the] only young women who have children are those too thick to do anything else? Girl Power is about doing what you want to do, allowing young women to be empowered to choose their own way in life.' (*Daily Mail*, 27 August 1998)

'France was treated yesterday to a lesson in student power – and also in girl power. All over the country, it was women of 16 to 18 who took the lead in a day of protest by lycée students.' (*Independent*, 16 October 1998)

girl talk A cliché which covers both what might be more staidly described as 'women's interests' in the media, and the sort of communication more often found among exclusively female groups. Very often it is little more than what gets said when women are being 'all girls together'. Use of the expression was no doubt boosted by the success of a song called 'Girl Talk' in 1966.

'Meanwhile, because what Ruby and Millie do best is girl talk, I asked them for their best-ever beauty secrets.' (*You* magazine, 20 September 1998)

'But Making Out highlights how important it is for women to have a job and be with other women workers – often in very crummy circumstances, but actually being very resilient with a lot of humour and girl talk.' (*Women: A Cultural Review*, 1991)

. . . are a girl's best friend This formula phrase, popular with advertisers, comes from the song 'Diamonds are a Girl's Best Friend', written by Leo Robbins and Jule Styne, from the 1953 show GENTLEMEN PREFER BLONDES, based on Anita Loos's book of the same name. The song in turn was based on words from Loos's 1925 book: 'So I really think American gentlemen are the best after all, because kissing your hand may make you feel very very good but a diamond and safire [*sic*] bracelet lasts forever' – words which may also have inspired the slogan 'A diamond is for ever', which has been used to advertise diamonds since 1939.

'Vitamins are a girl's best friend. Boots new range of advanced formula vitamins and supplements.' (Advertising campaign, Autumn 1998)

give and take This expression for reciprocal concessions or a fair exchange has been in use since the eighteenth century, and is found even earlier in the literal sense. Burke, for instance, speaking of America said in 1775, 'Every prudent act is founded on compromise and barter . . . we give and take; we remit some rights, that we may enjoy others.'

'There has to be a willingness among all the members of such a group to be prepared to give and take, to offer criticism and receive it, to encourage and to be encouraged etc.' (Anne Long, *Approaches to Spiritual Direction*, 1988)

give it your best shot see BEST SHOT

give someone a kick in the pants see KICK IN THE PANTS

give someone a tough time see TOUGH TIME

give someone the benefit of the doubt see BENEFIT OF THE DOUBT

give the lowdown on see LOWDOWN

give the shirt off your back A symbol of generosity, a willingness to part with everything, this phrase dates back to at least 1771 when Smollett wrote in *Humphry Clinker*, 'He would give away the shirt off his back'. A lack of a shirt as a sign of poverty goes back at least to Chaucer, but the idea of giving away essential clothing as a sign of generosity is even older. St Martin of Tours, one of the most popular saints of the Middle Ages, was famous for having cut his cloak in half with his sword to share it with a naked beggar, after which he had a vision of Christ wearing the cloak, and entered holy orders. Nowadays 'to give the shirt off your back' can also be used in the same way as 'to give your right arm' or 'to give your back teeth' for something – a hyperbolic way of saying you would give almost anything for it.

'A packed Underhill clubhouse heard George D. Maxwell, no relation to the late tycoon Robert, promise, "to give the shirt off my back", during an impassioned plea to a supporters' EGM.' (*Today*, 1992)

' "I can think of a few consultants, not to mention some very tired registrars," she added ruefully, "who'd give their right arm to work in conditions like these." ' (A. Jean Evans, *Dangerous Diagnosis*, 1993)

'Mom would probably give her back teeth to make a picture with McQueen but nobody would cast her if they could get Faye Dunaway.' (Celia Brayfield, *The Prince*, 1990)

glittering prizes This expression, for highly attractive rewards, dates from the late nineteenth century (and is found in a literal sense from at least 1713), but has only become a cliché more recently. It became better known after F. E. Smith delivered a much-quoted speech as Rector of Glasgow University in 1923 in which he said, 'The world continues to offer glittering prizes to those who have stout hearts and sharp swords', but the real leap to cliché status came in 1976, when BBC TV showed a series of six linked plays written by Frederick Raphael which charted the lives of a group of Cambridge students from their undergraduate days in the 1950s, through to the 1970s. It was both a critical and popular success. No doubt the title was chosen with Smith in mind.

'Newcastle won the Premiership last season – the wrong one. The Toon Army may have wanted English football's most glittering prize, but they had to be content with seeing Rob Andrew's Newcastle Falcons win the Allied Dunbar Premiership.' (*Evening Standard*, 1 September 1998)

global village The term 'global village' was first used in 1960: 'Postliterate man's electronic media contract the world to a village or tribe where everything happens to everyone at the same time: everyone knows about, and therefore participates in, everything that is happening the minute it happens. Television gives this quality of simultaneity to events in the global village' (E. S. Carpenter and M. McLuhan, *Explorations in Communication*). It is, however, better known from Marshall McLuhan's 1962 book *The Gutenberg Galaxy* in the form 'The new electronic interdependence recreates the world in the image of a global village.' This handy term, coined with great prescience long before the arrival of satellite television and mobile phones, let alone the world wide web, would not qualify as a cliché were it not repeatedly used loosely, often as nothing more than an alternative for 'it's a small world' (an expression in use since the late nineteenth century).

'Expect more from your holiday than a lobster tan and a skinful of sangria? *Stuff* explores the last of the global village's great frontiers.' (*Stuff*, October 1998)

gloom and doom see DOOM AND GLOOM

glory see BLAZE OF GLORY

glory days A shortening for 'days of glory', this is not recorded until the middle of the twentieth century. It is now often used as a variant of expressions such as 'the best days of your life'.

'Phil Read, the seven-times world grand prix champion, was not quite ready to hang up his leathers, even though the glory days of works rides for Yamaha and MV Augusta are a long way behind him.' (*Independent*, 1 September 1998)

'Queen Anne's London, from 1710 to 1714, saw him top pamphleteer in the war against the Whigs. These were his glory years.' (*Independent*, 5 September 1998)

glutton for punishment This expression seems to be a modern one, a development of the nineteenth-century 'glutton for work', and indeed 'glutton for punishment' can still have something of the aura of the workaholic about it. It is also found, used in an approving manner, of someone or something that keeps coming back for more, or is even DEAD BUT WON'T LIE DOWN.

'Regardless of the shape you're in at the finish, only a glutton for punishment will relish the long haul back down the road to the car.' (*Outdoor Action*, 1992)

go by the book see BY THE BOOK

go directly to jail, do not pass GO, do not collect £200 (or **$200**) These are the instructions on the Community Chest chance card in the game of Monopoly which was created by Charles Darrow in 1931. Any part of the instructions can be used as an alternative to 'bad luck!' or when someone has lost out. As the great wit Tom Lehrer put it in his song on the effects of all-out nuclear warfare, 'We Will All Go Together when We Go': 'You will all go directly to your respective Valhallas. Go directly, do not pass go, do not collect two hundred dolla's . . .'

go down a road (or a **long hard road**) Although 'road' has been used metaphorically since the days of Shakespeare, this expression seems to be modern. 'Royal road' for 'an easy path' has been used since the eighteenth century, but cannot really be taken back beyond that, for the saying attributed to Euclid (who lived about 300 BC) in which he told Ptolemy I 'there is no royal road to geometry' should strictly be translated 'no royal short cut'.

'Sales are not an indicator of quality, but of cost. Good-quality television costs money to make, unlike the talk show trash which exploits the vulnerability of people. If we must go down this road, let us at least be honest about it.' (*Independent*, 2 September 1998)

'It had been a long hard road for the fledgling station, but at least it had been a journey sustained by die hard supporters.' (*Independent*, 15 September 1998)

go pear-shaped see PEAR-SHAPED

go the extra mile see EXTRA MILE

go the whole hog A popular expression from the first part of the nineteenth century, but with no clear origin, although something to do with large-scale consumption of pork is implied.

'You could hire taxis, or go the whole hog and hire a chauffeur-driven car for the day.' (*Northern Echo*)

go with the flow Another cliché of the hippy era, this expression recommends tolerantly accepting things as they come, letting yourself be swept along by events, rather than swimming against the stream. It was well established by the mid-1970s.

'Just by opting for a more left field occupation you're putting yourself on the edge a bit. It really does take a bit of bottle to do that and find your own way through the maze rather than just go with the flow.' (Pete Silverton and Glen Matlock, *I Was a Teenage Sex Pistol*, 1990)

goalposts see MOVE THE GOALPOSTS

goes with the territory see TERRITORY

goes without saying A curiously contradictory expression since whatever is supposed to go without saying is always actually said. This filler-cliché, meaning no more than 'of course', has been common since the later nineteenth century, and is a literal translation of the French '*cela va sans dire*', which explains the odd form of words.

'It goes without saying that rare cars are more coveted than common ones – and rare convertibles are of blue-chip status.' (*Independent*, 7 October 1989)

'Of course it goes without saying that the aquarium glass must always be perfectly clear for best results.' (*Practical Fishkeeping*, 1992)

when the going gets tough, the tough get going This was a favourite saying of Joseph P. Kennedy (1888–1969), father of President J. F. Kennedy. It had become a cliché by 1970.

'In American sports, politics, business, even the literary world: when the going gets tough, the tough really get going.' (*Independent*, 9 September 1998)

'When the going gets tough, the women can get as tough as the men.' (*Business*, 1991)

going places Originating in the USA, this twentieth-century expression was first used in a literal sense, meaning to go out and about, but by the 1930s was being used to mean to get ahead or be successful, or to show GET UP AND GO.

' "I just wish Maggie were back," an old friend told me the other day. "As long as she was in charge, we were going places." ' (*Mail on Sunday*, 20 September 1998)

Goliath see DAVID AND GOLIATH

golden age The idea of a Golden Age, when things were perfect (or at least better), goes back to the ancient Greeks, whose Golden Age was a time when men and gods mixed together, and there was no evil – the Greek equivalent of the time before the Fall. 'In that golden age . . . they . . . ate roots for bread and fruits for flesh,' wrote North in 1557, in one of the earliest recorded uses in this sense in English. The term was then later used to describe a group of Latin authors, those who wrote between the times of Cicero and Ovid being considered the finest authors, those of the Golden Age, with the next generation of writers belonging to the lesser Silver Age. Now it is applied to the best or finest period of anything.

' "It could be a golden age for the club," said Radio 1 DJ, . . . Zoe Ball, described as a "die-hard Manchester United fan" by the Murdoch-owned *Sun*.' (*Private Eye*, 18 September 1998)

'One of the pioneers of cinema's golden age, producer Hal Roach, died last week aged 100.' (*Today*, 1992)

golden handshake (or **handcuff**, or **hello**) 'Golden', in these business clichés, refers to money or other reward. The earliest of the expressions, from about 1960, is the golden handshake, for a payment to someone who leaves a job before their contract is up, so that he or she goes quietly. In the 1970s, came the golden handcuff – an offer of such an attractive package of long-term benefits that the recipient cannot afford to disentangle him or herself from the company. Then in the 1980s came the golden hello, when someone is paid a generous bonus just for joining a company. A less common member of this group is the 'golden parachute', used when company directors who think they may lose their jobs, for instance in a takeover, give themselves a big pay rise or bonus, to cushion their fall.

'In fact the competition for audiences means stars are securing more money as long as they sign exclusive, golden handcuff deals with broadcasters.' (*Independent*, 21 August 1998)

'The Admiral who had been appointed as the boss of Playboy UK got a golden handshake of nearly £12 million for four months' tenure as the firm was taken over.' (*New Scientist*, 1991)

'This amount includes fees, taxable expense allowances, pension contributions, benefits in kind and amounts paid to obtain the services of a director ("golden hello").' (Stoy Hayward, *Model Financial Statements for Public and Private Companies*, 1990)

gone but not forgotten A cliché of memorials. Its use is closely linked with that other nineteenth-century mortuary cliché 'NOT LOST BUT GONE BEFORE', the title of a poem by Caroline Norton (1808–77), in which she wrote 'For death and life, in ceaseless strife,/Beat wild on this world's shore,/And all our calm is in that balm –/ Not lost but gone before.' This in turn was probably inspired by the writing of the third-century St Cyprian, who said: 'Our brethren who have been freed from the world by the summons of the Lord should not be mourned, since we know that they are not lost but sent before.'

gone for a Burton The origin of this expression has been hotly debated. The two front-running theories are that the 'Burton' referred to is the tailoring chain, in which case there is a possible link to the FULL MONTY; or that it refers to going for a Burton ale. Whichever it was, and the second seems the more convincing, the expression was used in the RAF in World War II to mean 'dead, missing', and spread to the general population from there.

'We asked my cousin if the poor laboratory rats had "gone for a Burton", and the sally caused to flit across our minds a phrase from *The Anatomy of Melancholy* condemning gluttony as "the source of all our infirmities and the fountain of all our diseases".' (Irene Young, *Enigma Variations*, 1990)

gone to a better place see BETTER PLACE

good as gold Why should it be gold that people are as good as? The alliteration is obviously important, and gold is something generally considered good, or at least rare and precious, as is, perhaps, good behaviour. The expression dates from the nineteenth century, when the value of money was still tied to the value of gold, so it also contains an element of 'as good as' in the sense found in the expression 'as good as money in the bank'. This phrase is usually described in reference books as used of children, but it is quite frequently found used of adults, although often with an air of condescension.

'She was good as gold; I don't know what he would've done without her!' (W. J. Burley, *Wycliffe and the Cycle of Death*, 1991)

'He had heard that the Feds at Lockerbie had been good as gold, working at the pace required, picking up on every small detail provided by the forensic team at Farnborough, where the 747 had been reconstructed.' (Gerald Seymour, *Condition Black*, 1991)

good as it gets see AS GOOD AS IT GETS

good chemistry see CHEMISTRY

good clean fun This expression has been in use since the 1920s, usually to mean 'not obscene', although similar terms are found earlier – 'sane, clean and wholesome', for example, in 1867, and 'good, clean, wholesome' in 1911. Nowadays it is often used defensively, to protest that something others may not approve of is only good clean fun – or it may be used ironically.

'Seduced by their own success, the Sultans stay on to wring one more blast of good clean fun out of "Are You Experienced" and finally leave.' (*New Musical Express*, 1992)

'And among the other questions this month: Is bathroom humour just good clean fun?' (*Esquire*, 1991)

good fight see FIGHT THE GOOD FIGHT

good friends see JUST GOOD FRIENDS

good housekeeping This expression was beginning to be used in the 1950s for routine business transactions, record keeping and computer maintenance, and was probably much older as a term for industrial maintenance, although this use is not recorded until the 1960s. However, its spread to government and other fields of life must owe much to the policies of Mrs Thatcher and her government, with their emphasis on running the country as you would run a household or a small shop.

'The administration of any society by government is never simply a technical matter of "efficient management" or "good housekeeping".' (A. Webster, *Introduction to the Sociology of Development*, 1990)

good in parts see CURATE'S EGG

have a good innings Innings has been used to mean a period of activity since at least the 1830s, about 100 years after it was first recorded of cricket. The modern-sounding, casual 'She's had a remarkably good innings, and persons can't expect to live for ever' is found as early as 1870.

'Geordie's dying . . . Well, you know, I get a bit fed up with people saying, perhaps it's for the best, he's had a good innings . . .' (*You* magazine, 20 September 1998)

good question see THAT'S A GOOD QUESTION

good Samaritan The parable of the Good Samaritan in Luke's Gospel (10:29–37) tells the story of how a man was mugged on the road to Jerusalem and left half dead by the roadside. Two people, including a priest, 'passed by on the other side' when they saw him lying there, but a Samaritan went to help him and tended his wounds, took him to an inn, and the next day left money with the inn-keeper, telling him to spend what was necessary to care for him. Jesus told this story after he had urged his followers to love their neighbours, and had been asked 'Who is my neighbour?' The point of the story is that Jews and Samaritans were traditional enemies but that this had not affected the Samaritan's behaviour. Nowadays, 'Good Samaritan' is generally used not to mean a good neighbour but someone who helps in time of trouble. In recent years use of the expression has been somewhat affected by Mrs Thatcher's comment in defence of her policies, in a television interview in 1989, 'No one would remember the Good Samaritan if he'd only had good intentions. He had money as well.'

'Davis from Richmond Road in Oxford knocked her unconscious, threw her cycle into the river and then posed as a good Samaritan, pretending to comfort her, before attacking her again and trying to strangle her.' (*Central News* autocue data)

good time was had by all This cliché of society reports and works outings, became a literary cliché after Stevie Smith used it as the title of a verse published in 1937. She said she got the expression from parish magazines. The crack that 'she was the original good time who had been had by all' has been attributed to various people, most frequently to Bette Davis.

good to talk This is a well-established expression which has been turned into a cliché as a result of its use in saturation advertising by British Telecom since 1994.

' "I don't talk to anyone about Jeffrey any more, except my wife." Why is this? "If anyone else says anything about him, he's on the phone to me asking what it was all about." Where Jeffrey's concerned, it's not always good to talk.' (*Independent*, 16 October 1998)

Goody Two Shoes This expression comes from an early children's book *The History of Goody Two-Shoes*, published in 1765 and which, although not published under his name, was probably written by Oliver Goldsmith. It is a story of a pitifully poor child who, through her own efforts, manages to get an education and become the village school-teacher, before eventually becoming lady of the manor. 'Goody' was a polite term of address used to lower-class women (it is a shortening of 'goodwife') but Goody Two Shoes was also a very good person, and this meaning was implicit from the start. With the loss of 'Goody' as a form of address (and the fact that the story is now rarely read) the term came to be used as an alternative to 'goody-goody' (originally the name of a kind of sweet).

'I was getting pissed off with having to be a little goody two shoes anyway.' (Val McDermid, *Dead Beat*, 1992)

(cut through) the Gordian knot According to legend, Gordius was the father of Midas (see MIDAS TOUCH). He was a peasant, who became king because an oracle had told the people of Phrygia to choose as king the first man to approach the temple of Zeus in a wagon. Having become king in this strange manner, Gordius dedicated his wagon to Zeus. The wagon was attached to the yoke with a very complicated knot, and the legend developed that whoever could untie it would become ruler of all Asia. Another legend has it that Alexander the Great, a master manipulator of propaganda, claimed Asia for his own, not by unravelling the knot but by cutting through it with his sword. Thus a 'Gordian knot' came to mean something impossible to unravel, and 'to cut the Gordian knot' to mean solving a problem not by finesse but by direct and often forceful means.

'A motion of censure in either House of Congress could be another option . . . it may be the best way to cut through the Gordian knot of legal wrangles.' (*Independent*, 22 September 1998)

'They had joined a Gordian knot of vans, taxis, and automobiles that was inching forward at a pace that had set that little muscle in his jaw to knotting and unknotting.' (Sandra Marton, *Roman Spring*, 1993)

gorgeous see DROP-DEAD GORGEOUS

gory details A set phrase which often retains its original connection with blood, but has also been extended to apply to the details of anything unpleasant. It does not seem to have been used before the twentieth century.

'She pictures the relationship between Katherine, the brash and rather unlikely features editor of *Woman Now* magazine (do these people really stand around in camisoles dictating gory details about gynaecological examination over radio-phones?) and a Russian exile, Slava.' (*Independent*, 2 October 1989)

gospel truth 'Gospel truth' to mean 'honestly; really true' is a cliché of the nineteenth century. It developed from the earlier use, from at least the seventeenth century, of Gospel truth in the literal sense, used to mean the word of God.

'He added: "I think Esther Rantzen does a tremendous amount of good work, but she is a media star and I would hope that she will realise that people accept what she says as gospel truth." ' (*Guardian*, 8 December 1989)

gottle of geer This expression is meant to represent a ventriloquist's pronunciation of the phrase 'bottle of beer', and is a catch-phrase often used when ventriloquism is mentioned. It can also indicate that someone is being manipulated like a ventriloquist's dummy, and is currently being extended to cover other fields, such as to indicate speech slurred or distorted by drink.

' "Gottle a geer" Gazza would undoubtedly be a tremendous asset to the team, but after Silver's recent professions of poverty, I tend to agree with the *Guardian* that this is a "We are still a big club" smokescreen.' (Leeds United e-mail list)

' "I had a gottle of geer too many," says ventriloquist.' (*Daily Mirror*, 1992)

grace under pressure When Dorothy Parker interviewed Ernest Hemingway for the *New Yorker* in 1929 she asked him what he meant by 'guts' and got the answer 'grace under pressure'. This phrase has become increasingly popular, although it will be interesting to see what long-term effect its use as the title of a television series will have.

'I guess you could call it "grace under pressure". All and sundry have been mightily impressed by my brave acceptance of the valetudinarian life.' (*Independent*, 5 September 1998)

'Both Rasta and Skin can be seen as bids for some kind of dignity, for what the late Pete Meadon, original mod and one-time manager of The Who once called "clean living under difficult circumstances": grace under pressure.' (Nick Knight, *Skinhead*, 1982)

of graduate calibre A cliché of job advertisements (see further on the subject under SELF-STARTER), a replacement for 'with a degree' or the simple 'graduate'.

'We are seeking to recruit 3 energetic and ambitious self starters of graduate calibre, who can contribute to Marks Sattin's current and future success.' (*Evening Standard*, 7 September 1998)

grain see AGAINST THE GRAIN

grasp with both hands; **grasp at straws**; **grasp the nettle** The image of grasping, of holding on hard, is a powerful one. It has given us 'grasp with both hands' – to take hold of something as fully as possible – which is probably a development of 'to grasp at', meaning to accept with alacrity. It has given us 'grasp the nettle' for to tackle a difficult problem head on, from the fact that a nettle touched tentatively will sting, but if taken hold of firmly will not. And it has given us 'grasp at straws', a development of 'A drowning man will clutch at a straw', a proverb found from the seventeenth century.

' "Grasp the nettle" by raising issues and problems that the group ought to face and tackle.' (Peter Honey, *Improve your People Skills*, 1992)

grass roots This expression has been current since the beginning of the twentieth century. Roots are of course in the ground, the lowest part of the plant, and the expression is obviously linked to the idea of doing something from the ground up. Indeed, it has often been used in the form 'from the grass roots up'. While 'grass roots' is often used to mean 'fundamental' or 'at the most basic level', it also has a long history of specifically political use, to mean the RANK AND FILE of an organization. Nowadays uses can also be found that are influenced by the ideas behind BACK TO YOUR ROOTS.

'Blackpool was the natural choice of venue to celebrate the grass-rootsiness of the Labour faithful. It briefly turned Labour MPs into pint-of-wallop-and-a-portion-of-chips men.' (*Independent*, 26 September 1998)

'As a result of grass roots pressure, city halls and private groups are encouraging people to take their 1989 Christmas trees in for recycling into mulch, fuel or erosion barriers.' (*Guardian*, 31 December 1989)

gravy train By the beginning of the twentieth century 'gravy' was being used to mean money that had been easily acquired, or that was extra in some way, such as a bonus or tip, in the same way that gravy is an extra on top of the basics of a meal. It could also be used for money obtained through extortion or other illicit means. A 'gravy train' was US railroad slang for an easy run where the pay was good. This was adopted into general speech in the 1920s.

'The recession abruptly derailed the gravy train on which most in the record industry had ridden through the 1970s; the generous salaries, inflated expenses and transcontinental junkets.' (M. Brown, *Richard Branson: The Inside Story*, 1989)

greased lightning see LIGHTNING

great see ALL-TIME CLASSIC

great and small see ALL CREATURES GREAT AND SMALL

the great and the good Defined by one wit as a group of people too eminent to need to be competent, the expression has been in use since at least the second half of the nineteenth century, frequently ironically. By 1904 it was enough of a cliché for the English classicist and humorous poet A. D. Godley to play on it, writing 'Great and good is the typical Don, and of evil and wrong the foe,/Good, and great, I'm a Don myself, and therefore I ought to know' (*Megalopsychiad*).

'The great and the good, roused from their beds, uttered with long practice the necessary platitudes, tragedy, the most abused of words, tripping easily from their tongues.' (*Evening Standard*, 28 August 1998)

great escape The 1963 film *The Great Escape* (written by James Clavell and W. R. Burnett, based on a book by Paul Brickhill) led to this expression becoming a journalistic cliché, with little meaning other than 'escape'.

'ERM – the great escape or a cold new world?' (*Accountancy*, 1992)

great expectations 'Expectations' in the sense of hopes of an inheritance has been in use since the seventeenth century, and 'great expectations' was already well-established by 1777 when Sheridan wrote in *School for Scandal*, 'I have a rich old uncle . . . from whom I have the greatest expectations'. When Charles Dickens used the expression for the title of his 1861 novel about a boy whose life was twisted by having a secret patron of whom he had great expectations – and who had great expectations of him – it was already a cliché, but it is this novel with which the expression is most closely associated today.

'We've very great expectations of a brand new pansy, an F1 hybrid called 'Imperial Gold Princess' with enormous scarlet blotches over deep yellow petals.' (*Gardeners' World*, 1991)

great minds think alike There has been a saying expressing this idea since the early seventeenth century, but it took the form of 'great minds [or wits] jump', 'jump' being used in an old sense meaning 'coincide'. The modern form of the saying is not recorded before the twentieth century, and is often used ironically.

'Anyway, I'd always believed great minds thought alike, until I found out that SEGA FORCE's Paul "if the cap fits, it's a miracle" Mellerick supports Leicester too!' (*Zzap 64!*, 1992)

great white hope This was originally a nickname given to James Jeffries, a white boxer defeated by the first black heavyweight boxing champion, Jack Johnson, in 1910 (see further under THE BIGGER THEY COME, THE HARDER THEY FALL). Users are now often unaware of the racist connotations, using 'white' as if it were the equivalent of 'shining' (as in 'shining example') or without any idea of its meaning.

'Once the great white hope of our consumer electronics industry, Amstrad lost £15.2m in the six months to December, a far cry from the £160m profits made only four years ago.' (*Punch*, 1992)

greater love has no man This is a quotation from the Bible (John 15:13), 'Greater love hath no man than this, that a man lay down his life for his friends'. It has been a cliché from at least the nineteenth century. It is used as a straightforward quotation on memorials and in similar situations, but nowadays, when it is used in general writing, it is nearly always with irony.

'"Greater love hath no man than that he lays down his jokes for his Prime Minister," a Cabinet minister said in Blackpool on hearing of the sacrifice made by Chris Patten, the Secretary of State for the Environment.' (*Independent*, 13 October 1989)

'Greater love hath no man for his three small grandsons than a 71-year-old friend of ours who sat in his car all night outside a Cardiff toy store to make sure he was first in line for a much-wanted Thunderbirds Tracy Island from Santa.' (*Today*, 1992)

greatest show on earth This started life as an advertising slogan for Barnum and Baily's Circus, used from 1881 onwards, and still in use by successor circuses. Its use was given a boost when a film about circus life was made by Cecil B. De Mille in 1952 with the same title.

'In 1965, in the Brezhnev era to which many old-style Communists were to look back with fond nostalgia, an Englishman observing the May Day festival on Red Square wrote: "The tourists, even the Americans, are delighted: they clap, cheer, photograph, and at the end simply gasp, as if they have just seen the greatest show on earth."' (*New Statesman and Society*, 1992)

greatest thing since sliced bread see BEST THING SINCE SLICED BREAD

Greek to me see ALL GREEK TO ME

grey suit A cliché of the 1990s, this expression comes from the dressing habits of the traditional businessman. Senior management has to wear sober, typically grey suits, and the dull conformity of this has come to be used to express the lack of individuality of a certain set of business mind. The expression is now often shortened to 'suit'.

'Wolff was a traditional workaholic grey suit, shackled by golden handcuffs to the major international company to which he'd sold his own thriving telecommunications business.' (*Sunday Express*, 4 August 1991)

'At stake is the priceless archive of audio and video material: paid for by the licence-payer, held in trust for the nation – and now at the mercy of suits who want to release money to pay for 24-hour digital, audience-free broadcast drivel.' (*Private Eye*, 18 September 1998)

grief see COME TO GRIEF

grind see AXE TO GRIND

grind the faces of the poor This is a quotation cliché, coming from Isaiah 3:15: 'What mean ye that ye beat my people to pieces and grind the faces of the poor?' It now has a rather old-fashioned ring to it, but together with the use of 'grinding' to mean 'oppressive, wearing' has helped to give rise to expressions such as 'grindingly poor' and 'in grinding poverty'.

'"They grind the faces of the poor and leave us only this," Boris continued morosely in a cunning bid for sympathy, picking up the vodka bottle.' (Amy Myers, *Murder at the Masque*, 1991)

grip see ICY GRIP

grit your teeth Under stress one automatically clenches one's teeth tightly. This can make a grinding noise, similar to that made when a bit of grit has got into food, hence 'to grit your teeth', used to describe such an action since the late eighteenth century. Nowadays it is often used metaphorically, in the sense of 'to brace yourself, keep your resolve up'.

'"If Dr Greene tells her it's best to wait another four weeks for the sake of the baby, she'll grit her teeth and wait another four weeks," Belinda added.' (Lilian Darcy, *A Private Arrangement*, 1993)

'She rubbed her face in a kind of fury now; a fury which she controlled, and through gritted teeth, said: "Saturday".' (S. Laws, *Darkfall*, 1993)

gross exaggeration A set phrase, exaggeration is for some reason always gross rather than great, definite or manifest. The other word often coupled with gross is overstatement. Gross exaggeration has been a cliché since the mid-nineteenth century, and gross overstatement probably dates from about the same time.

'Literary critics . . . have suggested that this account is probably a gross exaggeration – that is, that while Coleridge may have dreamed about Cublai Can, the poetry was not provided in the dream in its complete form, but required years of revision.' (Jacob Empson, *Sleep and Dreaming*, 1989)

ground-breaking Surprisingly, this journalistic cliché for 'innovative' is found as early as 1907 when William James, philosopher brother to the now more famous Henry, wrote in a letter, 'I am going to settle down to the composition of another small book, more original and ground-breaking than anything I have yet put forth.'

'I like some of the heavier stuff from America: I heard a couple of things by Superchunk that I really liked, and obviously the Nirvana album was a ground-breaking record.' (*Guitarist*, 1992)

guiding light This expression for a leader or example comes from the idea of a lighthouse, beacon or similar light being used to guide people through the night. Early uses were often theological, but its use received a boost in the 1960s when Selwyn Lloyd used the term for guidelines attempting to curb pay-rises.

'Graham Gooch will carry on using Geoff Boycott as a guiding light.' (*Today*, 1992)

'So Abram set out on a journey where faith rather than sight would be the guiding light, seeking a home, a city, a country.' (Anne Long, *Approaches to Spiritual Direction*, 1988)

(feel) gutted To be or to feel gutted for 'upset, very disappointed' is a cliché of the late 1980s. Its spread was helped by the way in which footballers took it up to replace the 1970s vogue term SICK AS A PARROT to express their feelings when they lost.

'We feel gutted, extremely gutted and completely gutted and in need of counselling, not at the loss of an Empire but of a football match.' (John Mortimer, *Evening Standard*, 28 August 1998)

guys and gals A general term for people, especially young people, this is a catch-phrase associated with the disc jockey Jimmy Savile, particularly in his role as presenter of BBC TV's long-running *Top of the Pops*. Savile presented the first ever *Top of the Pops* in 1964, and was a stalwart of the show for a long time. Not surprisingly, the expression now has a rather dated ring to it.

'But I know the feeling of being a member of a brave band of right-minded guys and gals, charged with responsibility no outsider can imagine, working all hours . . .' (Ann Wroe, *Lives, Lies and the Iran-Contra Affair*, 1991)

hale and hearty A set phrase, dating from the middle of the nineteenth century, 'hale' being otherwise unused outside dialect. 'Hale' is a northern dialect variant of 'whole' and in this context means 'sound, fit'.

'Uncle Hilbert, however, was only just sixty, very hale and hearty, still very much in practice as a solicitor, and Lewis could not imagine stepping into his shoes.' (Barbara Vine, *A Fatal Inversion*, 1987)

hallowed turf A sporting cliché, the sacred grass referred to being the pitch on which various games are played.

'Aussie flanker Brendan Nasser, who was a member of the Wallabies' World Cup-winning squad last year will be the only international on the hallowed turf of Twickenham.' (*Today*, 1992)

hand in glove The complex topology involved means that there can scarcely be a more intimate relationship than that between a hand and a glove. The expression, in use since the first half of the seventeenth century in the form 'hand and glove', is most commonly used of something nefarious, but it can also be used simply to suggest a very close co-operation or relationship.

'The Mayor and his friends were themselves the criminals, hand in glove with the smugglers whose leader Jake was clearly an old ally.' (John Ryan, *Captain Pugwash and the Huge Reward*, 1991)

'As I identified a minute or two ago, our approach to computerizing accounting applications fits hand in glove with the concept of relational database.' ('Enterprise Two Thousand Seminar', recorded, 24 March 1993)

hand of God This respected theological expression gained a new dimension for football fans after Argentinian footballer Diego Maradona used it to explain the scoring of a goal off his hand in the 1986 World Cup, thereby putting England out of the match. It quickly became a catch-phrase that was adopted as the title of a football fanzine.

'Tommy Johnson needed the hand of God to evade Nigel Martyn in goal.' (*The Central Match – Live*, 24 October 1993)

hand on heart The hand placed on the heart has long been a sign of sincerity and pledging your word, the heart being seen as the seat of life and the emotions. The children's oath 'Cross my heart and hope to die' is a relic of this. Thus 'hand on heart' – an expression used by Shakespeare – is an alternative way of saying 'I swear, truly'.

'I just feel he could have gone either way if he'd had a different mother. She succeeded in making him gay. Hand on heart I'd say that.' (*You* magazine, 20 September 1998)

hand out pills or drugs as if they were Smarties see SMARTIES

hand over fist This expression for making or losing money very rapidly comes originally from a naval expression. In the eighteenth century, sailors climbing ropes quickly were said to do so 'hand over hand'. This developed into the variant 'hand over fist' in the early nineteenth century, and this was soon applied to scooping up money with your hands as quickly as possible, and then used metaphorically. Although most often referring to money, it has always been used less commonly to mean 'rapidly' in general.

'Five years ago Vauxhall was losing money hand over fist and relations between management and workers was at a low ebb.' (*Liverpool Echo & Daily Post*, 1993)

'But a bar owner said: "Since this all began the town has been making money hand over fist."' (*Daily Telegraph*, 15 April 1992)

hand ... on a plate If you present something to someone on a plate it suggests care and preparation in advance. It is not something they have to force out of you, but it is given to them without their even asking. The expression probably arose in the first part of the twentieth century.

'The British state has presided over Ulster's long war for over 20 blood spattered years, all the time working hand in glove with our enemies in Dublin and Washington to eventually hand Ulster to Eire on a plate.' (*Ulster Dawn*, 1991)

hand that feeds you SEE BITE THE HAND THAT FEEDS YOU

handle with kid gloves Kid gloves are the softest and finest kind, worn by Victorian ladies in the evening, and rapidly wearing out despite the most delicate use. By the middle of the nineteenth century 'kid gloves' was being used to suggest daintiness: 'He was, in fact, a mere kid-glove sportsman,' wrote a reporter scathingly in 1856. By the late nineteenth century, 'with kid gloves' was being used to describe delicate negotiations and the handling of difficult problems.

'With the election out of the way, the Commission has called a halt to the period in which British questions were either postponed or handled with kid gloves.' (*Daily Telegraph*, 11 April 1992)

hands are tied If your hands are tied, or in a more extreme form if you are 'bound hand and foot' (a nineteenth-century cliché), you are unable to act freely. People's hands have been tied in this way since the seventeenth century, and the expression is currently a favourite with bureaucrats, belonging with DESPITE MY BEST EFFORTS.

'Does my right hon. Friend accept that to deal with military conflicts in the Province British troops must be able to deal with the Irish Republican Army in a professional, military way, without their hands being tied behind their backs for political reasons?' (*Hansard Extracts 1991–1992*)

hands down SEE WIN HANDS DOWN

hands-on This implies active, practical (rather than theoretical) involvement, a willingness to get your hands dirty. It appeared in the 1960s, and was particularly associated with computers, but has now spread to other fields.

'Hands-on, value-driven: management is about the implementation of values which are explicit and form the basis for action.' (Allan Osborne, *Education Management in the 1990s*, 1990)

handwriting on the wall SEE WRITING ON THE WALL

hang in the balance (or **by a thread**) 'Hang in the balance' is an old expression, dating from at least the fifteenth century, which uses an image, going back to biblical times, of the scales which can be turned by the least weight being added to either pan. It would have been a familiar visual image in the Middle Ages from the many paintings of the souls of the dead being weighed in judgement against the weight of a feather. Anyone who has ever used such an old-fashioned pair of scales will know that two almost equal weights can oscillate for some time before they come down on one side or the other. 'To hang by a thread' goes back to the world of the ancient Greeks, to the story of the Sword of Damocles. Damocles is said to have lived in the fourth century BC, and to have tried to flatter Dionysius, Tyrant of Syracuse, by telling him he was the most fortunate man alive. To teach him a lesson Dionysius held a magnificent banquet with Damocles in the seat of honour, but as he enjoyed the feast Damocles realized that suspended over his head was a sword, hanging by a single thread, by which Dionysius meant to convey to him the dangers and discomforts of supreme power.

'While hemlines hang in the balance, the fashionably correct can keep a foot in both camps.' (*Daily Telegraph*, 12 April 1992)

'Hopes of a title hat-trick hang by a thread, but all is not quite lost.' (*Independent*, 2 October 1989)

hang in there A cliché which developed in the USA in the mid-twentieth century. It is often found used of sport, where it probably originated.

'If there is one thing that Sweden taught me, it was to hang in there and not let my head go down, even if I don't play particularly well.' (*Golf Monthly*, 1991)

hangs a tale see THEREBY HANGS A TALE

not a happy bunny A fairly recently arrived ironic way of talking about people with problems or who are upset, a contrast between the Disneyesque image of the happy bunny and the grim reality he or she may have to face. 'Not a happy camper' is an earlier alternative.

'Neil Chalmers, director of the Natural History Museum, was not a happy bunny when the last *Eye* detailed some of the fraud, theft and mismanagement that has plagued what was once one of Britain's finest museums.' (*Private Eye*, 27 November 1998)

happy-clappy A recent introduction used to describe a type of evangelical Christianity involving enthusiasm and upbeat music. It is beginning to be used of this sort of approach to life in general, and is associated with the similar TOUCHY-FEELY.

happy event A euphemism-cliché for those who do not like to talk directly about childbirth, the expression in this sense dates from the 1880s.

'But not long after this happy event Fergie became depressed that Andrew would be away in Australia for some months and that she and her baby were being "abandoned".' (*Daily Mirror*, 1992)

happy ever after A conscious cliché taken from traditional stories such as fairy tales, this has been a cliché since the eighteenth century, and goes with the nineteenth-century clichés of the 'happy couple' or 'happy pair', who are to live in this way.

'In old age Flora would smile, remembering the child who believed that love was for one person, for ever, for Happy Ever After.' (Mary Wesley, *A Sensible Life*, 1990)

'You'll find the month stressful, arduous, demanding and difficult – but if you persevere in the most important area of all, you'll win your worldly battle and have a happy ever after in your emotional life too.' (*Esquire*, 1992)

hard (or **tough**) **act to follow** This expression developed in the USA about the beginning of the twentieth century, but did not become a cliché in the UK until the middle of the century. It comes from vaudeville, where a very successful or popular act would literally be a difficult one to follow, as unfavourable comparisons would inevitably be made.

'She has a hard act to follow; it is never enviable to be the successor of one very powerful founder director be it in the gallery sector or in commerce.' (*Photography*, 1991)

hard and fast 'Hard', in nautical terms, is used to mean 'secure, securely' so that a ship that is hard aground is not easily going to be refloated. 'Hard and fast' was used to describe a ship in dry dock or similarly out of the water. One would guess there was also an unrecorded use of 'hard and fast' to describe a securely tied rope, for early uses of 'hard and fast' as a cliché are nearly always 'hard and fast line', although today 'rules' is the most common word to go with it. The term became common in the second half of the nineteenth century.

'But there are no hard and fast rules about the physique of a racing cyclist.' (*Tour de France '92*, Channel 4, 1992)

hard as nails Anyone who has been clumsy while hammering in a nail will know that nails are not, in fact, particularly hard, but bend quite easily; but what they can do is 'take a hammering'. 'Hard as nails' replaced earlier expressions such as 'hard as a stone' (or as flint) in the second half of the nineteenth century.

'She was beautiful, with an air of fragility which, for all she suspected, hid a character as hard as nails, yet was guaranteed to bring out the male protective instinct.' (Jean Evans, *A Dangerous Diagnosis*, 1993)

hard man In football terms a hard man is someone who will tackle over-hard, and retaliate if he thinks he has been fouled. He is often also a BAD BOY. It is also used as a general term, a more polite version of 'thug'.

'Hughesy is renowned as a "hard man" although this appears to be a one way thing – he doesn't mind dishing it out but if anyone comes within a foot of him he crashes to the turf, usually clutching his face and rolling around frantically in an attempt to get a fellow professional booked/sent off.' (Leeds United e-mail list)

'Don Arden, hard man of the Sixties scene ... once dangled his rival Robert Stigwood from a fourth-floor window.' (*Independent*, 6 November 1998)

hard master see HARSH MASTER

hardened criminal A set phrase, often used without a clear indication of what is meant by 'hardened'. The word has been used in the sense of 'obdurate, set on a course' since the fourteenth century, and has been linked to 'criminal' as a cliché since the middle of the nineteenth century.

'Charles Bronson ... proved that prison *can* reform even the most hardened of criminals.' (*Guardian*, 26 August 1998)

harder they fall see BIGGER THEY COME, THE HARDER THEY FALL

a harsh (or **hard**) (**task**) **master** These terms for people or circumstances that demand hard work have not had their histories traced, but they appear to be twentieth-century uses.

'But the public is a harsh master. The new, inter-reactive politics mean the desire to preserve face – albeit a modern, cool, responsive face – at all times.' (*Independent*, 22 September 1998)

has to be seen to be believed see SEEN TO BE BELIEVED

hasn't got a dog's chance see DOG'S CHANCE

Hasta la vista, baby SEE I'LL BE BACK

have a nice day This has actually been a common phrase since the 1920s, but became ubiquitous in the 1970s. For some reason it irritates a lot of people, probably because they feel it is intrusive or insincere – although few people have the same reaction to 'How do you do?', equally impertinent if taken literally. It first became popular in the USA when in the 1960s the language of CB radio as used by long-distance lorry drivers became very fashionable. They had been using 'have a nice day' since the 1950s. It came to the UK a little later, and has always been felt to be something of an Americanism. It is now going out of fashion, even when shortened to 'nice day', and being replaced by the even more intrusive 'Take care' or even worse 'Take care, now'. The excessively twee 'Missing you already' is rarely used without irony.

'In the houses – never a window opened – in the cars, in the gruesome, echoing hypermarkets set in the middle of nowhere (where they wished you a "nice day" at 10 pm).' (Jean Bow, *Jane's Journey*, 1991)

have it both ways Usually negative in implication, if not in structure, this expression for wanting two contradictory things, has been in common use since the beginning of the twentieth century.

'What we are seeing is an "Iron" Chancellor up to all the old political tricks of his Labour predecessors, not to mention those of many of his Tory forerunners as well. It's called trying to have it both ways.' (*Independent*, 8 October 1998)

having said that A filler cliché, common in report writing and out of the mouths of politicians and their like. It appears to be a twentieth-century cliché.

'Ross admits to being a little disappointed at the level of basic skills when he arrived, adding: "A lot of the mistakes were down to the mental approach and lack of concentration, but, having said that, the attitude and determination of the players has been excellent throughout the season." ' (*Daily Telegraph*, 13 April 1992)

he who hesitates is lost SEE HESITATES

head above water SEE KEEP YOUR HEAD ABOVE WATER

head and shoulders above A cliché for something that stands out, or towers above the rest of its class, it is first recorded in the 1860s.

'On actual racecourse achievement, Rock City is head and shoulders above Cordoba and the rest of today's field.' (*Independent*, 5 October 1989)

head around SEE GET YOUR HEAD AROUND

with head held high Although this has only been a cliché since the nineteenth century, the idea behind holding one's head up, rather than bowed in shame, goes back much further. In fact, two expressions seem to have become blended here. Originally 'to hold one's head up' meant to behave arrogantly or proudly, while 'to hold up one's head' referred to keeping one's dignity or self-respect. Both these date from the sixteenth century.

'St Helens don't see it as a problem. They were grateful I'd told them what I was doing. Saints are still my priority. I'll give it my best shot and I want to be able to walk away with my head held high.' (*Daily Mail*, 27 August 1998)

head start SEE UP TO SCRATCH

heads will roll The earliest recorded use of this expression is a literal one by Adolf Hitler, who is reported as saying in 1930, 'If our movement is victorious there will be a revolutionary tribunal which will punish the crimes of November 1918. The decapitated heads will roll in the sand.' This statement made enough of an impact for a journalist to write of ' "Heads will roll" Hitlerism' ten years after this speech.

'Last night, Alun Michael, the Home Office minister, said "heads will roll" among police chiefs if they fail to meet tough targets on recruiting more black and Asian officers.' (*Independent*, 19 October 1998)

heady mixture A heady mixture is something that is exciting enough to make you act as if intoxicated, to 'go to your head' or 'turn your head'. It appears to be a modern cliché, but its history is not recorded.

' "There's a lot of method here; it's not as arbitrary as it seems," David says of the heady mixture of pattern and texture.' (*Country Living*, 1991)

hear a pin drop This expression for profound silence, now sometimes used to imply tension more than true silence, is implicit in Fanny Burney's diary entry for 11 June 1775 when she writes: 'Had a *pin* fallen, I suppose we should have taken it at least for a *thunder-clap*'; and must have been well-established by 1816 for Leigh Hunt to refer to it allusively in *The Story of Rimini* – 'A pin-drop silence strikes all o'er the place.'

'I still think the great moments in acting are when a theatre audience lets out a big laugh at just the point when you want them to laugh – or when you can hear a pin drop because you've got them totally captivated in the drama.' (*Woman*, 1991)

heart in the right place An expression for to mean well, to have good intentions, this has been in use since about 1800, and was certainly a cliché by the later part of the century. It is one of innumerable expressions, many of them clichés, where the heart represents emotions or feelings.

heart of darkness This comes from the title of Joseph Conrad's 1902 novel *The Heart of Darkness*, an account of human corruption and exploitation in Africa. The title of the book draws on associations with both the Dark Continent and the Prince of Darkness. Nowadays it tends to be used loosely to mean a hidden or central evil.

'The heart of darkness within American society in that racism remains strong and dangerous in the 1990s.' (*Independent*, 8 July 1998)

heart of gold Well used by writers in the sixteenth century, including Shakespeare, this appears to have been a translation of the earlier French *coeur d'or*. The well-known song of the period, often attributed to Henry VIII, says 'Greensleeves was my heart of gold . . .'. In the past it was used as a straightforward compliment, but in modern use it is nearly always used as a mitigating factor to balance something less complimentary. The image of the 'tart with the heart of gold' is almost an independent cliché.

'Rebuck, whom Gould describes as a "very formidable woman with a heart of gold", walked by the library at Sussex where Gould was sitting with another friend.' (*Harpers & Queen*, 1989)

'He may be an old moaner, but he's got a heart of gold.' (P. Ling, *Flood Water*, 1993)

heart of stone People have been described as stony-hearted since the time of Homer: 'Thy heart is even harder than stone' (*Odyssey*), and the Bible: 'His heart is as firm as a stone; yea, as hard as a piece of the nether millstone' (Job 41:24). More recently Oscar Wilde famously commented: 'One must have a heart of stone to read the death of Little Nell without laughing.'

'Here, as with most of Shostakovich, the content they locate is a projection of what they know of its circumstances – by which only a heart of stone would not be moved.' (*Independent*, 14 October 1989)

heart of the matter A cliché since at least the second half of the nineteenth century, this is also used with numbing frequency for headlines for articles on heart disease.

'They understand the many options available to savers and are trained to ask questions that get straight to the heart of the matter.' (Financial leaflet)

heart to heart In use from the beginning of the twentieth century, this originally implied getting close to someone, 'opening your heart' to them, but nowadays it is often used to mean a telling off or a warning. This development probably comes from the sort of situation in which parents say they want to have a heart to heart with their child, which turns into frank speaking, if not a list of complaints. Perhaps because of this change in meaning, 'heart to heart' is, at the time of writing, often replaced by the vogue phrase 'one-to-one' or 'one-on-one'.

'In union negotiations, for example, I always found that if you had a heart to heart with the opposition, the single leader, you could probably gain something.' (David Oates and Derek Ezra, *Advice from the Top*, 1989)

'He and I had had a heart to heart in the hotel following some comments supposedly made by him about me in the press, more particularly in the *Sun*.' (Linford Christie and Tony Ward, *Linford Christie: An Autobiography*, 1990)

after your own heart 'The Lord hath sought him a man after his own heart' is found in the Bible (1 Samuel 13:14) and the expression had been translated into the Anglo-Saxon forerunner of English by 825. However, in a non-religious context, to mean someone or something that agrees with you, it did not become a cliché until the nineteenth century.

'They had been thinking of a job in Parma to which I would commute daily; but this one sounded very interesting, something after my own heart.' (Wanda Newby, *Peace and War: Growing up in Fascist Italy*, 1991)

(to your) heart's desire (or **content**) These are two more expressions where the heart stands for the emotions or state of mind. They both date from the days of Shakespeare, but while 'heart's desire' has kept some feeling of emphasis, 'heart's content' is now often little more than a tag.

'There are two tragedies in life. One is to lose your heart's desire. The other is to gain it.' (George Bernard Shaw, *Man and Superman*, 1903)

'I'll leave you my keys and . . . you can rootle to your heart's content.' (Agatha Christie, *Cards on the Table*, 1936)

in the heat of the moment In the heat of the moment is the opposite of in COLD BLOOD, and depends on the same ideas of hot and cold emotions. It was an established cliché by the middle of the nineteenth century.

'Occasionally, courts and tribunals take the view that a dismissal or resignation given in the heat of the moment can be withdrawn.' (Martin Edwards, *How to Get the Best Deal from Your Employer*, 1991)

heat on see PUT THE HEAT ON

heaven and earth see MOVE HEAVEN AND EARTH

heighten (the) awareness Heighten the awareness is modern bureaucratic-speak for the simpler 'make more aware', used to make it sound more official.

'Like their colleagues in Manchester's better know [*sic*] hot spots, staff are being warned to don bullet-proof jackets. "It's a question of heightening the awareness of our staff for their own protection," he says.' (*Independent*, 14 August 1998)

heinous crime This has been a set phrase since the end of the sixteenth century, and was used regularly in political and forensic writing through to the eighteenth century. Nowadays 'heinous' is rarely found outside formal writing, except in this combination, and many people would be hard pressed to give a firm definition of it, let alone choose which is the preferred pronunciation. It comes from the same root as the word 'hateful'.

'In fact when you introduced me, I thought, "Oh my God, I'm going to be brought up in front of the assembly for some heinous crime and be humiliated.' (Michael Aspel, *Michael Aspel: In Good Company*, 1989)

hell see FROM HELL

hell has no fury like a woman scorned The popular version of William Congreve's lines from his 1697 play *The Mourning Bride*: 'Heav'n has no rage, like love to hatred turn'd,/Nor Hell a fury, like a woman scorn'd.' Usually appearing in a truncated form 'Hell has no fury . . .', it is also much parodied and used as a formula phrase. Partridge records a twentieth-century catch-phrase: 'Hell has no fury like a woman's corns.'

'A reasonable woman can forgive a man who goes straight into snore mode at bedtime. But hell hath no fury like that of a woman whose blueprint for new wallpaper and curtains has met with limp apathy.' (*Evening Standard*, 10 September 1998)

'Hell hath no fury like the wife of a South Korean naval captain passed over for promotion.' (*The Economist*, 1993)

hell of a way to run a railroad see WHAT A WAY TO RUN A RAILROAD

hell to pay Meaning 'serious consequences', this has been a popular expression since the early 1800s. There is an old verb 'to pay', meaning to cover a ship's seams with tar to make it waterproof, and a naval saying 'the devil to pay and no pitch hot', 'the devil' being a term for the seam at the point where the deck and the sides of the ship met, because it was so difficult to get at. This expression is still used in Newfoundland to mean 'to be unprepared for an emergency'; but it is not clear which is chicken and which egg with these expressions, or if they are connected.

'I was convinced that if the Democrats were perceived as stalling in the midst of a national economic crisis, there would be hell to pay in the midterm elections.' (David Mervin, *Ronald Reagan and the American Presidency*, 1990)

help from my friends see LITTLE HELP FROM MY FRIENDS

helping hand This self-explanatory expression has been in use since the fifteenth century, and a cliché since at least the eighteenth.

'It's the busiest time of the year for cooks, so this month's issue is packed with tips and advice to give you a helping hand.' (*Good Food*, 1992)

here and now To use both these terms is redundant, either 'here' or 'now' would usually do just as well as both, but the expression has been a cliché since the first part of the nineteenth century, and is often an alternative filler cliché to THIS DAY AND AGE.

'Eddie George, Governor of the Bank of England, spoke to our trade union leaders last week about the perils of inflation. "I'm interested in the here and now, and the livelihood of my members, not some academic lecture on economics," snarled one of the General Secretaries.' (*Mail on Sunday*, 20 September 1998)

here, there and everywhere It is, of course, unnecessary to have 'here' and 'there', if you are using 'everywhere', but that did not stop Shakespeare using the expression at least twice, nor Christopher Marlowe before him.

'If you leave a complicated estate with lots of bits here, there and everywhere and your affairs in a mess, and the solicitor's got to sort it out, he's going to have to do a lot of work for it.' (Legal advice: pre-retirement course, recorded, 26 April 1993)

here we go Once a simple resigned comment, this has now become most closely associated with the most mindless of football chants. Also known as 'The Earwig Song', this consists of endless repetition of the words ' 'ere we go, 'ere we go, 'ere we go' to the tune of the central section of Sousa's *Stars and Stripes*. As Fritz Spiegl says of the words, in his book on football, *A Game of Two Halves, Brian*, 'Even the thickest fan can memorise them after a little practice.'

he who hesitates is lost Although now most familiar in the form 'he who hesitates . . .' early uses of this proverb usually applied to women. The earliest known version is 'When love once pleads admission to our hearts . . . The woman that deliberates is lost', in Joseph Addison's *Cato* (1713). In modern use it is often a formula phrase.

'Of course I'd seen this one coming, but I still wasn't sure what I wanted to do. However, she who hesitates is lost in the detective biz, so I opted for partial disclosure.' (Sara Paretsky, *Indemnity Only*, 1982)

'She who hesitates, I'm afraid, just has to drink what she's given.' (Stephanie Howard, *Conspiracy of Love*, 1993)

hidden agenda The hidden agenda, for a secret motive behind actions, is one of the more useful recent clichés, fitting in well with our suspicious and conspiracy-theory-ridden society. Indeed, AGENDA is currently a very productive term, with the 'secret agenda' the nearest rival to the 'hidden' one.

'When will those with a hidden agenda stop trying to fool us that in the media "more" means more choice and a better service for the consumer?' (*Independent*, 2 September 1998)

'By making these charges, Labour has boosted its longstanding efforts to persuade voters that the Tories have a secret agenda for the NHS: privatisation.' (*The Economist*, 1991)

hidden depths This expression for there being more to someone than meets the eye has been in use since the middle of the nineteenth century.

'A lively and optimistic search to find hidden depths and insights and questioning within pupils must replace negative attitudes towards children's capacity for thinking.' (Brenda Watson, *The Effective Teaching of Religious Education*, 1993)

hide your light under a bushel In the Bible (Matthew 5:14–16), Jesus tells his followers to be open about their beliefs: 'Ye are the light of the world. A city that is set on a hill cannot be hid. Neither do men light a candle, and put it under a bushel, but on a candlestick; and it giveth light unto all that are in the house. Let your light so shine before men . . .' Bushel, here, is a container large enough to hold the equivalent of eight gallons. The passage has been used as an image in English since the sixteenth century, but the form 'to hide your light under a bushel' seems to be nineteenth-century.

'Always involved with every side of the production and never one to hide his light under a bushel, he was credited in every programme as co-writing, composing, designing, and making props and scenery – a one-man band.' (Doremy Vernon, *Tiller's Girls*, 1988)

high and dry This was originally a description of a ship stranded out of water or in dry dock, and therefore related to HARD AND FAST. It came to be used figuratively about the middle of the nineteenth century.

'It's all very well to plan for next year's holiday or a new home but there's little point if your family would be left high and dry by the death of the breadwinner.' (*Today*, 1992)

high and mighty First introduced as a literal expression in the fifteenth century, often as a term of address to a ruler, by the seventeenth century it was already beginning to move, via the sense of powerful, towards its modern sense of arrogant and conceited.

'The Bible also says God is understanding, merciful, compassionate and loving . . . not some high and mighty judgmental bigot.' (*Daily Mail*, 27 August 1998)

high dudgeon (or **horse**) 'High dudgeon' is so much a set phrase that no other type of dudgeon exists any longer, and even the origin of the word is lost. It first appeared in the sixteenth century, when you could simply be 'in dugeon' when angry or resentful, and even in 1816 Scott could write about 'deep dudgeon', but it has been fixed at high since about the middle of the nineteenth century. If you get in a high dudgeon, you might also be tempted to get on your high horse – to behave in a pompous or arrogant way. In the past the wealthy and powerful would literally ride higher horses than the poor on their ponies. The phrase has been used metaphorically since about 1800.

'He also knows that of 13 British chancellors since 1957, all but two – one of them John Major himself – have come to sticky ends: . . . removed by electoral defeat, forced to resign in high dudgeon.' (*The Economist*, 1993)

'Once, if addressed in such a tone, he would have denied his hunger stiffly, . . . but now it seemed he had learned sense enough not to climb on his high horse quite so easily and unprofitably.' (Edith Pargeter, *The Green Branch*, 1987)

high ground SEE MORAL HIGH GROUND

high hopes The idea of high hopes has been about since at least the seventeenth century. The playwright John Fletcher wrote that 'His jollity is down, valed to the ground Sir, And his high hopes. . . Are turned tormentors to him' (*Wife for a Month*, 1624) and Milton wrote in 1644 of people with 'High hopes of living to be brave men, and worthy Patriots'. Modern uses of the expression are sometimes influenced by the tone of the 1959 song 'High Hopes' from the film *Hole in the Head*, a hit for Frank Sinatra, with its account of ants and suchlike attempting the impossible, because of their 'high, apple-pie-in-the-sky hopes' (see also at PIE IN THE SKY).

'The ninth round of Arab–Israeli peace talks, which started in Washington amid unusually high hopes at the end of April, ended a fortnight later having achieved nothing.' (*The Economist*, 1993)

high horse see HIGH DUDGEON

high on the hog The best parts of a pig, from a butcher's point of view, are those from the upper part of the body, and living or eating high on or off the hog refers to this. The expression developed in the American South in the nineteenth century, but took until the middle of the twentieth century to become an international cliché.

'Living high on the hog at other people's expense is a UEFA trade mark.' (*Evening Standard*, 28 August 1998)

highly acclaimed 'Highly acclaimed' is a companion cliché to 'CRITICAL ACCLAIM', used in much the same way, and in the same contexts.

'Some of Britain's most highly acclaimed broadcasters are planning a boycott of a dinner hosted by Mr Hussey tomorrow night for Sir Michael Checkland, Mr Birt's predecessor, whom Mr Hussey squeezed out.' (*Scotsman*)

historic occasion (or **event**) This started out as a journalistic cliché, used by people such as radio commentators at state or royal events, but for some years now 'historic' has been popularly used as if it has the same meaning as 'memorable'.

'Aged from eighteen to eighty, some hadn't rung a bell for almost fifty years, but everyone pulled their weight on this historic occasion.' (Central Television news scripts, 1993)

'The 100th anniversary of the first street collection was of particular interest, as it was an historic event for volunteer fund raisers nationwide.' (Royal National Lifeboat Institution, *The Lifeboat*, 1991)

you're history Initially a tough-guy threat in films and television, as this has spread to more general use the threat has been diluted from death to a more general sense of dismissal, particularly from a job.

'Next they deliver this ultimatum: "Unless you get at least X clients in and on the market over the next week, you're history." ' (Alexander Davidson, *The City Share Pushers*, 1989)

history books see CONSIGN TO THE HISTORY BOOKS

hit a (new) high (or **low**) The use of 'new high' or 'new low' comes from the language of the stock market. Shares were hitting new highs in the USA in the 1920s, and by 1937 this was being used metaphorically in the headline 'Nazi epithets at U.S. set a new high.'

'The gap between top and bottom pupils at secondary school is growing, this year's GCSE results showed yesterday. The top-grade pass rate hit a new high – but so did the failure rate.' (*Daily Mail*, 27 August 1998)

hit the buffers The buffers are there on the railway line to make sure the train comes to a full stop, hence 'to hit the buffers' means to reach the end of the track, to come to an end. Its history is not recorded, but it would appear to be a twentieth-century cliché.

'Annabel Croft's comeback trail hit the buffers yesterday when she lost 6-4, 7-5 to 11th seed Sarah Bentley.' (*Today*, 1992)

hit the ceiling SEE RAISE THE ROOF

hit the ground running An American cliché from the 1970s, the exact origin of this expression, meaning to act as quickly as possible, is disputed. It has variously been derived from Pony Express riders changing horses on the run, rodeo riders getting out of the way of bucking broncos, hoboes jumping off trains to avoid being caught, and paratroopers in the Second World War being on the move the moment they land.

'In short, after promising to hit the ground running, people wonder why the President has become the leader of the Slow Is Beautiful Movement.' (*Independent*, 5 October 1989)

hit the road Meaning either 'to set out to travel' or 'Beat it!', and also found in the form 'hit the trail', these expressions have been in use since the middle of the nineteenth century, particularly in the USA. 'Hit the road' became more widely known after Ray Charles had a hit with Harold Arlen and Johnny Mercer's song 'Hit the Road, Jack' in 1961.

'But even before that happens he does not rule out a return – once McCann has hit the road, of course.' (*Daily Mail*, 27 August 1998)

'It's just from the way it came out, I thought you meant you decided to jack it all in and hit the road.' (Michael Falk, *Part of the Furniture*, 1991)

hit the spot Hit the spot comes from target practice, where if you hit the central spot on the target, you are 'spot on' or 'on target'. The sense was transferred to just the thing to satisfy hunger or thirst in the nineteenth century in the USA. While to the British 'hit the spot' conjures up images of the world of P. G. Wodehouse or a genial pub, in the USA it is closely associated with an advertising jungle of the 1930s and 1940s – 'Pepsi-Cola hits the spot, twelve full ounces, that's a lot.'

'The coffee hit the spot, though, and I drank my way through the whole pot and threw in a couple of cigarettes for good measure.' (P. Chester, *Murder Forestalled*, 1990)

'She sees the publication as a kind of . . . way of expressing her own belief – that fame, success and money . . . do not "hit the spot".' (*You* magazine, 20 September 1998)

hit where it hurts While this is often used literally as an alternative for 'hit below the belt', it is also used in a metaphorical sense, either of emotional violence, or of making an impact in some other way.

'My reaction was to hit him where it hurts; you are not with someone for 27 years without knowing that.' (*Today*, 1992)

'I for one rapidly lost interest in the one-dimensional, monotonous rapping and the constant . . . polemic, to say nothing of the music, a nondescript blur of indie-danceisms which needs some offensive noise of the guitar or techno variety to really hit us where it hurts.' (*New Musical Express*, 1992)

hither and thither (or **yon**) Despite the near redundancy of using both 'hither' and 'thither', this expression has been recorded for as long as English has, the first instance being in an Old English gloss to a Latin text, dated to about AD 725. 'Hither and yon', which sounds rather fey to English ears, is the preferred form in the USA, and is also found in English dialect from the eighteenth century. Neither shows any sign of going out of fashion, despite their long histories.

'Other boys and girls were flitting hither and thither among the trees, singly, without a word or a sign of communication with one another.' (R. George Thomas, *Edward Thomas: A Portrait*, 1987)

'The scene was rather like a bull-fight, with Betty, small-eyed, blundering hither and yon dazzled by the whisk of scarlet, the glancing slippers of the matador.' (Alice T. Ellis, *Unexplained Laughter*, 1985)

hive of industry Bees have long been considered particularly hard-working and industrious creatures and we still talk of someone being 'busy as a bee'. Hives have been used figuratively to mean places swarming with busy occupants since the early seventeenth century, although the actual wording 'hive of industry' is not recorded before 1863.

'The kitchen then became a hive of industry, with the fat being cut up and rendered for lard, kept in a big earthenware pot.' (Hannah Hauxwell and Barry Cockcroft, *Seasons of My Life*, 1989)

hog see HIGH ON THE HOG

hoi polloi This term from the Greek meaning literally 'the many' is used to mean the majority or the masses. It is rarely flattering. The hypercorrect will tell you that it should never be used in the form 'the hoi polloi' since 'hoi' already means 'the', and to use both shows your ignorance. In fact, this is a twentieth-century worry, 'the hoi polloi' being standard in earlier uses. John Dryden is the first recorded user of the term in English, and he set the pattern and the tone for its use when he wrote, 'If by the people you understand the multitude, the hoi polloi, 'tis no matter what they think; they are sometimes in the right, sometimes in the wrong: their judgement is a mere lottery' (*Of Dramatick Poesie*, 1668).

hoist with your own petard 'For 'tis the sport to have the engineer/Hoist with his own petar', wrote Shakespeare in *Hamlet* (III.iv), as he prepares to turn the tables on Rosencrantz and Guildenstern. An engineer in this context is the equivalent of a sapper in the modern army, and a petard – which gets its name from the French word for to fart – is a primitive type of bomb or grenade, used to blow open city gates. Explosives were, in those days, even more unreliable than today, and fuses were likely to ignite a device as soon as touched, so it would be no rare thing to have an engineer blown up ('hoist') by his own petard as he tried to use it.

'The leader writer depicted the Minister of Education Florence Horsbrugh as having been "hoist with her own petard": if she had hoped that her Committee of Enquiry would recommend financial cuts she had been disappointed, for if anything the proposals made some increase in expenditure likely.' (G. J. White and V. Williams, *Adult Education and Social Purpose*, 1988)

hold a candle to see CAN'T HOLD A CANDLE TO

hold a mirror up to This is another expression which is taken from Shakespeare. When Hamlet instructs the actors visiting Elsinore how he wants them act their parts, he advises them 'to hold, as 'twere, the mirror up to nature; to show virtue her own feature, scorn her own image, and the very age and body of the time his form and pressure' (III.ii). Sometimes, however, the term is simply used as an elaborate way of saying 'reflect'.

'Holding a mirror up to the story, the film found itself in a position oddly similar to its subject, in which it, too, didn't know which voices to trust.' (*Independent*, 4 September 1998)

hold back the tide Legend tells us that King Canute of England (*c*.995–1035), tired of the outrageous flattery of his courtiers, tried to show them his own limitations and his awareness of them by demonstrating that he could not hold back the tide. Canute has been badly treated by popular culture, which refers to him as if he was really trying to contain the uncontainable and get the sea to obey him. The expression is sometimes found in the alliterative 'turn back the tide'.

'Serious Crimes Squad: you chaps are like Canute these days, trying to hold back the tide.' (W. J. Burley, *Wycliffe and the Cycle of Death*, 1991)

hold forth The Bible instructs Christians that they should go through the world 'Holding forth the word of life' (Philippians 2:16). From this 'to hold forth' came to be used for delivering a sermon or bearing witness to the Word of God. Since people who are sermonizing tend to speak both at length and somewhat obsessively, it is easy to see how the modern senses of 'to hold forth' developed. This had happened by the eighteenth century, but since 'hold forth' could still be used at the time for 'hold out, present', some rather incongruous uses, to the modern ear, can be found, such as Burns's 'In plain braid Scots hold forth a plain braid story' (*Brigs of Ayr*, 1787).

'A master of spontaneous oratory, Asimov could hold forth on almost any subject with brilliant lucidity.' (*Daily Telegraph*, 7 April 1992)

hold on for dear life see DEAR LIFE

hold the fort 'To hold the fort' means, of course, to keep it out of the enemy's hands, and this has been used figuratively for centuries – a writer in 1592, for instance, describing women as 'Having but ... weak feeble Hands To hold their Honour's Fort unvanquished.' In the nineteenth century, however, two things happened to boost the use of the phrase. First, during the American Civil War General Sherman signalled another general 'Hold the fort!' during a battle in 1864, and this became something of a catch-phrase in the USA. Then, a few years later, the great American hymn-writers and evangelists Moody and Sankey picked up the expression, and produced a popular hymn with the immortal lines, ' "Hold the fort, for I am coming," Jesus signals still;/Wave the answer back to heaven, "By thy grace we will." '

'Insurance policies, wise investments, sensible diets and burglar alarms: if only we can lay down enough of them, the reasoning goes, we can maybe hold the fort against the chaos that rages outside.' (*New Statesman and Society*, 1992)

hold your horses This expression, meaning to wait, calm down, developed in the first part of the nineteenth century in the USA. If the horses were not restrained, then they were liable to 'dash off'.

'Irritably ... McAllister turned off the gas ring, blew out the match, and walked to the front door, grumbling to herself, Hold your horses, I'm coming, I'm coming, when another urgent series of knocks sounded.' (Paula Marshall, *An American Princess*, 1993)

hold your own Originally a military expression, but now used to mean holding your position against competition or other forms of attack rather than against enemy soldiers, this has been in use since the sixteenth century.

'This was to be Boomer's last appearance in the Ryder Cup, although he was still quite clearly a good enough player to hold his own against the best of the Americans.' (*Independent*, 10 October 1989)

(left) holding the baby If you are left holding the baby, you are left with a burden that someone else should be sharing if not taking full responsibility for. The expression seems first to have developed in business circles at the start of the twentieth century, to describe someone left holding shares that cannot be sold at a profit.

'Shearson was left holding the baby when the music stopped after the buyout: J. H. Whitney Co., leading the buyout, had persuaded Shearson to put up a bridging loan, and that it would easily be able to sell much of it on; in the event, the junk bond market collapsed and no one wanted it.' (*Unigram x*, 1993)

hole in the head This expression, usually in the form 'I need that like a hole in the head', started as slang in the USA in the 1940s, and had reached the UK by the 1950s, although it did not become really popular until rather later. It may be Jewish-American in origin, as there is an identical Yiddish expression, used in the States, '*ich darf es vi a loch in kop*'. Marshall McLuhan was an early user, when he wrote in *The Mechanical Bride* in 1951, 'A smart operator needs a dame like he needs a hole in the head', and in 1959 *Hole in the Head* was used as a film title.

holier than thou In the Bible, Isaiah (65:5) attacks those who have the attitude 'Stand by thyself, come not near to me; for I am holier than thou.' 'Holier than thou' has been used since the middle of the nineteenth century to describe people who are unpleasantly sanctimonious, or, more commonly now, those who are *self-righteous* rather than righteous.

'So I'm . . . I don't want to sit here holier than thou, start preaching that . . . you know things are not going to happen, because we're all human and we all make errors.' ('Defensive driving techniques', Lecture/seminar (Business), recorded, 27 March 1993)

hollow tones 'Hollow' has been used to describe sounds which are insubstantial or sepulchral since the sixteenth century, but the set phrase 'hollow tones' seems only to have ben used since the late nineteenth century. It usually suggests a certain degree of self-pity in the speaker.

'His hollow tone and his ridiculously red, swollen up appearance, made me laugh.' (Nina Bawden, *A Woman of My Age*, 1991)

Holy Grail The ultimate quest for the Knights of the Round Table was to find the Holy Grail, usually described as the cup used by Christ at the Last Supper, or a container that caught His blood at the Crucifixion. The subject was a popular one in nineteenth-century literature, and by the end of that century the expression was being used to describe anything much sought-after or desired.

'The man responsible for the Mach3 is British engineer John Terry, who has been working with teams of boffins at Gillette's two shaving research centres . . . to develop this Holy Grail of a razor.' (*Stuff*, October 1998)

home see DON'T TRY THIS AT HOME; IN THE COMFORT OF YOUR OWN HOME

(own) home ground 'Home ground' was being used to describe the pitch on which a team regularly played by the beginning of the nineteenth century, but it does not seem to have been transferred to familiar territory or a place of origin until the middle of the twentieth century.

'Mr Mandelson confronted the unions on their own home ground, at the TUC annual conference in Blackpool.' (*Evening Standard*, 17 September 1998)

home is where the heart is This proverb was well established by the 1870s, and has been popular ever since.

'The campaign has all the hallmarks of the Buy British crusade of the Sixties: sure, go and have a peek, but when you're done gawping, remember your local town centre. Remember that home is where the heart is.' (*Independent*, 2 September 1998)

(into) the home straight (or **stretch**) The home straight or stretch (the usual term in the USA) is the part of a racecourse leading up to the finish. By the middle of the nineteenth century the expression was being used for the final part of an enterprise or journey, often with the implication that there is not much left to be done. Thus an American newspaper wrote in 1864, 'Already we see the slave States . . . on the home-stretch to become free.'

home sweet home This sentimental view of home comes from the title of a song in the opera *Clari, or The Maid of Milan* (1823) with words by J. H. Payne, and music by Henry R. Bishop. Although the opera has sunk into obscurity, this song is still widely known, along with its line 'Be it never so humble, there's no place like home.'

'This is familiar David Lynch territory: beneath the reassuringly kitschy exterior of "home sweet home" lies a potentially life-threatening world of violent urges and toxic substances.' (S. Townsend, *Women's Art*, 1993)

home to roost see COME HOME TO ROOST

homework see DOG ATE MY HOMEWORK

hone your skills Although the image of using a honing stone to sharpen something seems an ancient one, the expression appears, in fact, to be modern. Indeed, while the noun 'a hone' goes back to Old English, the *OED* does not record it as a verb until the nineteenth century, and has no record of figurative use.

'It gave me an opportunity to study the great comics like Tommy Cooper and Dave Allen, and to hone my skills as a singer with the band.' (Marti Caine, *A Coward's Chronicle*, 1990)

honeymoon is over 'Honeymoon' has been used in a transferred sense for a period of goodwill or especial friendliness since the sixteenth century, although the expression 'the honeymoon is over' seems to be a cliché of the twentieth century.

'Merchant bank Morgan Grenfell says the honeymoon is over and the implications for building societies could be serious.' (*Today*, 1992)

honours see DO THE HONOURS

hook, line and sinker A fish that takes not just the bait and its hook, but the line and sinker as well, swallows all the fisherman has put in the water. The expression developed in the USA in the 1830s, and is used to mean 'entirely, completely'.

hoops see JUMPING THROUGH HOOPS

hope against hope This expression for hoping that something you do not really believe will happen does happen is a pared-down version of the biblical 'Who against hope believed in hope that he might become the father of many nations' (Romans 4:18). It has been used since the beginning of the nineteenth century.

'All she could do was to keep vigilant, and to hope against hope that Matthew would soon tire of the old man.' (J. Cox, *Don't Cry Alone*, 1992)

hopes dashed The idea of having your hopes dashed – destroyed, brought to nothing – has been around since the mid-sixteenth century, and was enough of a set phrase by 1645 for a book to appear, with the title *Hopes Deferred & Dashed*.

'Walsall's Worthington Cup hopes were dashed by a Danny Maddix goal in extra time last night.' (*Daily Mail*, 27 August 1998)

horses see HOLD YOUR HORSES

horses for courses Different race horses run better under different conditions, so the knowledgeable will modify their choice of horse to suit each track and its conditions. The expression was in use in racing circles by the late nineteenth century, and was in use metaphorically by the middle of the twentieth.

'It's a question of horses for courses, finding the best route forward and adopting the practices to fit that, rather than bulldozing your way through without perhaps realising the wider environment in which this needs to work.' (*Guardian*, 20 December 1989)

host of friends This has been a set phrase since the late nineteenth century. If your many friends are famous, then they may become a GALAXY OF STARS.

'They have made a host of friends who will greatly miss them.' (*Harpers & Queen*, 1990)

a hot potato A 'hot potato' is something embarrassing or difficult to deal with, something you want to get rid of. The expression was well established by the middle of the nineteenth century, when it was often used in the form 'drop like a hot potato'. Nowadays it is often used as 'pass on like a hot potato' or qualified as in 'a political hot potato'. To understand the image we should probably think in terms of potatoes baked in their jackets, which were sold as street food in the nineteenth century, or ones baked in the ashes of a hot fire. This links 'hot potato' to the expression 'to pull someone's chestnuts out of the fire', which comes from the fable telling how a monkey tricked a cat into letting him use the cat's paw to rake hot chestnuts out of the ashes. This is also the origin of the term 'cat's-paw'.

'This "McDonaldisation" of the traditional pub – such an essential part of our national identity – is something of a cultural hot potato.' (*Stuff*, October 1998)

hotly contested A set phrase of sports reporting – things are rarely contested in any other way – this has been in use since at least the late nineteenth century.

'The range includes the 1.6 Lantra in the hotly contested Ford Escort category.' (*Farmers' Weekly*, 1991)

house on fire see LIKE A HOUSE ON FIRE

household name A compressed way of saying 'a name known in every household', this term goes back to the nineteenth century. An early use of it, which now sounds rather incongruous, is in Tennyson's dedication of his Arthurian poem sequence *Idylls of the King* to Prince Albert: 'A Prince indeed,/Beyond all titles, and a household name,/Hereafter, thro' all times, Albert the Good.' The expression may owe something to the earlier 'household words', used by Shakespeare in the speech made by the king before Agincourt in *Henry V*: 'Then shall our names,/Familiar in his mouth as household words,/. . . Be in their flowing cups freshly remember'd' (IV.iii), and chosen by Dickens as the title of a magazine he edited.

'[It is] sponsored for the second year by YOU, and organised in conjunction with the Soil Association. Judges there will include household names such as Sophie Grigson and Clarissa Dickson Wright.' (*You* magazine, 20 September 1998)

how are the mighty fallen This is a quotation cliché, from David's beautiful lament for the death of Saul and Jonathan: 'The beauty of Israel is slain upon thy high places: how are the mighty fallen! Tell it not in Gath, publish it not in the streets of Askelon, lest the daughters of the Philistines rejoice . . . I am distressed for thee, my brother Jonathan: very pleasant hast thou been unto me: thy love to me was wonderful, passing the love of women. How are the mighty fallen, and the weapons of war perished!' (2 Samuel 1:19–24). As a cliché it is usually used as a statement of grim satisfaction that someone has got their come-uppance, a sentiment expressed by that German vogue word SCHADENFREUDE.

how was it for you? A conscious cliché used to enquire about sexual satisfaction, but rarely used seriously now. It is a companion cliché to 'DID THE EARTH MOVE FOR YOU?', and is not recorded before the second half of the twentieth century.

hue and cry Hue and cry has existed as a legal phrase since the thirteenth century, used to mean an outcry raised while hunting a criminal. It literally means 'noise and cry'. By the nineteenth century it was being used metaphorically, and nowadays is sometimes diluted from 'outcry' to mean little more than 'fuss'.

'Milosevic must be pretty confident that nothing much will come of the hue and cry over his latest atrocities in Kosovo, and that he has got away with it yet again.' (*Evening Standard*, 7 October 1998)

'No, let me – if I don't clean the place up there'll be a hue and cry.' (Celia Brayfield, *The Prince*, 1990)

humble abode A set phrase, 'abode' rarely being used otherwise. It is often used ironically or as a form of humorous modesty.

'I wonder, when you're allowed out of here if you'd like to come to my humble abode to recuperate?' (Pamela Street, *Guilty Parties*, 1990)

hundred and ten per cent SEE ONE HUNDRED AND TEN PER CENT

you always hurt the one you love This cliché comes from the title of a song written by Allan Roberts and Doris Fisher in 1944. Oscar Wilde's earlier 'Yet each man kills the thing he loves' (*Ballad of Reading Gaol*, 1898) probably lies behind it.

if it isn't hurting, it isn't working SEE NO PAIN, NO GAIN

I didn't get where I am today by . . . This was already a well-established cliché when it was given a new set of associations by its use by the pompous boss, C.J., in the enormously popular television series *The Fall and Rise of Reginald Perrin* (1976–80), written by David Nobbs, and based on his 1975 book *The Death of Reginald Perrin*.

'Mr Blair is perfectly happy ignoring large sections of his own party. Indeed, he got where he is today precisely by doing this.' (*Independent*, 22 September 1998)

I don't believe it Thanks to the success of the television series *One Foot in the Grave* (written by David Renwick, first shown in 1990) this has become a catch-phrase cliché. It is the outraged cry of the lead character, Victor Meldrew, played by Richard Wilson, as he finds yet something else to complain about.

I'll be back A catch-phrase cliché and quotation, used as a threat by the Terminator (played by Arnold Schwarzenegger) in the 1984 film *The Terminator* and its 1991 sequel *Terminator 2*. The latter is also the source of another catch-phrase cliché, 'Hasta la vista, baby'.

I'll drink to that see DRINK TO THAT

I've started so I'll finish see STARTED SO I'LL FINISH

icon the use of the word 'icon' to mean someone admired and seen as a symbol of a particular group or trend is a late twentieth-century development. It is often used loosely, just to mean someone popular, and is also common in combinations such as 'fashion icon' or 'gay icon'.

'At 30, the Canadian singer-songwriter is a lesbian icon, a country-and-western iconoclast and a Grammy award-winning performer.' (*New Statesman and Society*, 1992)

icy grip of . . . A journalistic cliché since the late nineteenth century, icy grips are usually those of fear or winter.

'Though my whole inside felt as if clutched in an icy grip, I had gone too far to retreat.' (Jack Caplan, *Memories of the Gorbals*, 1991)

'Mr Pourchet, a glaciologist from the University of Grenoble, devised a scheme to prise micrometeorites from the continent's icy grip using hot water and careful filtration.' (*The Economist*, 1991)

Ides of March see DIE IS CAST

if it ain't broke, don't (or **why**) **fix it** Bert Lance, US President Jimmy Carter's Director of the Office of Management was reported as saying 'If it ain't broke, don't fix it' when asked about government reorganization in 1977. Whether or not the saying originated with him, his use of it caught the public imagination at the time, and it rapidly became a catch-phrase cliché, although the grammar is sometimes tidied up.

'I'm just an ordinary middle-of-the road liberal, who believes British universities as they were 10–20 years ago weren't broke (other than financially), so why fix them?' (*Independent*, 23 July 1998)

if push comes to show see PUSH COMES TO SHOVE

if the cap fits 'If the cap fits, wear it' has been around since at least the early eighteenth century, and is probably older. A work of 1600 called *Pasquil's Fools-Cap* with the passage 'Where you finde a head fit for this Cappe, either bestowe it upon him in charity, or send him where he may have them for his money' suggests that the expression was known then, and also reminds us that the cap to be worn is a dunce's cap. In America this saying is more likely to be found in the form 'If the shoe fits . . .' or even, perhaps under the influence of the Cinderella story, 'If the slipper fits . . .'

'Anyway, I'd always believed great minds thought alike, until I found out that

SEGA FORCE's Paul "if the cap fits, it's a miracle" Mellerick supports Leicester too!'
(*Zzap 64!*, 1992)

if you can remember it, you weren't there see REMEMBER IT

if you can't be good, be careful see DON'T DO ANYTHING I WOULDN'T DO

if you can't beat them see BEAT THEM

if you can't stand the heat see STAND THE HEAT

if you've got it, flaunt it 'When you got it' flaunt it, is one of the earliest uses
of this expression. It occurs in the 1968 Mel Brooks film *The Producers*, and is possibly
the origin of it, at least as a popular expression. It is particularly, but not invariably,
used of physical assets.
   ' "If you've got it, flaunt it," thought Julia, when the long shapely high-heeled
legs flashed into even more prominence as the girl seated herself eighteen inches
away.' (Barbara Whitehead, *The Dean it Was that Died*, 1991)

ignorance is bliss 'Where ignorance is bliss/'Tis folly to be wise' wrote Thomas
Gray in his *Ode on a Distant Prospect of Eton College* (1742). In the poem the blissful
ignorance is of the future lying in store for the schoolboys, of whom he has already
said, 'Alas, regardless of their doom,/the little victims play!/No sense have they of
ills to come,/Nor care beyond to-day.' This had developed into the expressions
'blissfully ignorant' and 'blissful ignorance' by the late nineteenth century.
   'This is the stage where ignorance is bliss, when it looks easy and you don't realise
how much there is to it.' (Peter Honey, *Improve your People Skills*, 1992)

the same ilk, of that ilk This expression comes from the world of heraldry and
the aristocracy. In Scotland in particular the surname or title of a landholder is often
the same as the name of the land he holds. 'Ilk' means 'same' and 'of that ilk' is used
to avoid repetition of title and name, so that 'Sir Iain Moncreiffe of that Ilk' is a
handier, more elegant way of saying 'Sir Iain Moncreiffe of Moncreiffe'. However,
since the late eighteenth century 'that ilk' has been understood to mean 'kind, sort,
set' and used in a general way, despite the fact that 'the same ilk' is technically a
repetition.
   'In days of yore I worked on a gossip column. Back then there was no worthier
day's toil than "linking" some B-list celeb with another of the same ilk.' (*Evening
Standard*, 1 September 1998)

ill-gotten gains This is all that is left in general use of a proverb that ran 'Ill-gotten
gains never prosper.' This first appeared in English in 1519 in the form 'Evil gotten
riches will never prove long', and Shakespeare has it in the form, 'Didst thou never
hear/That things ill got had ever bad success' (Henry VI, part 3, II.ii). 'Ill-gotten
gains' had become separated from their proverb by the late seventeenth century,
and were a cliché by the nineteenth.
   'Energetic international regulation of banking and tax laws, making it impossible
for the mafiosi to launder their ill-gotten gains, would quickly destroy the Mafia and
with it the myth of an irrepressible global conspiracy.' (*The Economist*, 1990)

it's an ill wind . . . 'It's an ill wind that blows no one any good' has been established
in English since at least 1546 when it appeared in John Heywood's collection of

proverbs. The image is originally from sailing, but it has long lost any connection with the sea.

'The ill wind that blew one of the pre-tournament favourites out of the Selborne Salver sent a breath of good fortune over Mark Treleaven at a sun-drenched Blackmoor Golf Club on Saturday.' (*Alton Herald*, 1992)

impish grin Used to conjure up the image of a mischievous urchin, this set phrase has been in use since at least the middle of the nineteenth century.

'Meredith pointed at the third child, a pretty little girl with dark hair and an engaging, impish grin.' (Ann Granger, *A Season for Murder*, 1991)

implicit confidence A set phrase that now has a rather old-fashioned ring to it, this has been a cliché since the mid-nineteenth century. It has always been slightly ambiguous as a form of praise, for although 'implicit' has long been used to mean 'unreserved', it is also the opposite of 'explicit'.

'I then pointed out to him that I strongly deprecated a dissolution at this moment as I had implicit confidence in him and in the Conservative Party now in power.' (Rodney Brazier, *Constitutional Texts*, 1990)

in a real sense See REAL SENSE

in days of yore See DAYS OF YORE

in disguise See BLESSING IN DISGUISE

in extremis In Latin this literally means 'in the furthest reaches'. In English it is used to mean 'at the point of death', or, when it qualifies as a cliché, 'in an extremely difficult situation', or 'ultimately'. This latter sense is a twentieth-century development.

'Really, all this is no joke. It has created stress beyond measure . . . In extremis there have been suicides, nervous breakdowns, medical retirements. At best, many academics have adjusted to – even internalized – a mode of functioning where means replace ends.' (*Independent*, 23 July 1998)

in for a tough time See TOUGH TIME

in harness See DIE IN HARNESS

in the best possible taste See ALL DONE IN THE BEST POSSIBLE TASTE

in the cold See LEAVE OUT IN THE COLD

in the final analysis See FINAL ANALYSIS

in the heat of the moment See HEAT OF THE MOMENT

in the hole See ACE UP YOUR SLEEVE

in the land of the living See LAND OF THE LIVING

in the loop See LOOP

in the lurch See LEAVE IN THE LURCH

in the midst of An archaism and set phrase, 'midst' being otherwise unused outside poetry. The expression is a medieval one, although best known from the Burial of the Dead in the 1664 Book of Common Prayer: 'In the midst of life we are in death.'

As used in modern English it means the same as 'in the middle of', or even just 'in'.

'Does money provide our lives with a tragic subtext, a realisation that we will never have enough; that we will always be restless in the midst of abundance?' (*Mail on Sunday*, 20 September 1998)

in the picture see PUT IN THE PICTURE

in the post see CHEQUE IN THE POST

in the right place see HEART IN THE RIGHT PLACE

in the running see OUT OF THE RUNNING

in the throes of see THROES

in this day and age see DAY AND AGE

in three parts see DIVIDED INTO THREE PARTS

in your court see BALL IS IN YOUR COURT

in your cups This has been a cliché in English since the early seventeenth century, and the same image was well used by the Romans before. Nowadays, when 'cup' has been so totally replaced by 'glass' where alcoholic drink is concerned, it has something of the ring of a euphemism.

'Also she knew Shill to be a toper and, when in his cups, a man of violence.' (Roger Long, *Murder in Old Berkshire*, 1990)

in-your-face This expression, for behaviour which is aggressive or cannot be ignored, has only been in use since the 1970s, but has spread rapidly.

'I loved rap when it was raw and in-yer-face.' (*Stuff*, October 1998)

'Frankly, even in-yer-face Trotskyism, or a lengthy Helen Brinton disquisition on the Third Way, is preferable to this shifty vacuity.' (*Independent*, 29 September 1998)

in your own backyard see OWN BACKYARD

industrial action Famous for meaning the opposite of its surface meaning, 'industrial action' usually involves not doing what you would normally do. It was in regular use by the 1970s, the idea of collective action by the workers in an industry having somehow been compressed into 'industrial action'.

'FIgures yesterday also showed the number of industrial stoppages to be the lowest since 1929, and the number of working days lost by industrial action – 800,000 in the year to the end of March – was the lowest since records began 100 years ago.' (*Daily Telegraph*, 17 April 1992)

innate conservatism The history of this set phrase is not known, but it has been widely used in the twentieth century as a polite way of implying stubborn resistance to change.

'There is, indeed, much evidence to support such a view, especially on the corrosive effects of overmanning on productivity; practices which spring from fusion of innate conservatism and the creed of job protection.' (B. W. E. Alford, *British Economic Performance 1945–1975*, 1993)

inner man In the New Testament, St Paul says that Christ 'would grant you, according to the riches of his glory, to be strengthened with might by his Spirit in the inner man' (Ephesians 3:16). The expression has been used of the soul, mind or spiritual part of man since about the year 1000, but has also been used humorously to mean the stomach since the late eighteenth century.

'Left alone in solitary splendour, I could see them crouched behind the car, the flash of a hip-flask indicating that inner man and inner woman were being warmed.' (Bruce Sandison, *Tales of the Loch*, 1990)

ins and outs Although this is found from the late seventeenth century, it did not really become established until the nineteenth. The image is of the intricacies of the situation being similar to the twists and turns of a winding path.

'For the purposes of our argument here, it is not necessary to understand all the ins and outs of these various schemes, nor to grasp the increasingly complex rules of the centre invented to limit them.' (James Anderson and Allan Cochrane (eds), *Politics in Transition*, 1989)

inside track This is an image from horse-racing, where the inside track is the lane on the inside of a curve, which, being shorter, gives you an advantage if you can keep to it. Both literal and transferred uses of the expression, meaning having inside knowledge, developed in the USA in the mid-nineteenth century.

'Of course, radio and TV would be ahead of him with the broad outlines, but he knew he had an inside track.' (Frederick Forsyth, *The Deceiver*, 1992)

insult to injury see ADD INSULT TO INJURY

intents and purposes see ALL INTENTS AND PURPOSES

as interesting as watching paint dry A fairly recent simile which over-use has taken rapidly from the entertaining to the clichéd.

'I think Al Gore is about as interesting as watching paint dry.' (Lawrence Eagleberger, former President Bush aide, on possible successors to President Clinton, August 1998)

into every life a little rain must fall see LITTLE RAIN MUST FALL

into the home straight see HOME STRAIGHT

invidious see COMPARISONS ARE ODIOUS

iron fist (or **hand**) **in the velvet glove** The iron hand as a symbol of powerful control is found from the early 1700s (the iron fist appears in 1740), but Thomas Carlyle attributes the coining of the expression 'the iron hand in a velvet glove', to mean autocratic rule beneath a softer exterior, to Napoleon, although it has also been attributed to other, earlier, rulers. The expression is highly variable, 'iron fist' being as common as 'iron hand' and other variants including 'steel fist', 'MAILED FIST' and 'silk glove'.

'This theology slipped over the iron hand of the capitalist market like a silk glove.' (*New Statesman and Society*, 1992)

'The second is based on a latter day philanthropy, which, like its nineteenth-century antecedent, muffles the iron fist of control in the velvet glove of sentiment.' (Tom Lovett, *Radical Approaches to Adult Education: A Reader*, 1988)

irons in the fire If you have several irons in the fire you have several courses of action open to you; if you have too many, you have taken on more than you can manage; and if you put all your irons in the fire you are trying every possible course of action. All these come from the blacksmith and the pieces of iron he has heating in his forge before he works on them. The image has been in use since the mid-sixteenth century.

'Others have interpreted it as tactical manoeuvring, a manifestation of his habitual tendency to have two or more irons in the fire.' (Andrew Shennan, *De Gaulle*, 1993)

isn't broken why fix it see IF IT AIN'T BROKE

it was a dark and stormy night see DARK AND STORMY NIGHT

it was the best of times see BEST OF TIMES

it will all end in tears see END IN TEARS

it's a dog's life see DOG'S LIFE

it's an ill wind see ILL WIND

it's not for me see NOT FOR ME

ivory tower A tower of ivory is an ancient image. 'Thy neck is as a tower of ivory' appears in the Bible (Song of Solomon 7:4), and this became a standard image of beauty in medieval literature – Chaucer, for instance, uses it of the heroine of his *Book of the Duchess* – as well as being used of the Virgin Mary. However, the image associated with an ivory tower changed radically after 1837. Sainte-Beuve used it to describe the French poet Alfred de Vigny 'in his ivory tower', and the phrase changed to mean a privileged seclusion, sheltered from the realities of the harsh world outside. This is now used particularly of academics, perhaps under the influence of some loose association with 'dreaming spires', a description of Oxford by Matthew Arnold in his 1866 poem *Thyrsis*.

'There is a widespread feeling in the country that universities are "ivory tower" institutions, whose staff are ignorant of the realities of the modern commercial world.' (David Lodge, *Nice Work*, 1988)

jam tomorrow This is a quotation cliché, used to indicate something good that is unlikely actually to happen, PIE IN THE SKY. The full quotation is, 'The rule is jam tomorrow and jam yesterday – but never jam today', which comes from *Through the Looking Glass* by Lewis Carroll (1872). However, it is rarely used in full.

'Mr Lamont forecasts that the economy will be growing at the rate of three per cent per year in 12 months' time; he would have carried more conviction, if he had not made the same "jam tomorrow" forecast a year ago.' (*East Anglian Daily Times*, 1993)

jaundiced eye (or **view**) Webster wrote in his 1612 play *The White Devil*, 'They that have the yellow jaundice think all objects they look on to be yellow.' By the late eighteenth century this idea of jaundiced sight being different from the norm was beginning to be detached from the idea of the actual disease, and so the idea of looking at life with a jaundiced eye, or having a jaundiced view of life, came to mean to be cynical, resentful or bitter.

'Standing apart from these films is Lindsay Anderson's feature début, *This Sporting Life* (1963), where the director's jaundiced view of the world seeps into every frame of the film.' (James Park, *British Cinema: The Lights that Failed*, 1990)

je ne sais quoi This French expression, literally 'I don't know what', has been a clichéd way of expressing an indefinable quality, that special extra something, since about the 1880s. Nowadays it sounds rather dated, and is associated with affectation of the 'Pretentious, moi?' (a quote from the TV comedy *Fawlty Towers*) sort.

Jekyll and Hyde In the original novel, *The Strange Case of Dr Jekyll and Mr Hyde* (1886) by Robert Louis Stevenson, Dr Jekyll was a benign doctor and researcher who discovered a potion that could change him physically and mentally into someone he called Mr Hyde who expressed all the evil impulses Jekyll had suppressed. With time the change became irreversible. It took only a year or two for these names to be taken up to describe someone with conflicting characteristics. Modern use is becoming detached from the details of the story, and it is now being used more and more loosely to describe any kind of conflicting trend.

'The insider/anthropologist is therefore somewhat schizophrenic, something of a Jekyll and Hyde, for he knows that publication and explication might be career-suicidal but are necessary intellectual tasks.' (Malcolm Young, *An Inside Job*, 1991)

jewel in the crown This is an old phrase for the finest part of something, its CROWNING GLORY, in use since at least the eighteenth century. It became a common-place of Victorian Britain to describe the colonies, particular India, as the jewel in the crown of the Empire. It was this use that Paul Scott picked up when he called the first of his Raj Quartet novels *The Jewel in the Crown* (1966). Modern use of this cliché really took off after these novels were televised in 1984 under the title of the first one.

'The architectural commentator Lucinda Lambton lauded the Victorian gents on Rothersay Pier, on the Isle of Bute, as "jewels in the sanitarian's crown".' (*Independent*, 5 September 1998)

piece together a jigsaw (or **pieces of the jigsaw**) The jigsaw puzzle was not invented until the beginning of the twentieth century, but by the middle of the century the metaphorical use, for information that had to be assembled before something could be understood, was already well established. The idea is expressed in a number of different ways, and is becoming increasingly common.

'One paragraph in Mr de Klerk's statement on Tuesday announcing the release of Mr Mandela's old associate Walter Sisulu provided the final piece of the jigsaw.' (*Independent*, 12 October 1998)

jobs for the boys This expression for giving appointments to your friends or contacts – cronyism is the current vogue-word for it – was well established by the middle of the twentieth century.

'The use of it was scarcely unprecedented: "jobs for the boys", Tory MPs had cried as Harold Wilson infiltrated another trades union general secretary or a congenial academic on to the board of one or another of the great national institutions in his gift.' (Jeremy Paxman, *Friends in High Places*, 1990)

jobsworth see JUST DOING MY JOB

join the club This is a colloquial cliché, used to indicate sympathy and fellow-feeling or as a sardonic comment, when someone has described a problem or made a complaint. It has been in common use on both sides of the Atlantic since the 1940s.

joking apart see NO JOKE

jot or tittle This expression for 'the least bit' comes from the Bible, where Jesus says: 'Till heaven and earth pass, one jot or tittle shall in no wise pass from the law, till all be fulfilled' (Matthew 5:18). The expression has been in use since the Middle Ages, although it was mainly restricted to religious contexts until the sixteenth century. 'Jot' is the old form of the word 'iota', the Greek letter 'i', and 'tittle' is an old word for an accent or mark such as the dot over the 'i'.

'Just as under Mrs Thatcher, the crucial choices were decided in small committees: although there were open discussions at full cabinet meetings during March, there is no evidence that they changed a jot or tittle of the tax.' (*The Economist*, 1991)

the joy of . . . A cliché of headlines and book titles derived from *The Joy of Sex*, the title of a bestselling 1972 book by Alex Comfort. He in turn based the title on earlier instructional books such as *The Joy of Cooking* (1932).

'Joy of sex can help conception.' (Headline, *Independent*, 9 September 1998)

joy unconfined SEE LET JOY BE UNCONFINED

jump on the bandwagon SEE BANDWAGON

jumping through hoops The image here is of performing animals doing tricks. Such an act is first recorded in English in the late eighteenth century, but the expression's use to describe having to do something difficult or complicated to get what you want is from the early twentieth century.

'I'd dearly like to see a time-budgeting study of British academics. I bet it would show that most now spend more time filling in forms, jumping through hoops, and generally dodging the slings and arrows of outrageous quangos, than in actually doing their jobs.' (*Independent*, 23 July 1998)

blackboard, asphalt or **concrete jungle/it's a jungle out there** 'Jungle' was established as a term applied to something non-vegetable by 1859 when Thomas Carlyle writes of a 'jungle of redtape'. The concept of the 'law of the jungle' was established by Kipling in *The Jungle Book* of 1894. By the first decade of the twentieth century, 'jungle' had been given an urban context as a place where the homeless lived. 'Asphalt jungle' for the city as a jungle dates from 1920, but was made better known when W. R. Burnett used it for a book title in 1949. 'Blackboard jungle' became a well known expression for a difficult or out of control school when it was used as the title of a film in 1955, based on the novel of the same title by Evan Hunter, published the previous year. The popularity of 'concrete jungle' also comes from film, having been used as the American title of a 1960 British film released in the UK as *The Criminal*. These expressions have also been the source of many journalistic formula phrases.

the jury's out When a jury is out it has not yet reached a decision, so no verdict has been given. As a cliché this is a recent expression, dating only from the 1980s.

'The jury is out on whether the Government is ushering in a new golden age of private railways or whether, in the words of one of its sworn enemies – Jimmy Knapp, the RMT transport union leader – rail privatisation will turn out to be "the poll tax of the nineties".' (*Accountancy*, 1992)

just deserts 'Deserts', in the sense 'what you deserve', is obsolete, except in this set phrase, outside the world of hymns (such as the translation of St Francis Xavier's Latin hymn that starts in English, 'My God, I love thee: not because I hope for heaven thereby', which has the lines, 'But all this not for my desert, But for his holy name'). It does not seem to have been used before the twentieth century, but its history is obscure.

'The inevitable short drop resulted in strangulation, and many of those responsible received their just deserts, albeit with a more merciful long drop, after the Nuremberg War Trials.' (Geoffrey Abbott, *Lords of the Scaffold*, 1991)

just doing my job/jobsworth 'Just doing my job' is a twentieth-century cliché, used to justify actions, or stonewall objections to a lack of co-operation. One step up from this is the dreaded 'It's more than my job's worth to . . .' which has given rise to that useful insult 'a jobsworth', for the sort of person who uses it.

'Dorothy explained that . . . she was here as a reporter for a journal whose name they knew; her membership of the feminist abortion campaign to which PopCon had just made a large grant was irrelevant to the present discussion; she was just doing her job.' (M. Wandor *et al.*, *Tales I tell my Mother*, 1978)

'I wish therefore to nominate this uniformed halfwit for a Jobsworth Award (First Class).' (*Guitarist*, 1992)

just for the record This is a filler cliché, often no more than a verbal tic, there being no change in the meaning of a sentence if it is removed. It has been common since the 1950s.

'Just for the record, the picture was taken with a Nikon F4, fitted with a 600mm lens and a ×2 converter, on a tripod.' (*Today*, 1992)

just good friends Often a conscious cliché, although still used straight to signal the fact that the speaker wants a relationship to be seen as non-sexual. It is used particularly by journalists about the relationships of celebrities.

'We were "just good friends", however much I wished we could be more than that.' (James Kirkup, *A Poet Could Not But be Gay*, 1992)

'She was making these excuses that they were just good friends, and all she did was his typing.' (*Today*, 1992)

just one of those things A cliché used to show philosophical acceptance of the inevitable. It became popular in the 1930s and got a tremendous boost from the Cole Porter song 'Just One of those Things' (written in 1935, but not a big hit until 1941). The song's popularity was assured by its being used in at least six films.

' "It is just one of those things," said Adams, attempting to shrug off the ultimate disappointment for a jump jockey.' (*Daily Telegraph*, 6 April 1992)

just the job This expression for just what is needed was Forces' slang in the 1930s, and had spread to the general population by the 1950s.

'A bit of companionship with fellow climbers and walkers is just the job at the end of a hard day.' (Muriel Gray, *The First Fifty*, 1991)

keep an eye on the ball SEE ON THE BALL

keep (someone) posted This is an Americanism from the first half of the nineteenth century, originally in the form 'posted up'. It comes from accounting where you 'post' a figure into the accounts and 'post up' the books to bring them up to date. If someone is kept posted they are therefore supplied with the latest figures or information.

'I told Bernard to infiltrate the team so that he can keep us posted on their movements.' (Alastair MacNeill, *Time of the Assassins*, 1992)

keep the wolf from the door Wolves have long been associated with hunger – 'ravening' is almost only used of wolves – and 'to keep the wolf from the door' originally meant to keep starvation away, although it is used more generally now. The expression is found as early as 1470 in the image of warding off the wolf from the gate, and by the middle of the next century is found in the form we now use.

'No sign of any more money than is needed to keep the wolf from the door.' (Ruth Rendell, *The Best Man to Die*, 1981)

keep your head above water This expression, like to GRASP AT STRAWS, uses the image of a drowning person struggling to survive. It has been used of someone threatened with being drowned by their debts or other financial worries since the early eighteenth century, but its use for someone at risk of being overwhelmed by work or responsibilities is more recent.

'With the economy in the doldrums and the Pound struggling to keep its head above water, it was no time for Terry to splash out a couple of hundred quid beside the seaside.' (*Daily Mirror*, 1992)

keep your nose clean An expression which has been in use since the late nineteenth century, this is the opposite of 'poking your nose into other people's business', or getting into trouble by 'nosing around' to see what is going on.

'What I know of Moscow is that you keep your nose clean and do the work you've set out to achieve, and that way there's no hassle.' (Gerald Seymour, *Archangel*, 1983)

keep your shirt on In the days when the ordinary men had but two shirts, if that, he would strip his precious shirt off as well as his jacket before getting into a fight. Thus stripping off would be a sign of being ready to fight. Thus, 'to keep your shirt on' meant staying calm and avoiding a fight. It is first recorded in the USA in George W. Harris's 1854 book *Spirit of the Times*: 'I say, you durned ash cats, just keep yer shirts on, will ye?' 'Keep your hair on', perhaps a humorous development of this, dates from the 1880s.

keynote speech (or **statement**) A keynote is the note which determined the key of a musical piece. It has been used for the main idea of something, something that 'sets the tone', since the later eighteenth century, but expressions such as 'keynote speech' date from US politics in the early twentieth century. It has become very common in recent years.

'Sinn Fein's statement yesterday was issued by its press centre in Belfast on a single page headed "Keynote statement from Gerry Adams MP".' (*Independent*, 2 September 1998)

'A photograph on the front page of *The Sun* newspaper claiming to show three Labour Party delegates asleep during Neil Kinnock's keynote speech was criticised yesterday.' (*Independent*, 5 October 1989)

kick against the pricks Surprisingly, this expression comes from the Bible, from the passage in the Acts of the Apostles (9:5) when Saul, on his way to Damascus to persecute the Christians, has a vision of Jesus and converts to Christianity, becoming St Paul. In his vision 'The Lord said, I am Jesus whom thou persecutest: it is hard for thee to kick against the pricks.' The image here is of a horse that rebels when it feels the pricking of spurs, or the oxen the goad. Something very similar is also found in the second-century BC Roman playwright Terence. The expression originally meant resisting authority to your own harm, but nowadays it is used more generally, to mean to be recalcitrant, rebellious, or just plain bolshy – often with a play on the term 'prick' as an insult.

'Frank Field's apparent desire to speak the unspeakable on welfare reform is not the first time he had kicked against the pricks in his party.' (*Private Eye*, 21 August 1998)

kick butt (or **ass**) Currently very popular, these Americanisms are felt to be more vigorous than the English equivalent of a 'kick in the arse'.

'Ride down to Brands Hatch and Donington next year to watch Aprilia's race versions of the RSV kicking butt in the World Superbike Championships.' (*Stuff*, October 1998)

'The model for the mad air force generals of Dr Strangelove are widely believed to be the cigar-chomping, ass-kicking Curtis E. LeMay and the steely-eyed Thomas Power, who ran America's nuclear bomber force from 1948–57 and 1957–63 respectively.' (*Independent*, 8 September 1998)

(give someone a) kick in (or **up**) **the pants** This is a more polite version of a kick in the backside or the more emphatic kick in the arse (see above). It has been well established since the 1930s both in the literal and metaphorical sense.

'The Mall is doing the North-west the world of good. It's given councillors, businessmen and town centre managers the kick up the pants that they've deserved for years.' (*Independent*, 2 September 1998)

kick in the teeth While a KICK IN THE PANTS may make you pull your socks up, a kick in the teeth is purely negative. A more emphatic version of a slap in the face, it seems to be a fairly recent expression, not recorded until the 1970s. Some uses may be a polite version of a kick in the pants, but the main idea is likely to come from the fact that the teeth are one of the places you can 'kick a man when he is down'.

'Pam Carless, 46, an employee for nearly 30 years, said "There are a lot of people in tears in the factory – we just stopped work as soon as we heard the news. We have given our working lives to Yardley and now it feels as if we've been kicked in the teeth." ' (*Daily Mail*, 27 August 1998)

kick into touch In rugby, when the ball is kicked into touch, it is out of play, and the game is temporarily suspended. Thus it has come in recent years to mean to postpone, shelve or get rid of a problem.

'US manufacturer GT reckons it has finally kicked the old bumpy suspension, "rides like a pogostick" reputation into touch.' (*Stuff*, October 1998)

kicking and screaming (**into the twentieth century**) 'The Republican Party has to be dragged kicking and screaming into the twentieth century' is a saying attributed to the American politician Adlai Stevenson (1900–65). This popularized the expression, but with the approach of the millennium the expression has necessarily become variable.

'The old-style Selfridges, being pushed grunting and sweating into the twenty-first century, is represented by two in-house, middle-aged female detectives who, in between fags, puff down the street after suspected shoplifters.' (*Evening Standard*, 1 September 1998)

'The next morning I was a day older, no wiser and put in a bad mood right from the off because I was dragged from the Land of Nod kicking and screaming (well, grunting and stumbling actually) by the Celtic Twilight hammering on my door.' (Mike Ripley, *Angel Hunt*, 1991)

kid gloves see HANDLE WITH KID GLOVES

kill or cure This harks back to the early days of medicine, not entirely gone, when treatment could be as dangerous as the disease. The expression was in regular use in the eighteenth century, and a cliché by the nineteenth.

'The spring Budget, therefore, will be kill or cure.' (*Today*, 1992)

kill with kindness The best-known source of this expression is Shakespeare's *Taming of the Shrew* (IV.i) when Petruchio says, 'This is the way to kill a wife with kindness.' However, Shakespeare was using an already well established saying, in its full form 'to kill with kindness as fond apes do their young', a reference to the belief that apes could literally hug their young to death. Although this sounds like a companion saying to the biblical proverb 'Spare the rod and spoil the child', it is in fact usually used of adults and in kinder, domestic situations, rather than of the more abstract principles of upbringing.

killer instinct A sporting cliché, in use since at least the 1930s as a dramatic alternative to 'a determination to win'.

'He decided that the only way to become the best team in the world was to adopt a killer instinct; to play fairly and sportingly, but to be tough and uncompromising.' (Gerry Cotter, *England versus West Indies*, 1991)

killing fields This expression for a place of mass execution came to public notice through the 1984 film about genocide in Cambodia called *The Killing Fields*. The story of an American journalist caught up in the horror of events under the Khmer Rouge in the 1970s, it was written by Bruce Robinson, based on a newspaper article by Sidney Schanberg about his experiences in Cambodia. The actual title was taken from a comment about that country made by an American diplomat in 1980. The impact of the film was very powerful, and the expression rapidly passed into the language, although its meaning has now been diluted in some uses.

'The republic saw brutal ethnic violence in the Second World War, when its wooded hills and lush valleys were transformed into killing fields.' (*Daily Telegraph*, 7 April 1992)

'Celtic farmed him out to Blantyre Celtic to toughen him up and it was in the killing fields of Blantyre that he won his first honour, a Scottish Junior cap.' (Stuart Cosgrove, *Hampden Babylon*, 1991)

kindred spirit A quotation cliché, although not generally recognized as one. In his *Elegy Written in a Country Churchyard* (1751), after he has mused over the poor who are buried in the churchyard, Thomas Gray imagines Nature speaking to him of what may happen when he dies, and what may be said, 'If chance, by lonely contemplation led,/Some kindred spirit shall inquire thy fate.' The expression was picked up over half a century later by John Keats, who wrote in 1817 in his *O Solitude! If I Must with Thee Dwell*, 'and it sure must be/Almost the highest bliss of human-kind,/When to thy haunts two kindred spirits flee.'

'She recognised him as a kindred spirit, with the same happy-go-lucky, questing attitude to life which she herself possessed.' (Margaret Sunley, *Fields in the Sun*, 1991)

king's ransom This expression appears to go back at least to the 1530s, when the proverb 'A peck of March dust is worth a king's ransom' is first recorded. It is one of many country proverbs dealing with the importance of a dry March, and is said still to be current.

'Of course, the truth about how he has done it will probably only emerge in a ghosted autobiography that will cost some newspaper a king's ransom.' (*Today*, 1992)

kiss and tell Although this is a modern journalistic cliché, which has developed the variant 'kiss and sell' from the large amounts of money that have been made from selling salacious information to the media, the actual expression is an old one. In his *Burlesque* of 1675 Charles Cotton wrote, 'And if he needs must kiss and tell,/ I'll kick him headlong into Hell', and a few years later Congreve was writing, 'Oh fie Miss, you must not kiss and tell' (*Love for Love*, 1695).

'The kiss-and-tell industry, consolidated as a multi-million-dollar vested interest, setting its own standards, at the same time both nurturing and pandering to the public appetite.' (*Evening Standard*, 15 September 1998)

kiss of death This expression is usually linked to the Judas kiss, the kiss Judas Iscariot gave to Jesus to identify him to the officials who had come to arrest him. However, the expression is not recorded in the *OED* until the late 1940s, which seems rather late for it to be a Christian allusion. In most people's minds the expression is probably more strongly associated with Hollywood's depiction of the Mafia, and the Judas kiss that marks a fellow Mafiosi as doomed. The expression has a further film and criminal association, in that it had a lot of exposure from the lyrics of the highly successful theme song of the James Bond film *Goldfinger* (1964).

'Financial problems aside, the company had already received the kiss of death in that, two years ago, the Department of Trade and Industry chose to feature it as a prime example of the Enterprise Initiative.' (*Independent*, 10 July 1989)

knee-jerk response (or **reaction**) This term for an automatic or unthinking reaction comes from the fact that if the tendon just below the kneecap is hit the leg will give an involuntary kick or jerk, a response exploited by doctors testing the body's reflexes. The metaphorical use developed in the 1960s.

'They accepted that the popular will is capricious and transient and that governments and other institutions will make better decisions in our long-term interest if they ride out some of our knee-jerk responses.' (*Independent*, 22 September 1998)

knobs on see WITH KNOBS ON

knock me down with a feather The idea behind this saying is that you are so amazed, so staggered by the information or events, that the very least thing would be sufficient to 'bowl you over'. The expression has been in use since the early nineteenth century.

' "I'm telling you," she said, "when I heard that big clock in the hall striking the five, you could've knocked me down with a feather!" ' (Rachel Anderson, *Paper Faces*, 1991)

don't know what hit you In origin this refers to someone being killed, shot so effectively that they literally did not know what hit them before they died. This use is recorded from the 1920s, and its use to mean 'taken by surprise' or 'overwhelmed' is recorded from the 1960s.

'Then he'd tell Phil Simpkin that he was having trouble with one of the staff, and she'd be out on her wiggly bottom before she knew what hit her.' (*Best*, 1991)

labour of love This expression for something that is done for the sheer pleasure of it rather than for money or reward is a quotation from the Bible, the expression 'your works of faith and labours of love' occurring at both Thessalonians 1:3 and Hebrews 6:10.

'In a remarkable labour of love Charles Bohi categorised all the Canadian National stations west of Lake Superior and visited all the surviving ones in the early 1970s.' (Jeffrey Richards and John M. MacKenzie, *The Railway Station: A Social History*, 1988)

'It is very evidently a thorough piece of work; the judgements seem well justified, and the whole exercise must surely have been a labour of love.' (*Art Newspaper*, 1993)

ladies first see LADY WIFE

ladies who lunch If Stephen Sondheim did not coin this expression for a class of women who have the money and time to meet for leisurely lunches, then he certainly popularized it in his song 'The Ladies who Lunch' from the 1970 show *Company*. The words define the type: 'Here's to the ladies who lunch/. . . Off to the gym/Then to a fitting/Claiming they're fat/And looking grim/. . . Another long exhausting day,/Another thousand dollars/A Matinée, a Pinter play,/Perhaps a piece of Mahler's/ . . . A toast to that invincible bunch/The dinosaurs surviving the crunch/Let's hear it for the ladies who lunch.'

'In the tactfully beige interior designed by Emily Todhunter the ladies who were lunching the day we visited all possessed the advantage of interchangeability.' (*Evening Standard*, 7 October 1998)

lady doth protest too much see PROTEST TOO MUCH

lady wife The use of the word 'lady' is full of dangers nowadays, both on grounds of political correctness and as a class marker. To some it is as offensive as the FAIR or WEAKER SEX, marking the speaker as outdatedly sexist. Expressions such as 'ladies first' or 'the lady of the house' are seen as vulgarisms (although 'Is the lady of the house at home?' is used as a conscious cliché to mark the typical speech of the door-to-door salesman). 'Lady wife' is even more complicated, for while it is used as a conscious cliché to indicate working-class attempts at elegance or chivalry, it is also used to indicate stereotypes of the retired Colonel type, from its use in the services. In addition, it conjures up memories of the old music-hall cliché joke 'That's no lady, that's my wife.'

'MPs, trade unionists, delegates, and attendant journalists established a rich biennial tradition: meeting at the Winter Gardens, staying at the Imperial, toying with a glass of draught champagne at Yates's Wine Lodge . . . dancing with their lady wives to Reginald Dixon on the mighty Wurlitzer at the Tower Ballroom.' (*Independent*, 26 September 1998)

laid back An expression as redolent of the hippy era (it is first recorded in 1969) as to DO YOUR OWN THING, but, like the latter, surviving none the less. This is probably because it is a convenient, quick way of expressing a mental attitude and approach to life that would otherwise take many more words.

'I was still young and very laid back, and I was enjoying my life, but we had never bothered to find out if anything was wrong, and as time went on I thought, "Oh dear, I must do something about this."' (*You* magazine, 20 September 1998)

(like a) lamb to the slaughter In the Book of Jeremiah the prophet tells of God's plans for Babylon, and says 'I will bring them down like lambs to the slaughter' (51:39). Similar images occur elsewhere in the Bible – 'Yea, for thy sake are we killed all day long; we are counted as sheep for the slaughter' (Psalms 44:22), and 'He was led as a sheep to the slaughter; and like a lamb dumb before his shearer, so opened he not his mouth' (Acts 8:32, quoting Isaiah 53:7). This last quotation has probably been the most influential, but, while 'sheep' is sometimes found, Jeremiah's 'lamb' is the more common, perhaps because it is more emotive and gives a greater sense of innocence, of the helpless victim, than 'sheep'.

'I was a bit worried when Damon took his first [Viagra] pill. With all the five-times-a-night reports I had heard I felt a bit like a lamb to the slaughter.' (*Daily Mirror*, 21 July 1998)

land of Nod This was a pretty feeble joke when Jonathan Swift used it in the 1730s in his *Polite Conversation*, and it has not improved with repetition. In the book of Genesis (4:16) Cain was exiled to the Land of Nod after he killed Abel. Since you 'nod off' when you go to sleep, this became a punning way to say you were going to sleep.

'The next morning I was a day older, no wiser and put in a bad mood right from the off because I was dragged from the Land of Nod kicking and screaming (well, grunting and stumbling actually) by the Celtic Twilight hammering on my door.' (Mike Ripley, *Angel Hunt*, 1991)

(in) the land of the living This elaborate way of saying 'alive' is another quotation from Jeremiah (11:19), and closely linked with the previous entry, as it is another version of the same image: 'But I was like a lamb or an ox that is brought to the slaughter; and I knew not that they had devised devices against me, saying, Let us . . . cut him off from the land of the living, that his name may be no more remembered.'

'Only the odd bouts of involuntary twitching in his sleep reassured his owner that Jess was still safe and sound in the land of the living!' (*Dogs Today*, 1992)

'Of the five big recent City fraud cases, only one was satisfactorily concluded (the first Guinness case), and only two are still in the land of the living.' (*The Economist*, 1993)

lap of luxury The image of the lap as a place of control or protection is an ancient one. The Greeks placed the outcome of events 'in the lap of the gods', and we 'land something in somebody's lap', meaning we make it their responsibility. The child is taken on to the parent's lap for comfort and protection. The 'lap of luxury' is thus a place where you are protected from the harsher things of life. It has been in use since the beginning of the nineteenth century, and usually carries an element of disapproval or envy.

'But, as Peter immediately tells his father, this is just the sort of bon mot to expect from an idler who is being kept in the lap of luxury.' (John Jones, *Dostoevsky*, 1983)

large as life (and twice as natural) This expression comes from the world of art, where 'large as life' was used as an alternative to 'life-size'. 'And twice as natural' therefore becomes a fairly obvious extension of 'and (looking) as natural', or similar expressions. Although 'It's as large as life and twice as natural' is best known from Lewis Carroll's *Through the Looking-Glass* (1872), it was already well established by the time Carroll used it, being found at least 40 years earlier. It is now used as a formula phrase. 'Larger than life' for 'imposing', 'impressive', 'on a grand scale', is easily transferred from a gigantic statue such as Michelangelo's 'David' to a large-scale personality.

'The Shop (BBC1), a satisfying ramble around Selfridge's, has now found its stars ... the camp salesman in Shirts and Ties, the vaudevillian furniture-buyer from Italy, the two larger-than-life female store detectives.' (*Independent*, 18 September 1998)

'But now you're telling me different, you're telling me he wasn't hanged at all, that he's still walking around as large as life and twice as ugly.' (J. Herbert, *Creed*, 1991)

last but not least Found since the middle of the nineteenth century, this expression serves to make it clear that things are not being listed in order of merit, but can too easily become merely ingratiating or a filler.

'Here were: John and Norman, Maureen and Linda, Jim and Klaus and, last but not least, Robin, the Rev. Robin, with whom Kenneth shared so many long and intense telephone conversations.' (Kathleen Conlon, *Distant Relations* 1990)

last chance saloon This expression, usually 'drinking in the last chance saloon' is a media cliché of the 1980s, a more emphatic version of 'last chance'. It may, however, be quite a bit older. It was in The Last Chance Saloon that Frenchie (Marlene Dietrich) sang in the 1939 Western *Destry Rides Again*. Whether the saying gave the saloon its name, or vice versa, is not clear, but a similar expression was in use soon after, when Eugene O'Neill used 'It's the No Chance Saloon' in his 1946 play *The Iceman Cometh*.

'David Mellor, the man who warned journalists they were drinking in the Last Chance Saloon, was about to call last orders on himself.' (*Daily Mirror*, 1992)

last ditch (effort) Originally a military term, the last ditch of your defences would be the final rallying point, your last chance to avoid defeat. William III of England (1689–1702) is supposed to have claimed 'I will die in the last ditch', and during the American War of Independence the Citizens of Westmoreland issued a grandiloquent proclamation in 1798 saying, 'In War We know but one additional Obligation, To die in the Last Ditch or uphold our Nation.' The expression was being used figuratively by the 1820s.

'It was probably effective the first time, but now it is looked on as a desperate move, a last ditch attempt to gain attention.' (Norton York, *The Rock File*, 1991)

'In a last ditch effort to keep the public sector buoyant, bank credits to the private sector were yesterday frozen by the Governor of the Bank of Crete who ordered private enterprises to pay back state loans as soon as possible.' (*Guardian*, 11 November 1989)

last gasp/last legs Both these expressions originally meant close to death, but are now also used to mean near-exhaustion or being at one's limit in some way. 'Last legs' goes back to at least the late sixteenth century, the idea being that you are on your feet for the last time; 'last gasp' is recorded only a little later.

'At the other end Sudbury began to launch some promising attacks, but their final delivery was off-key, until their last gasp equaliser came with a minute left when defender Ian Williams drove low into the net after two previous shots had been blocked.' (*East Anglian Daily Times*, 1993)

'There's a flower bed of sorts over by the fence but the flowers look to be on their last legs, as far as I can make out.' (E. Nash, *Strawberries and Wine*, 1993) (**have**) **the last laugh** This is based on the saying 'He who laughs last laughs longest', itself based on an earlier proverb, 'He laughs best who laughs last', first recorded from about 1607. The modern version is not recorded before 1912, but by 1925 'the last laugh' was well-enough established to be used as a film title.

'Manchester City player-manager Peter Reid shared a joke with Mike Sheron yesterday, and is banking on his ace winger to hit the goals which will give City the last laugh on rivals United tomorrow.' (*Today*, 1992)

last nail in the coffin see NAIL IN THE COFFIN

the last (or **final**) **straw** (**that broke the camel's back**) The proverb 'It is the last straw that breaks the camel's back' has been in use in English since the seventeenth century. The shortened 'the last straw' came into use in the nineteenth century, while the variant 'final straw' seems to be a twentieth-century innovation.

'The NHS had been grossly abused by many people, including doctors, for many years. It would be the last straw, if its finances were pushed over the edge in the ludicrously frivolous cause of providing the public with free orgasms.' (*Evening Standard*, 15 September 1998)

'The final straw, according to inside source, was when Mr Zhivkov tried to bring his widely disliked son, Vladimir, who has a reputation as a drunkard and a womaniser, on to the politburo.' (*Guardian*, 11 November 1989)

last to the tape see FIRST PAST THE TAPE

the late great Although the associations we have with this cliché are of glib journalism and popular music, this is not a modern expression, having been popular in the seventeenth century, and a favourite of Samuel Pepys. The first recorded use is from 1656 when a priest was described as 'That late great Anti-sabbatarian prelate'.

'Laurie Lee, the late, great writer, revered the company of women.' (*You* magazine, 20 September 1998)

late in the day This expression, often used simply to mean just 'late', but sometimes with the implication 'too late', dates from around the 1800s. An early use is found in Jane Austen, who wrote in *Emma* (1816), 'It was rather too late in the day to set about being simple-minded and ignorant.'

'It seems a bit late in the day to be getting shirty, but under the headline "Whose food is it anyway?" a recent *Guardian* article written by an Asian woman takes the British to task for embracing curry – currently said to be the most popular dish in Britain – so wholeheartedly.' (*Evening Standard*, 1 September 1998)

late lamented This expression is often used in the same way as LATE GREAT, but can also refer to non-animate things that are no longer with us. 'Late lamented', which came into use in the mid-nineteenth century for people, but seems to be modern when used of things, is often used ironically, with a tone of voice that suggests that the thing or person is anything but lamented.

'DG has an invaluable asset in "Dokumente", a series devoted to top class individual artists of the recent past and today – Hungarians Foldes, Anda, Fricsay and Kodály . . . Gieseking, Streich and the late lamented Fritz Wunderlich.' (*CD Review*, 1992)

'According to the *Wall Street Journal*, former IBM Corp chairman John Akers is "still technically an IBM employee, though he has lost his title, his board seat and his office at IBM's Armonk, New York headquarters . . ." We seem to recall something similar happening to an editor of the late lamented Datalink ...' (*Computergram International*)

laugh out of court 'Out of court' is a legal expression used of someone who has lost their right to be heard in court. Thus 'laughed out of court' originally meant something so ridiculous or comic that it would have no right to be considered. As a concept it goes back to ancient Rome where Horace wrote 'The case will be dismissed with a laugh. You will get off scot-free' (*Satires*, book 2, no. 3). As an expression of general ridicule it dates from the early twentieth century.

laughed (or **cried**) **all the way to the bank** The flamboyant American pianist Liberace (1919–87) was enormously successful with audiences, but viciously attacked by critics. His frequent response to this, from about 1954 onwards, was to say that he had cried all the way to the bank, and there was no doubt that despite the critics he became very rich. In the UK the more obvious 'laughed all the way to the bank' is now far more common than the original.

'I don't know if they're laughing all the way to the bank, but they can certainly afford to get there in a cab.' (*Punch*, 1992)

'There may be a significant fall in volume in the first year or so, but while the third party suppliers to Technology may feel that they have no alternative but to withdraw their products, they look like being the net losers as a result, while ICL sheds crocodile tears all the way to the bank.' (*Unigram x*, 1993)

law and order Aristotle wrote that 'Law means good order' in his *Politics*, in the fourth century BC, and the two concepts are a natural coupling. As a cliché, however, it is particularly favoured by politicians, and 'law and order' has been used as a political rallying cry since at least the mid-nineteenth century. In recent political history the call for more law and order, along with slogans such as BACK TO BASICS and FAMILY or VICTORIAN VALUES, has often led to newspaper stories which have done the politicians involved more harm than good.

'The Prime Minister's personal style, together with his handling of the economy and the issue of law and order, had been the subjects of particular critical attention.' (*Keesing's Contemporary Archives*, 1991)

law of the jungle see JUNGLE

law unto himself 'These [Gentiles] ... are a law unto themselves' is a quotation from the Bible (Romans 2:14). Although the *OED* does not record its use, before the 1930s, as an expression meaning to set your own rules, to be unconventional, unpredictable, it was in use by the middle of the nineteenth century as can be seen from Nathaniel Hawthorne's *The Scarlet Letter* (1850): 'It was as if she had been made afresh out of new elements, and must perforce be permitted to live her own life, and be a law unto herself without her eccentricities being reckoned to her for a crime.' In modern use it is often used with resignation, if not outright disapproval, but in the original biblical epistle it was used approvingly, for Paul says that those outside the law of the Jews, by following it, become part of the law.

'Yet in this respect as in many others, few families are a complete law unto themselves, and many children are able to participate in the culture of the playground or the street in happy ignorance or gleeful defiance of adult wishes.' (S. Reedy and M. Woodhead (eds), *Family, Work and Education*, 1988)

lay down the law 'To lay down', here, is used in an old sense of 'to establish, formulate', and 'to lay down the law' originally meant, and in some cases still does, 'to interpret the meaning of the law, to legislate'. In the sense dogmatic or pontificating it dates from the nineteenth century.

'Those whose task it is to lay down the law on matters of ethics and morality need to ensure that their views are based on a wide knowledge of human institutions and their history.' (Richard Hoggart, *Liberty and Legislation*, 1989)

lay it on the line Like 'up front', this expression originally referred to paying money. It is found in this sense in the 1920s in the USA, and then, presumably via a similar idea to PUT YOUR MONEY WHERE YOUR MOUTH IS, came to be used to mean to be frank about something. This change came about around the 1950s. This is the dominant sense in the UK, but the paying sense was still strong enough in the USA for the sense 'put at risk, pay dearly' to develop in the 1960s.

'But soon – perhaps very soon – I am going to have to lay it on the line, tell them what really has been happening.' (Gavin Lyall, *The Crocus List*, 1993)

lay it on thick or **with a trowel** The image here is of someone piling on flattery or similar, like a bricklayer spreading a thick layer of mortar. The expression comes from Shakespeare (*As You Like It*, I.ii): 'Well said, that was laid on with a trowel.' As a cliché it dates from the nineteenth century, although that century offers interesting alternatives such as the comment from *Law Times*, 1893, 'It is nauseous to hear the adulation of Mr Neville, who laid butter on with a spade.' 'To lay it on' is simply a shortened version, which has largely ousted the full version in the USA.

' "Life is no longer easy for a well-bred girl," she exclaimed, determined to lay it on thick to please him.' (P. Falconer, *War in High Heels*, 1993)

lay your cards on the table see SHOW YOUR HAND

leader see TAKE ME TO YOUR LEADER

leading edge Used in much the same way as CUTTING EDGE, to mean in the forefront, particularly of technology, the expression originally came into use in the 1870s to mean the foremost edge of the ship's propeller and later of an aeroplane wing. The figurative use developed some 100 years later. Cynics battered by too many unfortunate encounters with 'the leading edge of technology' have developed a new cliché, christening it the 'bleeding edge'.

'This deal reflects the growing convergence of telecoms operators and Internet service providers. Planet Online adds leading edge Internet and intranet products together with a significant and rapidly growing customer base.' (*Evening Standard*, 28 August 1998)

leading light A 'leading light' is a nautical expression, an alternative to GUIDING LIGHT, a light which shows a ship the way into harbour. Thus it came to be used to mean someone who is prominent, who shows others the way. 'Luminary' is a more grandiloquent term that shares the same image. The expression's popularity may have been influenced by an association with Cardinal Newman's well-known 1834 hymn 'Lead, kindly light'.

'The third member of the team is Michael Simmonds, a leading light in right-wing think tank, the Adam Smith Institute.' (*Independent*, 5 October 1989)

learning curve Originally a graph plotting the rate at which a skill was acquired (first found in 1922), in recent years this has become first a general term for the rate something is learnt, then used loosely as a vogue term for 'experience'. It is now also found used as a warning to do something about your learning rate, an alternative to 'pull your socks up'.

'Oh, there's such a great learning curve! You pick up a whole new culture, being with a generation with a different mind-set and different experiences.' (*You* magazine, 20 September 1998)

lease on or **of life** SEE NEW LEASE OF LIFE

leave in the lurch This expression has nothing to do with 'lurch' in the sense of a sudden movement, but rather comes from an obscure gaming term. '*Lourche*' was a sixteenth-century game, said to resemble backgammon, although the exact nature of the game has been lost. In the form 'lurch' it was adopted as part of the scoring for games such as cribbage, when it meant a resounding defeat. From that developed the expression 'to give someone a lurch' meaning to get the better of them, put them in a bad position, and from this we get 'left in the lurch' – left in a difficult position, abandoned. All these terms are first recorded in the sixteenth century, and 'left in the lurch' became so well acclimatized, that by 1600 when Philemon Holland translated Livy's *Histories* he could write: 'The Volscians seeing themselves abandoned and left in the lurch by them, . . . quit the campe and field.'

leave no stone unturned An alternative for 'EXPLORE EVERY AVENUE', the image here is of thoroughness. The source of this expression goes back to the fifth-century BC Greek playwright Euripides, who tells the story of the Persians' defeat at the battle of Plataea in 477 BC. Their general, Mardonius, was said to have left behind a great treasure, and when Polycrates of Thebes could not find this, he asked the Delphic Oracle for help. He was given the advice, 'Move every stone', which, in the form we now use, had entered the language by the middle of the sixteenth century. The reversed form 'leave no turn unstoned' has all but become an independent theatrical cliché.

'Rod, working on his own life story with a ghost writer, has promised: "I am going to leave no stone unturned – I intend to delve deeply into the numerous stains I have left on the tapestry of life." ' (*Today*, 1992)

leave out in the cold To be left out in the cold is the opposite of to be given a WARM WELCOME. The expression has been in use figuratively since the middle of the nineteenth century. John Le Carré's 1963 spy novel, *The Spy Who Came in from the Cold*, where 'the cold' referred to the communist Eastern Bloc, echoing the term 'Cold War', gave a new twist to the old saying, which is often used by headline writers.

'This idea does leave out in the cold some of us who are not moved that much by emotion.' (George Carey, *I Believe*, 1991)

leave someone standing The image here is probably that of someone so quick off the start that the competition appears to be left behind, not moving. From this it has come to be used of someone who has figuratively 'seen off the competition'.

'She joined in the training sessions, but soon found to her chagrin that in the personal fitness stakes he left her standing.' (Kristy McCallum, *Driven by Love*, 1993)

leave (or **let**) **well alone** In the form 'let well alone' this was the motto of the eighteenth-century Prime Minister, Sir Robert Walpole, although as a proverb it goes back to the sixteenth century. In the UK today 'leave' is often substituted for 'let' which is now rather archaic, but in the States 'let' is still current.

'Only an exceptionally hungry or courageous predator will risk attacking such a creature, and most prefer to play safe and leave well alone.' (Desmond Morris, *Animal Watching – A Field Guide to Animal Behaviour*, 1991)

left hand doesn't know what the right is doing In the Bible (Matthew 6:3) Jesus says, 'When thou doest alms, let not thy left hand know what thy right hand doeth: that thine alms may be in secret.' In other words do good by stealth. Modern adaptations of the expressions can either mean this, or that someone is unco-ordinated, or it can be used of different parts of an organization not knowing what the others are doing.

'As she ate Maltesers from the box on her knee, apparently engrossed in the antics of Mickey Mouse, Donald Duck or Pluto her left hand seemed not to know what her right was doing.' (Ian Breakwell and Paul Hammond (eds), *Seeing in the Dark*, 1990)

left holding the baby see HOLDING THE BABY

a leg to stand on If you haven't got a leg to stand on, you are totally without support. Thus the expression is used to mean to be without any kind of supporting argument or defence on your side. It is first found in the sixteenth century in Thomas Nashe's *The Unfortunate Traveller*.

'Any solicitor will tell you, if you're cohabiting and the man leaves you, you haven't got a leg to stand on.' (*She* magazine, 1989)

legal loophole This expression for something that allows you to ignore the spirit of a law while sticking to the letter of it, has a surprisingly long history. Why a narrow opening designed to shoot an arrow through or to let in light should become a means of escape is not quite clear. Perhaps the idea is of something you can just squeeze through; perhaps it is influenced by the old Dutch word *loopgat*, of much the same meaning, where '*loop-*' comes from 'to run' and '*-gat*' means 'hole'. Whatever the reason for the change in the meaning of 'loophole', it had occurred by the middle of the seventeenth century, and the term is generally used in the context of the law. The alliterative 'legal loophole' is first found in 1768, in the very modern-sounding 'a legal loop-hole . . . for a rogue now and then to creep through'.

'A new bill, which will become law in October, will close a legal loophole which allows unscrupulous badger diggers to avoid prosecution by claiming they are digging for foxes.' (*Outdoor Action*, 1991)

legend in his (or **her**) **own lifetime** 'She was a legend in her own lifetime, and she knew it', Lytton Strachey wrote of Florence Nightingale in *Eminent Victorians* (1918) in what is the first recorded use of the expression. The jocular variant 'legend in his own lunchtime' was in use by the mid-1970s, usually of journalists, media types and other exponents of the three-hour lunch. A 'living legend' is a further form of the cliché.

'Czech president Vaclav Havel described him as a "living legend" . . . Praise indeed for rocker Lou Reed.' (*Independent*, 17 September 1998)

legendary Originally meaning 'mythical, out of legend', the development of the clichéd sense 'famous' is comparatively recent, perhaps starting in the middle of the twentieth century.

'The legendary Australian cricketer, Sir Don Bradman, is 90 today.' (*Today*, BBC Radio 4, 27 August 1998)

'There have been worrying signs that the Conservative MP for Kensington and Chelsea is losing his legendary sense of humour.' (*Independent*, 1 September 1998)

legs up to her armpits A twentieth-century cliché to describe a woman with long legs, this is often used in contexts which are sexist, or at best laddish.

'"Christ!" he said. "Legs up to her armpits, fit as a butcher's dog, wouldn't kick her out of bed for eating crisps." Then, as the cataract of clichés came to an end: "The sponsors will be falling over themselves." ' (*Independent*, 13 August 1998)

lend an ear The expression 'to lend a deaf ear', meaning to refuse to listen, is found as early as the fourteenth century, and 'to lend an ear' for 'to listen' was already very popular, if not already a cliché, by the time Shakespeare used it in its best-known context: 'Friends, Romans, countrymen, lend me your ears' (*Julius Caesar*, III.ii). Despite all the childish jokes made about the Shakespeare quote, the expression is still well used if getting a bit old-fashioned, both in the form 'lend an ear' and in forms echoing Shakespeare.

less means more see MORE MEANS WORSE

less than meets the eye see MORE THAN MEETS THE EYE

less than the dust see CAN'T HOLD A CANDLE TO

lesser of two evils The sentiment behind this goes back to the ancient world. It was obviously well known by the fourth century BC when Aristotle wrote in his *Nicomachean Ethics*: 'We must as a second-best course, it is said, take the least of two evils.' It is also found in Roman writing, and from there was passed on to the medieval world, Chaucer writing about 1385, 'Of harmes two the less is for to choose', and the fifteenth-century theologian Thomas à Kempis, 'Of the two evils the lesser is always to be chosen.' From this proverb it is an easy step to our usual use of identifying some particular thing as the lesser of the two evils.

'Regarding the Nationalists as the lesser of two evils he joined with them to resist Japanese encroachments.' (J. Hunter, *The Emergence of Modern Japan*, 1992)

let it all hang out This expression for being uninhibited or relaxed, the opposite of 'uptight', developed in American Black slang in the 1960s and spread rapidly to the rest of the English-speaking world. There has been much speculation as to what 'it' might be.

'After years of listening to and reading Anglo-Saxon women letting it all hang out, it was refreshing to be among women who so rigorously kept it all in.' (*Daily Telegraph*, 10 April 1992)

let joy be unconfined This is a quotation cliché, from Byron's *Childe Harold's Pilgrimage* of 1812–18. 'On with the dance! let joy be unconfined;/No sleep till morn, when Youth and Pleasure meet/To chase the glowing Hours with flying feet' (canto 3, stanza 12). Since it has a ring of artificial enthusiasm, modern uses are often ironic.

'Let joy be unconfined. England win.' (Headline on England's cricket Test Match win, *Independent*, 11 August 1998)

let me just say (or **tell you**) Modern filler clichés, these generally add nothing to the basic sense of what is said.

'First of all, let me just say that everything I am going to tell you is the complete and absolute truth.' (Mary Gervaise, *The Distance Enchanted*, 1983)

let me take you away from all this see TAKE YOU AWAY FROM ALL THIS

let or hindrance see WITHOUT LET OR HINDRANCE

let sleeping dogs lie In his *Troilus and Criseyde* of about 1385 Chaucer wrote: 'It is nought good a sleeping hound to wake', and the proverb has been well used ever since, although not recorded in the modern wording until the early nineteenth century. The image is that of not disturbing a watch-dog, and it is used to mean LEAVE WELL ALONE, or IF IT AIN'T BROKE DON'T FIX IT. It is quite often used as a formula phrase.

'In my opinion it would be better to let sleeping dogs lie as there would be no mileage to be gained from such a move.' (*Alton Herald*, 1992)

'Why you should let sleeping flowers lie.' (Headline, *Independent*, 5 September 1998)

let someone go A euphemism cliché of the second half of the twentieth century. In the form, 'We're going to have to let you go', it is a particularly offensive way of telling someone they have been sacked.

let well alone see LEAVE WELL ALONE

let's do (or **put on**) **the show right here** This is a conscious cliché, supposedly a line from a 1930s American musical film, although no such line has ever been traced. It is used to indicate naïve enthusiasm for a project, usually with an implication of success. Some kind of location, particularly 'in the old barn', is often added.

'With a "let's-put-on-the-show-right here" enthusiasm, the pair have come up with fashion-forward colours and commissioned futuristic packaging.' (*You* magazine, 20 September 1998)

'We can all agree that we need good political debate in this country. But too often the last place we'll find it is at party conferences. No, readers, we'll just have to do the show here, in the old barn.' (*Independent*, 29 September 1998)

letter of the law see BY THE BOOK

letters of fire The history of this cliché is something of a mystery, as it has been ignored by all the major dictionaries and reference works. It sounds biblical, but is not. In ancient Scottish law there was a process known as letters of fire and sword, a licence for the authorities to use force against a wrongdoer. Such warrants, for instance, were drawn up in the expectation of trouble from the Highlanders when James II was deposed, and provided some legal basis for the massacre of Glencoe. Perhaps this lies behind the expression. Whatever its history, it seems to have been a cliché by the early twentieth century, when, for example, Baroness Orczy used it in *The Scarlet Pimpernel* (1905): 'This she had read quite distinctly, then came a blur caused by the smoke of the candle, which obliterated the next few words; but, right at the bottom, there was another sentence, like letters of fire, before her mental vision, "If you wish to speak to me again I shall be in the supper-room at one o'clock precisely."'

'Eliot proclaimed the impersonality of great poetry, and yet his own personality and experience are branded in letters of fire upon his work.' (Peter Ackroyd, *T. S. Eliot*, 1988)

level best This expression is said to have originated in the California goldfields in the nineteenth century. People panning for gold would shake the matter in the pans until it was level, the better to spot the fragments of gold. It was well established in the USA by the middle of the nineteenth century, and in the UK by the end.

'What with Anna being such a charmer and what with the fact that he is now sleeping with her, he does his level best to find some small saving grace in her writing, something he can praise without hypocrisy.' (*Daily Telegraph*, 4 December 1992)

a licence to print money The Canadian-born industrialist Roy Thomson (later Lord Thomson of Fleet) is supposed to have commented, in 1957, on his commercial television company, 'You know it's just like having a licence to print your own money.' By the 1970s, this expression, in its shortened form, had become a cliché.

'Microsoft is reported to be bidding for De La Rue, the British company which prints banknotes in 150 countries. *Sneak* always thought Windows was a licence to print money, but it looks like Microsoft has finally decided to stop worrying about making software and get right down to the real business.' (*IT Week*, 26 October 1998)

lick into shape 'Why, love forswore me in my mother's womb;/And, for I should not deal in her soft laws,/She did corrupt frail nature with some bribe,/To shrink mine arm up like a wither'd shrub;/To make an envious mountain on my back,/ Where sits deformity to mock my body;/To shape my legs of an unequal size./To disproportion me in every part,/Like to a chaos, or an unlick'd bear-whelp/That carries no impression like the dam.' In these words Gloucester (later Richard III) describes his deformities in Shakespeare's *Henry VI*, part 3 (III.ii) referring to a legend, inherited from the ancient world, that bear-cubs are born a shapeless mass, and have to be licked into shape by their mothers. This is the origin of 'to lick into shape', first found in the late seventeenth century, although the idea had been expressed in similar words since the early fifteenth century.

lick your wounds The image here is of an animal treating its injuries by licking them. Just as an animal will retreat into shelter to do this, the expression often carries a sense of withdrawal or isolation with it.

'The Magpies' fans were still in London for the big game, licking their wounds after Kenny Dalglish's team lost the FA Cup Final to Arsenal the previous day.' (*Evening Standard*, 1 September 1998)

'I've changed, she thought, I'm not the same shallow little girl who first came here to lick her wounds before returning to her life of perpetual glamour and moneyed ease.' (Cathy Williams, *A French Encounter*, 1992)

lie back and think of England A cliché of sexual innuendo which has a some-what clouded history. In the form 'close your eyes and think of England' it seems to have been a late nineteenth-century catch-phrase, not particularly associated with sexual intercourse, but with doing anything unpleasant. The story that one of her ladies-in-waiting said it to Queen Victoria on her wedding night has no known foundation. A diary entry by Lady Hillingdon (1857–1940) for 1912 is sometimes cited as a source, but it is far more likely that she was already using established expressions when she wrote, 'I am happy now that Charles calls on my bedchamber less frequently than of old. As it is, I now endure but two calls a week and when I hear his steps outside my door I lie down on my bed, close my eyes, open my legs and think of England.'

'Nice smokers will sometimes ask whether we mind them smoking . . . For friendship's sake, like dutiful wives in the age before they invented foreplay and clitorises, we lie back, take a deep breath and think of England.' (*Independent*, 8 October 1998)

'Lie back and think of – well, certainly not England when you're soaking up the sun in St Tropez.' (*Daily Mirror*, 1992)

(risk) life and limb This is another cliché where alliteration wins out over common sense, for if you are risking your life you are obviously risking your limbs. It has been current since the seventeenth century.

'Our research shows that Amex members generally lead active social lives, regardless of whether or not they spend their weekends risking life and limb and that there is a need for this sort of cover.' (*Independent*, 14 October 1989)

life and soul (of the party) This expression for vivacity and sociability dates from the nineteenth century, and is quite often used ironically.

'People liked her. If she were down the pub, she'd be the life and soul: "Oh, she's a good 'un, Elsie Orton is . . . salt of the earth." ' (*You* magazine, 20 September 1998)

life begins at 40 *Life Begins at Forty* was the title of a self-help book written by Walter B. Pitkin in 1932. It is often used as a formula phrase.

'I would like to become a computer programmer after I finish the course. I think life really begins at 71.' (*Independent*, 8 September 1998)

'Perhaps it is true that "life begins at 40" (or 50) for those who recognize the opportunities available to them after parenting ceases, and are prepared to take advantage of them.' (Steve Scrutton, *Counselling Older People*, 1991)

life blood of The image behind this expression for an indispensable element comes from blood pouring from a mortal wound carrying away someone's life with it. Shakespeare uses it in his *Merchant of Venice* (III.ii) when he writes: 'Every word in it a gaping wound/Issuing life blood.'

'Town centres are the life blood of the community. Dependable souls running independent shops, restaurants and pubs are what makes Britain what it is.' (*Independent*, 2 September 1998)

life goes on As a cliché this is either an expression of resignation, implying there is nothing you can do about the circumstances you find yourself in, or used to protest that whatever someone else's circumstances may be, other people have to get on with living their lives.

'There have been spells back in Harefield, particularly last year, but the one true lesson is that life goes on, with the proviso that you take the medication every day – without fail.' (*East Anglian Daily Times*, 1993)

life in the fast lane see FAST LANE

life in the old dog yet To call a man 'a dog' for 'a chap', 'a good fellow', is an old expression. 'An old dog' is a term which developed from this in the eighteenth century, meaning someone who is experienced or adept at something (which is why you 'cannot teach an old dog new tricks'). This history explains the rather jovial feeling about 'there's life in the old dog yet' – an expression which has been in use since the middle of the nineteenth century.

'There's life in the old dog yet – even if it has trouble learning new tricks.' (*The Economist*, 1993)

life in your hands see TAKE YOUR LIFE IN YOUR HANDS

life is too short to . . . This is a cliché of the stressed-out later twentieth century, most famously exemplified in Shirley Conran's 1975 book *Superwoman* which contains 'OUR MOTTO: Life is too short to stuff a mushroom.'

'Life is too short to do your own washing, ironing, shopping and all those other dull but necessary jobs.' (*Stuff*, October 1998)

it's life, Jim, but not as we know it A catch-phrase from the original *Star Trek* series, first shown in 1966 and repeated almost without pause ever since. Unlike such quotes as 'to boldly go' this did not immediately become popular, but has gradually grown in use. It is popular with caption writers, and is now well established as a formula phrase.

'As Bones himself might have reported, "It's pop, Jim, but not as we know it." ' (*New Musical Express*, 1992)

'It's a care manager, but not as we know it.' (J. King and K. Bowry, *Community Care*, 1993)

the life of Riley There is confusion about the exact origin of this expression. In the 1880s in America a performer called Pat Rooney was a popular success with a song called 'Are You the O'Reilly?' which described all the things O'Reilly would do if he were rich. Then, around 1900, there was another popular song by Lawlor and Blake called 'The Best in the House is None too Good For Reilly'. By this time Reilly or Riley must have been proverbial for someone who is living a comfortable or carefree life, so it is hardly surprising that the actual wording of the expression is first found in yet another popular song 'My Name is Kelly' which has the words 'Faith and my name is Kelly Michael Kelly,/But I'm living the life of Reilly just the same.'

'The tabloid press will publish stories of dole scroungers laying in bed all day, living the life of Riley on the dole, blaming the unemployed and making them feel guilty for a desperate plight.' (Trade Union Annual Congress (Business), recorded, 9 June 1993)

life or death see MATTER OF LIFE AND DEATH

the light at the end of the tunnel This expression for a distant hope first came into use in the early twentieth century. The image has been a productive one, giving rise to graffiti such as, 'Will the last person to leave the tunnel please turn the light off', and 'The light at the end of the tunnel is the light of the oncoming train' (later used by Robert Lowell in his poem *Day by Day* (1977)).

' "I suppose . . . I could try to perform some great service?" said Rincewind, with the expression of one who knows that the light at the end of the tunnel is an oncoming train.' (Terry Pratchett, *Interesting Times*, 1994)

light dawned There is a whole set of images linking perception with light, ranging from the cartoonist's use of a light bulb to indicate understanding or a 'bright idea', to things coming to you in a 'blinding flash'. 'The light dawned' seems to have come into use about 1800, and was well established by 1874 when L. Carr wrote: 'A light dawned through the thick opacity of his brain.'

'Fabia echoed, and hoped as light dawned on her that she had got it right, "You're saying that Mr Gajdusek is going to Prague?" ' (Jessica Steele, *West of Bohemia*, 1993)

(skip the) light fantastic This is an adaptation of Milton's lines from *L'Allegro*

(1632), 'Come, and trip it as ye go/On the light fantastic toe.' 'Trip' was probably changed to 'skip' to avoid ambiguity, although 'trip' is still sometimes found. The second citation below seems to show a further change as this expression is blended with STRUT YOUR STUFF.

'On Saturday, 3rd October, the Cathedral Local Centre in Lancaster saw members, friends and well-wishers of the Lancaster Life Group, tripping the light fantastic . . . at the first Barn Dance to be held by the group.' (*Lancaster Diocesan Catholic Voice*, 1992)

'As an 18-year-old Prague law student, the Czech beauty was spotted by a model agency strutting the light fantastic in the local equivalent of Come Dancing.' (*Stuff*, October 1998)

light the blue touchpaper and retire Quoting this instruction frequently found on fireworks is used to indicate that 'sparks will fly', or is used as an alternative for to set the CAT AMONG THE PIGEONS.

'Despite Dick Crossman's native love of a row, there was not sufficient of the political fighter about him to light the blue touchpaper regardless.' (*Independent*, 4 October 1989)

light under a bushel see HIDE YOUR LIGHT UNDER A BUSHEL

as fast (or **quick**) **as lightning** or **like** (**greased**) **lightning** These are tired comparisons. Because lightning comes and is gone almost before the eye can register it, it has been used as a comparison for speed since at least the sixteenth century. The usually humorous 'greased lightning' developed in the first part of the nineteenth century from the use of grease to make things slide more quickly.

'Tweed calculated the combined speeds of the two vehicles as best he could, his mind moving like lightning.' (Colin Forbes, *Shockwave*, 1990)

lightning never strikes twice The proverb 'lightning never strikes the same place twice' is a comparatively recent one, not being found until the middle of the nineteenth century. Nowadays it is often used in a shortened form, to indicate that something unpleasant or unusual is unlikely to be repeated.

'Trainers are never satisfied, are they? I've bred top-class sprinters and stayers. Now my main trainer Ian Balding wants something between! They say lightning never strikes in the same place twice, but it's got to strike somewhere.' (*Evening Standard*, 1 September 1998)

like a house on fire A burning house can get out of control surprisingly quickly, so the image came to be used both for 'very quickly', and 'very well'. The first recorded use, by Washington Irving in 1809, suggests from its emphatic exaggeration, that it was already well established: 'At it they went like five hundred houses on fire.'

'The service at the crematorium went off like a house on fire and on returning home I received a phone call from Pybus to say that, at a meeting of directors, Carter and Tilley had quit.' (M. Gist, *Life at the Tip*, 1993)

like a man see TAKE IT LIKE A MAN

like clockwork This simile can be used to indicate smooth running, efficiency, or mechanical regularity, all aspects of clockwork. The most common forms are 'to go' or 'to work like clockwork'. Things were being compared to clockwork from the early seventeenth century, and by 1679 John Goodman, in *The Penitent Pardoned*, was approaching our modern use with 'Their Religion was a kind of clock-work . . . moving in a certain order, but without life or sense.' However, the actual wording 'like clockwork' is not recorded until the end of the next century.

'All went like clockwork until they reached the top, where a keen wind cut through their thick overalls, making them shiver.' (P. Falconer, *War in High Heels*, 1993)

like the plague see AVOID LIKE THE PLAGUE

lion's share This comes from one of Aesop's *Fables*, in which a group of animals – the exact membership of the group varies from version to version – goes hunting. When they have caught their prey, the lion used his size and strength to keep the whole of the kill for himself. Thus, the term should strictly be used to mean *all* of something, not, as it is, *most* of it. However, as it has been used since the eighteenth century as we use it today, it is a bit late to quibble.

lip service If you pay service to something with your lips, but not your inner self, then you are either not going to do it, or are insincere in your intentions. The expression comes from the Bible, from Isaiah 29:13 (and is echoed at Matthew 15:8): 'this people draw near me with their mouth, and with their lips do honour me, but have removed their heart far from me.'

'There is an awesome truth here that managers at all levels must act upon rather than pay lip service to – that is, there will be no educational progress without the full commitment and motivation of the teaching force.' (Allan Osborne *et al.*, *Education Management in the 1990s*, 1990)

lips are sealed Although it was known before the 1930s, this expression really took off only after the then Prime Minister Stanley Baldwin made a speech on the Abyssinia crisis on 10 December 1939, saying: 'I shall be but a short time tonight. I have seldom spoken with greater regret, for my lips are not yet unsealed. Were these troubles over I would make a case, and I guarantee that not a man would go into the lobby against us.' After this speech the cartoonist Low took to drawing him with a piece of sticking plaster over his mouth, and 'my lips are sealed' became something of a catch-phrase.

'In fact his father-in-law had congratulated him on the perfectly splendid bit of crackling Hugh had in his arms in Chancery Lane, and naturally mum was the word, and his lips were sealed as far as Molly Coddle was concerned.' (J. Mortimer, *Summer's Lease*, 1988)

literally Originally used to emphasize that what has been stated is not figurative, this word is increasingly used for mere emphasis, frequently with ridiculous effect. Although this is often deplored as a modern trend, it has been used in this way since the middle of the nineteenth century.

'Most of the nations that supply our oil and gas supplies are, literally, social and political powder kegs.' (*Independent*, 27 November 1998)

a little bird told me The origin of this expression seems to go back to the Bible (Ecclesiastes 10:20): 'Curse not the king . . . for a bird of the air shall carry the voice, and that which hath wings shall tell the matter.' The concept was current in the Middle Ages – when, for example, Christian propaganda against Mohammed claimed he was a renegade priest who fooled people into thinking he had a direct line to God by training a bird to fly down to his shoulder to take a nut he had hidden in his ear, telling witnesses that it was whispering God's word in his ear. The actual expression, however, is not found until the sixteenth century, and did not become a cliché until the twentieth.

'A reliable little bird tells this column that Frank may not be long for this world either.' (*Liverpool Daily Post and Echo*)

little did he know A filler cliché, an elaborate way of saying 'he did not know', although it can sometimes be used to imply something unexpected.

'When the first caveman scraped the stubble off his chin with a discarded tiger's tooth, little did he know what he was setting in motion.' (*Stuff*, October 1998)

'When one quiet weekend this February Mr Grosz left the country on a short trip to Switzerland, little did he know what would await him on his return.' (*Independent*, 7 October 1989)

with a little help from my friends Although this was already a cliché when used as the title of a Beatles' song in 1966, the popularity of this song not only boosted use of the expression, but, through the lyrics of the song, added a whole new dimension to its meaning.

'Henderson did get a little help from his friends, in particular a massive 484ft third-inning home run from Jose Canseco on Saturday that came within 13 rows of hitting the roof of the SkyDome but dropped instead into the hands of a surprised Toronto fan.' (*Independent* 10 October 1989)

'With a little help from your friends and the specially adapted boats, you can do just about anything.' (Central Television news scripts, 1993)

little local difficulty In 1958, shortly before the Prime Minister Harold Macmillan (Lord Stockton) was due to go on a Commonwealth tour, his Chancellor of the Exchequer Peter Thorneycroft, and two other Treasury Ministers, Enoch Powell and Nigel Birch, sensationally resigned over government spending targets. At the airport Macmillan, a master of words, nonchalantly dismissed the uproar this caused with 'I thought the best thing to do was to settle up these little local difficulties, and then turn to the wider visions of the Commonwealth.' In political circles this saying still carries overtones of the original circumstances, but elsewhere it can be used without irony.

'Is the Prime Minister aware that, after a little local difficulty in the House, there was a meeting this morning between the Engineering Employers Federation and the northern group of Labour Members, at which one of the representatives of the federation said that the Department of Trade and Industry suffered from inertia?' (*Hansard Extracts 1991–1992*)

'America's Liz Downing took advantage of Melissa's little local difficulty to take the women's prize.' (Central Television news scripts, 1993)

into each (or **every**) **life a little rain must fall** This is a modern proverb with a complex history. In 1842 the American poet Henry Wadsworth Longfellow published a poem called 'The Rainy Day' which contained the lines 'Thy fate is the common fate of all,/Into each life some rain must fall,/Some days must be dark and dreary.' This was picked up in 1944 by Allan Roberts and Doris Fisher, who used Longfellow's line in a song: 'Into each life some rain must fall,/But too much is falling in mine.' Despite the fact that the song uses the poem's words, it is usually known by the title 'Into Each Life a Little Rain Must Fall', and from this comes the proverb.

'The disappearance of vast tracts of Britain underwater by the year 2020 will mean so-long Swansea, bye-bye Bristol and adios Aberdeen. But it will also be farewell Fleet Street and pip! pip! party conferences by the sea. Never mind. Into every apocalypse a little rain must fall.' (*Independent*, 7 August 1998)

the little woman This expression started life as a term of affection (first found in 1765: 'My poor little woman had been in the drooping mood for two or three days') which merges imperceptibly into an affectionate term for 'wife'. As a clichéd term for a wife, usually in the form 'my little woman' or 'the little woman', in the twentieth century it seemed too condescending and proprietorial to be acceptable to the modern woman. From around the middle of the century it began to be used to indicate both such old-fashioned, possessive attitudes to wives and as shorthand for the role of woman as a stereotyped homemaker rather than an individual. These developments were no doubt helped by the fame of Louisa M. Alcott's 1868 book *Little Women*.

'I think he wanted me to be the little woman at home, but I'm just not that kind of person.' (*Daily Mail*, 10 August 1998)

'The report explodes the myth that men are the bed-hopping rogues while the little woman waits at home.' (*Today*, 1992)

live and learn A proverb found in the sixteenth century in English (but inherited from the ancient world) an extended version of which ran, 'One may live and learn, and be hanged and forget all.' It is used almost as a catch-phrase, to indicate that one can learn from experience, or as an exclamation of surprise when discovering something new.

'I've always said you've got to learn by experience, books tell you nothing, you live and learn, right?' (D. Smith and J. Eyles, *Qualitative Methods in Human Geography*, 1988)

live and let live A proverbial saying encouraging tolerance, in use since the seventeenth century, this was given a new twist by the 1973 James Bond movie *Live and Let Die*.

'It teaches a child to let go of his own will for the sake of others, with whom he has to live and let live.' (Michael Lawson, *Facing Conflict*, 1991)

(those who) live by the . . . die by the . . . The origin of this formula phrase is a proverb from the Bible: 'All they that take the sword shall perish with the sword' (Matthew 26:52). It was adapted as a variable saying, most often 'They who live by the sword shall die by the sword', and this has become a common formula. Indeed the pattern was set as early as 1601, when we find 'Those that live by blood: in blood they die.'

'The Clinton White House lived by the opinion polls, so it will only be poetic justice if it dies by them.' (*Independent*, 22 September 1998)

live fast, die young This companion cliché to I WORK HARD AND I PLAY HARD and to 'live dangerously' (a saying of Nietzsche), has a rather obscure history. 'Live fast' by itself has been used to mean live dangerously since the late seventeenth century. The fuller 'live fast, die young' or 'live fast, die young and have [or make] a good-looking corpse' is a modern quotation, strangely neglected by the major dictionaries. Although it is often associated with James Dean, who died young in a car crash in 1955, it actually comes from a 1948 novel by the Black American writer Willard

Motley called *Knock on Any Door*. This is the story of Nick Romano, a good Catholic boy corrupted into a heartless killer by poverty, resentment and the callousness of those with power over him. The expression is introduced in chapter 34 of the book: 'When the beer came Nick lifted and tilted the brown liquid in past the yellow foam. "Live fast, die young and have a good-looking corpse" he said with a toss of his head. That was something he had picked up somewhere and he'd say it all the time now. Always with a cocky toss of his head.' The expression was introduced to a wider public in 1949 when the novel was made into a film starring John Derek and Humphrey Bogart.

'Live fast, die young.' (Headline on the death, aged 38, of the sprinter Florence Griffith-Joyner, *Independent*, 23 September 1998)

live life in the fast lane see FAST LANE

live off the fat of the land see FAT OF THE LAND

lo and behold Although both 'lo' and 'behold' are ancient words, meaning the same thing, the combination of them is not. The first recorded use is at the very beginning of the nineteenth century, and it has always been used in a light-hearted way, as if a showman were producing something unexpected.

'Lo and behold, you have the full twelve-month series from Jan. to Dec. done and dusted, in the format you typed the first one.' (*Practical PC*, 1992)

local difficulty see LITTLE LOCAL DIFFICULTY

lock, stock and barrel An expression from the late eighteenth century, this is used to mean 'everything', because in origin it refers to the three main parts that make up a gun: the firing mechanism (lock), the stock that holds it and the barrel.

'They appeared to have every advantage in the world and the money to buy the City as well as Wall Street, lock, stock and barrel.' (*Evening Standard*, 10 September 1998)

lock the stable door after the horse has gone This is a highly variable proverb, found in forms such as 'It's no use shutting (or bolting, as well as locking) the stable door after the horse has fled (or bolted, or gone).' All mean to take action after the damage is done, or do TOO LITTLE TOO LATE. The earliest uses, from the middle of the fourteenth century onwards, refer to securing the stable after the horse is stolen, while in the USA a barn may be substituted for a stable.

'If the information has been divulged to sufficient people so that it can be said to be no longer confidential, an injunction will not be of any help; it would be like locking the stable door after the horse has bolted.' (David I. Bainbridge, *Introduction to Computer Law*, 1993)

lonely furrow (or **road**) see WALK A LONELY ROAD

long ago and far away see DAYS OF YORE

the long and the short of it This summing-up phrase is often no more than a pompous filler, adding nothing to the sense. It has been current since the late seventeenth century.

'Because she hadn't known what to expect, she'd expected too much: that was the long and the short of it.' (Elvi Rhodes, *Cara's Land*, 1992)

long arm of the law see STRONG ARM OF THE LAW

long hard road SEE GO DOWN A ROAD

a . . . is a long time in . . . A formula phrase, based on the saying attributed to Harold Wilson in about 1960 that 'a week is a long time in politics'. It is still used of circumstances where events can change radically in a short time, but as a formula phrase it is also used facetiously.

'A month is a long time in modelling, but in four short weeks Marisa Heath has posed for *iD*, *Russian Vogue*, and *The Face*.' (*Evening Standard*, 24 September 1998)

long walk A sporting cliché, in football it is mainly used of someone leaving the pitch after being sent off, in which case it may also take the form 'the long and lonely walk to the dressing room', while in cricket it refers to a batsman's walk back to the pavilion after being given out. Compare TAKE AN EARLY BATH.

'There was a time at Luton when I got a lot of stick from the fans after having to sell Roy Wegerle so I started keeping my head down when making that long walk at Kenilworth Road from the tunnel to the dug-out.' (*Daily Mail*, 27 August 1998)

look back in . . . A formula phrase found particularly in headlines, and based on the title of John Osborne's 1954 play *Look Back In Anger*.

'Look back in panic.' (Headline, *Independent*, 18 September 1998)

'Separatism: a look back in anger.' (Bob Cant and Susan Hemmings (eds), *Radical Records*, 1988)

look on the bright side This has been in use since at least the 1830s, but has never been the same since the song 'Always Look on the Bright Side of Life' (words Eric Idle, music Geoffrey Burgon) sung from the cross in the 1979 film *Monty Python's Life of Brian*, particularly after the song became a popular choice with football crowds.

'Always ready to look on the bright side she expected that the remission would last for a long time.' (E. Murphy, *A Nest of Singing Birds*, 1993)

looks as if butter wouldn't melt SEE BUTTER WOULDN'T MELT

in (or **out of**) **the loop** A modern cliché from the world of computing used to describe your access to the latest information. A loop is an element of programming that repeats itself, and this has been transferred to the idea of an information loop, a continuous pattern of passing information between a group of people. If you are in this loop, you get the information, if you are out of it, you do not.

'Blocked Internet access at universities will contribute to the sense of isolation and being out of the loop, which is already badly affecting the confidence of young scientists and engineers.' (*Independent*, 10 August 1998)

'Rennie tried to persuade them that the *Telegraph* is very influential in Britain, but for some reason they expressed doubts that the paper was "still in the loop with the government".' (*Private Eye*, 4 September 1998)

loose cannon In the days of sailing ships, conditions were very cramped, and in naval ships the cannon used to fight the enemy took up a good proportion of the below-decks living room. Weighing several tons, they were only secured by ropes, and if one came loose in a storm or battle it could do incalculable damage to both people and the ship. The transfer of this image to an unpredictable or destructive person does not seem to have happened until the twentieth century.

'From the evidence here, she was a loose cannon of the left, espousing causes in an antagonistic manner that would be called ultra-leftism, were any principles discernible behind her actions.' (*New Statesman and Society*, 1992)

lose the plot see LOST THE PLOT

(**fight a**) **losing battle** A vivid, if over-used, image for the feeling caused by working hard at something but knowing that the situation is getting worse all the time.

'The mountain of studies that must be mastered before that distant date assumes daunting proportions and you see nothing but a losing battle against time.' (W. Fisher Cassie and T. Constantine, *Student's Guide to Success*, 1989)

lost in the mists of time see MISTS OF TIME

lost souls Originally a term for the souls in hell, it began to be applied to those in torment in this world, the outcast or the hopeless, in the nineteenth century.

'In reality, those who took O levels were automatically regarded as successes while those who took CSEs were lost souls.' (*Daily Mail*, 27 August 1998)

lost the plot When a television series starts showing episodes that do not seem to be going anywhere, that have no point, then you know that the scriptwriter has lost the plot – his sense of purpose, what the series is trying to say. This idea is easily transferred to life in general.

'There are weeks when the North Stand is awash with the most ridiculous garb you've ever seen . . . It looks mad, but football fashion victims have lost the plot.' (*Stuff*, October 1998)

lost the war see WON THE BATTLE

loud and clear 'Loud and clear' used to mean 'understandable', 'emphatically', comes from the use of the expression in military circles to confirm that the message is getting through on communications systems. 'Receiving you, loud and clear' became a well known expression during World War II.

'Well, I always knew you'd get your side of the story across loud and clear, Viola.' (Robert Barnard, *Posthumous Papers*, 1992)

'On the level of language she was frightened, confused and unsure what to do, but her body spoke loud and clear.' (Michael Dibdin, *Dirty Tricks*, 1991)

love and war see ALL'S FAIR IN LOVE AND WAR.

love–hate relationship A useful expression when truly describing such a condition, it has become diluted through over-use.

'His love–hate relationship with reporters made headlines, especially when he came to blows with a columnist in a nightclub.' (Michael Munn, *Hollywood Rogues*, 1991)

'The love–hate relationship goes on: you voted Margaret Thatcher both most interesting and most boring woman.' (*Good Housekeeping*, 1992)

love that dare not speak its name This clichéd description of homosexual love comes from the line 'I am the love that dare not speak its name' in Lord Alfred Douglas's 1896 poem *Two Loves*. Because of Douglas's role in the trial of Oscar Wilde, the line is often misattributed to Wilde. Since the arrival of gay pride and a greater openness about sexuality, the expression has become rather coy, and is now much used as a formula phrase.

'The same applies, I believe, to the question under discussion, except that while our sexual desires are now the subject of free and frank discussion, our homicidal ones still dare not speak their name.' (Michael Dibdin, *Dirty Tricks*, 1991)

'This is the architecture that dare not speak its name.' (*Independent*, 4 October 1989)

(it's better to have) loved and lost A quotation cliché, from Alfred, Lord Tennyson's 1850 poem *In Memoriam*: ' 'Tis better to have loved and lost/Than never to have loved at all.' However, although Tennyson's words give us the form in which we use it, the sentiment was not original to him. In 1700 Congreve wrote, 'Say what you will, 'tis better to be left, than never to have lov'd' (*Way of the World*, II.i), and Crabbe in 1812 wrote 'Better to love amiss than nothing to have lov'd' (*Tales*, 14).

'For now it is sufficient to assert that John, having loved and lost, felt he would be tempting providence to allow himself to love again.' (Janet Mattinson and Christopher Clulow, *Marriage Inside Out*, 1989)

give (or **get**) **the lowdown on** This expression for the truth, or inside information, is first recorded in America in 1915. 'Low-down' had been in use for 'underhand' since the mid-nineteenth century, and the noun probably evolved from the idea that those who are low-down can 'keep their noses to the ground' and 'sniff out' things that people might prefer to keep secret.

'I mean, you get the lowdown on stuff that writers never get, because you're working with these people and you get the real story – not the stuff that goes on in books and magazines.' (*Guitarist*, 1992)

'But Machiavelli, who one gathers is a favourite source of the author, gave us the lowdown on this a few centuries ago.' (*Management Today*, 1991)

lowest form of life A cliché from the world of science, where it was used to describe single-celled creatures. From there it developed into an insulting term for the humblest, least significant person in a team or group, and from there it was but a short step to a general insult.

'Now I was an AC2, the lowest form of life in the RAF, and the "Hey you!" was a reflection of my status.' (James Herriot, *Vets Might Fly*, 1977)

'Anyone who's prepared to use a child as a pawn just to score points in some personal vendetta has to be just about the lowest form of life.' (Stephanie Howard, *Battle for Love*, 1991)

lunatic fringe This term was coined by American President Theodore Roosevelt who used it a number of times. In his *Autobiography* (1913) he wrote, 'There are the foolish fanatics always to be found in such a movement and always discrediting it – the men who form the lunatic fringe in all reform movements.'

'More futuristic, but by no means on the lunatic fringe, solar energy is now generating power to pump groundwater.' (*New Scientist*, 1991)

'While a lunatic fringe was organising a new party, leading conservatives such as Karoly Grosz . . . were refusing to reveal their intentions.' (*Independent*, 11 October 1989)

mad for see ALL THE RAGE

(far from) the madding crowd *Far from the Madding Crowd* is the title of a novel by Thomas Hardy published in 1874, now used to suggest a remote and peaceful spot. Hardy in turn took the words from Thomas Gray's *Elegy in a Country Churchyard* where Gray describes the churchyard as 'Far from the madding crowd's ignoble strife'. It is sometimes misquoted as 'maddening' – indeed, this is the original meaning of 'madding' – but since 'maddening' has developed the sense of 'irritating', 'madding' conserves the sense of 'insane'.

'The secret is to be based at the centre, but to make sure that you do your getting lost well away from the madding crowds.' (*Independent*, 5 September 1998)

it made me what I am today This is a self-satisfied cliché, used to imply either that the hearer is not as tough as the speaker, or that he has failed to make use of his opportunities to LIVE AND LEARN. It is a companion piece to I DIDN'T GET WHERE I AM TODAY, and nowadays is usually as much of a conscious cliché.

made my excuses and left An expression used by tabloid journalists to show they did not become involved in the improper behaviour they are exposing. It was coined by Duncan Webb, the chief crime reporter of *The People* in the 1950s.

'Miss Tapping said usually, when police officers visited the prostitutes, they "made their excuses and left" but on some occasions they paid for services so they could trace the banknotes.' (*Evening Standard*, 13 October 1998)

magic! see WORKED A CHARM

mailed fist This term for armed force or superior might is translated from the German. In 1897 Kaiser William II made a speech in which he said, 'But should any one essay to detract from our just rights or to injure us, then up and at him with your mailed fist.' At first 'mailed fist' was used to describe Germany's aggressive foreign policy, then used of similar behaviour by other countries, and from there spread to general use. It is sometimes used to replace the 'iron' in the IRON FIST IN THE VELVET GLOVE.

'And like every other passenger I fume at the traffic jams, the illegal parking and the wanton irresponsibility of drivers who regard their vehicles as a mailed fist to get their own way.' (*Daily Mirror*, 21 July 1998)

make a clean breast of In use since the mid-eighteenth century, this expression comes from the fact that since earliest records the breast or heart has been regarded as the seat of the emotions. The 'clean' element links with words such as 'purify' and 'purge' and even 'candid', which comes from the Latin for white.

'For one brief, but not very compelling moment, Creed was tempted to make a clean breast of everything, to confess that their son had been kidnapped by crazies who worshipped demons . . .' (J. Herbert, *Creed*, 1991)

make a decent life see DECENT LIFE

make a drama out of a crisis see DRAMA OUT OF A CRISIS

make a rod for your own back see ROD FOR YOUR OWN BACK

make a song and dance see SONG AND DANCE

make a stand Defeated troops, rather than retreating, can 'stand and fight', possibly in the LAST DITCH. Hence, someone who makes a stand refuses to be pushed about, but 'takes up arms in defence of' their cause. 'Make a stand' has been used in a military sense since the seventeenth century, and figuratively since the late eighteenth.

'Vernon Pugh, the IB chairman, is adamant that the clubs are trying to take control of the game in the Northern Hemisphere and this battle of friendly games is where he wants to make a stand.' (*Evening Standard*, 28 August 1998)

make an offer he can't refuse 'I'll make him an offer he can't refuse' is a line from the 1972 film *The Godfather*, based on Mario Puzo's best-selling 1969 novel of the same name. In film and novel it is said by a member of the Mafia and the 'offer' involves coercion, but although it was often used in this way at first, it has now largely lost its violent overtones.

'Travel: An offer you can refuse. Mark Edmonds is all for haggling – but not when it turns to meanness.' (*Daily Telegraph*, 4 April 1992)

'The cash, if not the equipment, was an offer impossible to refuse.' (*Northern Echo*)

make do and mend This comes from a World War II propaganda slogan, used to encourage people to conserve materials in a time of shortages by mending things rather than replacing them, or by making do with what they have (or doing without). It was based on an earlier naval term 'make and mend', a term for the half-day off-duty sailors used to have to give them time to make and mend their clothes and equipment.

'It was a long tale of low-cost facelifts, make do and mend, and cover up the cracks in a coat of Network SouthEast red, white and blue paint.' (David St John Thomas and Patrick Whitehouse, *BR in the Eighties*, 1990)

make head or tail of It is not clear whether this expression refers to the two sides of a coin or to the literal top and bottom of something. The chances are the latter, if the Latin usage, which translates as 'neither head nor feet', used by Cicero to mean total confusion, is anything to go by. 'Neither head nor tail' is found from the middle of the seventeenth century, although the construction with 'make' is not recorded until the eighteenth.

'Not for a moment am I suggesting that these figures, always in billions, are not important; only that I, an innumerate, cannot make head or tail of them.' (*Daily Telegraph*, 5 April 1992)

make it big This comparatively recent Americanism, not recorded until the second half of the twentieth century, seems to have pulled together two early senses of the verb 'to make'. One, common from the early seventeenth century, is usually found in the form 'to be made', meaning to be rich or established in a career. It is first found in 1614: 'If riches be that that makes men happy (according to the foolish phrase men use when such things befall one, "O he is made!")' The other usage started life in the same century, as a nautical expression meaning to travel a certain distance, then to reach a place, and from that, to achieve a goal.

'I read stories about novelists who make it big and suddenly retreat to vast rural compounds, surround themselves with assistants.' (*Mail on Sunday*, 20 September 1998)

make my day To make someone's day, in the sense of giving them pleasure, has been in use since the early part of the twentieth century. However, the expression was given new resonance after the 1983 film *Sudden Impact* written by Joseph C. Stinson and starring Clint Eastwood as Dirty Harry. In a famous scene in this film, Harry invites a robber to 'make my day' by giving him a chance to shoot the robber. Because of this, the expression is now aggressive if used alone, although not in forms such as 'he made my day'. The Dirty Harry line is often misquoted as 'Make my day, Punk', which is a blend of the *Sudden Impact* line, and one from the earlier film in the series, *Dirty Harry* (1971) in which Harry says to a villain, as he urges him to take the risk that there are no bullets left in his gun after a shoot-out, 'What you need to ask yourself, punk, is are you feeling lucky?'

'She gave it as her opinion that New Age travellers made no worthwhile contribution to society . . . but that she was going to visit one of their sites with an open mind. Roughly translated, this read: "Come on, New Age travellers, make my day!"' (*Evening Standard*, 17 September 1998)

make my excuses see MADE MY EXCUSES

make no mistake Although designed to add emphasis, this is often a filler cliché, that rarely adds anything to the meaning of a sentence. It has been in use since the nineteenth century.

'Make no mistake about what I mean by selling: it doesn't matter if you are trying to get people to buy tins of beans, contribute money to starving millions, or vote for a certain politician, you are selling the product, social cause, or person.' (Stafford Whiteaker, *A Career in Advertising and Public Relations*, 1986)

make or break This expression originally meant that you would either be 'made' (see under MAKE IT BIG) or a 'broken man', depending on the outcome. In use since the middle of the nineteenth century, it is still popular.

'And allied to this are concerns about "not getting the results" and about one's reputation with colleagues in general, and especially with the senior staff whose opinion can make or break a career.' (Guy Claxton, *Being a Teacher*, 1989)

make waves If you make waves you upset people by disturbing their calm. This watery image only came into use in the 1960s.

'Colin Barnes, the fashion illustrator, who has known her since St Martin's, says, "Of course outspoken people tread on toes, but they are often the ones who make waves and achieve something."' (*Independent*, 14 October 1989)

make your mark If you make a mark on something you change what it looks like, so this expression, in use since the mid-nineteenth century, implies leaving a permanent impression on the world or to being recognized as someone who can change things. 'Your' probably comes from an earlier use, where 'make your mark' referred to a cross or similar mark used by an illiterate to sign a document, an image that has been blended with the previous one.

'After making her mark at the Olympics, Griffith stepped out of the limelight for two years, working in a bank and as a beautician before making a comeback in 1987.' (*Independent*, 23 September 1998)

makes . . . look like a choirboy see VICARAGE TEA PARTY

makes . . . what it is A modern formula phrase used in vague praise of the subject, often found in the form '. . . what it is today'. It is often used in the same contexts as BEST . . . IN THE WORLD.

'Town centres are the life blood of the community. Dependable souls running independent shops, restaurants and pubs are what makes Britain what it is.' (*Independent*, 2 September 1998)

makes you think A catch-phrase cliché, current from the 1920s, popular from the 1930s, and often indicating a singular lack of thought on the part of the speaker.

'And so when something like that happens, it makes you think about it all, about the dangers, about all the travelling you do as a musician.' (*Guitarist*, 1992)

male menopause see MID-LIFE CRISIS

malice aforethought This is a legal term for premeditated harm, that which in law distinguishes murder from manslaughter. The date at which it was transferred to more general speech is not known, but is probably relatively recent.

'"But Louis Luyt had deliberately and with malice aforethought stuffed things up," recalled French.' (*Rugby World and Post*, 1992)

man about a dog see SEE A MAN ABOUT A DOG

man and boy This expression for 'all his life' has been used so much in caricatures of a certain type of elderly man, that it is now rarely used other than as a conscious cliché. The tone was set by the first recorded, and best-known use, in Shakespeare's *Hamlet* when the comic gravedigger tells Hamlet, 'I have been Sexton here, man and boy, thirty years.'

'They had got in through a cellar window at the back and made their way up to a small office on the third landing where, according to Cyril, the sole employee had been there man and boy until he became fossilized and had to be removed feet first from his station.' (Bette Howell, *Dandelion Days*, 1991)

man for all seasons see FOR ALL SEASONS

man of the world This expression originally meant a married man, the expected status of someone who was not a man of the church who had rejected the things of this world for those of the next. It seems to have taken on the suggestion of experience and sophistication that it has today some time in the nineteenth century.

'He leans back against the mantelpiece with his coffee, mastering the situation, a man of the world entertaining his oldest friend in his mistress's house.' (Michael Frayn, *Sweet Dreams*, 1976)

man on the Clapham omnibus 'The man in the street' is a nineteenth-century expression for the ordinary man, and should perhaps escape the stigma of being a cliché on the grounds that substitutes usually have a political or social implication, introducing ideas of class or socio-economic group. The elaboration, or elevation, of this comes from Lord Bowen, the judge at a trial in 1903. During it he asked the jury to interpret part of the case from the point of view of the average man, saying: 'We must ask ourselves what the man on the Clapham omnibus would think.'

'Are they truly objective in the sense they represent the average nose, i.e. the nose of the reasonable man: the now famous man in the Clapham omnibus?' (Denise Artis, *Odour Nuisances and their Control*, 1984)

'He was the one person within his household who had told him the truth; he had been his eyes and ears in the community, voiced the opinions of the man in the street.' (Penny Junor, *Charles and Diana*, 1991)

man or mouse It is hard to take the question 'Are you a man or a mouse?' seriously after it has been used of so many cartoon mice, but nevertheless it *is* still used in all seriousness, albeit more rarely than in the past. The expression was a popular one in the sixteenth century, but then carried the implication of financial success or failure rather than timidity, and this continued through to the nineteenth century. The idea of the mouse element being like Robert Burns's 'wee . . . tim'rous beastie' seems to be a modern one.

the man who . . . Found less commonly nowadays than in the recent past, this is a quotation from the cartoons of H. M. Bateman (1906–1970). He became famous for a series of cartoons that showed some poor man shrinking in embarrassment at having committed some minor social gaffe, while pompous types around him swelled with indignation. These cartoons carried the caption 'The Man Who Passed the Port the Wrong Way' or whatever the *faux pas* was.

'One of the most cultivated officials in the room turned to his professor neighbour and inquired: "What's a RAE?" This produced a slightly muted equivalent of a Bateman Cartoon: "The Mandarin who had never heard of the Research Assessment Exercise!" ' (*Independent*, 24 September 1998)

man who has everything An advertising cliché, offering luxury, and usually useless, goods 'for the man who has everything'. It became widely used in the USA in the 1920s or 1930s, and is still used both seriously and as a conscious cliché.

a man's gotta do what a man's gotta do Although this cliché of tough-guy heroics sounds like a quotation, a source has yet to be traced. It sounds like something from a Western film, but claims that it comes from the John Wayne 1939 film *Stagecoach* have not been substantiated. The nearest quote that has been found is in John Steinbeck's 1939 novel *The Grapes of Wrath* which contains the line, 'A man got to do what he got to do', but this may well only reflect an expression that was already current. It has been in popular use since about 1945. It is now usually used as a conscious cliché.

manna from heaven This expression for an unexpected benefit, help or treat, comes from the Bible, where the Children of Israel, stuck without resources in the desert, are miraculously sent manna to keep them from starvation. It appears in the form 'He rained down manna also upon them for to eat: and gave them food from heaven' in Psalm 78:25 in the version used in the Book of Common Prayer, and is repeated in several other places in the Bible.

'Tea dances with cakes; it all sounds rather dull in 1991, but to us then the cakes were manna from heaven and the dances were the greatest of fun.' (Wanda Newby, *Peace and War: Growing up in Fascist Italy*, 1991)

to the manner (manor) born A quotation-cliché, from Shakespeare's *Hamlet* (I.iv). A conversation between Hamlet and Horatio is disturbed by the noise of guns and trumpets used to mark the court's drinking session. Hamlet finds this objectionable and comments, 'But to my mind, – though I am native here,/And to the manner born, – it is a custom/More honour'd in the breach than the observance.' Thus the original sense is that of growing up with a custom. However, since it has been used so often of people at ease with wealth or position, it has come to be written sometimes in the form 'manor' as if of someone born into a privileged background, a form which will no doubt become more common after the success of the television series *To the Manor Born* (1979–81).

'The cast enter into this Lancashire hot-pot as to the manner born and only a snob will fail to enjoy: "By gum!"' (Joan Lawson, *A Ballet-makers Handbook*, 1991)

'On the day Nicol fitted in as to the manor born, his electrifying pace very much in evidence, notably in a touchline burst that almost led to a try by Gavin Hastings.' (*Rugby World and Post*, 1991)

many to the pound see YOU DON'T GET MANY OF THOSE

march to a different beat (or **tune** or **drummer**) see DIFFERENT TUNE

mark my words A cliché since the nineteenth century, this is either aggressive or simply a filler.

'Mark my words, a few slippery leaves, or later on some snow and ice, and I shall have some old people in my surgery with sprains and breaks.' (Miss Read, *The World of Thrush Green*, 1990)

marriage made in heaven Used literally, this is an old expression, represented in two sixteenth-century proverbs: 'Marriages be done in heaven and performed in earth', and 'The first marriages are made in Heaven, and the second in Hell.' Figurative use is mainly a twentieth-century development.

'For a start, 80% of its staff come from the former graphics system builder, which was itself born of a marriage made in hell between bitter rivals Ardent Computer Inc and Stellar Computer Corp back in 1989.' (*Unigram x*, 1993)

massive exposure, massive investment Two clichés of journalism, this diluted use of 'massive' dates only from the middle of the twentieth century.

'The commentator enjoyed massive exposure during the Beeb's coverage of the World Cup, but his contract came to an end on the same day as the final.' (*Independent*, 26 August 1998)

'It's clear that there would have to be massive investment in the playing strength if the club is realistically going to be challenging for major honours.' (*Daily Mail*, 27 August 1998)

master of my fate This is a quotation cliché, taken from W. E. Henley's 1888 poem *Invictus* ['Undefeated']: 'I am the master of my fate: I am the captain of my soul.'

'I wish to be wholly responsible for my acts, to be master of my fate; I shall make my own choice of ends, distance myself from my own reactions and learn to manipulate them like external events.' (A. C. Graham, *Reason and Spontaneity*, 1985)

material girl The title of a song written by Peter Brown and Robert Rans which was a great hit for Madonna in 1985. A precursor to GIRL POWER, it was used to indicate the attitudes of a certain type of emancipated, post-feminist young woman.

'She has created pop's answer to Barbarella, dressing her up in clothes fit for a material girl.' (*Clothes Show*, 1991)

as a matter of fact see FACT OF THE MATTER

matter of life and death As a cliché this dates from the middle of the nineteenth century, although it goes back originally to the sixteenth century. In sense it has become very diluted, often meaning no more than 'important' or at best 'urgent'. A similar dilution is currently going on with the expression 'life-threatening' and has already happened with 'vital', which originally meant 'concerning life, essential for life'. Perhaps the most famous example of 'a matter of life or death' is the comment made in 1981 by the Scottish footballer and Liverpool manager Bill Shankly: 'Some people think football is a matter of life and death. I don't like that attitude. I can assure them it is much more serious than that.'

mean streets 'Down these mean streets a man must go who is not himself mean', wrote Raymond Chandler in his essay 'The Simple Art of Murder' (1944). Chandler himself is probably echoing 'I am . . . a citizen of no mean city' (St Paul, in Acts 21:39), once a popular quotation. St Paul's 'mean' signifies 'insignificant', but Chandler probably meant to be deliberately ambiguous in his use of the word. Certainly the expression is also well known as the title of a 1973 Martin Scorsese film, which is used to mean both socially deprived and violent.

'My dad grew up in less-than-prosperous circumstances on New York's mean streets.' (*Mail on Sunday*, 20 September 1998)

meat and drink to In use by 1533, this expression covers a range of intensities from something that is essential, to something that gives great pleasure. 'Meat' here does not mean 'flesh', but retains its old sense, the more general 'food'.

'They are people to whom the Conservative party is meat and drink and there are few enough eccentrics among them.' (Jeremy Paxman, *Friends in High Places*, 1990)

'Certainly, the multi-studio techniques used for the famous 1959 Decca *Aida* were meat and drink to Karajan.' (Richard Osborne, *Conversations with Karajan*, 1991)

medicine see TAKE THE MEDICINE

meet an untimely end see UNTIMELY END

meet the eye see MORE THAN MEETS THE EYE

melt in her mouth see BUTTER WOULDN'T MELT

men of goodwill A literal translation of the Latin used by that brilliant propagandist Cicero in the first century AD. In Latin it is the elegantly simple *boni*, 'the good', in its masculine, plural form. When told by one so eloquent as Cicero that certain behaviour patterns are those of the *boni*, it takes a man of great courage to mark himself as a member of the opposite side, and this clever way of blackening the character of the opposition was eagerly picked up by later politicians.

'But the appointments he has given Mr Heseltine and Mr Patten in no way compromise their freedom to criticize the government when this seems necessary. They merely give a signal that men of goodwill can cross party boundaries, to address issues of common importance and concern.' (*Evening Standard*, 7 October 1998)

mend fences The proverb 'Good fences make good neighbours' has been recorded in various forms since the seventeenth century. In 1879 the American Senator John Sherman made a speech in Mansfield, Ohio, saying, 'I have come home to look after my fences.' Whatever Sherman may have meant by this, it was interpreted, no doubt under the influence of the proverb, to mean that he had come to campaign. Within ten years 'mend fences' had become an Americanism for looking after your interests, and since then has mutated to suggest the rebuilding of good relationships. Perhaps some of this change, and certainly a greater awareness of the proverb, comes from Robert Frost's poem *Mending Wall* (1914) which includes the lines, 'My apple trees will never get across/And eat the cones under his pines, I tell him. He only says, "Good fences make good neighbours." '

'Opening a debate on public spending, the Prime Minister tried to mend fences with the Tory Right by vowing that Britain would not join a single European currency in the next seven years.' (*Liverpool Daily Post and Echo*)

merry (or **merrie**) **England** As a literal description, using 'merry' in an obsolete sense meaning 'delightful', 'merry England' dates back to at least the fourteenth century. The form 'merrie England', used to indicate all that is 'olde worlde', is found by 1839 in a title *Merrie England in the Olden Time*, but received a great boost with the enormous success of a comic opera with the name *Merrie England* (by Hood and

German) in 1902. It is now rarely used without irony, at least outside the tourist industry.

'Indeed, the powerful imagery of pastoral will often suggest that the true location of the golden age lies in pre-industrial Merrie England – a traditional lament that was already well established in Queen Victoria's golden era.' (G. Pearson, *Hooligan: A History of Respectable Fear*, 1983)

merry men Based on Robin Hood and his Merry Men (although in the past Robin was by no means the only one to have his gang described as merry men), this term, found in the original sense from the fourteenth century, is first recorded in 1873 in the modern sense of 'followers' or 'supporters': 'Moderate Liberals had been glad to give Mr Daubeny and his merry men a chance' (Anthony Trollope, *Phineas Redux*).

'Remake of the old classic in which Senator Joe McCarthy and his merry men held the whole of America to ransom. In this update, it's Ken Starr and his merry men who try to paralyse America by crucifying the President.' (*Independent*, 23 September 1998)

on (or **off**) **message** Being 'on (or off) message' means saying, or failing to say, the right things as instructed, or even simply what you've been told to say. It has been associated with the Labour Party since its election campaign of 1997, and has spread from there to more general use. It is particularly associated with following the advice of SPIN DOCTORS and has to some extent replaced the similar 'sending the right signals'.

'Everyone is "on message" even if not all of them have quite got it. "The new buzz word is contemporary," says one of the sales ladies, "but I don't know what it means." ' (*Evening Standard*, 1 September 1998)

'Thousands of churches remain smoothly on message, while modern media and marketing methods ensure that the programme can be disseminated with breath-taking efficiency.' (*Independent*, 17 September 1998)

methinks he doth protest too much see PROTEST TOO MUCH

method in his madness This is a quotation cliché: 'Though this be madness, yet there is method in it', from *Hamlet* (II.ii), indicating that there is in fact a rational purpose underlying seemingly irrational actions.

'Their unpolished tastes are being labelled "ugly fashion" – but designer Joe Casely-Hayford claims there's method in the madness.' (*The Face*, 1992)

Midas touch Midas, son of Gordius of GORDIAN KNOT fame and king of Phrygia, looked after Silenus, drunken companion of the god Dionysus, when he became separated from the other revellers who followed the god of wine, and as a reward Dionysus offered him whatever gift he might want. Midas chose the gift of changing anything he touched to gold, but when he found that this was taken more literally than he intended, even turning the food he tried to eat to gold, he had to beg for the gift to be removed. The unpleasant results of the gift are usually forgotten, and 'a Midas' is used to mean someone with a golden touch, who can turn ordinary things into great wealth.

'One minute a mere tomboy Neighbour with a habit of putting a spanner in the works, the next Kylie was an overnight sensation, a pop princess with the Midas touch, so ordinary and yet so electrifying.' (Sasha Stone, *Kylie Minogue: The Superstar Next Door*, 1989)

Middle England This term, rarely used to flatter, covers the middle classes outside

London, particularly those with conservative or old-fashioned views, living in the Home Counties. It has only become a cliché in the last few years. The equivalent expression, Middle America, can be found in the USA.

'I love that other-worldly, rather abandoned feel English sea-side towns have – the people are outsiders, very definitely not Middle England, and there is a whole subterranean world of scandals and deals and feuds.' (*You* magazine, 20 September 1998)

'The fact that so many of Glover's judgements are rooted in or affect a kind of snobbery may explain why when he writes for Middle England in the more serious but uni-dimensional *Daily Mail*, he lacks sparkle.' (*Independent*, 22 September 1998)

. . . is their middle name As an expression to describe a quality for which someone is notable this is an American creation from the early years of the twentieth century.

'Bridget Jones' middle name is Vulnerability.' (*Guardian*, 5 September 1998)

middle of the road This expression has acquired a variety of connotations, which can range from approval of moderation to outright scorn. In politics it can still be used to indicate lack of extremism; in general application it indicates average, for good or bad; but in music, while it can just mean music with mass appeal, it is often a term of condemnation, particularly when shortened to MOR.

'I'm just an ordinary middle-of-the-road liberal, who believes British universities as they were 10–20 years ago weren't broke (other than financially), so why fix them?' (*Independent Education*, 23 July 1998)

'In 1983, for example, Gallup found that of voters who placed themselves on the political left and right, 22 percent placed themselves at various ranges of the left end of the scale (from "far" to "slightly" left), 51 percent placed themselves on the right, and 13 percent regarded themselves as middle of the road.' (Dennis Kavanagh, *Thatcherism and British Politics*, 1990)

'Anyone under 21 might not realise that Rod Stewart was not always a smug, smarmy middle of the road crooner.' (*Today*, 1992)

mid-life crisis An expression used to describe the dissatisfaction with one's achievements, a feeling that life's opportunities have passed one by, that can begin to set in as middle age approaches and which often leads to depression or a radical change in lifestyle. The expression came into use in the 1960s and was well established by the 1970s. 'Mid-life crisis' is used more often of men than women (who may suffer from the EMPTY NEST syndrome), but exclusively male is the more extreme 'male menopause', a term coined as early as the 1940s, but only recently over-used.

'How useful it would be to be able to turn for guidance to one of our great and wise novelists . . . Howard Jacobson would pitilessly explore the male mid-life crisis . . .' (*Independent*, 7 November 1998)

'Her peer group was struggling with the male menopause, of course, but the sting of rejection had been no less sharp.' (Stella Shepherd, *Black Justice*, 1988)

midst of see IN THE MIDST OF

with might and main A lasting monument to the staying power of alliterative phrases in English, both 'might' and 'main' mean 'power, force', so the repetition is unnecessary. 'Main', in this sense, has been obsolete since the sixteenth century, except in this set phrase. 'Might and main' is first found as a set phrase in Old English poetry, which depended on alliteration. It occurs in *Beowulf*, one of our oldest recorded poems, and has been in regular use ever since, although it is now, not surprisingly, rather old-fashioned.

'If He's not with you every single moment of the day and night and you praying to Him with all your might and main – if that's not there, then you become like that poor young man with the monkey taking lice out of his hair.' (John Allan *et al.*, *The Licensing (Scotland) Act 1976*, 1989)

mighty fallen see HOW ARE THE MIGHTY FALLEN

milk of human kindness In Shakespeare's *Macbeth*, Lady Macbeth is trying to nerve her husband to murder his way to the throne, but expresses her fears that he is not ruthless enough: 'Yet do I fear thy nature;/It is too full o' the milk of human kindness' (I.iii), and it is from here that the expression has passed into the language. The image behind it is probably a combination of ideas: of the baby at the mother's breast (Lady Macbeth later says (scene v), 'Come to my woman's breasts,/And take my milk for gall, ye murthering ministers' and (scene vii), 'I have given suck, and know/How tender 'tis to love the babe that milks me:/I would, while it was smiling in my face,/Have plucked my nipple from his boneless gums,/And dash'd the brains out, had I so sworn as you/Have done to this'); and derived from this, the association of milk with being childish and weak, found in words such as 'milksop'.

'Dear old Martha had much of the milk of human kindness about her; she had pensioners who shared with her such things as she had: one was a lame robin redbreast, who came and sat on a bush opposite the door till he was fed; another was a pigeon whose cot was quite a mile away.' (Mairi Hedderwick, *Highland Journey*, 1992)

mince words (or **matters**) If meat is tough, it is minced to make it easier to eat: so words that are not minced – the expression is always negative – amount to 'talking tough'. The expression dates from the sixteenth century.

'It is unkind – perhaps I should not mince words – it is cruel to keep albino fish under bright lights.' (*Practical Fishkeeping*, 1992)

mind boggles To 'boggle', which probably comes from the type of mischievous spirit called a bogle, originally meant to shy at something like a startled horse, an apt description of the mind when you do not want to think about something. As used today, the expression is largely a development of the second half of the twentieth century and is usually humorous.

'The mind boggles at the complexity of a system using twelve slide projectors producing 4,000 pictures during the 2¼ hour performance.' (*Bishop's Castle Railway Society Journal*, 1990)

'And Mike from Pearl Jam has fractured his foot in the studio (the mind boggles).' (*New Musical Express*, 1992)

mind over matter This expression, indicating the use of willpower to overcome obstacles, is recorded only from 1914, but is probably much older. The concept is an old one, for Virgil uses a similar expression (which translates as 'mind moves matter') in his *Aeneid*, written in the 20s BC.

'With a combination of every kind of scientific equipment and a psychological "mind over matter" approach, he got players fit again in a fraction of the time it took other trainers.' (Stephen Studd, *Herbert Chapman. Football Emperor*, 1981)

mind set This is a vogue cliché, currently popular as an alternative for terms such as 'attitude', 'way of thinking' or 'outlook on life'. It is recorded from the 1930s, but did not start to become fashionable until the 1970s.

'Oh, there's such a great learning curve! You pick up a whole new culture, being with a generation with a different mind-set and different experiences.' (*You* magazine, 20 September 1998)

'One could not teach a chimpanzee to grow bananas nor a dolphin to farm fish, for these are quite alien to its mind set and require the foresight, the ability to see and plan ahead, which only man possesses.' (John Davidson, *Natural Creation and the Formative Mind*, 1991)

. . .-minded The use of 'minded' to mean 'interested in', 'enthusiastic about', is a twentieth-century development. It is first recorded in the *Daily Express* in June 1928: 'At last, I believe, people are becoming "air-minded"', and for a while the term 'air-minded' – interested in aeroplanes and their development – was the dominant form. Since then, use has grown steadily.

'Sports minded national advertising company specialising in sports, entertainment and telecommunications clients are opening 4 new offices.' (Advertisement, *Evening Standard*, 1 September 1998)

'They will look about for someone in touch with the spirit of the age – classless, sensitive, tearful, family-minded . . . the people's poet.' (*Independent*, 7 November 1998)

mine host A conscious archaism, which, although to some ears it sounds affected, is still very common. The facetious use of this term for the person running a place to eat, drink or stay – the temptation is to use the term 'hostelry' to match 'mine host' – probably dates from the early nineteenth century.

'I hope mine host won't mind when he finds we're only going to have coffee and bread and cheese – because we really oughn't to have a banquet!' (Mary Gervaise, *The Distance Enchanted*, 1983)

mine of information This term for a rich source of information, current from at least the beginning of the twentieth century, is not entirely a dead metaphor, for it has been extended to cover the art of extracting relevant information out of the vast databases computers have now made possible, which is now known as 'data-mining'.

'The research team acquired a mine of information, which they decided to put into a teaching pack for midwives and other health professionals.' (*Nursing Times*, 1992)

'Wendy and Mary take along large selections of books and yarns each month, give talks and demonstrations . . . and are a mine of information on all things knitting.' (*Machine Knitting Monthly*, 1992)

mirror see HOLD A MIRROR UP TO

miss the boat This expression for being too late for something, or being unable to take advantage of an opportunity dates from the 1930s.

' "Isn't it incredible that religion missed the boat with the whole self-help thing?" He is not only on the boat, but steering it, thus *Kosher Sex* and *Dating Secrets of the Ten Commandments*.' (*Independent*, 21 September 1998)

missing link The original image here is of a chain of events, which will not be complete without all its links. This idea has been almost completely overtaken by the idea of the missing link in evolution – particularly that which links man to the apes – which developed in the 1860s, and most contemporary uses come from this.

'She is the missing link between the European ballad and torch-song tradition and Anglo-American white soul, and she chooses her material bravely.' (*Guardian*, 21 December 1989)

'For a long time Cindy's only competition was a sad show called Style With Elsa Klensch, a yapping Aussie who looks like the missing link between Morticia and Uncle Fester in The Addams Family.' (*The Face*, 1992)

mission statement Currently one of the most pervasive of the ever-changing list of business jargon clichés, a mission statement is simply an account of the intentions and purposes of a group or company – what a few years ago would have been called its remit. The term developed from the military use of 'mission', and has always run the risk of comic overtones by association with the long-running 1970s television series *Mission Impossible*, with its opening catch-phrases 'Your mission, should you choose to accept it . . . This tape will self-destruct in five seconds.' 'Mission impossible' has itself become a popular cliché of headline writers, particularly since the series was turned into a film in 1996.

'MSSL is funded by the Particle Physics and Astronomy Research Council, the only research council handing out government money that does not include wealth-creation in its mission statement.' (*ES Magazine*, 23 October 1998)

'Wool has never felt so soft as in the new season's collections . . . In fact, the Woolmark mission statement – "Take comfort in wool" – has never been more appropriate.' (*Daily Mail*, 27 August 1998)

(back in/lost in) the mists of time Usually in the form 'lost in the mists of time', this is a companion cliché to the DIM AND DISTANT PAST. Its history is yet to be traced, but is probably similar to that of its companion.

'Deborah Dean had been nicknamed Dimity so long ago that the reason for the diminutive had been lost in the mists of time.' (Miss Read, *The World of Thrush Green*, 1990)

'Travel back into those mists of time and you will meet many who have gone before and who also may have experienced these sudden sea frets, for that is what these mists are.' (*The East Yorkshire Village Book*, 1991)

in . . . mode Although similar uses have been around since the seventeenth century, the current vogue for describing people as acting in some sort of mode probably comes from computing, where a click of a button can change the way or mode of its operating.

'Institutions are in panic mode. They do not need economists, they need psychiatrists.' (*Evening Standard*, 28 August 1998)

Mom and apple pie see APPLE PIE

moment in time see AT THIS MOMENT IN TIME

the . . . of the moment The use of 'of the moment' to mean 'fashionable, popular' seems to have developed in the second half of the nineteenth century, and to have been a well established cliché by the turn of the century. See also MOOD OF THE MOMENT.

'There are just 200 coming to the UK this year, then another 1,000 or so in 1999, so move fast if you want to score the bike of the moment.' (*Stuff*, October 1998)

moment of truth This is a term from bull-fighting (in Spanish, *el momento de la verdad*), which is, not surprisingly, first recorded in English in Ernest Hemingway's *Death in the Afternoon* (1932). In bull-fighting, it is the moment of the final thrust with the sword that dispatches the bull; in general use it refers to a crisis or turning point, although its use is being steadily diluted.

'With fewer than 500 days before the moment of truth, the air industry has hardly begun to resolve the [millennium] bug problem.' (*Independent*, 20 August 1998)

'They felt sure that at the moment of truth in the polling booth most voters will consider their wallets.' (*Daily Telegraph*, 5 April 1992)

money can't buy you love (or **happiness**) The proverb that money can't buy happiness would seem, from the strange absence of reference to it in dictionaries of proverbs, to be a modern saying, but it has been around long enough to develop a cynical extension – 'Money can't buy you happiness, but it can rent you some for a while.' The currency of 'money can't buy you love' is largely due to the Lennon and McCartney song 'Can't Buy Me Love' (1964). Compare the BEST THINGS IN LIFE ARE FREE, a saying also given prominence by the Beatles. A further variant is 'Money can't buy you friends', or, as Spike Milligan put it in *Puckoon* (1963), 'Money can't buy friends, but you can get a better class of enemy.'

money talks This concept, perhaps best summed up by Mrs Aphra Behn's version, 'Money speaks sense in a language all nations understand' (*The Rover*, 1681), has been around since the time of the Greek playwright Euripides, and in English since the sixteenth century. Bob Dylan brought the saying up to date with his comment, 'Money doesn't talk, it swears' ('It's Alright, Ma', 1965).

'At Geneva airport, there is an advertising hoarding welcoming travellers "to a city where money talks but wealth whispers".' (*Guardian*, 11 November 1989)

'But usually money talks in football, no matter what the club, and if United do raise their bid, Wednesday – despite their protestations – may find it hard to resist.' (*Today*, 1992)

money under the mattress This is a conscious cliché to do with the hoarding peasant who does not trust institutions with his wealth. It reflects the material progress of the peasant, in that it replaced an earlier image of money buried under a brick in the fireplace or in a hole dug in the earth floor.

'Russians with any real wealth have sensibly channelled dollars overseas or kept them in cash under the mattress.' (*Evening Standard*, 28 August 1998)

money where your mouth is SEE PUT YOUR MONEY WHERE YOUR MOUTH IS

monumental effort It is difficult to see the connection between 'monumental' from something as massive and solid as a monument, and a word with the associations of 'effort'. 'Monumental' has travelled from its original sense of something connected with a tomb or memorial to our modern sense of 'great' via a number of semantic shifts since it first appeared in the early seventeenth century. 'Monumental' came to be used of actions that were great enough to deserve a monument. This was combined with the idea that monuments were usually physically large, to give the word a general sense of 'large' or 'massive'. By the middle of the nineteenth century this had been diluted to our modern vaguely emphatic meaning.

'She swallowed and with monumental effort said, "Look, I'm sorry I'm late." ' (Laura Martin, *Garden of Desire*, 1993)

'The Encyclopedia of World Rugby is a monumental effort by Keith Quinn the NZTV commentator.' (*Rugby World and Post*, 1992)

mood of the moment A sub-cliché of the formula phrase 'THE . . . OF THE MOMENT', this expression tends to be used particularly by those writing about fashion or in a particularly fey style. It does, however, avoid that fashionable alternative, *Zeitgeist* (literally, in German, 'the spirit of the time').

'Part of the charm of a sale is that the financial result is in itself a sort of critical judgement, reflecting even if not defining the taste and mood of the moment.' (Joseph Darracott, *Art Criticism: A User's Guide*, 1991)

moot point 'Moot' started life as an Anglo-Saxon term for a meeting, and by the early Middle Ages had acquired the sense of a 'discussion'. From the sixteenth century it was also used for a special gathering of law students, where interesting points of law were examined via hypothetical cases (a practice and term that lives on at university law departments). Thus 'a moot point' was originally something worthy of debate in a moot. By the eighteenth century the term had spread to cover any debatable question.

'Redpath had been called in because the body on the mud had been reported by PC Clifford from a land-based patrol car, but whether it was properly a land or a river matter was a moot point.' (J. Anderson, *Death in the City*, 1980)

moral high ground The image behind this modern cliché is of military activity, where to have the high ground is to have a 'superior' advantage from which you can 'look down on' anyone attacking you from below. The verbs such as 'occupy' and 'take' that go with this phrase often reflect this military ancestry and are meant to represent PROACTIVE, militant behaviour, rather than passive acceptance of the way things are.

'While their representatives in Paris doubt the conference delegates will discard the Minerals Convention, they are confident that they, for the moment, occupy the moral high ground.' (*Independent*, 10 October 1989)

'In vetoing repeated efforts by the state legislature to adopt the death penalty . . . Mr Cuomo has taken the moral high ground – and does not seem to have lost votes by doing so.' (*The Economist*, 1990)

more ado SEE WITHOUT MORE ADO

more equal than others In George Orwell's political satire *Animal Farm* (1945) the pigs justify their power and privilege in a society where everything is supposed to be shared, with the slogan 'All animals are equal but some are more equal than others.' This cynical manipulation of the truth has become a popular description of privilege, particularly when power has been used to obtain unfair perks. Orwell's words are themselves an echo of the American Declaration of Independence: 'We hold these truths to be self-evident, that all men are created equal . . .' In the same vein, politicians of all types like to use 'equal but different' to justify inequalities.

more in sorrow than in anger This is one of the many contributions of Shakespeare's *Hamlet* to the English language. In this case Hamlet's friend Horatio is giving an account of the appearance of the ghost of Hamlet's father, and describes him as having 'A countenance more in sorrow than in anger' (I.ii).

'Finally, more in sorrow than anger, he said, "Well, thanks a lot, Hercules. I must say, you've been a great help so far. I think I've had about as much as I can take for now." ' (Timothy Boggs, *Hercules – The Eye of the Ram*, 1997)

more means worse; less means more Kingsley Amis, writing on the expansion of higher education in *Encounter* in 1960, famously said, 'More will mean worse.' One year earlier, the architect Mies van der Rohe had written in the *New York Herald Tribune*, 'Less means more.' Between them these two statements have spawned a whole family of variants.

'This is all of the white water with none of the rafting, and less is definitely more.' (*Stuff*, October 1998)

'Unconvinced by such sales patter, some of the more hirsute members of the *Stuff* office lined up for a go with the new order of shavers, and found that more is indeed better.' (*Stuff*, October 1998)

'I simply do not accept that "more has meant worse" in our seminar rooms: it may mean that in the Cabinet Room.' (*Independent*, 24 September 1998)

more sinned against than sinning A quotation from Shakespeare's *King Lear* (III.ii), the outcast king describing himself as 'a man more sinned against than sinning'. It still tends to be used in self-justification, but not invariably.

'But never forget that snakes are more sinned against than sinning.' (*Practical Fishkeeping*, 1992)

more tea, vicar? see VICARAGE TEA PARTY

more than meets the eye This is a set phrase, popular since the nineteenth century, and used to express vague or unformulated doubts. It is often now reversed as 'There is less in this than meets the eye', a comment supposedly made by Tallulah Bankhead of one of the plays of the difficult Belgian dramatist Maeterlinck.

' "I don't give a stuff " was the far from elegant response of Her Majesty's Secretary of State for Health to suggestions that there is less to his good news than meets the eye.' (*Daily Mail*, 27 August 1998)

more than you can chew see BITE OFF MORE THAN YOU CAN CHEW

more things in heaven and earth ... Yet another quotation from *Hamlet*. Horatio questions the exact nature of the ghost of Hamlet's father, and is reproved by Hamlet with the words, 'There are more things in heaven and earth, Horatio,/ Than are dreamt of in your philosophy' (I.v).

'*The Secrets of Sleep* aims for scientific composure but its manner is very much "there are more things than are dreamt of in your philosophy".' (*Independent*, 24 July 1998)

mother of all ... This formula phrase really took off after the Iraqi President, Saddam Hussein, declared at the start of the Gulf war in January 1991, 'The great, the jewel and the mother of battles has begun.' During the war 'the mother of all battles' was much cited, often, given the emptiness of Hussein's rhetoric, ironically, and the expression caught on as a formula phrase. Previously, from the beginning of the century, 'Daddy of . . .' had been used, but usually only in a light-hearted or highly colloquial way. 'Mother of all . . .' is popular with headline writers, as in a piece on plays about the Phaedra legend headed 'The mother of all dramas' (*Independent*, 9 September 1998).

'Of the 250 hours of piano-playing made available by this mother of all compilations, only 90 minutes will never have been heard before.' (*Evening Standard*, 1 September 1998)

motley crew, on with the motley 'Motley' is a medieval word, originally meaning variegated, mixed in colour, and hence also the term for the many-coloured costume worn by a court jester. 'Motley' then developed the sense of 'various things', a 'mixed bag'. 'Motley crew' with 'motley' used in this sense of 'mixed' is found used literally by 1748 in 'With this motley crew . . . Pizarro set sail.' It had become a set phrase by the beginning of the nineteenth century. 'On with the motley', the older version of 'the tears of a clown' (the title of a 1970s hit written by William Robinson, Henry Cosby and Stevie Wonder) comes not from this, but from the words of the tragic jester in Leoncavallo's opera *I Pagliacci* (1892), as he struggles, despite his broken heart, to carry on. It is used to indicate both a SHOW MUST GO ON mentality, and the idea of struggling to carry on as normal in the most difficult circumstances, putting on a brave face.

'*Stuff* assembled a motley crew of former CD buyers and prescribed a radical course of music therapy.' (*Stuff*, October 1998)

'On with the motley, the show must go on, smile though your heart is breaking and other assorted clichés.' (Adele Geras, *The Green Behind the Glass*, 1989)

mouths of babes and sucklings see OUT OF THE MOUTHS OF BABES AND SUCKLINGS

move heaven and earth This expression for making every possible effort dates from the middle of the eighteenth century. Presumably the original idea behind it was that you tried every possible way of changing things – to move heaven with your prayers combined with taking practical action on earth.

'The Germans failed to honour this undertaking and Nicolle and Symes were court-marshalled and sentenced to death by firing squad . . . It was later established that Bandelow, who had been on leave at the time of their surrender, moved heaven and earth in his endeavour to keep his word.' (*Independent*, 3 October 1998)

'But if members tell us they are in dire straits, without a job, gone bankrupt, and the wife's run off with the milkman, then we will move heaven and earth to help them.' (*Accountancy*, 1993)

move the goalposts A recent image, taken from the world of football. If the goalposts are moved after you have kicked the ball, you have little chance of getting the ball into the net. So, 'moving the goalposts' is used for a situation where the target is changed after you have started doing something.

'The exam itself has been the subject of considerable dispute, with accusations that . . . the homelands education authorities frequently "move the goalposts" by altering the pass levels year by year.' (Sarah Graham-Brown, *Education in the Developing World*, 1991)

movers and shakers Although it was known beforehand, the use of this expression as a cliché comes from Arthur O'Shaughnessy's 1874 *Ode*, which contains the lines 'We are the music makers,/We are the dreamers of dreams . . ./Yet we are the movers and shakers/Of the world for ever, it seems.' It is a poem in praise of the power that poets wield through their words and imaginations, yet the modern use is far from the idea of 'dreamers of dreams', but is applied very much to men of action, who get things changed through their vigour.

'And from Spike Lee to Reverend Jesse Jackson, Michael Jordan to Philip Michael

Thomas, black movers and shakers now shape US opinion on more than just race.' (*The Face*, 1990)

moves in a mysterious way This tag is from a 1779 hymn written by William Cowper which starts, 'God moves in a mysterious way/His wonders to perform.' Nowadays it implies that there is no understanding the hidden motivations or workings behind something.

'Lottery regulator Oflot moves in a mysterious way its wonders to perform. Charged with the simple duty of maximising the revenue for "good causes", it has continually sanctioned higher and higher prize payouts . . . at the expense of these selfsame good causes.' (*Private Eye*, 21 August 1998)

'moving finger writes . . .' see WRITING ON THE WALL

moving the deckchairs on the *Titanic* see DECKCHAIRS ON THE *TITANIC*

(no more) Mr Nice Guy This expression, also often found in forms describing someone as the nice guy of some occupation or grouping such as, 'X, soccer's Mr Nice Guy . . .', is a twentieth-century creation. It came to prominence in the early 1970s when it was announced that Senator Ed Muskie had decided that it was going to be 'No More Mr Nice Guy' in his 1972 campaign to stand for the presidency. Then, in 1973, Alice Cooper had a hit record with a song of the same name. The expression may well be a development of the saying attributed to the American baseball player and manager, Leo 'The Lip' Durocher: 'Nice guys finish last.' Pedants will point out that what Durocher actually said, in 1946, after listing his players' names, was 'Take a look at them. All nice guys. They'll finish last. Nice guys. Finish last', but such was Durocher's reputation, that the words were interpreted in the way we now use them.

'TV beauty Davina McCall last night praised soccer firebrand Stan Collymore as a Mr Nice Guy.' (*Daily Mirror*, 21 July 1998)

'Furthermore, the speed and ease of yesterday's negotiations shows that, unlike Glenn Hoddle . . . the Dutchman is capable of learning from his mistakes. No more Mr Greedy.' (*Evening Standard*, 28 August 1998)

mum's the word This expression dates from the eighteenth century, and now has a rather dated feel to it. 'Mum', an imitation of the sound made through closed lips (and source of mumble), means 'not a word, silence', and dates from the Middle Ages.

'In fact his father-in-law had congratulated him on the perfectly splendid bit of crackling Hugh had in his arms in Chancery Lane, and naturally mum was the word, and his lips were sealed . . .' (J. Mortimer, *Summer's Lease*, 1988)

murder most foul One of the many quotations from Shakespeare's *Hamlet* that have become clichés. In Act I Scene v the ghost of his father, telling Hamlet how he died after his own brother poured poison into his ear while he was asleep, describes it as 'Murder most foul, as in the best it is;/But this most foul, strange and unnatural.' 'Murder most . . .' has become a formula phrase for headline writers, particularly in the form 'murder most horrid'.

mute, inglorious Milton Like FAR FROM THE MADDING CROWD, this is a quotation from Thomas Gray's *Elegy Written in a Country Churchyard*. Gray writes of the apparently ordinary people who are buried there, who might in their own ways have been

as heroic as those who are more famous. 'Full many a flower is born to blush unseen
... Some village-Hampden, that with dauntless breast/The little tyrant of his fields
withstood;/Some mute inglorious Milton here may rest,/Some Cromwell guiltless
of his country's blood.'

'But the untimely death of thousands of mute inglorious Princess Dianas doesn't
cause weeping crowds.' (John Mortimer, *Evening Standard*, 28 August 1998)

my wife doesn't understand me A conscious cliché, the chat-up line of an
errant husband, trying to convince the object of his desire that she is more sensitive
and understanding than the woman he is married to. Its history has not been traced,
but it is by no means recent, and has probably been in use at least throughout the
twentieth century. Eric Partridge, in his *Catchphrases*, describes it as 'prob[ably]
almost immemorial, both in Britain and the US'.

mysterious way see MOVES IN A MYSTERIOUS WAY

(final, or last, or another) nail in the coffin The subject under discussion may
not yet be DEAD AND BURIED, but the image here is of people working towards that.
This macabre expression dates from the late eighteenth century.

'It's a shrewd move. It's another nail in the coffin of the London art market and
a rather dramatic one at that.' (*Evening Standard*, 28 August 1998)

'Allowing it to become an executive toy of yet another millionaire would drive
the final nail in the coffin of the Government's green credentials – both at home
and abroad.' (*Climber and Hill Walker*, 1991)

naked truth The naked truth is the truth *unadorned* by prevarication. A favourite
with journalists, the expression has been a cliché since the nineteenth century. It
comes from the fable in which Truth and Falsehood are bathing; Falsehood gets out
first and steals Truth's clothes. Truth prefers to go naked rather than be seen dressed
in Falsehood's clothes. An alternative is the UNVARNISHED TRUTH.

'Some of the gringa women are imitating me and trying to dress "a la Mexicana",
but the poor souls only look like cabbages and to tell you the naked truth they look
absolutely impossible.' (*Oxford Art Journal*, 1991)

name and shame This is a recent development of the journalistic cliché to 'name
names', itself a development of the expression of 'name no names'. The latter is first
recorded in Fanny Burney's *Diary* from June 1792 where she writes, 'She desired he
would name no names, but merely mention that some ladies had been frightened.'
'Name and shame' or 'naming and shaming' is very popular at the moment, reflecting
a growing awareness of the power of publicity to affect the behaviour of corporations
or those in power.

'I have just received a short letter from an insurance company (I'll not name
and shame it here). It contained more than a dozen spelling, grammatical and
punctuation mistakes.' (*Independent*, 6 August 1998)

'Naming and shaming is futile.' (Headline to article on proposed public humiliation
of criminals, *Independent*, 19 June 1998)

name of the game An expression used to indicate that something is important
or central to a situation. It probably developed in sporting circles in the USA, and
had spread to more general use there by the beginning of the 1960s, reaching Britain
some ten years later.

'English rugby's top clubs assemble in London today to signal the start of a league season that still threatens to land the game in court. Brinkmanship is still the name of the game for England's top 28 clubs in the Allied Dunbar Premiership and the Rugby Football Union.' (*Evening Standard*, 28 August 1998)

nanny state In the 1980s, opponents of the idea of the CRADLE TO GRAVE welfare state started attacking it by talking in terms of a dependency culture and describing as a 'nanny state' one that looked after its citizens in this way. Since the Labour victory of 1997 the term has been expanded in the UK to cover any interference in private life by the state. Although it is so new, the terms 'nannyist' and 'nannyism' have already developed from it.

'Nicholas Ridley was a political firebrand even keener than Mrs Thatcher to dismantle what he called the nanny state and roll back the effects of years of nationalisation.' (*Central News* autocue data)

nasty, brutish and short 'No arts; no letters; no society; and which is worst of all, continual fear and danger of violent death; and the life of man, solitary, poor, nasty, brutish and short', wrote Thomas Hobbes of the state of uncivilized man in *Leviathan* (1651). The expression is very widely used, sometimes as a jibe against individuals.

'To talk of "mistresses" and "courtesans" may risk glamorizing, romanticizing or exoticizing a life that was in most cases nasty, brutish and short.' (James Davidson, *Courtesans and Fishcakes*, 1997)

nature red in tooth and claw see RED IN TOOTH AND CLAW

naughty but nice A cliché since it was used to promote cream cakes in the 1980s in an advertisement campaign said to have been written by the novelist Salman Rushdie, who once worked in advertising. The phrase was, however, in use before then, for example as the title of a film released in 1939.

'The pleasures of the romance novel are not dissimilar from those of the chocolate bar; naughty but nice.' (S. Ewen *et al.*, *Consumption, Identity and Style*, 1991)

navel gazing In the mid-nineteenth century the word 'Omphalopsychic', the name of a religious sect whose members achieved a trance state by gazing at the navels, was translated into ordinary English as 'navel-contemplators'. From this the term 'navel-contemplating' for complacent self-absorption, or a narrow view of things, came into use. By the early twentieth century this had been simplified to our modern 'navel gazing'.

'Too many trade unionists, sadly, have been happy to dismiss such fundamental questions about their role as just so much navel gazing.' (*Independent*, 17 September 1998)

near and yet so far see SO NEAR AND YET SO FAR

nearest and dearest This term for close friends and relatives has been common since the sixteenth century, its longevity no doubt helped by its rhyme.

'Revealing a gritty fortitude that was hitherto unsuspected by even my nearest and dearest, I have steeled myself sufficiently to face up to the regular consumption of restorative viands.' (*Independent*, 5 September 1998)

neck of the woods This is an American expression from the days of frontier settlement. Originally a neck of wood was a narrow, neck-shaped, stretch of woodland. However, in the States the idea was reversed, and by the 1830s 'neck of the woods' was being used for a settlement cut out of wooded country. From there it came to be used for any remote area, and then applied more generally to mean region or neighbourhood.

'However, I must admit that there is not a great deal of variety at fishmongers in this neck of the woods.' (*Independent*, 5 September 1998)

neck or nothing An expression in use since the early eighteenth century, meaning a willingness to risk all or 'go flat out' to achieve something. In horse-racing, a neck is a measurement of the distance by which a horse has won.

(I) need it like I need a hole in the head see HOLE IN THE HEAD

needle in a haystack This expression for an impossible search is only found in the form in which we now use it from the mid-nineteenth century, but the idea is much older. In the past the image was a little less ambitious, as people looked for the needle, not in a whole haystack, but in a 'bottle of hay', the old equivalent of a bale – still an all but impossible task. However, the origin of the expression may be LOST IN THE MISTS OF TIME, for it exists in a number of other languages, and may have reached English from one of them.

'If you have to use files created by someone else, finding out which file you want to retrieve can be like looking for a needle in a haystack, particularly if that person is out of the office.' (Hari Andralojc et al., *Microsoft Word: Training Guide*, 1990)

needless to say A companion cliché to GOES WITHOUT SAYING, and, like it, usually little more than a filler.

'The householders who lived above the valley bottoms were not happy about paying two sets of rates, needless to say, especially when the towns on the tops of the hills found themselves subsidizing drainage benefits for lowland farmers.' (J. Purseglove, *Taming the Flood*, 1989)

needs no introduction A pompous-sounding introduction formula, loved by chairpersons through the land. It is not very encouraging for the person being introduced, for the very fact that it is nearly always a preamble to an introduction means that it carries the subtext, 'You probably don't know who this person is, so I'm going to tell you about them.'

'Gary Moore, a born again bluesman who certainly needs no introduction from us, had broken off from his European tour especially to take part in the event.' (*Guitarist*, 1992)

neither here nor there An alternative for 'irrelevant', this expression is often used as bluster by someone reluctant to answer a difficult question or deal with inconvenient facts. It has been in use since the sixteenth century.

'His Honour said that J's dyslexia "would appear to give him significantly greater difficulty in learning than the majority of children of his age", and that J's high intelligence was "neither here nor there" in relation to the specific cause of the learning difficulty.' (Susan Johnstone et al., *The Legal Context of Teaching*, 1992)

nerve centre Coined about the middle of the nineteenth century as a term for a group of nerves, this was transferred by the 1870s to the administrative centre from which an organization was controlled.

'Repairing the midsole, often the nerve centre of the modern shoe, can be more difficult.' (*Running*, 1991)

'For Cologne, although not the capital city of North Rhine Westphalia, which is Düsseldorf, is the closest to Bonn and as the capital of the republic Bonn is the nerve centre of government.' (Frederick Forsyth, *The Deceiver*, 1992)

nest see FOUL YOUR NEST

never a dull moment This originated in the 1880s, but took on an ironic tone in the Second World War when it became a naval catch-phrase used in times of danger or frantic activity.

'The hotel also has a great variety of light meals/snacks and also has its own TV and video – so there'll never be a dull moment!' (Club 18–30 Summer Holiday Brochure 1990)

never darken my door again A conscious cliché, used to evoke the image of the stern Victorian father casting off the errant child, an image summed up by Tennyson in his poem *Dora* (1842): 'You shall pack/And never darken my doors again.' The earliest recorded use of the expression is by Benjamin Franklin of someone who had taken offence, 'I am afraid she would resent it so as never to darken my door again' (*Busy-body*, 1729), but as is clear from the way he uses it, it was obviously already well established. 'To darken a door' by itself was used in the past simply to mean 'to enter'.

never did me any harm Usually now a conscious cliché, due to the stereotype of the old buffer asserting that if something had been good enough for him in the past, it should be good enough for the young now. A comparison to I DIDN'T GET WHERE I AM TODAY BY . . .

'Writing captions for the legendary "Bootiful Baby" competition in the *Diss Express* or venturing a hard-hitting critique of the Hedgehog Rescue scheme for the *Bury Free Press*, never did me any harm.' (*Independent*, 26 August 1998)

never knowingly undersold This is a slogan associated since the 1920s with the John Lewis Partnership shops. It is used sarcastically of the flamboyant.

'Never knowingly undersold in terms of body language, Fergie has been supplying us with fascinating insights into her private life for years.' (*You* magazine, 20 September 1998)

never mind the . . . , feel the . . . A formula phrase, based on 'never mind the quality, feel the width', a catch-phrase meant to parody the patter of a market salesman, dating from the mid-twentieth century. It became much more widely known and used after it was the title of a successful television sitcom which ran from 1967 to 1971.

'Never mind the ethics, feel the warmth.' (Headline, *Independent*, 27 September 1998)

never the twain shall meet This is a quotation cliché, indicating mutual incompatibility, taken from Rudyard Kipling's *The Ballad of East and West* (1892): 'Oh, East is East, and West is West, and never the twain shall meet.'

'Inside a packed-to-capacity press box, national passions were running high, Scottish press corps to the right, English press to the left, and never the twain shall meet.' (*Liverpool Echo & Daily Post*, 1993)

new age Originally used by self-designated New Agers for an approach to life that emphasized the spiritual and natural, this has been taken up to describe anything vaguely alternative (another cliché) or concerned for the environment.

'A joint European Community statement described unification as heralding "a new age for Germany and all of Europe".' (*Keesing's Contemporary Archives*, 1990)

'She said he'd got into all this New Age stuff, and kept telling her they were soul mates and must be together.' (Val McDermid, *Dead Beat*, 1992)

new broom This way of describing a newly appointed person who arrives at a job full of ideas and enthusiasm for change, comes from the saying 'a new broom sweeps clean'. It dates from at least the mid-nineteenth century.

'As the new man at Century wielding the new broom, he expected that decisions and policies would come to his desk.' (Gerald Seymour, *Archangel*, 1983)

new high or **low** see HIT A NEW HIGH

new lease of life The image of a lease on something abstract goes back to the sixteenth century – the Countess of Pembroke wrote of 'A lease of bliss with endless date'. The idea of someone who has recovered from illness taking on a new lease of (or on) life is recorded from the beginning of the nineteenth century, and before the end of that century had been transferred to mean a more general renewal.

'I must say, moving to Wimbledon has given me a new lease of life. I am encouraged by Joe to go out and express myself and it is a pleasure to be there.' (*Evening Standard*, 10 September 1998)

'Video was supposed to supersede cinema; instead, it has given the big screen a new lease of economic life.' (*Independent*, 17 September 1998)

new rock and roll A journalistic vogue phrase dating from the early 1990s, and used to suggest that something is so popular that it has replaced music in popularity, although quite why a term so dated as rock and roll is used is unclear. Variants on the formula '. . . is the new . . .' abound, particularly '. . . is the new black'.

'In the world of profitable business, customer service is the new rock n' [*sic*] roll.' (*Around Resources* magazine, quoted in *Private Eye*, 24 July 1998)

'Is interior design the new rock'n'roll, I ask. "I prefer to think of it as the new chocolate. Not particularly necessary, but indulgent and delicious." ' (*Independent*, 3 August 1998)

'A steep price tag accompanied it, setting me back an alarming £550. But how could I have resisted it in my quest for all things grey? It is the new black, after all.' (*Daily Mail*, 27 August 1998)

nice day see HAVE A NICE DAY

nice guys finish last see MR NICE GUY

nice little earner Although it was already well established beforehand, this expression became much more widely used thanks to the popularity of the television series *Minder* (written by Leon Griffiths and running 1979–85, 1988–94), where it was a catch-phrase of the lovable rogue Arthur Daley.

'Few can rival the Natural History Museum's offer of drinks beneath its dinosaur, but Christmas and new-year parties have become a nice little earner for museums and galleries right across the country.' (*The Economist*, 1991)

nice work if you can get it This expression was popularized by a 1937 George and Ira Gershwin song. Ira Gershwin later said that he had got the expression from a *Punch* cartoon by George Blecher, but this has yet to be traced.

'Nice work if you can get it, I thought as the tail lights of her Daimler (or was it a Rolls?) disappeared into the night.' (*Today*, 1992)

nicely see THAT'LL DO NICELY

nick of time The history of this expression, meaning just in time or at the critical moment, is rather obscure. It appears to be the same word as that meaning a small cut or notch, and, in the simple form 'the nick', is used to mean 'the exact moment' from 1577 ('nick of time' is dated 1674). One possibility is that it comes from the use of 'the nick' to mean 'the exact point aimed at', although this is not recorded until 1602. However, records of these colloquial terms are so erratic and unreliable, that thirty years' difference may not be significant.

'If anyone thinks my language exaggerated or highly coloured – and such there might well be, considering that no one here under pensionable age can have any recollection of a world without rent restriction or subsidised rents – let him recall another upas tree which we only managed to cut down in the nick of time ten years ago.' (Enoch Powell, *Reflections of a Statesman*, 1991)

night follows day see SURELY AS NIGHT FOLLOWS DAY

night of the soul see DARK NIGHT OF THE SOUL

nip in the bud This is generally thought to come from the effect of a late spring frost that kills flower buds and causes them to drop off. In use since the sixteenth century, it is famously part of the standard illustration of the mixed metaphor, attributed to the Irish politician Sir Boyle Roche (1743–1807): 'Mr Speaker, I smell a rat; I see him forming in the air and darkening the sky; but I'll nip him in the bud.'

'The problem is dauntingly vast. But had Unicef and its partners in the international aid community not been so dazzled by their own success, they might have nipped it in the bud years ago.' (*Independent*, 5 September 1998)

no accounting for taste see TAKES ALL SORTS

no alternative see ALTERNATIVE

no comment A standard response to intrusive enquiries from the media, this is often taken to be a confirmation of the question. It has been used as a conscious cliché or catch-phrase since the middle of the twentieth century.

'The ANC yesterday made a discreet "no comment" on the latest rumours that the couple are on the verge of divorce.' (*Daily Telegraph*, 6 April 1992)

' "No comment" means "as guilty as hell".' (Environmental Health Officers' Conference: lecture)

no expense spared This expression, dating from the nineteenth century, is now often used ironically.

'They promised a "Rolls Royce" solution to the problem – no expense spared.' (Crispin Aubrey, *Melt Down: Collapse of a Nuclear Dream*, 1991)

'Let me assure all you good citizens and voters of Riverbank that no stone shall remain unturned, no avenue unexplored, no expense spared in ridding our fair community of this dreadful menace.' (Stephen Lawhead, *A Tale of Anabelle Hedgehog*, 1990)

no flies on ... If you have no flies on you, you are active, alert and know what is going on, like the livelier cows in a field whose twitching and tail-swishing means the flies do not settle on them but choose the dull, sluggish ones instead. The expression is recorded from the mid-nineteenth century in both the USA and Australia (which suggests it was in use by immigrants from the UK, though it is unrecorded there). By 1900 it was so well established in the USA that there was a Salvation Army hymn entitled 'There Are No Flies on Jesus' which contained the immortal lines, 'There may be flies on you and me,/But there are no flies on Jesus', something to give pause to anyone who thinks HAPPY-CLAPPY evangelism is something new.

no fury like a woman scorned see HELL HATH NO FURY LIKE A WOMAN SCORNED

no hiding place The history of this expression is unrecorded although its inspiration might be Psalm 139 which describes how there is no hiding place from an omniscient God, a theme taken up by a number of later poets. It is an alternative to HE CAN RUN, BUT HE CAN'T HIDE, and has been well used in the twentieth century, appearing as the title of at least two books, in 1951 and 1962. To anyone middle-aged it has very strong associations with adventure and bringing criminals to justice, from its use as the title of an enormously successful police drama which ran from 1959 to 1967, the theme tune of which entered the pop charts in 1960.

'We will leave no hiding place for terrorists.' (Jack Straw, Home Secretary, 27 August 1998)

no joke/no joking (or **laughing**) **matter** Things have been described as 'no laughing matter' since the sixteenth century, but 'it's no joke' dates only from the early nineteenth century, although 'joking apart' is found from a century earlier. There is often an element of indignation or bluster in the use of these expressions.

'Really, all this is no joke. It has created stress beyond measure ... In extremis there have been suicides, nervous breakdowns, medical retirements.' (*Independent*, 23 July 1998)

'The coordinating of the various world pick-ups did try the patience of all concerned and the long waits at 5am on a chilly Christmas morning were no laughing matter.' (Roy Dunlop, *In All Directions*, 1986)

no more Mr Nice Guy see MR NICE GUY

no pain, no gain A proverb which seems to date from the middle of the nineteenth century, although the sentiment appears earlier. It is also found in the form 'no gain without pain'. John Major tried out a substitute when he said of his economic policy in 1989, 'If it isn't hurting, it isn't working.'

'For years, America's unions shied away from strikes because the pain wasn't worth the gain.' (*Evening Standard*, 10 September 1998)

there's no peace for the wicked This is an adaptation of the biblical 'There is no peace, saith the Lord, unto the wicked' (Isaiah 48:22). It has only been in use since the 1940s, as a resigned or wry comment by the busy when yet more work is thrust upon them.

no picnic A picnic is meant to be a time of relaxed enjoyment in a quiet pastoral setting. It had come to be used as a colloquial term for a treat or lively time by the early years of the nineteenth century (Keats writes, in a letter of 1818, 'you may like a little picnic of scandal'), and by the 1880s the ironic 'no picnic' has come to mean the opposite of this.

'Like with the conditions at Holloway, I knew it would be no picnic, but I just didn't think they would treat human beings like that, anywhere.' (Una Padel and Prue Stevenson, *Insiders: Women's Experience of Prison*, 1988)

no place or **nowhere to go** see ALL DRESSED UP AND NO PLACE TO GO

no stone unturned see LEAVE NO STONE UNTURNED

no such thing as a free lunch Around about the 1840s, American bars began advertising 'free lunches' when you bought a drink. These were usually salty snacks put out to encourage you to drink more. John Farmer's *Americanisms* of 1889 contains the entry: 'The free lunch fiend . . . is one who makes a meal of what is really provided as a snack. He pays for a drink, but shamefacedly manages in this way to get something more than his money's worth.' So the free luncher does not really get his lunch for free – he must not only buy his drink, but if he is really to make a lunch out of it, must pay in subterfuge or embarrassment. The expression is sometimes attributed to the American economist Milton Friedman as it was much used by him and was the title of one of his books, but it antedates him. It may have been formulated by a group of economists at the University of Chicago school of economics, possibly based on some unrecorded folk saying. Robert Heinlein's 1966 novel *The Moon is a Harsh Mistress* used a slightly different wording as a repeated motif: 'There aint no such thing as a free lunch', which could be shortened to the acronym TANSTAAFL. The expression is usually used allusively or as a formula phrase.

'American experts think the drug might impede the absorption of vitamins, or might lead to an increased susceptibility to breast cancer. There are no free lunches.' (*Independent*, 22 September 1998)

'There's no such thing as a free holiday.' (*Out of Sight*, CITV, 22 September 1998)

no two ways about it This expression, recorded in America as early as 1818, means that there is no alternative, it is not to be doubted.

'I'm frightened of the probation and the social services finding out that I'm using again, 'cos when I came out this time, they said to me that, if I ever went back on the smack, the kids'd be took off me, no two ways about it.' (R. Newcombe *et al.*, *Living with Heroin*, 1988)

no-win (or **win–win**) **situation** 'No win' has been a cliché since the 1960s. It is particularly popular in works on business, negotiating and inter-personal relationships. These books often advocate a change from the macho, confrontational style of business in which if negotiations fail neither side gets what it wants – a no-win situation. Instead they recommend a more consensus-based style of doing business in which negotiation leads to both sides getting what they want – a win–win situation. In modern business theory, as Gerard Nierenberg, president of the Negotiation Institute, put it in the *Wall Street Journal* in 1987, 'In a successful negotiation, everybody wins.' 'No win' has spread to have a more general sense of 'a loser', while win–win' has started to be used of personal relationships.

nodding acquaintance In the days when manners were more formal, someone you had been introduced to, but did not really know, would be recognized with a nod, rather than with a more complicated form of recognition such as a bow or curtsey. 'Nodding acquaintance' in this sense is recorded from the early nineteenth century, but it does not seem to have been used of things until the later part of the century or the beginning of the next.

'When the 1976 championship year began for Hunt, he was driving a car with which he had no more than a nodding acquaintance.' (Keith Botsford, *The Champions of Formula One*, 1988)

nose clean see KEEP YOUR NOSE CLEAN

not a happy bunny or **camper** see HAPPY BUNNY

not a pretty picture see PRETTY AS A PICTURE

not as such This expression, probably originally legal jargon of the nineteenth century, is now largely used as a filler, as obfuscation, or as a weasely way of saying 'no'.

'They lay down minimum standards, and do not as such provide an incentive, exerting upward pressure to achieve top quality performance.' (J. E. Parkinson, *Corporate Power and Responsibility*, 1993)

'There are exceptions, but the fact that information is held in confidence is not as such a sufficient reason for exemption.' (Susan Johnstone, Penelope Pearce and Neville Harris, *The Legal Context of Teaching*, 1992)

not every day that you see . . . A platitudinous way of expressing surprise, this is a favourite of journalists.

'Astonished eyewitness Maggie LeMorvan, 26 . . . said: "It's not every day you see the future king and his brother going over the edge of a sheer drop like that." ' (*Daily Mail*, 10 August 1998)

not fit to hold a candle to see CAN'T HOLD A CANDLE TO

it's not for me, it's for my . . . A standard excuse when asking for such things as an autograph. While this is still to be found in all seriousness, it is most often nowadays a conscious cliché.

not lost but gone before see GONE BUT NOT FORGOTTEN

not to put too fine a point on it Although this has been described by one writer on clichés as obsolescent it is ALIVE AND WELL among the over-sensitive. It is used to mean to put bluntly, generally apologetically. It is first recorded in Dickens's *Bleak House* (1852) in a way that can still be found today: 'He was – not to put too fine a point upon it – hard up.'

'Not to put too fine a point on it, Washington could save millions of dollars and industry years of wasted time by privatising this snail's-pace bureaucracy.' (*Business*, 1991)

'I'm sure you know, Inspector, how impossible it is for even the most committed clergy to avoid incurring – not to put too fine a point on it – hatred.' (D. M. Greenwood, *Unholy Ghost*, 1991)

not wisely but too well Shakespeare's Othello describes himself as 'One that loved not wisely, but too well', to excuse his murder of his wife (V.ii). It has been a cliché since the early nineteenth century, and is usually used to describe over-indulgence in food and/or drink.

'Having dined "not wisely, but too well" on one of Georgina's extra-special Sunday lunches, they were relaxing in the garden of their Buckinghamshire home when Mark broke the news.' (M. Kilby, *Man at the Sharp End*, 1991)

not with a bang but a whimper A quotation from T. S. Eliot's 1925 poem *The Hollow Men*: 'This is the way the world ends/Not with a bang but a whimper.' While it is still associated with the end of the world or other cataclysmic event, it is often used today either with a sexual innuendo (the quotation below refers to President Clinton's apology for his dealings with Monica Lewinsky), or else as a formula phrase.

'The second and minor chord – over rehearsed yet poorly produced – is that of plaintive whining. This was the day when bang met whimper.' (*Evening Standard*, 10 September 1998)

not worth the candle SEE GAME IS NOT WORTH THE CANDLE

nothing ventured, nothing gained This is a proverbial saying, found in various forms since the Middle Ages, and from the early sixteenth century fixed in the form we use it today.

'I know I run the risk of being informed by some disdainfully incredulous reader that it's just a paraphrase of some dog-eared puzzle settled by the Pythagoreans two millennia ago. Yet, as I tell myself, nothing ventured, nothing gained.' (*Independent*, 5 September 1998)

now or never Although this saying was used by the ancient Greeks, and is recorded in English from Chaucer onwards, for many the words are irrevocably associated with the adaptation by Aaron Schroeder and Wally Gold of the Italian song 'O Sole Mio' which was a hit for Elvis Presley in 1960 under the title of 'It's Now or Never'.

'With further government setbacks in by-elections in Bradford and Bootle on 8 November, there was a strong feeling that Heseltine's reputation would be irreparably damaged if he did not stand: it was now or never.' (*Parliamentary Affairs*, 1991)

nowt so queer as folk 'Nowt' is a northern dialect form of the word 'nought' or 'nothing'. 'There's nowt so queer as folk' is only recorded from the beginning of the twentieth century, and is still to be found used proverbially, but is often a conscious cliché, used to indicate rusticity.

'My father used to say, "Nowt so queer as folk", Imogen remarked.' (Jill Paton Walsh, *A Piece of Justice*, 1995)

nuf said This is a colloquial form of 'enough said' and is used, often humorously, to indicate that no more explanation is necessary, or that it would be indiscreet to elaborate further.

numerous SEE TOO NUMEROUS TO MENTION

nuts and bolts of Used figuratively to mean either the basic, practical, HANDS ON aspects of something, or else the mechanics of it; the image coming from the small but essential bits of metal that keep things together. This use has only come in since the second half of the twentieth century.

'Sir Adrian Cadbury is not one of those who subscribes to the popular theory that a truly professional manager can take over the helm of any type of business with only a superficial knowledge of the nuts and bolts.' (David Oates and Derek Ezra, *Advice from the Top*, 1989)

O tempora! O mores! The great Roman orator Cicero, who also coined the expression MEN OF GOOD WILL, used this expression in one of his most telling political speeches. In the year 63 BC Cicero was one of the two Consuls – most senior officials – of Rome, when Catiline, a poor but capable rival, tried to foment revolution. What exactly was going on is not quite clear, since the main evidence we have against Catiline is Cicero's speech attacking him, and Cicero was quite capable of twisting facts. In the speech he gives an account of the depravity and general worthlessness of Catiline and his followers, lamenting that such things should be possible, exclaiming 'O tempora, O mores!' The reason that this expression is usually kept in Latin is that it is difficult to translate into English. While the first part is easily translated as 'O what times!', the word *mores* presents problems. It is used in modern English to mean the customs and conventions embodying the fundamental values of a society. In Latin it literally means 'customs' and is used by Cicero in a sense that falls about halfway between the modern English 'morals' and 'lifestyle'. It has been a cliché since about 1770.

'O tempora, O mores: or as Bill Clinton would say, "Why wasn't I president 30 years earlier?" ' (*Independent*, 18 September 1998)

odious see COMPARISONS ARE ODIOUS

of age see COME OF AGE

of that ilk see ILK

off message see MESSAGE

off the cuff In the past men who were about to give a speech would make notes of what they wanted to say on their shirt cuffs; by taking surreptitious glances at these, they were able to speak without a fully prepared script. This was easier in the days when shirts, particularly those worn by after-dinner speakers, were made of stiff cotton, heavily starched. Nowadays people may use biro on their hands for the same purpose, but still use the old expression to mean 'impromptu' or 'unplanned'. It is recorded from the 1930s, but may well be older.

'This fuller appreciation may result from a short or a long article, even occasionally some unexpected insight or well-phrased judgement; but it will not come from a brief comment off the cuff, an item of gossip, or a mere listing.' (Joseph Darracott, *Art Criticism: A User's Guide*, 1991)

off the wall This expression, recorded from the mid-1960s, is most often found used to mean unconventional and eccentric but can also mean angry or be an alternative for OFF THE CUFF. It is thought to come from the image of a squash ball or ice-hockey puck bouncing off a side wall unpredictably, but it may also have been influenced by the idea of someone mad or angry after being 'driven up the wall', coming down to give their views from another perspective.

'You've got to try so hard to get people's attention today that advertisers are increasingly turning to more off-the-wall techniques.' (*Independent*, September 1998)

off your own bat This expression is first found in a literal sense in 1742, used of runs at cricket scored by an individual by his own hits. It became a cliché meaning on your own initiative, by yourself, some 100 years later.

'The challenge for ITV, which has earned a peerless reputation for sticking with dog-tired formulas and not developing fresh shows off its own bat, was simple: to come up with a new Saturday-night entertainment.' (*Independent*, 7 September 1998)

an offer he can't refuse see MAKE AN OFFER HE CAN'T REFUSE

OK, Yah? The key expression identifying the 1980s Sloane Ranger type, it can still be heard today in regular use by both sexes of a certain age and class.

old as the hills An image reflecting the immensity of geological time, this dates from the beginning of the nineteenth century.

'Amaranth's eyes wandered: the hotel foyer was almost empty, and the only other couples seemed as old as the hills.' (Julian Critchley, *The Floating Voter*, 1993)

old block see CHIP OFF THE OLD BLOCK

old dog see LIFE IN THE OLD DOG YET

on a pedestal see PUT ON A PEDESTAL

on a plate see HAND SOMEONE SOMETHING ON A PLATE

on a roll In gambling, especially dice-playing, 'on a roll' is used to mean a winning streak, with the dice rolling in your favour. Both the gambling sense and the transferred sense of experiencing success or good luck in general are first recorded in the 1970s.

'By common consent the management accountants are on a roll. Chartered accountants have tended to look down on a qualification that is associated with factory floors . . . but leading firms are now starting to . . . stress the value of management accountancy to a whole range of businesses.' (*Independent*, 9 September 1998)

on message see MESSAGE

on the back burner see BACK BURNER

on the ball This expression for being efficient and alert dates from the beginning of the twentieth century and comes from the USA. The original image behind this term is of a baseball pitcher putting spin on the ball, but for most British users it is more likely to be associated with 'to keep an eye on the ball' (which has the same meaning and dates), or with soccer.

'They have good days and bad days: days when things seem relatively easy, they are on the ball, and a lot gets done, and days when they just can't face it and phone in sick.' (Guy Claxton, *Being a Teacher*, 1989)

on the brink see BACK FROM THE BRINK

on the (or **your**) **case** The image here is that of a lawyer, doctor or, most probably, a detective dealing with a case. Such work involves asking questions and investigating the details of a person's life. In the 1960s urban Blacks in the USA began to use 'case' to mean someone's personal affairs, and 'to get on someone's case' to mean to harass, badger or interfere.

'You do not have to agree with Greenslade's view that "the British tabloid press were the indirect underlying cause" of the car crash that killed Princess Diana to be glad that he is on the case about press ethics.' (*Independent*, 22 September 1998)

on the side of the angels Used to mean 'on the right side, the side of good', or even 'virtuous', this comes from a speech given by Benjamin Disraeli in 1864, on the then hotly debated subject of evolution, when he said 'Is man an ape or an angel? Now I am on the side of the angels.'

'Lonrho's ethics have been publicly queried in the past, so many in Whitehall are galled to see it cast on the side of the angels by its opposition to the Al Fayeds, after they had thwarted Lonrho's own designs on Harrods.' (*The Economist*, 1989)

on with the motley see MOTLEY CREW

on your (or **yer**) **bike** Originally 'on your bike!' was a British expression that came into use in the 1960s, meaning 'push off', 'go away', the sort of thing a policeman might say to a youth he suspects is up to no good (the Americans, meanwhile, could use 'on your horse' in the same way). From this, it also developed a more general sense of 'get a move on'. However, in 1981, shortly after a series of violent poll-tax riots, the then Conservative Minister of Employment, Norman Tebbit, said in a speech at his party's Political Conference, 'I grew up in the thirties with our unemployed father. He did not riot, he got on his bike and looked for work.' This was interpreted by the tabloid newspapers as an unsympathetic minister saying 'On yer bikes' to the unemployed, and ever since then the expression has had both the original sense, and the sense of 'go and look for work'.

once and for all In the form 'once for all' this expression dates from the fifteenth century. In the sense of 'finally and decisively', it is often found as a cliché of political and similar rhetoric.
'According to this, any theoretical statement, or political initiative, is supposed to tackle racism as a whole, all at once, and once and for all.' (J. Donald and A. Rattansi, *Race, Culture and Difference*, 1993)

once in a lifetime see CHANCE OF A LIFETIME

once more into the breach This is an adaptation of a line in the speech made by Shakespeare's Henry V at the siege of Harfleur, where he encourages his faltering troops to go back into the attack of the city walls with 'Once more unto the breach, dear friends, once more;/Or close the wall up with our English dead!' (III.i). It is used as a wry or resigned comment when getting back to the task in hand. Compare STEP INTO THE BREACH.

one brick short of a load see BRICKS SHORT OF A LOAD

one day all this will be yours, my son A conscious cliché, a favourite with cartoonists, representing a proud father displaying to his son his potential inheritance.
' "And when we are gone, all this" – he waved his hand – "all this will be yours." ' (Thomas Hayden, *The Killing Frost*, 1991)

one hundred and ten per cent A modern term for maximum or extra effort. Users seem to have no problem with the mathematical impossibility of the expression.
'Because if you achieve a hundred per cent of what's in your plan, there's always a danger that they could've achieved a hundred and ten per cent of what was in your plan and haven't been working hard.' (Tarmac Construction Ltd: training session (Business), recorded on 28 January 1994)

one in a million 'One in a million' (earlier the more moderate 'one in a thousand') is a twentieth-century cliché used to indicate the exceptional excellence of someone.
'And he'll tell you that each of us would-be Marines is one in a million – one in a

billion – except for he who sets himself above the rest of his brothers, and that one is less.' (Ian Watson, *Warhammer 40,000: Space Marine*, 1993)

one of those things see JUST ONE OF THOSE THINGS

one on one; one to one see HEART TO HEART

one that got away Originally a fishermen's saying, describing the giant fish they failed to land. When used in this way it is a conscious cliché. During the Second World War it was transferred to someone escaping from danger, and nowadays it is also found used of potential partners of the opposite sex.

the only game in town This expression comes from the USA and is still not fully naturalized in the UK. Used to mean the only important thing that is happening or the most important thing of its kind, it reflects the feelings of sports fans for whom there may be only one game out of the many worth watching at any one time.

'Eddie is downsized into redundancy when he blows the whistle on a corrupt deal that his boss has struck with a muck-spreading mining magnate; after all, "deregulation is the only game in town".' (*Independent*, 5 September 1998)

the only good . . . is a dead . . . Originally 'the only good Indian is a dead Indian', a cliché of old Westerns no longer acceptable because of its racism, it is now used as a formula phrase. The history of the original is obscured by folklore. Traditionally, General Phil Sheridan is supposed to have said this when he met the Comanche Chief Toch-a-way at Fort Cobb in 1869. In fact Toch-a-way introduced himself as 'Me Toch-a-way, me good Indian', and Sheridan is said to have responded 'The only good Indians I ever saw were dead.' If Sheridan did say this, he was merely repeating the sentiments expressed earlier by Montana Congressman James Cavanaugh who said, 'I have never in my life seen a good Indian . . . except when I have seen a dead Indian.'

'"There are more than enough killer whales around – we don't need to import them," he said. "Anyway, the only good killer whale is a dead one."' (*Independent*, 15 September 1998)

only in the mating season see DO YOU COME HERE OFTEN?

only skin deep see BEAUTY IS ONLY SKIN DEEP

open a can of worms see CAN OF WORMS

open and above board Meaning 'patently fair and honest', this phrase comes from card playing, where 'board' is the old word for table, and players were expected to keep their cards and dealings above board, where they could be seen, to avoid suspicion of cheating. Both 'above board' and the now obsolete 'under board' (for 'secretly', 'deceivingly'), are found from the early seventeenth century, although the combination with 'open' is not recorded until the mid-nineteenth century.

'But if your private affairs were open and above board you wouldn't be worrying about having to conceal a phone caller's identity – which is what you are doing.' (Miriam Macgregor, *Wilder's Wilderness*, 1993)

the opera ain't over till the fat lady sings see AIN'T OVER TILL THE FAT LADY SINGS

opium of the people (or **masses**) Karl Marx said, 'Religion . . . is the opium of the people' (*A Contribution to the Critique of Hegel's Philosophy of Right* (1843–4)) – but this was not a particularly original idea. About the same time (1848) the Rev. Charles Kingsley was writing in his *Letter to the Chartists no. 2*: 'We have used the Bible as if it was a constable's handbook – an opium-dose for keeping beasts of burden patient while they are being overloaded'. Marx's version is much snappier and caught on, the word 'masses', so common in Communist writing, often replacing the original 'people'. It is now a formula phrase, with a variety of palliatives being substituted for 'religion'. In Roman times the poet Juvenal expressed much the same idea in BREAD AND CIRCUSES.

'Romanticism . . . has in the twentieth century replaced religion as the opium of the people.' (Simon Reynolds, *Blissed Out*, 1990)

'William's grandad blamed it all on the Television, like most things, the cathode god, the new opium of the masses.' (A. Rush, *Adam's Paradise*, 1989)

out for the count Meaning 'unconscious', this expression refers to a boxer who is stunned or unable to get to his feet for the full count of ten seconds that results in a knock-out. The phase is also used figuratively in much the same way as that other sporting image, KICK INTO TOUCH.

'And there she was, the huge figure of the Headmistress, stretched full-length on her back across the floor, out for the count.' (Roald Dahl, *Matilda*, 1989)

out of court see LAUGH OUT OF COURT

out of hand see REJECT OUT OF HAND

out of line Currently a very popular expression for behaving unacceptably or in a way that does not conform to the norm, this is a shortening of 'to get (or step) out of line', an action that makes you stand out as different from all the others. Modern uses can often be rather threatening. It is recorded from the 1930s, an early example being 'He is out of line in giving Frankie the hot foot' (Damon Runyon, *Furthermore*, 1938).

out of the blue see BOLT FROM THE BLUE

out of the loop see LOOP

out of the mouths of babes and sucklings 'Out of the mouths of babes and sucklings hast thou perfected praise' is from the Bible (Matthew 21:16), which in turn derives from an earlier line in the Old Testament: 'Out of the mouths of babes and sucklings hast thou ordained strength' (Psalms 8:2). But the shortened expression, in use since at least the nineteenth century, is used nowadays not of praise, but to exclaim at some unusually perceptive or witty remark by a young person, particularly when they hit upon some truth missed or clouded by adults.

out of the running In horseracing the only horses considered 'in the running' – with a chance of winning – are the first few, and the rest are 'out of the running'. It was being transferred to other things that had no chance of winning by the second half of the nineteenth century.

out on a limb This image of someone or something stuck, dangerously exposed at the end of a tree branch, and unable to escape by climbing elsewhere, is originally an Americanism, used since the end of the nineteenth century to mean being in an isolated position or at a disadvantage. The first recorded use is the splendidly Western:

'Seven of us . . . seein' whatever can we tie down an' brand, when some Mexicans gets us out on a limb' (A. H. Lewis, *Wolfville*, 1897).

'Oliver Sacks is hardly putting himself out on a limb when he affirms that the brain is not like a computer: neuroscientists have been telling the Artificial Intelligence buffs that for years.' (*New Statesman and Society*, 1992)

(cast into) outer darkness 'But the children of the kingdom shall be cast out into outer darkness: there shall be weeping and gnashing of teeth' comes from the gospel of St Matthew (8:12) and he repeats the exact words from 'cast' to 'teeth' twice more (chapters 22 and 25). The variant 'wailing and gnashing of teeth' comes from yet another similar passage in Matthew (13:42). 'Outer darkness' here is the equivalent of Hell, the state of being cut off from the Light of God. It has been used since the nineteenth century to mean being rejected as a social outcast.

'After all, the postal map of London S.W.1 had been drawn with a special excrescence to enable Harrods to be included in it and thus avoid the ignominy of falling within the outer darkness of S.W.3 or 7.' (Peter Lewis, *The Fifties: Portrait of a Period*, 1989)

over a barrel This expression, which started life in the USA, derives from the former custom of putting someone rescued from drowning head-down over a barrel to help clear their lungs of water, hence its use to mean 'helpless', 'in someone's power'. It is not recorded until the 1930s, but is probably older.

'Lange admitted that he had "been over a barrel" after the French government had threatened that unless the accord was accepted, New Zealand would be denied access to French markets for its agricultural exports, the mainstay of its economy.' (*Keesing's Contemporary Archives*, 1990)

over and done with This set phrase, useful for emphasis, but often used when none is necessary, was a cliché by the middle of the nineteenth century.

'Wright's spot kick was so hurried it was as if he wanted to get it over and done with while no one was looking.' (*Today*, 1992)

over bar the shouting SEE ALL OVER BAR THE SHOUTING

over-egg the pudding Eggs added to a pudding make it richer, but put too many in and it is spoilt. Dating from the late nineteenth century, this was originally used to mean to exaggerate or argue something over-forcefully, but has now been extended to include going too far in general.

'The proposals sensibly resist any temptation to over-egg an already rich international pudding by staging more one-day internationals than are presently staged in England.' (*Daily Telegraph*, 17 April 1992)

over the hill The image behind this expression is of someone 'going downhill', no longer at the top of their achievements. It is comparatively recent, being recorded only since 1950.

'Scott knew that Annabel was now facing the worst moment any model can face: she was officially over the hill, gaining weight, losing her looks and on the downward path to wrinkles and sag.' (S. Conran, *Crimson*, 1992)

over the moon Although this expression of joy, a cliché since the 1970s, is chiefly associated with footballers and their managers, its origins are very different. It was part of the special slang used by a group of aristocratic, art- and philosophy-loving

Victorians and Edwardians known as 'The Souls', who used to communicate with each other in a highly precious, specialized language which effectively excluded outsiders. They used it in much the same way as the footballers, to express great pleasure, a desire to 'jump for joy', and took it from the nursery rhyme in which 'The cow jumped over the moon'. The earliest recorded use goes back as far as 1857.

'What about relatives' reactions? "His mum wasn't over the moon and mine . . . well, mine is still waiting for me to get a proper job." ' (*You* magazine, 20 September 1998)

overwhelming response A common, modern, cliché used by organizers of events to puff their own success, who rarely actually drown under the flood of responses despite the literal sense of 'overwhelm'.

'The response to our campaign to find Britain's best organic food has been so overwhelming . . . that the judges of today's awards are preparing themselves for a mouthwateringly difficult choice.' (*You* magazine, 20 September 1998)

in your own backyard An American equivalent of 'on your own HOME GROUND', which is now naturalized in English, this does not seem to have become a cliché until about the middle of the twentieth century.

'[Football fans] seem to love the fact that famous foreigners are ready to come and play in their own backyards.' (*Evening Standard*, 17 September 1998)

own bat see OFF YOUR OWN BAT

own goal If you score an own goal in soccer, you are working against your own side and helping the opposition. Thus the phrase is used to mean something you score against yourself, that works to your disadvantage. The expression reached a wider public in the 1970s when it was the sardonic term used by the British Army in Northern Ireland to describe terrorists who were blown up by their own bombs before they could use them to kill others.

'His admission that Central Office had put a tabloid newspaper in touch with the consultant at the centre of the case was a spectacular own goal.' (*Daily Telegraph*, 4 April 1992)

own home ground see HOME GROUND

own worst enemy The idea of someone who does more harm to himself than others can do to him goes back to Greek and Roman times, but in the form we have it is twentieth century. A famous comment by Ernest Bevin (1881–1951) involving the phrase is recorded by Sir Roderick Barclay in his book *Ernest Bevin and the Foreign Office* (1975): 'A Ministerial colleague with whom Ernie [Bevin] was almost always on bad terms was Nye Bevan. There was a well-known occasion when the latter had incurred Ernie's displeasure, and one of those present, seeking to excuse Nye, observed that he was sometimes his own worst enemy. "Not while I'm alive 'e ain't!" retorted Ernie.' Similar exchanges have been attributed to others.

'In reviewing some Scriabin discs in your March issue, RM wrote that "in some respects, of course, Scriabin acted as his own worst enemy by surrounding his works with a pseudo-philosophical aura of largely incomprehensible mysticism." ' (*CD Review*, 1992)

packing see SEND PACKING

pain in the neck Used to mean someone irritating, and often shortened to simply 'a pain', this is a polite version of 'pain in the arse', although it could be argued that there is a slight difference both in the meaning of the two expressions and the people about whom you use them; the pain in the neck being more cerebral than that lower down. Both are recorded from the early twentieth century, but are probably older.

'Many who professed to revere the principle found it hard to like the example they were faced with in Mr Rushdie's case: the book unreadable and the writer a pain in the neck.' (*The Economist*, 1991)

painstaking see TAKE PAINS

paint dry see INTERESTING AS WATCHING PAINT DRY

pale into insignificance An expression dating from the early twentieth century, 'pale' is used here in the same way as 'fade' might be.

'The amounts of money involved, however, pale into insignificance when compared with the vast sums spent each year on older areas such as "big physics".' (*New Scientist*, 1991)

pan out This comes from panning for gold, where gold is said to be 'panned out' of the gravel it is mixed with. The expression is found literally from the 1830s, and used figuratively to mean 'to end up', 'to have a result', from about thirty years later.

'As the movie industry would soon learn, this cool-headed assessment of the way he hoped his career would pan out would soon include his rejection of many scripts including *The Godfather*, *The Sting* and *The Great Gatsby*.' (John Parker, *The Joker's Wild: Biography of Jack Nicholson*, 1991)

pants down see CATCH WITH YOUR PANTS DOWN

par for the course In golf, 'par' is used to mean the number of strokes an excellent player should need to complete a hole, and 'par for the course' the number he should need to complete a round. The expression was coined in the late nineteenth century, and was in use figuratively to mean average, normal, what you would expect, by the 1920s.

'Long hours and tough working conditions are often par for the course in catering.' (*Caterer & Hotelkeeper*, 1991)

part and parcel Many of our English expressions which repeat the same idea in two ways come from legal language, when lawyers have tried to cover themselves against misinterpretation of their words or people weaselling out of the spirit of the law while obeying the letter, and this is no exception. 'Parcel' here is used in the original sense of the word, which is a small part, a particle – rather than in its modern sense of something you get through the post. Thus 'part and parcel', in use in a legal sense from the sixteenth century, means 'part and sub-division of that part'. It has been used more generally to mean 'all, every bit' since at least the beginning of the nineteenth century.

'Keeping our dogs alive longer, and buying a second dog as company for the first are part and parcel of modern living; but both have associated problems which are in danger of being misunderstood.' (*Dogs Today*, 1992)

a parting of the ways A parting of the ways is a crossroads or junction, used in the King James Bible in this sense: 'For the king of Babylon stood at the parting of the way, at the head of the two ways' (Ezekiel 21:21). It took until the nineteenth century before it was transferred to mean people 'going down different paths' in their lives, a separation of some sort.

'Norman comes in looking solemn, and only then do the warning bells start going off in my head . . . Why does Norman have a face like a turbot? He sits down, fidgets a bit, then looks up and says, "I'm afraid we've come to the parting of the ways."' (*Independent*, 23 September 1998)

parting shot All the might of the Roman Empire could never manage to subdue the Mesopotamia-based Empire of the Parthians, their only serious rivals as a world power. One reason for this was that the Romans fought as massed infantry, while the Parthian army was of lightly armed skirmishing cavalry, that the Roman army could never get to grips with. If the Romans tried to engage them they would scatter, turning round over their horses' rumps to fire devastating arrows at the Romans. This ability to attack while running away became known as the Parthian shot, found in the form 'Parthian blow' as early as the sixteenth century. Since the shot was fired while parting from the scene, it is probable that this expression mutated into our 'parting shot', a term for getting the last word in, usually a cutting remark made on leaving, which is found from the nineteenth century.

'As he reached the end of the quay, where the road ascends steeply from the harbour, he turned for one parting shot: "You marry him, then!" he shouted.' (Charles Gidley, *Armada*, 1988)

partner in crime This expression is used figuratively as a jocular extension of the word partner. Its history is not known.

'The Yorkshire-based player selected his old "partner in crime" Ken Brown . . . as his first lieutenant.' (*Daily Mail*, 27 August 1998)

pass in the night see SHIPS THAT PASS IN THE NIGHT

pass muster In military jargon, a 'muster' meant an inspection, and 'to pass muster' meant to pass the inspection. It is found used figuratively from 1574, and by the eighteenth century was being used frequently enough to count as a cliché.

'Critically surveying her reflection, she told herself she would pass muster.' (Philippa Wiat, *The Child Bride*, 1990)

pass on a hot potato see HOT POTATO

pass the buck see BUCK STOPS HERE

passion and pride see PRIDE AND PASSION

past (or **passed**) **its sell-by date** A term, derived from the dates on supermarket food labels, used to describe something that is getting rather tired or has become stale. It dates only from the 1980s, when such labels became common.

'The answer is that the placenta, the baby's life-support system, is apt to get a bit past its sell-by date around week 42: it's not necessarily a dramatic decline, but there is evidence that babies can lose weight and fail to thrive as it gradually packs up.' (*Independent*, 22 September 1998)

' "I don't want to seem to be making trouble here," he said, "but it doesn't strike you, does it, that these men are a bit, well, past their sell-by date? A little, not to put too fine a point on it, old?" ' (Terry Pratchett, *Interesting Times*, 1994)

pastures new see FRESH FIELDS AND PASTURES NEW

path to someone's door SEE BEAT A PATH TO SOMEONE'S DOOR

patter of little (or **tiny**) **feet** The probable source of this expression is Longfellow's *Tales of the Wayside Inn* (1862), a popular poem in its day: 'I hear in the chamber above me/The patter of little feet,/The sound of a door that is opened,/And voices soft and sweet.' It became a general term for small children, either actual or expected, but since at least 1920 has rarely been used straight, but instead ironically, or twisted into something like 'the thunder of little feet'.

'It was obvious Irene could already hear wedding bells, and the patter of little feet.' (Alice Grey, *Hearts in Hiding*, 1993)

pave the way If you pave a road or path you make it easier for someone to get where he wants to go; thus to pave the way for something or someone has been used since the sixteenth century to mean to make it easier for them to do what they want.

'In a case which could pave the way for other people living near Sellafield to bring similar claims, the couple are suing British Nuclear Fuels, which weekly pumps millions of gallons of low-level nuclear waste into the Irish Sea from Sellafield.' (*Independent*, 3 October 1989)

pay the price Most cultures have stories that tell of heroes who have to sacrifice something of enormous value to get what they want. Jephthar finds out after the event that the price of victory is the sacrifice of his only child; Woden sacrifices an eye to acquire wisdom. 'Pay the price' is recorded in the sense of 'suffer a penalty' from the sixteenth century, and most modern uses relate to this; but the older idea of sacrifice is also found from the nineteenth century, and is illustrated by Woodrow Wilson's 1916 speech: 'There is a price which is too great to pay for peace, and that price can be put in one word: One cannot pay the price of self-respect.'

'Dalglish paid the price for that lack of success last week when the board replaced him with Dutchman Ruud Gullit.' (*Evening Standard*, 1 September 1998)

pay your dues To pay your dues is literally to pay what you owe, whether it be a tax or a subscription for membership of some group. The expression is used to mean both to fulfil your obligations, pay what you owe (usually to society) in a figurative sense, and also to mean to undergo hardship or gain experience, a use not dissimilar to 'It's the price you have to pay for . . .' This latter use developed in the USA in the 1940s, possibly among urban Blacks.

'However, I state again that enforcement procedures offer plenty of opportunities for someone to pay their dues and so avoid imprisonment.' (*Hansard Extracts 1991–2*)

'It sounds like a meteoric rise, but Dermot says: "We've all paid our dues in other bands so it's not quite as spectacular as it looks." ' (*Belfast Telegraph*)

peaches and cream A description of a woman's complexion, in use since the very beginning of the twentieth century, it has also been transferred to conjure up a whole aura of attractiveness (compare ENGLISH ROSE).

'By now the "peaches and cream" teenager was in her forties, and grey haired, with nine children to feed and clothe.' (Wendy Green, *Getting Things Done: Eva Burrows – A Biography*, 1988)

go pear-shaped A cliché of the 1990s, the expression was originally RAF slang.

Presumably the idea behind it is that if something you are dealing with is meant to be spherical or round, and ends up pear-shaped, you are in trouble.

'Then, in the early Nineties, everything went pear-shaped. The tabloids were screaming blue murder, a girl on ecstasy died, and rival security firms were waging a "door war" over control of the now lucrative bouncing contracts.' (*Independent*, 14 August 1998)

(to cast) pearls before swine In the Bible (Matthew 7:6), Jesus says, 'Give not that which is holy unto the dogs, neither cast ye your pearls before swine, lest they trample them under their feet', the pearls here being pearls of wisdom, or at least of the holy word. From this the expression has come to mean to offer things you value to people who will not appreciate them, a use found from at least the seventeenth century, and clichéd by the nineteenth. (See further at AGE BEFORE BEAUTY.)

'Course Television Coverage of the Arts is mainly a matter of pearls before swine and horses before carts.' (Liz Lockhead, *True Confessions and New Clichés*, 1985)

pecking order In the 1920s scientists observed that hens have a social system whereby a hen will peck at any hen less dominant than it is, but not at those more dominant. In this way they establish and maintain a social hierarchy. By the 1950s this has been transferred to other animals and to humans, although this possibility has been present from the start, for the first recorded use of 'pecking order', by the novelist Aldous Huxley, brother of the zoologist Julian Huxley, from whom he may have learnt it, makes a comparison between hens and human hierarchies.

'He has started just two matches so far, having been pushed down the pecking order by the arrival of £2 million David Rocastle from Arsenal.' (*Today*, 1992)

pedestal see PUT ON A PEDESTAL

pen to paper see PUT PEN TO PAPER

people (power), the people's . . . These are very productive cliché generators at the moment. The emotive use of 'people' in this way goes back to nineteenth-century socialism, but became particularly active as a source of slogans from the 1960s. 'Power to the people', the obvious ancestor to 'people power', was used by the American Black radical party, the Black Panthers, from about 1968, and was also used as the title of a John Lennon song of 1971. 'People power' has spawned a number of expressions, the most prominent of which has been 'GIRL POWER'. 'The people's . . .' has the same background, being used in the reform movement of the nineteenth century, with the Chartists in the 1840s, for instance, campaigning for the adoption of the People's Charter, and this has had a strong influence on modern politics. 'The people's choice' is an old political campaign slogan. With the election of the Labour party in the UK in 1997 and the death of Diana, Princess of Wales in the same year, the formula took on a new lease of life. 'The people's Princess' was coined by the Prime Minister's press secretary, Alastair Campbell, in the aftermath of Diana's death, and subsequent uses of 'the people's' have been so prolific, that it is now used ironically.

'She [Princess Anne] shook 218 hands, accepted 12 bouquets, unveiled three plaques, patted one dog and asked "Are you local" at least 146 times. Just another 48 hours in the life of the other (and very much unsung) People's Princess.' (*Daily Mail*, 27 August 1998)

'They will look about for someone in touch with the spirit of the age – classless, sensitive, tearful, family-minded . . . the people's poet.' (*Independent*, 7 November 1998)

petard SEE HOIST WITH YOUR OWN PETARD

pick and choose This expression uses the repetition of meaning so common in set phrases, and has been current since the seventeenth century.

'The unique Options section provides a vast menu of extra activities from which you and your students can pick and choose according to your own needs.' (OUP English Language Teaching promotional leaflet, 1992)

pick of the bunch SEE BEST OF THE BUNCH

pick up (or **take up**) **the gauntlet; thrown down the gauntlet** These expressions come from the medieval custom of throwing down a glove or gauntlet (hand-armour) to challenge someone to a fight, and of picking it up as a sign of acceptance. They were being used metaphorically by the seventeenth century.

'At least nine brave souls have declared that they will take up his mocking gauntlet. They should be under no illusion that he will treat them kindly should they fail.' (*Independent*, 4 September 1998)

'Do you want me to apologise for picking up the gauntlet you threw down?' (Amanda Richmond, *The Stolen Heart*, 1992)

pick yourself up Use of this cliché as an alternative to 'pull yourself together' was reinforced in 1936 by the Jerome Kern/Dorothy Fields song with its instructions to 'Pick yourself up,/Dust yourself down,/And start all over again.'

'We have to pick ourselves up now for the home match against Liverpool. When you're 3-0 up there is no way you should be beaten.' (*Evening Standard*, 10 September 1998)

picture of health This was probably already well established when Jane Austen used the expression in *Emma* (1815), for she says, 'One hears sometimes of a child being "the picture of health".' 'Picture' here is used in much the same way as 'image' might be.

'In spite of the anxiety she had recently undergone, she was the picture of health, and Roger's heart warmed – as everyone's did – when she gave him her radiant smile.' (Mary Gervaise, *The Distance Enchanted*, 1983)

pie in the sky In the 1911 satirical song 'The Preacher and the Slave', written as a parody of the sort of hymns put out by the Salvation Army, the slave is promised, if he works hard and is subservient, 'You will eat, bye and bye, in the glorious land above the sky! Work and pray, live on hay, you'll get pie in the sky when you die.' It was written by Joe Hill, unionist and leader of the International Workers of the World, as part of their campaign to improve working conditions. For a similar sentiment see JAM TOMORROW.

'He expressed the hope that my presence would "give a boost to the standing of art history in the school", but unfortunately that wish was pie in the sky.' (Michael Falk, *Part of the Furniture*, 1991)

piece of cake This expression passed into general use from Second World War RAF slang, where an easy mission was described as 'a piece of cake'. Its origin is not clear. It has been suggested that it may be linked to 'cakewalk' which dates from the 1870s and refers to a Black American custom in which people would gather for a party, with a cake being given as a prize to the best dancers. From that, 'cakewalk' evolved to something pleasurable in general. However, although the first recorded use of 'piece of cake' is from America, there is really no need to suppose this link, as an easy time, rather than a tough one, could readily be compared to something soft, sweet and luxurious without the influence of 'cakewalk'.

'The American scene should be a piece of cake for these lads after several years of sharing a camper and traversing huge chunks of arid land to play in one-day pro-ams that may net them a couple of hundred pounds.' (*Daily Telegraph*, 7 April 1992)

piece of the action An Americanism that still has a slightly transatlantic feel for British users, this developed from the concept of buying a piece of some business or activity (recorded from the 1920s), which was blended with the slang use of 'the action' for an important or significant activity (recorded from the 1930s). The two together are not recorded before the 1960s, but the phrase is probably older. Nearly every article on pizza in newspapers or magazines puns on this.

pillar of society (or **church**) A person who is a pillar of society or the church is one of its main supports, someone who upholds what it stands for. 'Pillar of the church' dates from the fourteenth century, when 'pillar' was used much more generally for any supporter. 'Pillar of society' is comparatively recent.

'In fact, he was the archetypal "pillar of society": flour-miller, magistrate and county councillor.' (Philip Heselton, *The Elements of Earth Mysteries*, 1991)

pillar to post see FROM PILLAR TO POST

pilot see DROP THE PILOT

pin drop see HEAR A PIN DROP

place in the sun The use of this expression to mean a chance of advancement or something that is rightfully yours, comes from the period building up to the First World War. Germany wanted to expand its Empire in both the East and Africa, and in 1897 Bernard von Bülow made a speech saying: 'We desire to throw no one into the shade, but we also demand our own place in the sun.' The demand for a place in the sun was used on several later occasions by the Kaiser, Wilhelm II.

'Edwin Gooch, the former President of the NUAAW, once demanded that the farm worker be given his "place in the sun", by which he meant not only better pay and conditions but a more deserving recognition by the rest of society and equality of opportunity within it.' (H. Newby, *Green and Pleasant Land*, 1985)

plague see AVOID LIKE THE PLAGUE

plain sailing This was originally 'plane sailing', the art of navigating by plotting your position as if the world were a flat plane rather than a sphere, which works for short, simple journeys. By the mid-eighteenth century this had become 'plain sailing' used in the sense of easy sailing, not 'sailing in troubled waters', an expression used figuratively from the early nineteenth century.

'As a professional cook, Caroline finds the Christmas meal plain sailing – but she knows it's a task which sends many people into a flap.' (*Today*, 1992)

play a straight bat Playing with a straight bat is generally accepted as the best way to bat well in cricket. This advice is recorded from the mid-nineteenth century, but the expression is not recorded figuratively until the later twentieth century, although by then it was already regarded as representing old-fashioned values.

'All her life she had played it safe, done what others expected of her, hidden her emotions behind the stiff upper lip the Colonel was so fond of, played the straight bat he always wanted her to.' (Susannah James, *Love over Gold*, 1993)

play for see EVERYTHING TO PLAY FOR

play the game Although this expression for playing fair or honourably, closely related to the previous entry, is recorded earlier, it really came into its own in the nineteenth century. Two enormously popular poems used it in a way that established its associations. In the UK Sir Henry Newbolt wrote *Vitaï Lampada* (1897) which uses it as a chorus. The poem opens 'There's a breathless hush in the Close to-night –/ Ten to make and the match to win –/A bumping pitch and a blinding light,/An hour to play and the last man in./And it's not for the sake of a ribboned coat,/Or the selfish hope of a season's fame,/But his Captain's hand on his shoulder smote –/ "Play up! Play up! And play the game!" ' (The rest of the poem explains how this experience trains you to die for the Empire.) Then in 1941 in the USA sports writer Grantland Rice wrote in *Alumnus Football*, echoing Newbolt's sentiments, 'For when the One Great Scorer comes to mark against your name,/He writes – not that you won or lost – but how you played the Game.'

play the market This image from the stock market is used in a similar way to 'pick and choose', but with a greater sense of manipulating the material from which you have to choose.

'Nigel de Gruchy, head of the National Association of Schoolmasters/Union of Women Teachers, said schools could not be blamed for "playing the market" and concentrating on pupils likely to achieve at least a C grade [GCSE].' (*Daily Mail*, 27 August 1998)

play with fire The proverb 'if you play with fire you get burnt', meaning that if you involve yourself in dangerous things you must expect to be hurt, is first recorded in 1655 in the allusive form we use today: 'I played with fire, did counsel spurn . . . But never thought that fire would burn' (Henry Vaughan, *Silex Scintillans*).

'Those who play with fire, however archly, must expect to get their fingers burnt once in a while, and when ironic lyrics are allied to questionable public utterances and clearly provocative imagery, then it is reasonable to question the man's motives and intentions.' (*New Musical Express*, 1991)

plot thickens Used to mean things are getting more complicated or melodramatic, this expression is first recorded in George Villiers' play *The Rehearsal* of 1671. A cliché of Victorian melodramas, it is now rarely used except in joke or as a conscious cliché.

plough a lonely furrow see WALK A LONELY ROAD

point in time see AT THIS MOMENT IN TIME

poisoned chalice A poisoned chalice, for an apparent benefit which is in fact a disadvantage, started out as business jargon in the later twentieth century. The image is of nefarious goings-on in melodrama and films set in the Middle Ages, of the sort so admirably parodied in the 1955 Danny Kaye film *The Court Jester* (written by Norman Panama and Melvin Frank), although in that case 'The pellet with the poison's in the vessel with the pestle. The chalice from the palace has the brew that is true.'

'Salisbury looks certain to get another chance this week, though he may regard the match against Aravinda De Silva and company as something of a poisoned chalice.' (*Daily Mail*, 27 August 1998)

pole position A cliché of the second half of the twentieth century, 'pole position' refers to the most advantageous position at the start of a motor race, given to the person with the best practice lap times. As well as meaning in the best position, 'pole position' is sometimes used in a similar way to PECKING ORDER.

'Planet Online adds leading edge Internet and intranet products together with a significant and rapidly growing customer base . . . We are now in pole-position in the fastest growing sector of the business telecoms marketplace.' (*Evening Standard*, 28 August 1998)

'Driving Me Crazy mercilessly records the squalls, the vibrant performances and the inertia of the production team, who spend most of their time solemnly discussing what black music means to them and jockeying for pole position.' (*Independent*, 12 October 1992).

poles apart Nothing on earth can be further away from each other than the North and South Poles. 'Poles apart' has been used for 'completely separate' or 'different' since the early twentieth century.

'In many ways the two men ought to be poles apart, from opposite ends of the spectrum and also the United Kingdom, but rarely has a partnership flourished like theirs did during the Jack Walker revolution at Blackburn.' (*Daily Mail*, 27 August 1998)

political dynamite see DYNAMITE

politically correct Originally coined, in the early 1980s, to describe words or behaviour that was sensitive to the feelings or need of minorities or the disadvantaged, this rapidly became a cliché used to attack and condemn those trying to reform usage.

'This is a very funny, very quirky film, and politically correct it ain't: Evans plays a comedy cripple.' (*Evening Standard*, 10 September 1998)

'Although I welcome any move towards a more open society I am a little disturbed by the relentless way in which childhood is being forced to be politically correct.' (*Today*, 1992)

poor but honest A cliché of the Victorian age, this has rarely been used straight since the popularity in the First World War of the music hall song 'She Was Poor but She Was Honest' with its chorus, 'It's the rich wot get the pleasure, but the poor wot get the blame.' The companion cliché, 'the deserving poor', from the same era, used to mean those deemed to deserve help as opposed to those who have brought their troubles upon themselves, has suffered a similar fate.

'Yet back in the 1950s there was the "Teddy Boy" to alarm the public and to set against the allegedly poor but honest inter-war years when people could leave their doors unlocked.' (Richard Holt, *Sport and the British*, 1989)

'The underlying moral assumption is the smug conviction that the good and just prosper because they so deserve: lack of success is proof of immorality – there are no deserving poor!' (I. M. Lewis, *Social Anthropology in Perspective*, 1992)

poor little rich girl This was the title of a 1917 film starring Mary Pickford, which satirized the rich, but, ironically, made her the richest actress in the world. The expression was then picked up by Noel Coward and used as the title of a popular song in 1925.

'Kate, a poor little rich girl with her own private rink, can barely keep a partner long enough to get to the Olympics, let alone win a gold medal.' (*Daily Mirror*, 1992)

is the Pope a Catholic? This is a highly colloquial rhetorical question used to suggest incredulity when someone doubts a statement, or just to mean 'of course'. The formula has been taken up and produced many variants. These can be pretty obvious such as 'Does a fish like to swim?' or 'Do kangaroos hop?' and 'Is the Pope Polish?', which is well used in the USA; but can also reach such baroque splendours as 'Does Dolly Parton sleep on her back?' and 'Do one-legged ducks swim in a circle?'

posted see KEEP POSTED

the pound in your pocket The clichéd use of this expression for the money you actually have to dispose of, comes from a radio broadcast made in 1967 by the Prime Minister Harold Wilson after the devaluation of the pound: 'It does not mean, of course, that the pound here in Britain, in your pocket or purse or in your bank, has been devalued.' This was immediately adopted in the form 'the pound in your pocket'.

pound of flesh This was the interest payment demanded by the money-lender Shylock in Shakespeare's *Merchant of Venice*, if the loan he made to Antonio was not redeemed. Since the nineteenth century it has been used to signify an unjust or excessive payment, or something exacted in revenge.

'Humphrey Carpenter's book, *Dennis Potter: Under the Skin* . . . duly extracted its pound of flesh, and merely proved what we already knew: that however noble and majestic a human being might seem from the outside, his innards and vitals are unlikely to make very pleasant viewing.' (*Evening Standard*, 10 September 1998)

Pour encourager les autres see ENCOURAGE THE OTHERS

power without responsibility This set phrase comes from a speech made in 1931 by Stanley Baldwin attacking the popular press for not being newspapers but propaganda machines: 'What the proprietorship of these papers is aiming at is power, and power without responsibility – the prerogative of the harlot throughout the ages.' The then Duke of Devonshire is supposed to have exclaimed when he heard this, 'Good God, that's done it, he's lost us the tarts' vote.'

'And when the public believes a leader has failed . . . they will not be rescued by objecting that they only did what we wanted. For the first time it is the ruled, not the rulers who have power without responsibility.' (*Independent*, 22 September 1998)

powers of darkness see DARKNESS

powers that be This expression for those in control, a cliché since the nineteenth century, comes from the Bible: 'The powers that be are ordained by God' (I Romans 13:1).

'My suggestion, a fortnight ago, that Spurs should get rid of Christian Gross was not well received by the powers that be at White Hart Lane.' (*Evening Standard*, 28 August 1998)

practice see BEST PRACTICE

precious few 'Precious' developed an emphatic sense in the early nineteenth century, being used to mean 'very' or 'extremely'. It has been linked in a set phrase with 'few' since that time.

'Given the choice, and assuming that precious few of us are blessed with the ideal soil type, it is probably better for garden land to err on the heavy side.' (*Gardeners' World*, 1991)

prejudice see EXTREME PREJUDICE

here's one (or **something**) **I prepared** (or **made**) **earlier** An expression chiefly associated with demonstrations of model-making on the children's television programme *Blue Peter*, but also used from the earliest days of television cookery demonstrations. It is now used ironically.

'Like many ideas, this one has been prepared earlier, in North America.' (*Independent*, 19 June 1998)

'Here's something I prepared earlier – Cheap, quick and easy to make, TV cookery shows are a staple of the schedules.' (*Independent*, 7 September 1998)

'Of course it is hard to get meaningful data out of a trawl of 200 volunteers over three days in a shopping centre . . . But, like Fanny and Johnny Cradock, I will have the results of something I prepared earlier.' (*Independent*, 8 September 1998)

present and correct see ALL PRESENT AND CORRECT

press buttons see PUSH BUTTONS

press the flesh Originally an Americanism meaning simply to shake hands (recorded from the early twentieth century) this then became a term for politicians going round shaking hands with large numbers of people, and from there developed the sense of campaigning in general.

'Reduction in guaranteed funding for research with each student place has led to senior academics increasingly being required to forsake the laboratory and library to go and press the flesh with research directors on the Government's councils and of the big companies, charities and foundations.' (*Edit*, 1992–3)

'Pretentious, moi?' see JE NE SAIS QUOI

pretty as a picture; not a pretty picture 'Pretty as a picture' has been used as a term of praise since the nineteenth century, although it now has a rather dated ring. 'Not a pretty picture' is a more recent development and is still well used.

'Shearings, a charming listed, timber-framed, thatched cottage, dates back to 1575 and is, as they say, "as pretty as a picture".' (Mike Stone and Roger Russell, *Warm Welcomes in Britain*, 1990)

'However, we were able to obtain the results for 1989 through 1991, and they do not paint a pretty picture.' (*Unigram x*, 1993)

pride and joy This term for something greatly prized, either a possession or a person, comes from a line from Sir Walter Scott's *Rokeby* (1813) which describes children as 'a mother's pride, a father's joy'.

'Strolling quietly together down the gravel paths of the old-fashioned Elizabethan knot garden, which was her mother's pride and joy, Laura found the evening taking on a completely different complexion.' (Stephanie Howard, *Battle for Love*, 1991)

pride and (the) passion This is a cliché of sports journalism, trying to evoke the feelings of those playing in important matches.

'He had also managed to instil in his troops all the pride and passion which comes with pulling on the England sweater.' (*Daily Mail*, 27 August 1998)

'Ireland tagged along, trying to prove that playing on reserves of passion and pride was good enough.' (*Rugby World and Post*, 1992)

prime of life The concept of a period of life when you are at your peak is an ancient one, going back to Plato's *Republic*, but the expression has only been a cliché in English since the nineteenth century. The alternative version 'in your prime' is particularly associated with Muriel Spark's 1963 novel *The Prime of Miss Jean Brodie*, who considered herself to be in hers and told her pupils 'One's prime is elusive. You little girls, when you grow up, must be on the alert to recognise your prime at whatever time of life it may occur. You must live it to the full.'

'It was melancholy to see in the civil prisons of the metropolis, remarked Grant, men whose birth, education, manners and appearance would have fitted them for occupying the highest positions in society and consequently of proving benefactors to their species, spending no inconsiderable portion of the prime of life amid scenes of deepest degradation.' (Hugh Barty-King, *The Worst Poverty*, 1991)

prisoners see TAKE NO PRISONERS

proactive Not coined until the 1930s, and rare before the 1970s, this is one of the most active current vogue words. In form it is the opposite of 'reactive', and means dealing with a situation by controlling what happens through your actions rather than by reacting to what has already happened. At first used mainly in fields such as psychology and the social sciences, it has now got into the hands of those dealing with marketing, business studies and advertising, and is beginning to be little more than an emphatic form of 'active' (when it means anything).

'I just started thinking, Jesus himself was a very proactive marketer.' (*Independent*, 7 November 1998)

'A useful distinction can be made between the defensive factors that cause companies to look beyond their domestic markets (reactive factors) and proactive influences.' (*KBS Open Learning MBA Programme*, 1989)

protest too much 'The lady doth protest too much, methinks', comments Hamlet's mother, Gertrude, about the Player Queen's protestation of fidelity in Hamlet's 'Mousetrap' play (III.ii) – not realizing that she is meant to see herself in the Player Queen. The whole line is rarely quoted in full now, but is frequently alluded to.

' "I don't give a stuff " was the far from elegant response of Her Majesty's Secretary of State for Health to suggestions that there is less to his good news than meets the eye. He was not going to let the "two-bit accountants" rain on his parade – even if they are experts. Mr Dobson protests too much. Something to hide, perhaps?' (*Daily Mail*, 27 August 1998)

proves the rule see EXCEPTION THAT PROVES THE RULE

public speaking see UNACCUSTOMED AS I AM

publish and be damned A comment attributed to the Duke of Wellington (1769–1852) in reply to a former mistress who tried to get him to pay her money to leave their relationship out of her KISS AND TELL autobiography. Nowadays the 'damned' element usually refers not to a curse from the person written about, but to public reaction to the published work.

'By over-reaching himself, Mr Starr has thrown him a lifeline. If Mr Clinton survives it will be because Mr Starr published, and was damned.' (*Independent*, 14 September 1998)

'Publish and be blessed.' (Headline, *Independent*, 15 September 1998)

pull out all the stops On an organ the stops control which pipe the air can pass through to make the sound. If you want to use a particular set of pipes, you pull out the stops that govern them. If you pull out all the stops, then the organ is played at maximum volume. Thus, in the nineteenth century, 'to pull out all the stops' came to be used for 'to do your utmost', 'to work as hard as possible'.

'With shutdowns and redundancies already hitting British Aerospace, Mr Major is determined to pull out all the stops to save the £22 billion project.' (*Today*, 1992)

pull someone's chestnuts out of the fire see HOT POTATO

pull someone's strings see PUSH BUTTONS

puppy's privates see DOG'S BOLLOCKS

pure and simple Although this expression was in use by the middle of the fifteenth century, it does not seem to have become a cliché until the nineteenth, when it was very common. Oscar Wilde put it in its place when he wrote, 'The truth is rarely pure, and never simple' (*The Importance of Being Earnest*, 1895). A related phrase is 'pure genius', which is again old – Dryden used it – but which is a twentieth-century cliché. Wilde's comment applies to it equally well.

'Shareholders will be circulated with details of this "in a matter of weeks", according to yesterday's statement, and they will be interested to hear the details of what was dismissed by London as a "piece of financial engineering, pure and simple".' (*Independent*, 4 October 1989)

push (or **press**) **buttons** To push or press someone's buttons means to know how to get an automatic emotional response from them, as if you were using a machine. The idea has probably been around for as long as the sort of machinery that is operated in this way has been common – a writer in the 1930s got close to it when he said: 'These terms ... have become push buttons which touch off emotional reflexes' – but it has not become a cliché until recently. A related term, although used for a rather different meaning, is 'to pull (someone's) strings', where the imagery comes not from machinery but from puppets, where a pull on the right string will get the response you require.

'A skilled comedy craftsman such as, say, Jerry Seinfeld, who pushes all the right buttons and is undeniably funny, is not really in the same business.' (*Independent*, 7 November 1998)

'I don't know if different women press different buttons with Stan. I would not dare go into it because even if someone does press buttons, it does not justify violence.' (*Daily Mirror*, 21 July 1998)

when (or **if**) **push comes to shove** The great commentator on the American language, William Safire, has linked this expression to the rugby scrum, but the expression is undoubtedly American in origin, and this explanation does not convince. More likely is the view that it reflect the progress of a quarrel, or even an escalating temper while trying to shift a heavy load. Whatever the origin, this expression, which has largely replaced the older 'when the chips are down', is recorded from the 1950s, but not generally used until the 1970s.

'Ron had a small greyish-brown, torn-eared terrier on the end of a string, although in truth it would be hard for an observer to know exactly who was leading whom and who, when push came to shove, would be the one to fold at the knees if the other one shouted "Sit!" ' (Terry Pratchett, *Feet of Clay*, 1996)

to push the boat out A boat-builder's term, originally (recorded from the 1930s) used to mean to pay for a round of drinks, but now extended to mean to be generous or extravagant in general. It would have originated in the custom of breaking a bottle over the bows of a ship being launched, and having a celebratory drink afterwards.

'They will receive £225m out of next year's £535m cash for higher and further education. Although colleges will not quite be able to push the proverbial boat out, it is a good start.' (*Independent*, 23 July 1998)

put a brave face on 'Face' has been used in the sense of 'appearance' since the Middle Ages, but although expressions such as 'put a good face on' are recorded from early times, there is no record of the history of this particular version, although there is no reason to suppose it is recent.

'The Allied Dunbar launch party today will feature Rob Andrew, director of rugby at champions Newcastle, and everyone involved will be putting on a brave face and accentuating the positives of a new season.' (*Evening Standard*, 28 August 1998)

put all your eggs in one basket The proverb 'Don't put all your eggs in one basket' has been used in English since at least the 1660s, but the expression is more often found in the form 'to put all your eggs in one basket' today.

'City wisdom suggests that you shouldn't put all your eggs in one basket, so for most people it is best to consider a single company PEP only after you've taken out a £6,000 general plan.' (*Accountancy*, 1993)

'When Gilbert arrived at The Oval in 1995 he inherited a lot of egos in one basket.' (*Independent*, 1 September 1998)

put down roots see BACK TO YOUR ROOTS

put in the picture The image here is probably one of belonging, of knowing what is going on because you are a part of a group, and are in a photograph of a team or of friends. The expression dates from the early years of the twentieth century.

'The players are still in the dark about the sale of the ground, and have asked to be put in the picture before the end of the season.' (*Northern Echo*)

put on a pedestal The image of putting something or someone on a pedestal as if they were an idol to be worshipped goes back to the middle of the nineteenth century. Woody Allen, in his monologue *I Had a Rough Marriage* (1964), played on the expression when he said: 'It was partially my fault that we got divorced . . . I tended to place my wife under a pedestal.'

'Even now, while being the consummate professional, he shuns the star system which puts footballers on pedestals.' (*Daily Mail*, 27 August 1998)

put pen to paper As an elaborate way of saying 'to write', this was obviously already considered objectionable by the 1650s, when a certain Mr Osborne wrote in a letter, 'The fellow thought that putting "pen to paper" was much better than plain "writing".'

'He has written about his time in jail, but it is not for public consumption. It was for his grandchildren, he says, that he put pen to paper.' (*Independent*, 8 October 1998)

put the cat among the pigeons SEE CAT AMONG THE PIGEONS

put the fear of God into Although recorded in a literal sense from early times, as an expression meaning to terrify, or to frighten into submission, this dates from the 1890s.

'News of The Mall's three miles of shops caused open rebellion among husbands and boyfriends within a 45 minutes' drive. The prospect of being dragged around by the missus, screaming kids in tow ... put the fear of God into their hearts.' (*Independent*, 2 September 1998)

put the heat on An expression from underworld American slang of the 1930s (when 'turn the heat on' was more common), 'the heat' in this sense is pursuit of a criminal by the police or a similar pressure from such people as fellow criminals.

'He is also quite deliberately putting the heat on the Bank of England to start moving interest rates downwards, earlier than it might wish.' (*Independent*, 8 October 1998)

put through the mangle A self-explanatory image, assuming you are old enough to have seen wet washing passed through a mangle to squeeze the water out of it. Its history is not known, but it is probably twentieth century.

'I can see why abattoirs need checking up on all the time – but universities? Have other countries put their higher education systems through the mangle like this?' (*Independent*, 23 July 1998)

put through your paces In horse dressage a horse may still be tested for its skills and training by literally being put through its paces. This was transferred to more general use by the later nineteenth century.

'Many of the products that the judges are putting through their paces right now will soon be commonplace.' (*You* magazine, 20 September 1998)

'By late March they were in Bologna, where Wolfgang was put through his paces by the famous theorist Padre Martini, who professed himself amazed at the boy's ability to work out complex fugues on a brief given subject.' (Wendy Thompson, *Mozart: A Bicentennial Tribute*, 1989)

put too fine a point SEE NOT TO PUT TOO FINE A POINT ON IT

put up or shut up A nineteenth-century expression, its origin has been connected either with gambling, demanding that a player produce his bet or keep quiet (the more probable source) or else from a simple challenge to put your fists up or keep silent.

'Harsh words are their regular currency. Do not believe the public proclamations of peace. The market economy takes no prisoners. It's time to put up or shut up.' (*Independent*, 2 September 1998)

put your money where your mouth is This is an American expression which originated among poker players as a challenge to back your boasts with a bet. It is recorded from the mid-twentieth century.

'Everyone wanted this scheme to work, including many corporate investors who were busy promoting the Thames. But not one of them put their money where their mouth was.' (Peter Lay, chief executive of White Horse Fast Ferries, quoted in the *Independent*, 1 August 1998)

(like) putty in the hands of As anyone who has reglazed a window will know, putty, when fresh out of the tin, is both stiff and sticky. To make it into a substance that is soft and malleable and will hold any shape you want it to, you have to knead it in your hands, working the oil back into it and warming it. Thus someone who is like putty in your hands has been worked on until they will do what you want. The expression dates from the first quarter of the twentieth century.

'Psychologically illiterate sales directors were putty in the hands of such experts in the unconscious mind, with their battery of mumbo-jumbo such as word-association lists, ink-blot tests, lie detectors and eye-blink counters.' (Peter Lewis, *The Fifties: Portrait of a Period*, 1989)

Pyrrhic victory This is an allusion to the experiences of the Greek general Pyrrhus. He was a skilful general and had ambitions to emulate his second cousin, Alexander the Great. He agreed to lead the Greeks of southern Italy against the encroaching Romans, and the two forces met at the battle of Asculum in 279 BC. Pyrrhus and his forces were victorious, but lost so many men that they never recovered their power, and Rome was the real winner in the long run. After the battle Pyrrhus, it is said, exclaimed, 'One more such victory and we are lost.' 'Pyrrhic victory' began to be used to describe this sort of situation in the nineteenth century, but now has a rather old-fashioned ring, and has been superseded by the expressions 'real winner' or 'WON THE BATTLE BUT LOST THE WAR', both of which sum up the same situation.

'But, very often, the victories on the track and pitch or in the ring are Pyrrhic: they are costly in other areas.' (Ernest Cashmore, *Black Sportsmen*, 1982)

quality of life This useful expression from medicine and the social sciences has now become so fashionable that it can be stretched to cover almost anything, although it is most usually used of leisure, the environment and the non-materialist – although this might not be what those in the third world would count as adding to the quality of life.

'These include issues to do with the environment, product markets and prices, farm structures, human attitudes including the quality of life, transportation and rural population trends.' (The Arkleton Trust, *The Agricultural Potential of Marginal Areas*, 1981)

'There's a great temptation to move to the middle of Exmoor where the quality of life is fantastic.' (*Daily Telegraph*, 8 April 1992)

quality time This is an expression used to mean time you concentrate on actually being with the person or people concerned (it is particularly used of children or family) as opposed to the quantity of time a stay-at-home mother, say, might spend with her children when she is actually trying to do other things. It developed in the 1980s as a way of justifying parents working long hours, who, could argue it was quality not quantity that mattered.

'I can now speak from experience and say that it's much easier to spend a day at the office than it is to spend a day at home, and you have the benefit of spending "quality time" with your baby at evenings and weekends.' (NCT Birmingham Central Branch Newsletter, 1989)

quantum leap Strangely, in the world of nuclear physics, where this expression comes from, a quantum leap is a sudden change that happens at a subatomic level, about the smallest scale you could be working on; but in popular usage, 'quantum' has come to mean the exact opposite, something vast, a quantum leap being a big leap forward. The term in its original sense came into use about 1950, and was being used figuratively some five years later.

'The new arts programme, fronted by Mark Lawson and Francine Stock, is a quantum leap forward from the sterile élitism of *Kaleidoscope*.' (*Independent*, 22 October 1998)

'In France, for example, there was a "quantum leap" from small shops to hypermarkets, by-passing the "supermarket phase" in retailing evolution. (*KBS Open Learning MBA programme*, 1989)

question see CALL INTO QUESTION

question (mark) hanging over A journalistic cliché expressing uncertainty, that has flourished since the 1980s.

'It all looked too good two weeks ago when a British League appeared to be within the grasp of everyone in the game. That move failed and now we are left with yet more questions hanging over the sport with just seven days to go until the English leagues start.' (*Evening Standard*, 28 August 1998)

quick as lightning see LIGHTNING

quick fix A quick fix is usually a bodged job, and when this is used figuratively there is an implied recognition of long-term inadequacy.

'Now that we have 25 years of sexual revolution behind us, we know only too well that quick fixes do not cure people of their cultural prejudices and only serve to ossify them . . . Quick fix chemical cures are based on an impoverished view of what life is about.' (*Independent*, 22 September 1998)

. . . R us Taken from the name of the chain of toyshops, Toys R Us, this is a fashionable way of poking fun at people or institutions.

'I was naturally very grateful to our good friend Mr Conran, of Sofas R Us, who last week made special arrangements to allow me into his shop after hours.' (*Private Eye*, 4 September 1998)

'The dome-coiffed author was a trifle upset when someone described his book as "Hagiography 'R' Us".' (*Independent*, 5 November 1998)

a race against time A useful expression spoilt by journalistic over-use. It dates from the twentieth century.

'Passengers were ordered to fasten seat belts and some received oxygen as the pilot began a race against time to land the plane before the screen blew out.' (*Today*, 1992)

(w)rack and ruin Historically the 'rack' of rack and ruin is related to 'wreck' and WREAK HAVOC, and means destruction, ruin, so we have here another example of a set phrase where each half has the same meaning. The expression dates from the sixteenth century, and 'rack' is otherwise obsolete. Although it can be used of a wide range of things, including abstracts, it is most frequently used of buildings and gardens.

'His parents kept it spick and span, but when they died, he lived there alone until it went to rack and ruin.' (Roy Kerridge, *Jaunting through Ireland*, 1991)

rage see ALL THE RAGE

rags to riches A three-word summary of the Cinderella story, this expression nearly always has 'like a fairytale' associations, even when the climb from poverty to wealth has involved extremely hard work. The reverse process, 'riches to rags', is not uncommon.

'Channel 5 was first to the tape with an autopsy on Fashanu, and while it delivered essentially the same what-went-wrong story of rags-to-riches-to-rags, . . . it failed to assemble as many pieces of the jigsaw.' (*Independent*, 4 September 1998)

railroad or **railway** see WHAT A WAY TO RUN A RAILROAD

rain must fall see LITTLE RAIN MUST FALL

rain on your parade The image of spoiling someone's plans or enjoyment, just as rain would spoil an outdoor event, has been in use since about 1900 in the USA, but has only recently become fashionable in the UK.

' "I don't give a stuff" was the far from elegant response of Her Majesty's Secretary of State for Health to suggestions that there is less to his good news than meets the eye. He was not going to let "two-bit accountants" rain on his parade – even if they are experts.' (*Daily Mail*, 27 August 1998)

raise Cain This expression must have been well-established by the 1840s, when the St Louis *Daily Pennant* published the riddle, 'Why have we every reason to believe that Adam and Eve were both rowdies? Because . . . they both raised Cain.' Cain, son of Adam and Eve, was the first murderer – of his brother Abel – and a social outcast, he and his descendants for ever bearing the mark of Cain. Thus 'to raise Cain [from the dead]' was to behave in a way that Cain might have done: to make a disturbance, be noisy, 'cry blue murder'.

raise the roof, hit the ceiling 'To raise the roof' can be used for both 'to be very angry' or 'to make a lot of noise', the more common sense now. In both cases the image is of anger or noise explosive enough to lift off a roof. The similar 'hit the ceiling' is restricted to anger. Both expressions date from the early twentieth century.

'Dolly wanted to scream, to raise the roof and to wake Joe.' (Mary Jane Staples, *Sergeant Joe*, 1992)

'There will be a great variety but over the day some carols may be repeated because we want to make sure we have enough truly popular ones so people can sing along and raise the roof.' (*Today*, 1992)

rank and file The image here is a military one, the mass of the troops being lined up in ranks (side by side) and files (one behind another) forming a platoon – and easy 'cannon fodder' – while the officers stand apart. The term has been used literally since the sixteenth century, and figuratively since the eighteenth, and is a cliché particularly applied to members of political parties.

'Peter Calvocoressi has very acutely (if somewhat smugly) described the sort of people who worked at Bletchley – both brilliant high-flying code-breakers and the rank and file of graduate clerks milling round them.' (Irene Young, *Enigma Variations*, 1990)

'Even Bevan reckoned that if the Labour Party were to campaign on a programme fully reflecting the aspirations of the rank and file party activists "we could say goodbye to any Labour government being elected again in Britain".' (A. Cottrell, *Social Classes in Marxist Theory*, 1984)

rat race This expression comes from experimental psychology, and the discoveries made by studying rats under stressful conditions, which appears to have been combined in popular imagination with work done on rats' learning abilities by racing them through mazes. The development of this expression, used of a highly competitive working life, was no doubt helped by the fondness of cartoonists for showing such experiments in their work. It first developed in the USA in the 1930s.

'Many of the drop-outs eventually left their flowers, cut their hair and dropped back in to the "rat race" of business, commerce and industry.' (Kevin Logan, *Paganism and the Occult*, 1988)

at a rate of knots This is a naval image; a knot in this sense having originally been one of a series of knots on a rope used to judge the speed of a ship by measuring the rate the knots ran out behind the ship in a given time. This system of measurement led to the nautical mile being called a knot. 'At a rate of knots' has been used for 'very fast' since the late nineteenth century.

'Restrictive practices, which Clapper had fought so hard to introduce, were being discarded at a rate of knots in the quest to increase efficiency, output and earnings.' (M. Kirby, *Man at the Sharp End*, 1991)

raw deal; **square deal** 'Raw deal', for unfair treatment, comes from the use of 'raw' to mean crude, unrefined, rough (as in 'raw silk'). 'Square', on the other hand, refers to a carpenter's square, indicating that something is carefully finished, made FAIR AND SQUARE. Although 'square dealing' has been around since the seventeenth century, 'square deal' really took off as a cliché after US President Theodore Roosevelt used it to describe his policies, particularly his statement that 'If elected, I shall see to it that every man has a square deal, no less and no more' (1904). 'Raw deal' dates from the same period.

'In practice it means that people from black and ethnic groups get a raw deal because their particular problems are seldom acknowledged.' (*New Internationalist*)

'When the cameras had long since departed, I was left to carry the can and answer any angry participants who felt they had been given a raw deal.' (*Liverpool Echo & Daily Post*, 1993)

razor's edge, **razor sharp** The image of the razor's edge for an acute dilemma, where things could 'cut either way' is adopted directly from a quote in Homer's *Iliad*. It first appears in English in Chapman's translation of the *Iliad* (1611): 'Now on the eager razors edge, for life or death we stand.' 'Razor sharp' is used for incisive or cutting intellectual ability, and, along with 'razor' by itself used as an adjective ('razor wit' most typically) is a cliché of the twentieth century.

'But behind the make-up there still lies a razor sharp intellectual who has been quoted for the past several years as one of the top 100 lawyers in the US.' (*Today*, 1992)

read my lips An expression used for emphasis dating from the 1970s, this became a cliché after George Bush said, 'Read my lips: no new taxes', in a speech (written for him by Peggy Noonan) given in 1988 when accepting the Republican nomination to run for President.

'So, if you're out there spying on me, read my lips, little cheat: big brother is not going screwy, young lady, and your thin-ended wedges stop right here!' (I. Maitland, *Cathedral*, 1993)

read the riot act In 1716 the Riot Act set out provisions that if twelve or more were gathered together and someone in authority read a certain portion of the act out loud, those people automatically became criminals if they did not disperse within the hour. The act was not repealed until 1973. By the early nineteenth century, 'to read the riot act' had become an alternative for 'to issue a severe warning or telling off' about someone's behaviour.

'Every now and again, Albert's digestive system revolted, and his hard-pressed medical advisers were called in, prescribed tablets, and read the riot act again.' (Miss Read, *The World of Thrush Green*, 1990)

'The first time Jimmy Patino, who represented family interests on the board, came to a meeting, he read me the riot act about how of every £1 I was talking about, 51p was owned by the family, and of that 51p, 25p of it was his.' (*Accountancy*, 1993)

real McCoy The origin of this expression for the genuine article is muddled. The Mackay whiskey distillery was promoting its whiskey as 'the real Mackay' by 1870, and this expression seems to have had some currency, at least in Scotland, for Robert Louis Stevenson used it in 1883. Then in the 1890s there was an American boxer who boxed under the name of Kid McCoy. The expression is strongly linked to him, but this may be an echo of the earlier one. There are various stories about him being 'the real McCoy' rather than an imitation – either other boxers were trying to cash in on his fame, or he had to prove his identity in a bar by knocking out a challenger – but certainly in 1899, after he won a particularly spectacular fight, the *San Francisco Examiner* used as its headline, 'Now you've seen the real McCoy'.

'Walter stayed in the North, felt at home there, so his books are authentic – the real McCoy.' (Robert Barnard, *Posthumous Papers*, 1992)

in a (very) real sense This attempt to sound sincere, growing in use since the 1960s, often creates the opposite effect from that intended, and is at best a mere filler.

'In a very real sense there were two Glasgows and the second city was the one that clustered along either bank of the River Clyde and all the way to Clydebank.' (Edward Chisnall, *Bell in the Tree. The Glasgow Story*, 1989)

real time Originally this was an expression used in computing to distinguish data that was processed at the time of gathering rather than at a later date. For instance, accounts could be processed as the transactions were made, rather than all the information gathered and processed at the end of the month. The expression was coined in the 1950s, but it took until the 1980s before the general public was exposed to the exciting developments in the computing world that made this term a buzz word and started its transference into a clichéd way of saying 'as it happens, now'.

'The experiment in St Etienne is the first to link terminals in shops, in real time, with the banks' computers.' (*New Scientist*, 1991)

'Here at Cabarave, east London's black comedy club, the video monitors replaying his classic stage show Raw are turned down – displaced by the sound of jokes told in real time and laughter that's live, spontaneous, uncanned.' (*The Face*, 1992)

real winner see PYRRHIC VICTORY

real world As a cliché this is not a contrast between the real and the imagined, but between the practical and the theoretical. To tell someone that what they suggest will not work in the real world is to accuse them of being impractical, or living in an IVORY TOWER. This use became common from the 1960s.

'The lucky few are among the most highly paid people in the City – even though the types of product they create do not always work in the real world.' (*Evening Standard*, 7 October 1998)

reality check People who do not live in the REAL WORLD, or who have an over-lively imagination, probably need a reality check, something to remind them of how things really work or what is going on. The expression is a recent development from the USA.

'HM's troops can't scan a hard drive on a computer so easy to use that it's the choice of many primary schools ... Suddenly, my image of British technology complete with James Bond and the phlegmatic Q's whizzy gismos, is getting a sharp reality check.' (*Independent*, 21 August 1998)

reap the whirlwind 'They have sown the wind and they shall reap the whirlwind' comes from the Bible (Hosea 8:7), as a warning about the consequences of sin. It is still used, often rather smugly, to mean to suffer serious consequences from your actions.

'More orthodox critics feared that he was only stoking up a consumer boom which would reap the whirlwind in a vast price inflation.' (Kenneth Morgan, *The People's Peace*, 1990)

rearranging the deckchairs on the *Titanic* see DECKCHAIRS ON THE *TITANIC*

theirs not to reason why 'Their's not to make reply,/Their's not to reason why,/ Their's but to do and die', wrote Alfred, Lord Tennyson in his poem *The Charge of the Light Brigade* (1854), describing the fate of the troops who took part. The poem is also the origin of the expression 'to do or die'. 'Theirs not to reason why' is found nowadays used both seriously and jocularly.

'Ours not to reason why – ours just to read the ruddy instruments and let others sort the problems out.' (Nancy Fjallbrant and Ian Malley, *User Education in Libraries*, 1984)

recipe for disaster Although a figurative use of recipe was well established by the nineteenth century – Thomas Hood, for instance, published a book called *A Recipe for Civilisation* in 1826 – the set phrases a 'recipe for disaster' and 'recipe for success' do not seem to have been used until comparatively recently.

'Giving very young children too much choice over when to get up, what to wear or what they eat for breakfast can be a recipe for disaster – acrimonious arguments, delays and tantrums.' (Martin Herbert, *Discipline: A Positive Guide for Parents*, 1989)

reckoning see DAY OF RECKONING

record see JUST FOR THE RECORD

red carpet A red carpet is traditionally rolled out for honoured guests to walk on, although the practice is not recorded until the early twentieth century. By the 1930s the expression was being used to suggest special attention or treatment.

'Well, I must say I didn't expect the red carpet, but neither did I expect you all to look at me as though I were the devil incarnate!' (Emma Richmond, *Love of my Heart*, 1993)

(nature) red in tooth and claw This expression, at first used to indicate a view of nature as a struggle for survival between predator and prey, rather than the fluffy bunny approach, is now often used as an alternative for the rather old-fashioned DOG EAT DOG. It is a quotation from Alfred, Lord Tennyson's *In Memoriam* (1850): 'Man . . . Who trusted God was love indeed/And love Creation's final law –/Tho' Nature, red in tooth and claw/With ravine, shrieked against his creed.'

'He also liked to portray British social democracy as an alternative to the 'red tooth and claw' of American capitalism and Soviet communism.' (C. J. Bartlett, *The Special Relationship*, 1992)

redeeming feature A set phrase that has been in use since the very start of the twentieth century.

'This has not been publicised elsewhere to date, and that is the one redeeming feature of this otherwise unwelcome and ill-considered arrangement.' (*Climber and Hill Walker*, 1991)

'But it has one redeeming feature, for the claim that paperwork needs to be completed is used as an excuse to avoid other types of police work which are disliked even more.' (John Brewer and Kathleen Magee, *Inside the RUC*, 1991)

reinvent the wheel An expression from the second half of the twentieth century, meaning to waste time by redoing, usually elementary, work instead of building on it. Its development may owe something to the prevalence of cartoons showing the invention of the wheel.

'In any case, if a writer has managed to put some key point rather well, why not both give him the credit for doing so, and at the same time avoid struggling to reinvent the wheel?' (Judith Waters and Ray Lester, *Environmental Scanning and Business Strategy*, 1989)

reject out of hand While 'out of hand' was used early to mean 'without pausing for consideration, at once', its clichéd pairing with 'reject' seems to be modern.

'The problem, then, is not to be seen as one of whether we should continue to use concepts like "identity" or "autonomy" at all, or simply reject them out of hand.' (M. Whitford and M. Griffiths, *Feminist Perspectives in Philosophy*, 1989)

reliable sources A journalistic cliché of the twentieth century, meant to instil confidence in the anonymous informant, but often doing the exact opposite.

'He is said by reliable sources to be negotiating with both the US and Iran for compensation to give up the business, playing one nation off against the other.' (*Guardian*, 11 November 1989)

'Reliable sources . . . claimed that the Tianjin students were the only ones during the "winter of discontent" to experience serious confrontations with the police and receive violent injuries.' (Ruth Cherrington, *China's Students*, 1991)

(if you can) remember it, you weren't there A recent cliché with variant forms which has come to the fore with the recent spate of memoirs of the 1960s, the implication being that those who were really involved in 'the scene' were too high to have clear memories. Although used of other things, it is most frequently used of the 1960s, particularly of the SUMMER OF LOVE or the revolts of 1968.

'*The Sixties* Arthur Marwick Basically the most concise history of the sixties ever published, essential for those who can't remember or weren't born during those swinging times.' (*Stuff*, October 1998)

rendezvous with destiny see DAY OF DESTINY

rent-a-mob (or **crowd**) A cliché for crowds of supporters obtained on demand, or to suggest that they do not understand the reasons for their support, by the 1970s it was particularly used by the POWERS THAT BE to disparage popular protest. The expression was based on hire services using 'rent-a-. . .' in their title, such as 'rent-a-van' services. Compare DIAL-A-. . .

'Flying pickets and rent-a-mob Trots operated anywhere at will.' (*Daily Telegraph*, 6 April 1992)

response has been overwhelming see OVERWHELMING RESPONSE

rest in peace Another cliché of mourning, this is a translation of the Latin *Requiescat in pace* from the Requiem Mass, and the source of the letters RIP on gravestones. It is also used figuratively of a subject that is best not brought up again.

'Standing on the edge of the lake, they threw some small memento of their dead into the rippling water – a final request that their souls should rest in peace.' (Monica Connell, *Against a Peacock Sky*, 1991)

the rest is history A modern cliché of no known source, although its form may be modelled on Hamlet's dying words 'The rest is silence.' It is used to indicate that what happened next is too well known to need mentioning.

'Robert Graves, to whom one of these effusions was shown . . . advised a change of direction: write about what you know, he suggested . . . Sillitoe took the hint: the rest is publishing history.' (*Mail on Sunday*, 20 September 1998)

rest on your laurels In the ancient world both victorious athletes and generals were crowned with laurel wreaths to mark their success. The expression 'to rest on your laurels' developed in the nineteenth century to suggest satisfaction with the laurels you had already achieved, but quite what is behind the phrasing of this uncomfortable-sounding image is not clear.

'But Liverpool's inspiring light will not be allowed to rest on his laurels, as manager Graeme Souness has set Barnes fitness targets of Old Testament rigour.' (*Today*, 1992)

results-driven, **-orient(at)ed**, **-motivated** These are clichés of job advertisements. Until recently everyone had to be a SELF-STARTER; now the advertisements are more likely to be looking for someone concerned with results. The two sets of phrases are equally imprecise and obscure, and users of both are equally likely to demand a good TRACK RECORD as well.

'The successful applicants will be excellent communicators, have good attention to detail and be results driven.' (Advertisement, *Evening Standard*, 1 September 1998)

'We are looking for result-oriented achievers who are keen to make a major strategic impact.' (*Independent*, 7 September 1998)

rewrite the script Meaning to change or challenge the way things are, this expression is an up-and-coming cliché from the world of television and film, something to be done when you have LOST THE PLOT.

'Meanwhile, the wind of change may be blowing holes through the fabric of English football, but you can always rely on Wimbledon's mavericks to rewrite the script.' (*Evening Standard*, 10 September 1998)

rich as Croesus Croesus was King of Lydia in Asia Minor in the sixth century BC, and reputed to be the richest man alive, until he lost everything to the King of Persia.

Now rather old-fashioned, the expression is an alternative to 'rich beyond the DREAMS OF AVARICE'.

'Her father died when she was a kid, as did her uncle, which meant that her grandfather who was as rich as Croesus had no one else to leave his ill-gotten gains to.' (Ann Granger, *A Season for Murder*, 1991)

rich beyond the dreams of avarice see DREAMS OF AVARICE

ride off into the sunset A conscious cliché from the 1930s cinema, when the heroes of Westerns would typically ride off into the sunset, having done those things that a MAN'S GOTTA DO, and righted the wrongs of the townsfolk. Not quite a HAPPY EVER AFTER ending, because this sort of hero is often one who WALKS A LONELY ROAD, but still suggesting a job well done.

'Its heroes do not characteristically commit suicide or ride off into the sunset: they settle down, marry, and make comfortable and elaborate treaties with the world they live in.' (George Watson, *British Literature since 1945*, 1991)

ride roughshod Horses that are going to travel over slippery terrain can be roughshod – given shoes with the nails left projecting so that they give the horses a better grip on the ground. Cavalry horses could also have shoes like this, not only to prevent them slipping and disrupting a charge, but also to inflict more damage on the enemy as they rode over them. It was from this practice that the expression 'to ride roughshod over' comes; used literally from the seventeenth century, and by the nineteenth transferred to mean to domineer, to carry on regardless, trampling down other's opinions or desires.

'Hence, we do not need to think about how we will deal with the situation if the Government rides roughshod over all informed opinion and ceases to fund the fifth year of full-time education.' (*Royal Institute of British Architects Journal*, 1990)

right see THE CUSTOMER IS ALWAYS RIGHT

right arm see GIVE THE SHIRT OFF YOUR BACK

right chemistry see CHEMISTRY

right direction see STEP IN THE RIGHT DIRECTION

right place see HEART IN THE RIGHT PLACE

Riley see LIFE OF RILEY

ring a bell The source of this expression, dating from the 1930s, for a reminder or for something that seems familiar, is not clearly known. Rather than debate whether the image comes from doorbells or telephones or elsewhere, we should probably see it in terms of a ringing bell as something that gets our attention, makes us sit up and listen.

ring of truth, **ring true** When coins were made of precious metal it was worth forgers' while to make coins of base metal and cover them with gold or silver, or to make them out of an alloy that looked like a precious metal. As well as biting the coin to see if it was soft (a familiar scene from cinema), someone suspicious of the coin he was given could bounce it on a hard surface and listen to the sound. A forged coin would give off a much duller sound, but a genuine one would ring true or have the ring of truth about it.

'Although some doubt has been cast on the authenticity of this account, there are many vivid details which have a ring of truth about them.' (Graham Webster, *Archaeologist at Large*, 1991)

'Hand-on-heart declarations that rugby is an amateur game and that players have freedom to play when they choose, do not in this competitive, rewarding age, ring true.' (*Daily Telegraph*, 9 April 1992)

riot act see READ THE RIOT ACT

riot of colour A cliché since at least the 1960s, this expression implies not just strong colour, but variety as well. Although it is used of other things, it is most frequently found used of gardens.

'It was a riot of colour in the sunshine, with gaily striped tents and awnings, cloth of gold and scarlet on the royal box, ornately uniformed attendants and bandsmen, and the glinting steel of weapons and armour.' (Andrew Boyle, *Ayrshire Heritage*, 1990)

ripe old age Ripeness here is used to imply a natural process of ageing and a readiness to be picked by death at the proper time, rather than being cut off in your prime. The combination of ripeness and age was already current in Shakespeare's time.

'Maximum lifespans may be much greater, some narwhal and spotted dolphin living to 40–50 years, and the Baird's beaked whale possibly to the ripe old age of 70 years.' (Michael Donoghue and Annie Wheeler, *Dolphins: Their Life and Survival*, 1990)

rise and shine Originally an example of Forces humour, demanding that the sleeping troops should be like the sun and rise and shine at dawn. First recorded in the early twentieth century, this has now become a general term for 'wake up'.

'If I hadn't chucked away the rulebook shortly after Johannes Gutenburg invented printing, this would be the proper time for me to rise and shine.' (Ellen Galford, *The Dyke & the Dybbuk*, 1993)

rise from the ashes According to ancient legend, only one phoenix at a time is alive. When its time comes to die it flies to Egypt where it builds a nest from precious, sweet-smelling woods, settles in it and bursts into flames. From its ashes a new bird is born, which rises from its parents' ashes in all its beauty. The legend passed from the ancient world to the medieval one, being used to illustrate Christ's resurrection. Nowadays it is often used literally of something like a building that is rebuilt after a fire, as well as figuratively.

'He now hates to speak about the past and his rise from the ashes, claiming to hate the way his life is summed up in such clichés.' (*Independent*, 8 October 1998)

risk life and limb see LIFE AND LIMB

road see GO DOWN A ROAD

between a rock and a hard place This expression, meaning being faced with two equally unpleasant choices, dates from the 1920s in America, where it is originally recorded used to mean 'bankrupt'. Although it is a vivid image, exactly where it comes from is obscure, although it may be influenced by the expression between 'Scylla and Charybdis'. This comes from Homer's *Odyssey*. Odysseus and his crew needed to pass through the straits of Messina, between Italy and Sicily, where, according to legend, you ran the risk of being eaten alive by the monster Scylla whose lair overlooked one side of the strait, or sucked down into the whirlpool Charybdis if you passed through out of Scylla's reach. Thus if you are caught between Scylla and Charybdis, whatever choice you make will be a bad one.

'In 1987 Labour's local selection committee in this working class constituency had to choose between a rock and a hard place – either Hughes, a local Transport Union convenor with strong left-wing views, or the outsider, "Red Ted" Knight from Lambeth.' (*Daily Telegraph*, 9 April 1992)

rock and roll see NEW ROCK AND ROLL

rock the boat If you stand up or otherwise try to 'make waves' in a small boat it will start rocking and ultimately capsize. This expression for making things unstable has been in use since the 1920s, and was popularized by the hit song, 'Sit down, you're rocking the boat' from the 1950 musical *Guys and Dolls*, based on Damon Runyon's stories of New York low life.

'I was still trying hard not to rock the boat, not to upset either the FO or WTN, and was desperate to find a way of making uncontroversial remarks sound interesting.' (J. Morrell and J. McCarthy, *Some Other Rainbow*, 1993)

(make) a rod for your own back Meaning to do something likely to cause you difficulties later, this is probably an ironic adaptation of the Bible's 'A whip for the horse, a bridle for the ass, and a rod for the fool's back' (Proverbs 26:3), anyone who makes a rod for their own back being self-evidently a fool.

'Gloucester's actions after his brother's death are traditionally seen as the triumph of an over-mighty subject, and it follows that Edward IV had been making a rod for his own back when he allowed Gloucester to become lord of the north.' (R. Horrox, *Richard III*, 1992)

roll of a dice see DICE WITH DEATH

Rome see WHEN IN ROME

root and branch A biblical phrase, coming from the splendidly apocalyptic 'For, behold, the day cometh, that shall burn as an oven; and all the proud, yea, and all that do wickedly, shall be stubble: and the day that cometh shall burn them up, saith the Lord of hosts, that it shall leave the neither root nor branch' (Malachi 4:1). Meaning 'thoroughly', 'utterly', 'so that it can never happen again', it has been in regular use since the seventeenth century.

'I would say just this: that having got the legislation it would be wise to proceed by exemplar, by experiment, by demonstration of success rather than trying to do a root and branch revolutionary approach.' (*Independent*, 10 October 1989)

root of the matter Yet another biblical expression, from Job 19:28: 'Why persecute him, seeing the root of the matter is found in me?' Since 'root' has long been used to mean the fundamental, essential part of something (as in GRASS ROOTS), it was quite easy for the 1611 translators of the Bible to make a literal translation of the Hebrew to produce this expression, but even so, it did not become a cliché until the early nineteenth century.

roots see BACK TO YOUR ROOTS

rotten apple see BAD APPLE

rough and ready This expression for 'crude but effective', or simply an extension of 'rough', became a cliché in the early nineteenth century. The suggestion here is that there is not enough time to create a more finished version. As one writer has pointed out, we might expect the wording to be 'rough *but* ready', and it is tempting to counter this with a vision of a surly workman muttering about having something rough and ready, or properly finished and next year.

'Unused to the rough and ready answering-back of British socialism, he remarked next day that if he lived in Britain he would be a Tory.' (Peter Lewis, *The Fifties: Portrait of a Period*, 1989)

rough diamond A rough diamond is someone who has intrinsic value but whose 'lack of polish' initially obscures the fact. It is an old expression, the literal use for an uncut diamond going back to the early seventeenth century, the figurative use first being recorded in 1700, when Dryden wrote: 'Chaucer, I confess is a rough diamond.'

'A rough diamond in his earlier years, he has now become a sophisticated centre who was drafted into the Irish World Cup squad, although he languished on the bench and was never called upon.' (*Rugby World and Post*, 1992)

round up the usual suspects see USUAL SUSPECTS

rub it in An alternative for to ADD INSULT TO INJURY, used to emphasize something that is already a source of shame or embarrassment. It has been current from the mid-nineteenth century, and is assumed to be a shortening of the earlier 'rub salt into a wound'. This latter refers to making a punishment flogging even more painful by adding salt or vinegar to lash wounds, a practice that was common in the Navy in the seventeenth and eighteenth centuries. A modern alternative to this is to 'rub someone's nose in it' – a reference to the practice of trying to train a puppy not to defecate in the house by doing just this.

'And just to rub it in, while you're being impatient and grumpy they're always cheerful and chatty – despite the freezing cold and the pouring rain.' (*Woman*, 1991)

'To rub salt into England's wounds, Wales has produced an information technology policy to underpin the budgeting, pricing and payment demands of the coming health market.' (*Guardian*, 20 December 1989)

rub the wrong way This term for 'to irritate' or 'get on someone's nerves' comes from the effect of stroking a pet against the natural lie of the hair. It has been in use since at least the middle of the nineteenth century.

'Our personalities are different, and we rub each other up the wrong way almost immediately.' (Linford Christie and Tony Ward, *Linford Christie: An Autobiography*, 1990)

rub your hands The use of this gesture to express keen satisfaction and anticipation is recorded first in Fanny Burney's 1778 novel *Evelina*: 'He rubbed his hands, and was scarce able to contain the fullness of his glee', but is probably older.

'Lawyers all over London will be rubbing their hands with glee at the prospect of numerous legal actions when the clubs are taken to task by the various unions.' (*Evening Standard*, 28 August 1998)

Rubicon see DIE IS CAST

rude awakening This cliché for shaking someone out of complacency, a set phrase since the 1890s, springs so readily to the journalistic mind that it was used as a headline after Ruud Gullit's first match as manager of Newcastle United by no less than five newspapers.

'If you are intransigent, or are determined to stick to the letter of your contract come what may, you could be in for a rude awakening.' (Martin Edwards, *How to Get the Best Deal from Your Employer*, 1991)

rule the roost Originally this was 'rule the roast', a curious expression, the meaning of which is not clear, although the best guess is that it refers to some sort of custom of being master of a feast. It is first found in the fifteenth century, and was a cliché in the sixteenth. It is not surprising that by the eighteenth century the obscure expression had changed 'to rule the roost', as if describing a cock dominating the hen house, particularly as it then linked up to other expressions such as 'cock of the walk' (chief person in a circle or best person at something – early nineteenth century), the obsolete 'cock of the school' for the boy who leads others in games and fights (nineteenth century again) and 'dunghill cock' (in use since the fifteenth century for a coward).

'She ruled the roost with, literally, a rod of iron, taking up whatever cudgel came to hand to beat her children.' (*You* magazine, 20 September 1998)

rum do (**go** or **situation**) These rather dated uses of 'rum' to mean strange, odd, have nothing to do with the drink. Instead they are a hangover from eighteenth-century slang. The origin of the word is not known, although one attractive suggestion links it to the word Romany, gypsies already having a reputation both for mystic powers and as rogues by this date.

' "Don't laugh," he shouted and launched into the expletive-spattered story of how this rum situation had come to pass.' (*Mail on Sunday*, 20 September 1998)

'An election campaign in which the two principal parties find it difficult to believe what the opinion polls are telling them is a rum do.' (*New Statesman and Society*, 1992)

he can run, but he can't hide The boxer Joe Louis said this of his opponent, the swift-footed Billy Conn, before a match in 1946, showing that pre-match hype is no new thing. Nor was the sentiment new, being found in the Bible and elsewhere. However, Louis's form stuck, and was reinforced by US President Reagan who used it as a warning to international terrorists in 1985.

'Tommy Adams was certainly a member of the upper echelon of major criminals and we have proved that an untouchable strata of criminal does not exist. It sends a clear message to anybody else – you can run but you can't hide.' (*Independent*, 18 September 1998)

run for dear life see DEAR LIFE

run it up the flagpole (**and see if anyone salutes it**) An expression coined in the USA in about 1950, and popular in business and advertising circles, it means to try something out and see how people react to it. It has obvious links to the imagery of expressions such as 'to fly a kite' in the sense of raising an idea and seeing how it is reacted to, or to 'see which way the wind is blowing'. Since the UK has no tradition of saluting the flag, the full form of the expression can seem an affectation when used by the British, particularly after it was taken up by the writers of the cult television series *Drop the Dead Donkey*. They ridiculed the expression by showing the unpopular and vacillating yuppie boss Gus Hedges using ever more bizarre variants of the formula, culminating in such expressions as 'let's put it in the percolator and see if it makes coffee'. The shorter 'let's run it up the flagpole' is less likely to raise eyebrows.

run of the mill In this expression for ordinary, standard, 'mill' is used in the sense of 'factory'. 'Run of the mill' was originally a manufacturing term for goods as they are run off the production line, rather than after they have been specially finished or graded and sorted. It began to be used figuratively in the first part of the twentieth century.

'Lakes and Mountain holidays are very different to run of the mill summer holidays.' (*Enterprise Lakes and Mountains*, 1990)

run on empty The image of the car fuel gauge showing the tank is empty is used in this expression for to be out of reserves, near to grinding to a halt. It developed in the USA, and use spread after the success of Jackson Browne's 1978 song 'Runnin' on Empty'.

'The big oligarchies in Russia think he won't do anything to damage their interests; close down big businesses that have long been running on empty, for instance, or make Russian companies pay tax.' (*Evening Standard*, 1 September 1998)

run rings around A very similar sporting cliché to LEAVE STANDING, this was introduced in the late nineteenth century.

'You may well believe, in your bright cocky little way, that you can run rings round your gullible mother and you may, indeed, be right about this character.' (*Daily Mirror*, 1992)

run something past This modern business cliché originally implied letting someone have a quick look or check of something, but now tends to be used to mean consulting with, or getting authorization from someone.

'If I ever had to qualify an audit report, I'd run it past Claire first.' (*Accountancy*, 1993)

run the gauntlet The sort of gauntlet you run has nothing, in origin, to do with PICK UP THE GAUNTLET. It comes from the Swedish *gatlopp*, formed from words meaning 'lane' and 'course', and refers to a traditional military punishment for crimes such as theft from your fellows, in which the guilty party had to run, stripped to the waist, down a lane formed by two ranks of men who would strike at him as he passed. The word entered English in the form *gantlope*, and, because of a perceived similarity of sound, was changed to the more familiar 'gauntlet', although the two forms co-existed from the seventeenth to nineteenth centuries. The figurative use, for something difficult or dangerous that has to be passed through, has been used for as long as the literal sense.

'Councillors arriving for Leominster's Planning Committee meeting had to walk a silent gauntlet of children and parents to get to the council chamber.' (Central Television news scripts, 1993)

run to earth This image, taken from foxhunting, has been used since the middle of the nineteenth century to mean to find a thing or person long looked for.

'When a mail robber was run to earth there – he was living with his sister by whom he had three little boys – the local paper was bombarded with letters from the outraged citizens of our suburban town complaining on both counts: the threat to property and the affront to public morals.' (Nina Bawden, *A Woman of my Age*, 1991)

run to seed, seedy Any gardener will know what happens to a plant that is allowed to run to seed after flowering. First of all it gets untidy and scraggy; then, if it is an annual, it grows sickly and dies – all concepts covered by 'run to seed' and its derivative, 'seedy'. 'Run to seed' has been recorded figuratively since the middle of the nineteenth century, but may well be older, as 'seedy' is found as early as 1739.

'The rest of the College, like the theatre, seems in Paul Pry's day to have run to seed.' (Ernest Cotchin, *The Royal Veterinary College London*, 1990)

running see OUT OF THE RUNNING

S. H. One T. Like so many modern euphemisms, this one for 'shit' depends on the hearer knowing exactly what you are talking about, and so saves no blushes. Common only a few years ago, it has already lost its amusement value, and is declining.

sacred cow Cows are sacred in the Hindu religion, and the British in India coined the term 'sacred cow' for the animals that are left to roam there unmolested. By about 1900 the expression had been transferred to an institution, idea, or person considered above criticism or change.

'Another told her spying, again like police work, was a sacred cow, the subject of pompous statements of loyalty from overprotective politicians, and so should be regularly threatened with the abattoir.' (Trevor Barnes, *A Midsummer Killing*, 1991)

a sadder and a wiser man A quotation cliché, from Samuel Taylor Coleridge's *The Rime of the Ancient Mariner* (1789): 'He went like one that hath been stunned,/ And is of sense forlorn:/A sadder and a wiser man,/He rose the morrow morn.' Since the philosophy behind the poem is so obscure, it is tempting to feel that the immense length of the poem has as much to do with this as the ideas that underpin it.

'Now sadder but wiser, we are prepared to admit that the implementation of curriculum change is a complicated business.' (Colette Hawes *et al.*, *Curriculum and Reality in African Primary Schools*, 1979)

safe and sound This set phrase has been in regular use since at least the fourteenth century. As is typical of these alliterative phrases, each half adds little to the other, and 'safe and sound' rarely means more than a simple 'safe' would.

'The methods used and the pollution control systems fitted are sophisticated and provide a safe and sound disposal option, subject to rigorous operational controls and inspection.' (*Hansard Extracts 1991–1992*)

safe haven A haven is an inlet that provides shelter for boats, and in bad weather any sailor will look for a safe haven. It is easy to see how this could be transferred to the idea of a shelter from the troubles of the world. John Wesley used the idea for heaven in one of his popular hymns 'In Temptation' (1740): 'Jesu, lover of my soul,/Let me to thy bosom fly . . . Safe into the haven guide,/O receive my soul at last', an idea Gerard Manley Hopkins picks up in his 1864 poem *Heaven-Haven*. In worldly terms, a year after Hopkins, someone was writing in *The Times* about 'One safe haven where no nicotine perfume intrudes'. The expression was much used in the 1990s during the wars in former Yugoslavia, and is also popular jargon in the financial world for a safe investment.

'As the rouble collapsed against the mark in panic selling amid disappointment over terms of the Russian government's debt restructuring plan, safe-haven buying lifted the pound.' (*Daily Mail*, 27 August 1998)

safe pair of hands This is a term from cricket, in use by the middle of the nineteenth century, describing someone who can be relied on to hold a catch. At an unknown date it was transferred to politics and in recent years has spread to more general use, to mean someone who can be relied on not to make serious errors of judgement.

'Known as a "safe pair of hands", he has only had one noteworthy blip during his career, when he decided, as night foreign editor on the day of the Chernobyl reactor meltdown in 1986, that it was "not a story".' (*Independent*, 22 September 1998)

salad days A cliché for a time of innocence or ignorance, from Shakespeare's *Antony and Cleopatra*, when Cleopatra talks of her 'salad days,/When I was green in judgement', 'green' here meaning 'ignorant' (as in modern 'greenhorn'), a very common use in Shakespeare's day. Twentieth-century cliché status was reinforced by the success of the 1956 musical by Julian Slade, showing the *Salad Days* of newly qualified students just launching themselves into the adult world, and it is a very frequent caption for magazine articles dealing with salads.

'Having concentrated on choral conducting during his salad days in the early 1970s, he found himself in something of a career rut by the age of 28.' (*Gramophone*, 1992)

salt of the earth This is a biblical quotation: 'Ye are the salt of the earth: but if the salt have lost his savour, wherewith shall it be salted?' (Matthew 5:13). It has been used in the language since Anglo-Saxon times, but really took off as a cliché in the nineteenth century. In the past it was used to mean someone of great worthiness and reliability, but in current use it seems to be changing, perhaps under the influence of the idea of 'earthiness'.

' "He's a popular, rough diamond, salt-of-the-earth type," says a City commentator. "People like him." ' (*Independent*, 8 October 1998)

same ilk see ILK

same wavelength see WAVELENGTH

save the day A well-established term for preventing the loss of a battle in the nineteenth century, its figurative use for solving a difficulty seems to be twentieth-century.

'A posse of American financial backers was rounded up and rode in – although it was touch and go at the time – to save the day.' (*Independent*, 8 October 1998)

save your breath Although this cliché is to be heard all the time, the original proverb 'Save your breath to cool your porridge' of which it is a shortening is very rarely heard. It dates from the sixteenth century.

'I'll collect you and I'll take you home again afterwards, so save your breath and stop arguing.' (Jennifer Taylor, *Destined to Love*, 1992)

saved by the bell If a boxer is knocked down right at the end of a round, the count may be interrupted by the bell marking the end of the round, in which case he will not be OUT FOR THE COUNT but literally saved by the bell. The term was transferred to any last-minute reprieve in the middle of the twentieth century.

saving grace Used literally, 'saving grace' is a theological term, for the grace of God that allows sinning humans to reach heaven. This is recorded from the sixteenth century onwards, but in the nineteenth the term started to be used for a redeeming quality in someone, which is felt to compensate for other faults.

'The big liability of a politician in America is not sin but hypocrisy. Clinton's saving grace was never to have campaigned on a family values ticket.' (*Independent*, 12 November 1998)

say it with flowers One of the oldest advertising slogans still in use, this was adopted by the Society of American Florists in 1917, and has since become a part of the language.

'They said it with flowers again, but this time they brought picnics too. The sun was blazing down on Kensington Gardens yesterday, so the thousands of people who came to pay their respects to Diana, Princess of Wales, a year on from her death had clearly decided it was worth making a day of it.' (*Evening Standard*, 1 September 1998)

. . . says more about you than . . . A modern formula phrase, used by journalists to make a clever point, regardless of any truth in the statement.

'In the office, your pen says more about you than what you write with it.' (*Guardian*, 5 September 1998)

schadenfreude A cliché of the intellectually pretentious, used to some extent to replace the rather old-fashioned HOW ARE THE MIGHTY FALLEN. The word is German, a compound of 'harm' and 'joy' and means pleasure derived from another's misfortune.

'Anyone who has ever had a close encounter with that lethal spirit tequila . . . will experience an agreeable sense of schadenfreude as the characters toss back the shots with reckless abandon, while the evocation of the hideous, hungover morning-after is hilariously achieved.' (*Daily Telegraph*, 9 April 1992)

scrap heap SEE CONSIGN TO THE HISTORY BOOKS

scratch SEE UP TO SCRATCH

Scylla and Charybdis SEE DEVIL AND THE DEEP BLUE SEA

sea change This comes from Shakespeare's *Tempest* (I.ii), where Ariel sings to the shipwrecked Ferdinand, 'Full fathom five thy father lies;/Of his bones are coral made:/Those are pearls that were his eyes:/Nothing of him that doth fade,/But doth suffer a sea-change/Into something rich and strange.' 'Sea change' began to be used in the nineteenth century for a profound change, and is today a very popular journalistic cliché, often used where a mere 'change' is perfectly adequate.

'We are, it seems, in the middle of a spectacular sea-change in the way the British eat.' (*Independent*, 8 September 1998)

seamy side While the outside of a garment may be smooth and neat, a look inside the lining will reveal the rough edges of the seams and the hidden signs of how the outer appearance is achieved. This is the image that lies behind the term 'seamy', first recorded in Shakespeare's *Othello* (IV.ii): 'He turned your wit the seamy side without.'

'She was a tough girl with an abrasive manner, and seemed very knowledgeable about the seamy side of life.' (E. Murphy, *A Nest of Singing Birds*, 1993)

seats SEE BUMS ON SEATS

second nature 'Custom is second nature' wrote Plutarch in the first century AD.

This had been translated into English by the fourteenth century, and from this idea that something you habitually do becomes so much a part of you that it is indistinguishable from nature, comes our use of 'second nature'.

'Addressing the Supreme Soviet during a debate on emergency price curbs, Mr Ryzhkov was far blunter than a man accustomed to the velvety circumlocutions and understatements, second nature to Western central bankers.' (*Independent*, 11 October 1989)

secret agenda see HIDDEN AGENDA

see a man about a dog A joking catch-phrase cliché, used as an excuse for going away to do something. It is most usually used when leaving the room to go to the lavatory, or by men as an excuse to leave the house to go down to the pub. It developed in the later nineteenth century, and is still used today, although probably in decline.

seedy see RUN TO SEED

(has to be) seen to be believed A clichéd expression of amazement, in use since at least the beginning of the twentieth century, and a great favourite with advertising copywriters.

'Four of the relieving kicks he launched in this match had to be seen to be believed, particularly as he varied his kicking foot.' (*Daily Telegraph*, 6 April 1992)

self-made man A term from the first part of the nineteenth century, used to describe someone who has won wealth and position through his own efforts, rather than through the advantages of birth. It is rarely used without some element of snobbery or an implication that the person is at best a ROUGH DIAMOND. The quotation books abound in jokes at his expense, one of the best known of these being Disraeli's comment: on being told that he was perhaps being too hard on John Bright, a self-made man, he replied, 'I know he is and he adores his maker' (often quoted in the form 'a self-made man who worships his maker').

'But then Mrs Lawler came from a "good" background, while it was well known that Lawler was an entirely self-made man.' (Emma Blair, *Maggie Jordan*, 1990)

self-starter The language of job advertisements, especially in the financial sector, is one of the last strongholds of the sort of obscure business jargon once notoriously found in business letters. This cliché-ridden dialect is full of obscure terms such as RESULTS-DRIVEN people of 'GRADUATE CALIBRE' with good TRACK RECORDS, and self-starters – not, as the term implies to an older generation, an electrical device for starting a car, but someone 'self-motivated', 'able to act on their own initiative' (two more favourites of advertisers). The phrase seems to have come into use around 1960 and to have peaked in the mid-1990s.

'We are seeking to recruit 3 energetic and ambitious self starters of graduate calibre, who can contribute to Marks Sattin's current and future success.' (*Evening Standard*, 7 September 1998)

selling off the family silver see FAMILY SILVER

send packing 'To pack' has been used to mean 'to send someone away' since the beginning of the sixteenth century, and is still found in the expression 'to pack someone off somewhere'. It is from this that the term 'to send someone packing' comes. It is recorded from the late sixteenth century.

'Three armed gangsters burst into a businessman's house demanding money – but were sent packing by fourteen burly relatives.' (*Daily Mirror*, 1992)

serious The use of the word 'serious' to mean 'worthy of respect, substantial' became a cliché in the 1980s, particularly in the form 'serious money', although similar uses can be traced for about 100 years. 'Serious money' was used to sum up the whole of the yuppie culture when Caryl Churchill used it as the title of her 1987 play.

'Australia's first serious botanical range, Aesop, offers plant-based products to care for hair, face and body.' (*Evening Standard*, 28 August 1998)

'Most have a core of solid businesses that ensure that at least parts of the firm are making serious money.' (*The Economist*, 1991)

set the cat among the pigeons see CAT AMONG THE PIGEONS

seventh heaven In the ancient world people believed that there are seven levels or spheres of the heavens corresponding to the seven planets, a belief carried over into the Jewish and Muslim cosmologies. In a literal sense this seventh and highest level of bliss appears in medieval literature and can be found in Chaucer's work. In a figurative sense it occurs used in the same way as paradise or bliss, for a state of great happiness, from the early nineteenth century.

'And when the little bouncing balls came up onscreen, pointing out the subtitled lyrics for "Fixin' To Die Rag", the ciderheads were in seventh heaven.' (Ian Breakwell and Paul Hammond (eds), *Seeing in the Dark*, 1990)

sex and drugs and rock and roll This cliché of rock as rebellion and the lifestyle that goes with it comes from the title of a 1977 song performed and written by Ian Dury and the Blockheads, 'Sex & Drugs & Rock & Roll'.

sex kitten A cliché of the 1950s, which now seems rather dated as the helpless image of the kitten is no longer as admired in women. It was particularly associated with the French actress Brigitte Bardot, and then with actresses of similar looks. Blended with the earlier BLONDE BOMBSHELL, the expression produced the term 'sex bomb'.

'It was Von Unwerth who captured Claudia Schiffer's sex kitten quality and used it in the Guess advertising campaign which made the model famous.' (*The Face*, 1992)

sex, lies and videotape The title of this 1989 film is very popular with headline writers, and much alluded to whenever newspaper stories break involving scandal and secret recordings.

'It is not so much the sex and lies that matters, but the videotape – the way that the lie is conveyed to us which defines whether that magic trust factor remains intact or not.' (*Independent*, 14 September 1998)

'Sex, lies and telephone rates.' (Advertisement, October 1998)

sexual chemistry see CHEMISTRY

shake the dust from your feet This is an allusion to Jesus' instructions to his disciples: 'And whosoever shall not receive you, nor hear your words, when ye depart out of that house or city, shake off the dust of your feet' (Matthew 10:14) – in other words, eradicate all associations with them. The expression has been used for leaving, usually indignantly, since the eighteenth century. Fanny Burney wrote in 1782,

'I then paid off my lodging, and "shaking the dust from my feet", bid a long adieu to London.'

'It is this characteristic which renders fundamentalist religion open to large numbers of fissures in communities, with preachers or sections of congregations shaking the dust from their feet and moving off to build or buy another church.' (John Fulton, *The Tragedy of Belief*, 1991)

sharing see CARING AND SHARING

shave see CLOSE SHAVE

ships that pass in the night A quotation from Henry Wadsworth Longfellow's *Tales of a Wayside Inn* (1874), where he writes of 'Ships that pass in the night, and speak each other in passing;/Only a signal shown and a distant voice in the darkness;/ So on the ocean of life we pass and speak one another,/Only a look and a voice; then darkness again and a silence.' The cliché has to some extent been superseded by 'strangers in the night', the title of a song by Charles Singleton, Eddie Snyder and Bert Kaempfert, which was a hit for Frank Sinatra in 1966, and which seems to owe something to Longfellow's words.

shirt off your back see GIVE THE SHIRT OFF YOUR BACK

shirt on see KEEP YOUR SHIRT ON

shoe fits see IF THE CAP FITS

shoot yourself in the foot This expression originated in the USA, and has only arrived in the UK in the second half of the twentieth century. It refers to soldiers wounding themselves with their own guns, either by accident or, more often, deliberately as a means of disabling themselves to escape going into battle – although those doing this were still likely to find themselves shot, as it was a court-martialable offence, deemed the equivalent of desertion.

'But I don't see why they should be asked to shoot themselves in the foot by paying to train a competitor's workforce, and neither do they!' (*Independent*, 9 October 1989)

shooting the messenger Stories abound of tyrants in the past who punished the bearer of bad news with death, giving rise to the saying, 'Don't shoot the messenger who brings bad news.' From this comes our current use.

'The sort of scenes shown in the *Uncovered* series are precisely the kind of thing that those who want more regulation worry about . . . They are wrong. There could not be a clearer case of shooting the messenger. In fact, we should be grateful to the producers for revealing a new truth about what is going on, however unpleasant.' (*Independent*, 21 August 1998)

shop till you drop A cliché of the 1980s, part of the high-spending culture of the time. Its popularity provides interesting evidence that the rhymed set phrase is still alive and well in English.

'While the missus shops till she drops, husbands and boyfriends can sit in Ye Olde Arms and gaze at 28,000 "stars" twinkling in the "sky".' (*Independent*, 2 September 1998)

short and sweet An expression in use since the first part of the sixteenth century, often, even then, used ironically. It is particularly frequently used of the spoken word, the unspoken contrast being with 'long and tedious'.

'I think I've got five minutes which is probably more than some of you delegates have got so I'll keep it fairly short and sweet.' (Trade Union Annual Congress (Business), 7 June 1993)

short, sharp shock This is a quotation on the subject of execution from the Gilbert and Sullivan comic opera *The Mikado* (1885): 'Awaiting the sensation of a short, sharp shock,/From a cheap and chippy chopper on a big black block.' The political use of 'short, sharp shock', recommending it as a treatment for young offenders, while current before, dates particularly from a speech made in October 1979 by the Conservative Minister William Whitelaw when he introduced a particularly harsh new regime for young offenders.

shot in the arm This expression for a much-needed stimulant or for encouragement comes from 1920s America. Whether we should see it as an injection given by a doctor to put you back on your feet, or as the effect of narcotics, is in doubt: 'a shot in the arm' was certainly part of drugs slang in the 1930s.

'And although many architects still find it hard to say Charles's name without curling their lips, most of them do admit that by bringing the whole subject into the public domain, architecture has had a much-needed shot in the arm.' (Penny Junor, *Charles and Diana*, 1991)

shot in the dark Meaning a wild guess or something done without full information, this dates from the late nineteenth century, and reflects the effects of trying to shoot at something you cannot see.

'It had only been a shot in the dark; playing a hunch really, but Johnny's face reddened and he looked momentarily discomfited.' (E. Nash, *Strawberries and Wine*, 1993)

show SEE LET'S DO THE SHOW RIGHT HERE

show must go on This theatrical expression is very much a cliché of the Hollywood film between the 1930s and 1950s, but appears to have originated in the nineteenth-century circus.

'Perhaps the secret of all these people at the top is that they have vertigo but out of a feeling of "the show must go on" they smile in public and are sick off stage.' (Enoch Powell, *Reflections of a Statesman*, 1991)

show your hand and **lay your cards on the table** come from card playing. These actions let your opponents see what you have in the way of strengths and weaknesses, and how you will play your cards. As early as 1581 the Jesuit Edmund Campion is recorded as saying, 'I would I might be suffered to show my cards.'

'But in this, the great crisis of his reign, the Old King remained supremely cool, waiting for his enemies to show their hand before committing his own forces in sudden and decisive pounces.' (John Gillingham, *Richard the Lionheart*, 1989)

shut the stable door SEE LOCK THE STABLE DOOR

sick as a parrot This is a footballers' cliché, prominent in the 1970s and 80s, but now largely out of fashion, except for the fact that it has caught the public's imagination, and is often cited as a typical cliché. 'Sick as a dog' is the much older equivalent (in use from the 1700s). Various suggestions have been made as to the origin of the sick parrot: from a dialect 'sick as a peat' (pronounced pee-at), meaning 'feeling heavy', to a seventeenth-century expression, 'melancholy as a sick parrot', but its source is not really known, and it may just have started life as a joke.

'If I was to break my leg tomorrow I'd be as sick as a parrot, but it wouldn't be the end of the world.' (Ernest Cashmore, *Black Sportsmen*, 1982)

side of the angels see ON THE SIDE OF THE ANGELS

sideways look at A cliché of humourists, suggesting an unconventional or offbeat way of seeing the world.

'Until recently, the Guild of Columnists insisted upon a three-year apprenticeship of local training before one was allowed to take a sideways look at life on a national scale.' (*Independent*, 26 August 1998)

sight for sore eyes The image here is of something that is such a delight to see that it would cure sore eyes. It is often used of a welcome or unexpected visitor – Jonathan Swift cites 'The Sight of you is good for sore eyes' as an example of his *Polite Conversation* (1738) – or of something particularly beautiful.

'A visit to the Westonbirt Arboretum with its 13,000 trees and shrubs is always a sight for sore eyes.' (Mike Stone and Roger Russell, *Warm Welcomes in Britain*, 1990)

sign of the times In Matthew 16:2, Jesus says to the Pharisees: 'O ye hypocrites, ye can discern the face of the sky; but can ye not discern the signs of the times?' In modern use it is nearly always a signal of disapproval, the English equivalent of O TEMPORA! O MORES!

'Before we once-and-for-all set up our new tank . . . it's a sign of the times that we have to pause and consider the single most important item in our tank – water.' (*Practical Fishkeeping*, 1992)

silence see CONSPIRACY OF SILENCE

silent majority This became a cliché after being popularized by President Nixon in 1969 in a speech in which he said that he was sure that 'the great silent majority of my fellow Americans' would not want to get out of the Vietnam War except on honourable terms. Since then many politicians have claimed to speak for the silent majority, but without explaining how they know what they want. MIDDLE ENGLAND (or America) is an alternative term.

'Not only is there at present much special pleading which largely ignores the needs of children; but also, I believe, there is a large silent majority whose views, though unfashionable, deserve a hearing.' (S. Reedy and M. Woodhead, *Family, Work and Education*, 1988)

sing a different tune (or **song**) see DIFFERENT SONG

sink or swim This expression, used in various forms since Chaucer's time, is self-explanatory. There is no need to look for lurid antecedents in the trial by water of witches as some have, but simply to the art of basic survival.

'And former Tory chairman Lord Parkinson said the Prime Minister and Chancellor Kenneth Clarke would "sink or swim together", and talk of rivalry between them was nonsense.' (*Liverpool Daily Post and Echo*)

sinking feeling An expression from the late nineteenth century, originally used to describe hunger, and from there transferred to other things such as fear that affects the stomach, and from there applied to a similar mental state. The expression became well known from the 1920s when there was a vigorous advertising campaign which used the slogan 'Bovril prevents that sinking feeling.'

'Doug had a sinking feeling that he might be in the process of making a grave mistake, but he went on.' (C. F. Roe, *The Lumsden Baby*, 1990)

sinned against see MORE SINNED AGAINST THAN SINNING

sins see FOR MY SINS

sisters under the skin 'The Colonel's lady an' Judy O'Grady are sisters under their skins' is the chorus of the poem *The Ladies* by Rudyard Kipling (1896). From this the expression has been widely used to indicate similarity of feeling or reaction regardless of exterior differences.

'Women cast down, on whom life had left its mark, were to him sisters under the skin regardless of station.' (Philip Callow, *Van Gogh: A Life*, 1990)

sit tight Used either literally for to sit bunched up or without moving, or figuratively meaning to take no action. The expression is used in poker for someone who does not want either to bet or throw his cards in, and it has been suggested that this is the origin; but since the first recorded use is from 1738, used of women at their embroidery, this seems unlikely. It is far more likely to come from a physical description.

'They sit tight, are unlikely to budge unless really disturbed and can be easily shot with a .22 rifle or even a high-powered air rifle.' (Bob Smithson, *Rabbiting*, 1988)

'Quite frankly, we're advising all our clients to sit tight, at the moment, and neither to buy nor to sell.' (Alexander Davidson, *The City Share Pushers*, 1989)

sitting duck A sitting duck is literally an easy target for someone with a gun, and will swiftly become a DEAD DUCK, although no true sportsman would take any pride in shooting his target other than on the wing; hence the disparaging tone that the expression often involves. The figurative use dates from the middle of the twentieth century.

'Dug-outs at some [football] grounds have become chambers of horror, with visiting soccer bosses the sitting duck targets for verbal and, sometimes, physical abuse.' (*Today*, 1992)

skeleton in the cupboard E. Cobham Brewer, the author of *Brewer's Dictionary of Phrase and Fable* written in 1870, tells a story, to account for this expression, of a search for someone who had perfect contentment. The woman selected took the searchers to her bedroom, showed them a skeleton in the cupboard, and told them it was a rival killed by her husband in a duel years before, and that he forced her to kiss it every night. Alas, Brewer does not say where he got this fantastic rigmarole from, and it sounds suspiciously like something made up to account for the saying. It came into use in the early nineteenth century, at a time when the Gothic horror novels so well parodied by Jane Austen in *Northanger Abbey* were popular, so it may be inspired by them – perhaps one of these was the source of Brewer's story. In the USA the saying takes the form of 'skeleton in the closet', and since for many years homosexuality was considered such a skeleton, this has given rise to 'come out of the closet' for being open about one's homosexuality.

skin deep see BEAUTY IS ONLY SKIN DEEP

skip the light fantastic see LIGHT FANTASTIC

skittles see BEER AND SKITTLES

sky's the limit The image of climbing high to describe aspirations is an ancient one, but the idea of height so great that the sky is the limit only dates from the twentieth century.

'While high pay is not a myth, it is not as high as is generally supposed – but if you turn into a super advertising star, the sky's the limit.' (Stafford Whiteaker, *A Career in Advertising and Public Relations*, 1986)

slap in the face with a wet fish see BETTER THAN A SLAP IN THE FACE WITH A WET FISH

sledgehammer to crack a nut Although a sledgehammer has been used figuratively for something forceful since the middle of the nineteenth century, the expression 'to take a sledgehammer to crack a nut' to indicate the use of far more force or power than is necessary, does not seem to have come into general use until the 1970s.

'These measures could quite justifiably be regarded as something of a sledgehammer to crack a very small nut, since they are intended to deal with a problem the existence of which is almost totally unproven.' (Susan Johnstone *et al.*, *The Legal Context of Teaching*, 1992)

sleeping dogs see LET SLEEPING DOGS LIE

sliced bread see BEST THING SINCE SLICED BREAD

slings and arrows In his famous 'To be or not to be' speech, Shakespeare's Hamlet wonders 'Whether 'tis nobler in the mind to suffer/The slings and arrows of outrageous fortune,/Or to take arms against a sea of troubles,/And by opposing end them' (III.i). In the nineteenth century slings and arrows became a cliché for the problems life throws at you.

'I'd dearly like to see a time-budgeting study of British academics. I bet it would show that most now spend more time filling in forms, jumping through hoops, and generally dodging the slings and arrows of outrageous quangos, than in actually doing their jobs.' (*Independent*, 23 July 1998)

slip into something more comfortable see SOMETHING MORE COMFORTABLE

slippery slope This image of starting out on a path that will unavoidably lead to your falling into something worse, with little or no hope of climbing back, only dates from the middle of the twentieth century, but rapidly became a cliché.

' "It's the worst thing for a hangover and could put you on the slippery slope to alcoholism," warns the magazine.' (*Today*, 1992)

small beer (or **potatoes**) Small beer was weak beer, suitable for quenching thirst, but not for getting drunk. It came to be used early on for something that is insignificant. Shakespeare uses it several times in his plays – in *Othello*, for instance, Iago dismisses a virtuous woman as fit only 'to suckle fools and chronicle small beer'. 'Small potatoes', used in the same way, dates from nineteenth-century America, and is the more common expression in American English.

'If the truth were known, Sir Henry had never wanted to be a country gentleman, which must have seemed very small beer after such a distinguished and varied military career.' (Ray Harrison, *Patently Murder*, 1991)

'Novell is so rich that the Unix acquisition is relatively small potatoes.' (*Unigram x*, 1993)

small but perfect(ly formed) This set phrase, often used ironically of people, seems to have developed in the nineteenth century. The *OED* has an example of 'small but perfect' from 1863. By 1914 Duff Cooper could write to his future wife, Lady Diana, of 'Your two stout lovers, frowning at one another across the hearth rug, while your small, but perfectly formed one kept the party in a roar.'

'Small, compact and perfectly formed, the island at the heart of the Mediterranean offers a mix of cultures to suit all tastes.' (*Independent*, 5 September 1998)

small mercies see THANKFUL FOR SMALL MERCIES

small world see GLOBAL VILLAGE

handing out pills/drugs as if they were Smarties This clichéd description of doctors' prescribing habits or of drug taking, has become particularly common in the 1990s. The comparison arises from the similarity between the brightly coloured chocolate sweets and some pills – both have the same sort of shape and lurid sugar coating, and as a result there have been scares about children confusing the two.

'Cannabis isn't a new drug and clearly has relatively low toxicity. It shouldn't be dished out like Smarties (nor should Valium) but it shouldn't be denied to deserving cases.' (*Independent*, 2 March 1999)

snake in the grass Snakes hidden in grass are difficult to spot, and may not be seen until trodden on. As an image for something deceitful it was used by Virgil in his *Eclogues* of about 38 BC, and occurs again in Dante's *Inferno*. By the seventeenth century the phrase was well enough known in England to be used as the title of a book.

snare and delusion Dating from the nineteenth century, this was most famously used by Lord Denman, the Lord Chief Justice, in a speech in the House of Lords in 1844, when he said that without reforms 'trial by jury itself, instead of being a security to persons who are accused, will be a delusion, a mockery and a snare.'

'Olavide, in the later eighteenth century, dreamed of transforming the whole of lower Andalusia on the model of the English countryside, without seeming to suspect that climatic conditions were radically different and that the creation of artificial meadows was a snare and delusion under the arid sun of southern Spain.' (R. Carr, *Spain 1808–1975*, 1993)

snow see WRONG KIND OF SNOW

so near and yet so far This expression first appears in English in a 1755 translation of the Latin poet Martial's *Epigrams*, but probably owes its own clichéd status to a line in Tennyson's poem on his dead friend, *In Memoriam* (1850): 'He seems so near and yet so far.'

'So an extra place was laid, and Jennifer allowed to sit between Jill and Nathan, with . . . Tristram in a flame of embarrassment at having her so near and yet so far.' (Charles Gidley, *Armada*, 1988)

(we were) so poor that . . . Usually preceded by something like 'When I were a lad . . .', this is used to introduce some outrageous tale of deprivation. Since at least the 1970s it has been a conscious cliché, much used by comedians. It is a companion cliché to STILL HAVE CHANGE FROM SIXPENCE.

some are born great see BORN GREAT

someone, somewhere This set phrase became much more common after the British Post Office, from the 1960s, used the slogan 'Someone, somewhere, wants a letter from you.'

'That's right. Someone somewhere is laying out public money on the incubation of these groovy thoughts.' (*Private Eye*, 26 June 1998)

something I made earlier see PREPARED EARLIER

(slip or **change into) something more comfortable** A conscious cliché from the world of film, used by the vamp before reappearing in something seductive (and often very uncomfortable looking), usually a negligée. The line appeared in various forms in various films, most famously spoken by Jean Harlow in her 1930 film *Hell's Angels* (written by Howard Estabrook and Harry Behn), 'Would you be shocked if I changed into something more comfortable?'

son and heir In the days when property, and particularly titles, passed to the eldest son, 'son' and 'heir' were distinct ideas, which, combined, usually indicated an eldest son. This use is found from the thirteenth century, but by the nineteenth the second part of the expression was losing significance, and nowadays it often has little connection with inheritance.

'I had drifted into caddying, much to the disgust of my father, who had other ideas about careers for his eldest son and heir whom he had sent to the best public school he could afford.' (Malcolm Hamer, *Sudden Death*, 1991)

son of a gun This expression, a jocular or disparaging term for a person, or, in the USA, a largely meaningless exclamation, is recorded from 1708, used much as we do today. In Admiral W. H. Smyth's *Sailor's Word-Book* (1867) there is a statement that it is 'an epithet conveying contempt in a slight degree, and originally applied to boys born afloat, when women were permitted to accompany their husbands to sea; one admiral declared he literally was thus cradled, under the breast of a gun-carriage.' Some commentators, however, have doubted that it comes from being born on a gun-deck, and think that it is a euphemism for 'son of a bitch', 'gun' chosen because it rhymes with 'son'.

'Old Laz is a pretentious son of a gun, but he's got a heart of gold.' (Robert Rankin, *The Suburban Book of the Dead*, 1993)

(make a) song and dance Used to mean to make an unnecessary fuss about something, this expression developed in the mid-nineteenth century. By the end of the century, this idea of elaborating something simple into a show had spread, so that 'a song and dance' could also, in the USA, be used to mean a long, usually evasive, explanation.

'If any other part of the machine broke the farmer would be down at the dealer causing a song and dance.' (*Farmers' Weekly*, 1991)

'Surely people have better things to do than make a great song and dance about missing a dinner party.' (Claire Rayner, *The Meddlers*, 1991)

sore eyes see SIGHT FOR SORE EYES

sorry state Often found in the form 'sorry state of affairs', this set phrase is frequently used to avoid defining exactly what is wrong.

'Some banks have already begun to lay off staff to compensate for the sorry state of the markets.' (*Evening Standard*, 7 October 1998)

sorted Like DONE AND DUSTED, this is a cliché based on housework, meaning that a task has been completed or seen to. It is likely to be heard in a business environment, with the suggestion that the speaker is dynamic and efficient.

sound and fury This is another line from Shakespeare, this time from *Macbeth* (V.v). After he hears of the death of his wife, a despairing Macbeth says, 'Life's but a walking shadow, a poor player,/That struts and frets his hour upon the stage,/And then is heard no more: it is a tale/Told by an idiot, full of sound and fury,/Signifying nothing.'

'All those hundreds of thousands of electors stopped and questioned; all that "analysis" and number crunching; all those column centimetres filled with prognostication; all that sound and fury; all that nothing.' (*Marketing Week*, 1992)

sound of one hand clapping, sound of silence The first of these is the best known Zen conundrum, meant as an aid to meditation, and often found used to indicate mysticism in general. The second, well known as the title of a 1966 Simon and Garfunkel song, is also found used as a conundrum or poeticism.

'I am like the child spell-bound by the accumulated powers of the night – darkness, the sound of silence, loneliness, infinite possibility, all mingled in a vast horror.' (George R. Thomas, *Edward Thomas: A Portrait*, 1987)

sour grapes This is an allusion to Aesop's fable of the *Fox and the Grapes*, which tells of a fox's struggles to get at some grapes hanging out of reach. When at last it has to give up, it walks off muttering to itself that it knows they are nasty sour things anyway. From this comes our use of 'sour grapes' to mean running down something you cannot get for yourself.

'Many English fans even regard West Indian cricket as boring, but it is more impossible to know, as defeat follows defeat follows defeat, to what extent this is an objective judgement or to what extent it is just sour grapes.' (Gerry Cotter, *England versus West Indies*, 1991)

space, the final frontier see FINAL FRONTIER

spade a spade see CALL A SPADE A SPADE

spanner in the works Throw a spanner into the working parts of machinery, and everything will literally grind to a halt. The expression has been used to mean 'to cause disruption' since the 1930s.

'One minute a mere tomboy Neighbour with a habit of putting a spanner in the works, the next Kylie was an overnight sensation, a pop princess with the Midas touch, so ordinary and yet so electrifying.' (Sasha Stone, *Kylie Minogue: The Superstar Next Door*, 1989)

sparring partner In boxing, a sparring partner is someone with whom you fight in training, to HONE YOUR SKILLS, wearing special protective gear. The term is found from the beginning of the twentieth century, and by about the middle had been transferred to mean someone with whom you constantly argue or skirmish, but with whom you do not FIGHT TO THE FINISH.

'The image of . . . the endowment mortgage has been well and truly tarnished, and now another sparring partner, the PEP mortgage, is also down in the popularity stakes.' (*Independent*, 9 September 1998)

speak softly and carry a big stick see BIG STICK

speak with a single (or **one**) **voice** The idea of a group speaking unanimously (literally 'with one mind') has been expressed by 'with one voice' since the Middle Ages, and was so much a part of the language that in the seventeenth to eighteenth centuries the term 'univocal' was used as an alternative to unanimous. 'With a single voice' seems to be a recent variant, no doubt used because it alliterates with 'speak'.

'The two Richmond adult and tertiary colleges, Uxbridge College and West Thames College, are to "speak with a single voice" on matters of curriculum and good housekeeping.' (*Independent Education*, 23 July 1998)

that special moment Although this expression is still used straight, it is hard to do so since its over-use in advertisements.

'Now that summer is ending and I am heading back to England, I have trawled through the images of the past few weeks for that special moment to carry with me, something to savour on grey winter days.' (*Independent*, 5 September 1998)

spell it out A less aggressive form of 'TO LAY IT ON THE LINE', used to mean 'to make things clear', this has been in use since the 1940s.

'Don't expect everything to be crystal clear, or cut and dried for Monday's one of those times when you have to take the lead and not wait for folk to spell things out in words of one syllable.' (*Liverpool Daily Post and Echo*)

spend more time with your family A clichéd excuse, very often a conscious one, for high-fliers, particularly politicians who have been pushed from their posts, to give as their reason for leaving. It dates from the 1980s. Teenagers might describe it as a desire to GET A LIFE.

'The normally outgoing Garel-Jones has been looking tired lately, say his friends, who believe he genuinely wants to bow out of the spotlight and spend more time with his family.' (*Today*, 1992)

spick and span This expression, which keeps alive two otherwise obsolete words, was originally applied to ships, to mean 'brand new'. 'Spick' is a form of 'spike' and referred to nails; 'span' is a chip of wood, and a spick and span new ship would have everything new, down to these little bits. The expression is found used literally from the sixteenth century, and began to be applied to something so neat and tidy it looked new in the nineteenth.

'His parents kept it spick and span, but when they died, he lived there alone until it went to rack and ruin.' (Roy Kerridge, *Jaunting through Ireland*, 1991)

spill the beans This Americanism of the 1920s brings together two earlier bits of slang, 'to spill' meaning confess, give information, and 'beans' for information.

'With the VSX4 test suite already announced and starting to ship, X/Open Co is preparing to go public on XPG4 itself, and has set early October as the time when it will spill the beans.' (*Unigram x*, 1993)

spin doctor Coined in the 1980s in America, and a buzzword of the 1990s particularly in connection with the British Labour party, this term is used to mean someone employed to put a particular interpretation ('spin') on events in the public eye.

'Away went the shares in a razzle-dazzle of spin doctoring that would have left Downing Street envious as they sparked from 670p to 766p.' (*Evening Standard*, 28 August 1998)

spinning (or **turning**) **in your grave** The idea of the dead responding to the sins of the living, usually visiting them with dreadful warning, goes back to the ancient world, and this presumably lies behind the vivid image of someone's behaviour making the dead restless in their graves. 'Spinning' is a modern, emphatic use of the mid-nineteenth-century 'turning in his grave'.

'From the cover of the car seat I looked out at the other mothers – clean and efficient to a woman – with their neat and name-taped children. I felt my mother spinning in her grave and my former husband spitting in contempt.' (*Independent*, 21 September 1998)

'Captain Weatherall of the 20th Hussars, who founded the Cavalry Club in 1890, must be turning in his grave. For the new secretary of the Cavalry and Guards Club is a naval man.' (*Evening Standard*, 17 September 1998)

spirit of the age A more grandiose version of the MOOD OF THE MOMENT, and a favourite expression of politicians and journalists. It is a cliché of the nineteenth century, and probably owes something to the ancient concept of the genius, or spirit which represented the essential character of a thing, best known in the expression 'spirit of place', a translation of the Latin *genius loci* and a cliché from the same period.

'They will look about for someone in touch with the spirit of the age – classless, sensitive, tearful, family-minded . . . the people's poet.' (*Independent*, 7 November 1998)

spit and polish Spit and polish is literally the technique of raising the high shine so beloved by the army on boots by repeated rubbing with a polish-soaked rag lubricated with spit. From this it came, by the late nineteenth century, to mean all that goes into keeping things excessively neat and clean in barracks, and from then, by the 1920s, to mean exaggerated cleaning in general.

'She and Ellen between them had turned out the dining-room, giving it extra spit and polish because of Christmas.' (Elvi Rhodes, *Ruth Appleby*, 1992)

spitting image In the early nineteenth century it was possible to describe a child as 'the spit' of his father, or for emphasis the 'spit and image'. It has been suggested that this came from a saying that the child was as like his father as if he had been spit out of his father's mouth. This expression got corrupted into a number of forms, 'spitting image' being the dominant one by the beginning of the twentieth century.

' "Look at that expression – it's Uncle Harold!" they'll say or "She's the spitting image of her mum".' (*Today*, 1992)

splendid isolation In 1896 the Canadian politician Sir George Foster delivered his *Official Report of the Debates of the House of Commons of the Dominion of Canada* which contained the words, 'In these somewhat troublesome days when the great Mother Empire stands splendidly isolated in Europe'. *The Times* reported this the next day under the headline, 'Splendid isolation', and thus a new cliché was born.

'It is very difficult to stand aloof in splendid isolation, posing as moral arbiter, especially in Britain's position as a middle-ranking power.' (*Independent*, 23 September 1998)

springtime of life The springtime of life is its hopeful beginning. The expression is often found in the form 'cut off in the springtime of life' for an early death, one of the many clichés of death (see also gone to a BETTER PLACE, DEAR DEPARTED, etc.).

'"Well, I assumed after reading the *Sun-Times* that the boy was Thayer, but I certainly didn't know when I saw the body. To me, he seemed to be just another corpse. Snuffed out in the springtime of life," I added piously.' (Sara Paretsky, *Indemnity Only*, 1982)

square deal see RAW DEAL

stab in the back A cliché for treachery, which, perhaps surprisingly, is not recorded until the twentieth century although similar images, such as Chaucer's wonderful 'smiler with a knife beneath his cloak' in *The Knight's Tale*, are found from quite early on.

'There was quite a bit of hurt pride and some back-stabbing but a sense of failure amongst all those pin-striped suits and highly polished black Oxfords? Get real.' (*Independent*, 15 October 1998)

stable door see LOCK THE STABLE DOOR

staff of life Bread, or whatever else serves as the local staple, is the staff of life, because it *supports* life. The phrase is an allusion to the Bible's 'the stay and the staff, the whole stay of bread' (Isaiah 3:1). It was in use in English by the 1630s.

'Long queues for that symbolic food, the staff of life, will immediately materialise, despite the ready availability of many alternatives.' (Olive Stevenson and Michael Key, *Age and Vulnerability*, 1990)

stalking horse A hunted animal might not run away from a horse, when it will run at the sight of a man, so a hunter can stalk his prey by hiding behind his horse. This custom had already passed into figurative language when Shakespeare wrote, 'He uses his folly like a stalking-horse and under the presentation of that he shoots his wit' (*As You Like It*, IV.iii). Since the 1980s the expression has taken on a special political meaning, that of someone who stands for the leadership only to provoke an election and let a stronger candidate win.

'Unkind loyalists mocked him as "not so much of a stalking horse as a stalking donkey" who would get only his own vote.' (*Guardian*, 8 November 1989)

'It is clear that pre-Christmas Sunday trading has simply been a stalking horse for all-year Sunday trading.' (*Hansard Extracts 1991–1992*)

stand alone A cliché on two counts, first of all as a way of describing something that is unique. Second, as an adjective, often hyphenated, it was originally used of elements of computer hard or software able to operate independently of others, a usage which rapidly spread outside the computing world.

'It's a unique airport, and as a unique airport it stands alone.' (Cathay Pacific pilot on Hong Kong Airport, interviewed *Today*, BBC Radio 4, 2 July 1998)

'If the report is seen and used as a reminder note of discussions that took place during the consultation meeting rather than a stand alone document then the task of report writing becomes significantly easier.' (Mike Sullivan, *Marketing your Primary School*, 1991)

stand on ceremony 'Stand ' here means to be scrupulous or attentive. The older form of the saying used 'upon' and is first recorded in a sermon of 1751: 'There is no occasion to stand upon Complaisance and ceremony with writers who have done so much mischief.'

'Constables have a definite view about the style of authority they prefer in officers . . . they should not stand on ceremony and overtly assert their authority.' (John Brewer and Kathleen Magee, *Inside the RUC*, 1991)

stand proud see WALK TALL

if you can't stand the heat, get out of the kitchen This is a saying associated with American President Harry S Truman (1884–1972), but probably coined by Harry Vaughan. The original version is rumoured to have been much less polite.

'Mike Atherton . . . and Angus Fraser have clearly shown that they can step into the kitchen and withstand the heat.' (*Daily Mail*, 27 August 1998)

stand the test of time see TEST OF TIME

stand up and be counted A twentieth-century cliché which grew up in America, the image here is of a public meeting where votes are cast by people literally standing up to be counted.

'If, as Stop Hinkley Expansion suspected, such fatalism was not shared by the general population of the West Country, then it was vital to get the silent majority to stand up and be counted.' (Crispin Aubrey, *Melt Down: Collapse of a Nuclear Dream*, 1991)

stand your ground The alternative to standing your ground is to run away, for this is a military term, used from about 1700, meaning to hold your position. It began to be used figuratively in the nineteenth century.

'It is wise to be alert to this, and to stand your ground if asked to work in an area which is beyond your present capabilities.' (Alison Morton-Cooper, *Returning to Nursing. A Guide for Nurses and Health Visitors*, 1990)

start from scratch see UP TO SCRATCH

'I've started so I'll finish' Magnus Magnusson, chairman of the television quiz show *Mastermind*, first shown in 1972, used to say this when his question was interrupted by the signal that marked the end of a timed round. It soon became a catch-phrase.

a starving child in Africa would be glad to have that A variable expression, used by many parents to try to bully their children into finishing the food on their plates. As a cliché it probably dates from the second half of the twentieth century. In the first part of the century a child was more likely to be told to think of the starving children in Armenia or China.

'I finished my pasta – no child ever died in India because of my inhuman failure to clean my plate.' (Sara Paretsky, *Indemnity Only*, 1982)

'My attempt to justify leftovers consumption with "children-in-Africa-would-give-their-eye-teeth" spin meets with derision.' (*Independent*, 7 November 1998)

state of the art An alternative to LEADING EDGE, this expression is first recorded in 1889 in the form 'the present status of the art'. From being a description of where things had got to, it had, by the 1950s become an adjective describing how up to date something was, and nowadays has all but replaced 'latest' in some fields.

'Admittedly nodding dogs are kitsch, but if you want real state-of-the-art in the back of your motor then get contemporary with the Envoy Car Message.' (*Stuff*, October 1998)

steal a march This expression, for gaining an advantage by acting before someone else, comes from warfare. It was used literally in the Middle Ages for manoeuvring by stealth into a position without the enemy's knowledge, and was being used in the modern way by the eighteenth century.

'Graham and I had risen early, thinking to creep out and leave our host in peace, but he was a difficult man to steal a march on.' (*Climber and Hill Walker*, 1991)

steal someone's thunder This is an anecdote that grew into a cliché. The writer and critic John Dennis had devised a new way of creating stage thunder for his play *Appius and Virginia* in 1709. The play was a flop, but the thunder effect was not, and was used soon after in a production of *Macbeth*. Dennis is recorded as saying 'Damn them! They will not let my play run, but they steal my thunder', and the expression came to be used for stealing someone else's ideas or impressive gesture.

'It seems that one of the reasons why Mr Brown came to the House of Commons yesterday and stole his own thunder from his Mansion House speech last night was to put pressure on those of his colleagues who have yet to agree their budgets.' (*Independent*, 12 June 1998)

steely eyes (or **-eyed**) A cliché of popular fiction. People began to be described as having steely eyes in the second half of the nineteenth century, but did not become steely-eyed for another 100 years.

'The models for the mad air force generals of Dr Strangelove are widely believed to be the cigar-chomping, ass-kicking Curtis E. LeMay and the steely-eyed Thomas Power, who ran America's nuclear bomber force from 1948–57 and 1957–63 respectively.' (*Independent*, 8 September 1998)

steer clear of If a ship is said to have steered clear of rocks or shoals it has avoided them, 'clear' here meaning 'out of reach'. The expression was being used in the modern way by the early eighteenth century.

'Mr Gorbachev could be forgiven for wishing he could plead a diplomatic cold, and steer clear of celebrations where a wake would be more apt.' (*Independent*, 5 October 1989)

stem the tide According to the normal rules, this expression should not exist. Usually where there is ambiguity, one of two senses drops out of use. However, there is only one fixed rule in English, and that is that there are no invariable rules. There are two possible meanings to this expression, with opposite senses. A ship that stems the tide is one that is making headway against it. The other sense, the tide you cannot stem (and it is perhaps the fact that it is usually negative that has kept it alive), uses a word of different origin, where stem means 'dam, stop up', in a saying that evokes the same image as HOLD BACK THE TIDE.

'Government ministers tried to stem the tide of mounting public expenditure.' (Kenneth Morgan, *The People's Peace*, 1990)

step in the right direction A cliché from the later nineteenth century, this is one of a number of expressions, such as 'putting your best foot forward', that equates life with a journey.

'Brooks said last year's appointment of David Pleat to oversee the long-term strategy of the club was a step in the right direction.' (*Daily Mail*, 27 August 1998)

step into the breach Another military image: if the ramparts you are defending are breached, then if all is not to be lost, people must step into the breach and prevent the enemy getting through. 'Step into' seems to be a development of the earlier (seventeenth-century) 'stand in the breach'. Compare ONCE MORE INTO THE BREACH.

'Once all the intelligence officers have been killed by alien invaders, it will be left to the handful of techies who run the MI5 Web servers to step into the breach.' (*PC Week*, 1 September 1998)

step out of line see OUT OF LINE

sterling qualities (or **worth**) 'Sterling' here is the same word found in 'sterling silver'. The term comes from the name of the Norman English silver penny, the purity and reliability of which was recognized throughout Europe. Because of this it came, from the seventeenth century, to be used as a term of excellence. The word was linked as a set phrase with both 'qualities' and 'worth' in the first part of the nineteenth century. The origin of the word 'sterling' is uncertain, but it may come from the Old English for 'little star' as many of the coins were decorated with a star design.

'But he has sterling qualities, particularly courage and a total indifference to public opinion.' (A. Goodman, *Tell Them I'm on my Way*, 1993)

'But even as he lifted it, reflexes that she'd always prayed would be lightning-fast in a showdown proved their sterling worth, galvanising her into action.' (Rachel Elliot, *Lover's Charade*, 1992)

stick and carrot see CARROT AND STICK

stiff upper lip The image here comes from the way in which strong emotion can cause the upper lip to tremble. Keeping the lip free of such signs of feelings was equated with keeping them under control. Surprisingly, for an attitude that is felt to be so typically British, the expression is first recorded in the USA, in the 1830s.

'As far as I am aware, no other country, certainly none in which my company operates, so prizes the stiff upper lip, rigid control of emotions, and "politeness" which conceals rather than reveals, than the British.' (John Harvey-Jones, *Making it Happen*, 1988)

still have change from a sixpence/a shilling A comment on the effects of inflation, felt to be typical of old people reminiscing about the good old days, now usually found as a conscious cliché or joke.

'I had a bike and could pedal down to Middleton in Teesdale, meet Marie, take her to the pictures – not the best seats mind – then buy us both fish and chips and still have change out of that two bob.' (Hannah Hauxwell and Barry Cockcroft, *Seasons of my Life*, 1989)

stone see CAST THE FIRST STONE

stop you in your tracks There is a wide range of expressions expressing human movement in terms of tracks – 'make tracks', 'lose track of ', 'cover your tracks' and so on. This particular one seems only to have been in use since the middle of the twentieth century, although others are much older.

'The Manhattan fashion designer Donna Karan produced a brilliant advertising campaign based on the swearing-in of the first female President . . . It was a stop-you-in-your-tracks picture because it all seemed so unlikely.' (*Mail on Sunday*, 20 September 1998)

stout party see COLLAPSE OF STOUT PARTY

straight (or **strait**) **and narrow** 'Strait' is the more correct form here, being an old word for narrow, the expression coming from the Bible's: 'Strait is the gate, and narrow is the way, which leadeth unto life' (Matthew 7:14) – meaning that it is easy to wander off the narrow path to eternal life. In both forms it was a set pairing by the sixteenth century, but the expression 'the strait and narrow' for a socially acceptable way of living is not found until the late nineteenth century.

'I have no idea whether Merson, a reformed alcoholic and gambler, is correct in claiming that the lifestyle of Middlesbrough's players was threatening his efforts to stay on the straight and narrow.' (*Evening Standard*, 10 September 1998)

strange bedfellows This is derived from the comment in Shakespeare's *The Tempest* that 'Misery acquaints a man with strange bedfellows.' Since sharing a bed with other people was normal at the time, even in inns, there was no sexual element in the saying.

'Rugby and art may seem strange bedfellows, but as Parfrey says: There should not be this artificial divide between culture and recreation.' (*Rugby World and Post*, 1991)

strange but true An expression belonging with BELIEVE IT OR NOT, and similarly popular with journalists. The phrase has been used since the sixteenth century, and is connected with the proverb 'truth is stranger than fiction'. This is first recorded in a line from Byron's *Don Juan* (1823) which combines the two: ' 'Tis strange – but true; for truth is always strange; stranger than fiction.'

'It's a strange but true fact: the majority of guitarists who order custom electrics from a specialised builder actually ask for something that's pretty conventional.' (*Guitarist*, 1992)

stretcher case see WALKING WOUNDED

strike gold (or **oil**) A miner or prospector who strikes gold or oil is going to get rich. By the end of the nineteenth century enough people had done this for the expression to be transferred, along with 'strike it rich', to a more general sense of acquiring wealth or luck.

'She struck gold when she met Kenneth Kimes, a self-made multi-millionaire with interests in motels and the construction industry.' (*Mail on Sunday*, 20 September 1998)

strike while the iron is hot A blacksmith working at his forge needs to strike the iron with his hammer while it is hot if he is to shape it properly. The expression has been used to mean to make use of your opportunity while it is still there, since the fourteenth century.

'Wilcox, always one to strike while the iron was hot, signed a deal of his own with United Artists, then remade his silent film, Nell Gwynn, presumably thinking its mix of history and sexiness made it sufficiently like Korda's hit to clean up.' (James Park, *British Cinema: the Lights that Failed*, 1990)

at a stroke This has been used to mean 'with a single blow' since Chaucer's day, and had been transferred to mean 'at once, immediately', by the eighteenth century. It is particularly associated with claims by politicians, above all a statement issued by the Conservative leader Edward Heath two days before he became Prime Minister in 1970, in which he proposed tax cuts and a price freeze, claiming, 'This would, at a stroke, reduce the rise in prices, increase productivity and reduce unemployment.' Of course it did no such thing.

'It cannot really be compared with the enormous declines in 1987 which, at a stroke, wiped almost a third off market values.' (*Evening Standard*, 28 August 1998)

strong arm of (the law) In the days when might and right went hand in hand, a strong arm represented power, and has been used to mean this since the early seventeenth century. However, the form 'the strong arm of . . .' did not become common until the nineteenth century, then and now most commonly used of the law, perhaps because it is combined with the 'long arm of the law' in people's minds, to create the idea of something that can both reach far and impose its will.

'I've always envied the profligate, the improvident – those financial reprobates who cut a swathe through life and never seem to worry about the strong arm of American Express.' (*Mail on Sunday*, 20 September 1998)

strut your stuff It is tempting to try to link this to Shakespeare's 'Life's but a walking shadow, a poor player/That struts and frets his hour upon the stage' (see further under SOUND AND FURY), but this is not possible. The expression is in fact Black American slang, derived from their use of 'strut' as the name of a type of dance, 'strut your stuff' starting life as a general term to encourage someone to show off. Early uses are found from the 1920s, and tend to be in non-standard contexts, such as Blues lyrics. Only in recent years has it become an English cliché, and it still keeps some of its original sense, in that it is mainly used of popular music and the media.

'At any one time . . . fewer than 1,000 people are watching Gavin Esler and his colleagues strut their stuff.' (*Independent*, 22 September 1998)

the stuff that dreams are made of A popular misquotation of Prospero's speech in Shakespeare's *The Tempest* (IV.i) which begins, 'We are such stuff as dreams are made on.' As a cliché it dates from the twentieth century.

'The stuff that drams are made of.' (Headline to a piece on whisky, *Stuff*, October 1998)

'Concrete underpasses and plastic shopping precincts are not the stuff that dreams are made of.' (Jeffrey Richards and John M. MacKenzie, *The Railway Station: A Social History*, 1988)

stuffed shirt This is generally linked to the idea of a shirt on display in a shop window, stuffed to make it look occupied, the idea being of an underlying emptiness. However, the term 'stuffed shirt' is usually linked not just with pomposity, but with stiffness and formality, and it may be that the image also involves the highly starched formal dress shirts (of the kind that gave rise to OFF THE CUFF) worn at the turn of the century, when this expression was coined in America. These shirts were so stiff down the front that a wearer might well have about as much movement as he would were he stuffed, as well as being typically worn by those with well-stuffed bellies.

'This is hardly a stream of invective and obscenity but it's a long way from the stuffed shirt formality of the 50s interviews.' (*New Musical Express*, 1992)

stumbling block The rather odd grammar of this comes from the fact that it is a translation. In the Bible (Leviticus, 19:13) there is the injunction, 'Thou shalt not curse the deaf, nor put a stumbling block before the blind', where 'stumbling' means something over which one stumbles. It has been used figuratively since the sixteenth century.

'Although the course is free, accommodation and living are not, and for an unemployed teacher that is a major stumbling block.' (*National Congress on Languages in Education*, 1988)

style over substance Often expressed in terms of 'a triumph of style over substance' this is a modern put-down which implies that what is on offer is all contrived attraction rather than anything really worth having.

'What I would say to those people who have said we are offering something that is style over substance is, "Let them come and experience it for themselves."' (*Independent*, 16 October 1998)

(from the) sublime to the ridiculous The contrast between the sublime and the ridiculous was made in Latin literary criticism, but the expression we use today comes from a saying attributed to Napoleon, after the retreat from Moscow in 1812, 'From the sublime to the ridiculous is but one step.' This was not, however, original to Napoleon. Tom Paine had already written in *The Age of Reason* (1795), 'The sublime and the ridiculous are often so nearly related, that it is difficult to class them separately. One step above the sublime, makes the ridiculous; and one step above the ridiculous, makes the sublime again.' Napoleon may have read Paine, but the saying may well have been proverbial before either used it.

'It is to Alan Rough's eternal credit that he developed a sense of humour which carried him through experiences that ranged from the sublime to the ridiculous.' (Stuart Cosgrove, *Hampden Babylon*, 1991)

(he's) suffered enough A modern cliché often used to excuse the behaviour of some figure of popular culture, particularly football, suggesting that he should no longer be condemned because 'he's suffered enough' already.

'The jury that awarded her £600,000 may also have thought she had suffered enough in her life, he said.' (*Independent*, 5 October 1989)

suffice it to say A filler cliché, well used since the eighteenth century, with similar forms going back as far as the fourteenth.

'Suffice it to say, without getting into the tortured complexities of the US budget process, that everyone is fiddling with the numbers.' (*Independent*, 7 October 1989)

summer of love The 'Summer of Love' refers to the heyday of hippydom in 1968, or more generally to the period around then (see if you can REMEMBER IT . . .), but the expression has been a cliché of headline writers and journalists ever since.

'Sowing the seed of panic in my summer of love.' (Headline, *Independent*, 28 July 1998)

'Anyway, she got her way, and lived in fine style for a couple of weeks that heady summer of love and peace.' (Iain Banks, *The Wasp Factory*, 1990)

sumptuous repast A cliché of the society report and local journalism, this has been in common use since the 1880s. Perhaps it owes something to Milton's 'Their sumptuous gluttonies, and gorgeous feasts' (*Paradise Regained*, 1671).

'At 7 o'clock the office bearers, a number of the brethren and their lady friends sat down to a sumptuous repast in a granary tastefully decorated with evergreen and flags and after a long toast list the tables were removed for dancing.' (Islay Museum Trust, *An Islay Notebook*, n.d.)

Sunday best In the days before mass-produced clothes, those who could afford it would have two sets of clothes; an ordinary one for work days and a best outfit for Sundays and special occasions. The term, recorded from the late eighteenth century, was soon transferred to mean a smart outfit in general.

'Shell suits are not welcomed; this is a place to preen, to show off your Sunday best.' (*Independent*, 2 September 1998)

sundrenched A copywriters' cliché since the 1920s, used to describe anything from holidays to citrus fruit.

sundry see ALL AND SUNDRY

as surely as night follows day Despite the fact that this expression for the inevitable is not recorded in the *OED*, the comparison is an old one. Polonius' famous lecture to his son Laertes on how to behave (*Hamlet*, I.iii) ends with 'This above all: to thine own self be true,/And it must follow, as the night the day,/Thou canst not then be false to any man.' From the way Polonius talks in clichés throughout the play, we may guess that the idea was not original then.

'This is New Labour's favourite tactic . . . Create a few super-nurses or super-teachers as "role models" . . . and reform will follow as surely as day follows night.' (*Independent*, 17 September 1998)

surplus to requirements An unpleasant euphemism for someone about to get the sack, this is typical of modern management-speak in that it turns people into a commodity. It appears to have started life in America. Compare LET SOMEONE GO.

'Mitch Ward and Carl Tiler are likely to be the first casualties of Everton manager Walter Smith's rebuilding plans. The pair, labelled surplus to requirements after only 10 months at Goodison, have been linked with Nottingham Forest and Sheffield United respectively.' (*Daily Mail*, 27 August 1998)

surprise, surprise An irritating exclamation, not often used ironically, which only seems to date from the middle of the twentieth century.

'The top clubs are refusing to change their minds about playing Cardiff and Swansea in friendly matches that will, surprise, surprise, run alongside the normal Allied Dunbar fixtures.' (*Evening Standard*, 28 August 1998)

survival of the fittest This description of the process of evolution comes from Herbert Spencer's book, *Principles of Biology* (1865), not from Charles Darwin as is often assumed. 'Fittest' means here 'most suited, best adapted', but is now often used as if it meant 'in good physical condition'.

'A trip down the supermarket aisles . . . is simply an obsolete way of shopping for groceries in this new, information-rich age. Now it is the ability to process complex information that will drive the survival of the fittest.' (*Independent*, 7 September 1998)

swathe see CUT A SWATHE

sweetness and light This is an expression coined originally by Jonathan Swift, but popularized by Matthew Arnold who used it a number of times, for example: 'Hellenism, and human life in the hands of Hellenism . . . are full of what we call sweetness and light' (*Culture and Anarchy*, 1869). Arnold's use turned it into such a cliché that it is now rarely used without irony.

'Here was a woman whose wish it was to be the queen of all our hearts, to whom we had all surrendered when the shy, beguiling girl was presented to us as our future queen, sweetness and light personified, peaches and cream, unsullied innocence and girlish mischief.' (*Evening Standard*, 28 August 1998)

swim with (or **against**) **the tide/current** In the earliest uses of the expression people usually swam with or against a stream – Shakespeare has 'You must now speake Sir John Falstaffe fair, which swims against your stream of Quality' (*Henry IV*, part 2, V.ii) – but since the eighteenth century 'tide' or 'current' has been more common. This is such an obvious metaphor that it occurs independently in other cultures, for instance in Confucius' *Analects* of about 500 BC. A similar image is found in GO WITH THE FLOW.

'In early trading the only Footsie stock strong enough to swim against the current was Blue Circle.' (*Evening Standard*, 28 August 1998)

swings and roundabouts This is a shortened version of the fairground proverb, 'What you lose on the swings you win on the roundabouts', current from the beginning of the twentieth century in various forms. It is used to mean that things will balance out in the end.

'Many chairmen were content to adopt a "swings and roundabouts" approach to this, provided they broke even on sales overall.' (Leslie Hannah, *Engineers, Managers and Politicians*, 1993)

Sword of Damocles see HANG BY A THREAD

swords into ploughshares An allusion to the passage in the Bible (Isaiah 2:4) where there is a vision of a world of peace, where people 'shall beat their swords into ploughshares, and their spears into pruninghooks'. It was much used in the period of Russian and American disarmament in the 1990s when news stories showed the metal of armaments being recycled into domestic products.

'The United States crowned its greatest diplomatic triumph in the region, the peace treaty between Israel and Egypt, by distributing to both parties swords as well as ploughshares.' (David McDowell, *Palestine and Israel*, 1990)

systems see ALL SYSTEMS GO

T see TO A T

take a rain check This expression comes from the custom, in use by 1884, of issuing rain checks (or cheques) entitling you to a free ticket to another game when rain stopped play at a baseball match. From this it came to mean simply to postpone something until another time. However, in UK business circles the expression has been widely mis-analysed as coming from the verb 'to check', and understood to mean 'to check if it is raining' and used in a similar manner as 'to see which way the wind is blowing'.

take an early bath A sports cliché, particularly used of football. When a player is sent off, he must first make the LONELY WALK off the pitch and is then supposed to take the normal post-match bath earlier than usual. The expression is used to mean 'sent off' or 'retired early'.

'The blond-haired mid-fielder embarked on a pointlessly fierce challenge . . . and was immediately cautioned by Italian referee Graziano Cesari. The challenge never put Beckham in danger of another early bath but it does mean the midfielder is already under pressure when the real competition kicks off next month.' (*Daily Mail*, 27 August 1998)

take it like a man An attitudinal cliché, like A MAN'S GOTTA DO WHAT A MAN'S GOTTA DO, and associated with the same sort of film. It usefully avoids specifying what is involved.

'But although Ronson was seen to have taken punishment like a man . . . he emerged to find his business in ruins.' (*Independent*, 8 October 1998)

take me to your leader A cartoon cliché that became a catch-phrase. From about 1950 a series of cartoons of little green men used this expression in various comic circumstances (see quotation), but the expression itself probably echoed earlier tales of explorers and heroes in the wild dealing with 'primitive' tribes, and may well go back to the 1860s.

'It concerns a Ship from another world landing on this planet, and strange creatures get out and say to a petrol pump, dustbin, slot-machine or similar mechanical device, "Take me to your leader." ' (Terry Pratchett, *Wings*, 1992)

take no prisoners A fairly recent business cliché indicating a ruthless fight to the death in pursuit of the company's aims.

'Harsh words are their regular currency. Do not believe the public proclamations of peace. The market economy takes no prisoners. It's time to put up or shut up.' (*Independent*, 2 September 1998)

take on board see BRING ON BOARD

take pains This expression dates from the sixteenth century and is a development of the medieval 'to pain yourself', meaning to make an effort. This obsolete use of 'pain' also survives in the word 'painstaking'.

'Take pains to present a smart, efficient appearance and to show that you are beginning to master your subject.' (Stafford Whiteaker, *A Career in Advertising and Public Relations*, 1986)

take the medicine At the time when this expression is first recorded, in the mid-nineteenth century, it was common for people to take a 'purging potion' (strong laxative and/or emetic) as part of their general health-maintenance regime. This was known as 'taking a medicine', so when we think of the image behind this expression for doing something unpleasant, we should perhaps think of something much more stomach-churning than a dose of cough mixture or an aspirin.

'Many emerging nations have taken the medicine administered by the International Monetary Fund and Western governments.' (*Evening Standard*, 28 August 1998)

take to task As might be expected, the original meaning of this, in the sixteenth century, was to take on something as a task. From there it came to be used for to take a person or thing in hand, and it was but a small step from there to mean tell someone off for what they had done, a change which had happened by the eighteenth century.

'Lawyers all over London will be rubbing their hands with glee at the prospect of numerous legal actions when the clubs are taken to task by the various unions.' (*Evening Standard*, 28 August 1998)

take to the cleaners This expression, derived from being 'cleaned out', an early nineteenth-century gambling term for losing all your money, dates from the middle of the twentieth century. It carries a sense of being cheated that 'cleaned out' – a self-explanatory image – does not.

'Not only did the Kiwis get blown off the park at the Hong Kong Sevens by Fiji, but three gnarled members of their supporters club got taken to the cleaners in a local hostess bar.' (*Rugby World and Post*, 1992)

take umbrage Umbrage originally, in the fifteenth century, meant 'shade, shadow'; from this it came to mean both to be in the shadow of someone's displeasure, and, by way of a shadowy outline, to mean a suspicion. By the 1680s 'take umbrage' had developed the sense of 'to take offence', the suspicion having turned into something 'without a shadow of a doubt'.

'If there is an important and difficult question of law, however, I do not anticipate that senior judges will either feel "demeaned" or take umbrage at the possibility of the courts looking at the question again on fuller argument.' (*The Weekly Law Reports*, 1992)

take up the gauntlet see PICK UP THE GAUNTLET

(let me) take you away from all this A conscious cliché from film and romantic fiction, these are the typical words of the romantic hero either rescuing the heroine from an unpleasant situation, or tempting the woman to leave her unpleasant duty. Compare GET AWAY FROM IT ALL.

'One day, Eve, I'm going to take you away from all this.' (Caption of cartoon set in the Garden of Eden, *Private Eye*, 18 September 1998)

take your life in your hands A cliché of risk-taking, this seems to have come into use in the nineteenth century. It is often nowadays used exaggeratedly for something that is not really lethal.

'There are more motor vehicles around than ever and you take your life in your hands just crossing the road.' (David S. Mackenzie, *The Truth of Stone*, 1991)

it takes all sorts (to make a world) A tolerant proverb, current since the seventeenth century, expressing in a different way the earlier Roman proverb '*de gustibus non est disputandum*' – there's no accounting for taste.

'Interestingly [oysters] start life as female and then switch around as it suits them (well, it takes all sorts . . .).' (*Stuff*, October 1998)

tale of two . . . A cliché of journalists and headline writers, based on the title of Charles Dickens' 1859 novel *A Tale of Two Cities*.

'This is a tale of two postcodes, only a few minutes' walk from each other. Apparently a world apart.' (*Evening Standard*, 1 September 1998)

talk is cheap This appears to be a modern proverb, indicating that it is easy to say you will do something, but that does not mean that it will actually be done. It echoes an earlier proverb, current from the seventeenth century – 'talking pays no tolls'.

'Being a terminal pessimist, I didn't trust this wave of deranged ardour for my novel. "Talk is cheap," I kept telling myself. "It will add up to zilch." ' (*Mail on Sunday*, 20 September 1998)

tall, dark and handsome A clichéd description of the ideal man, this developed in the USA in the early years of the twentieth century, was the title of a song in 1928 and was used as the title of a 1941 film. It is now rarely used except as a conscious cliché, although 'darkly handsome' can still be found in romantic novels.

'He entered into the room, tall dark and handsome, looking like a character straight out of a Clarke Gable movie.' (Schoolchildren's creative writing, unpublished)

tea party see VICARAGE TEA PARTY

team player A business and management cliché meaning someone who works well as part of a team, this is taken from sport. It was being used of cricket in the 1880s, but as jargon it is probably modern.

'The successful candidate will be a strong team player with good organisational skills and possess the ability to work unsupervised.' (Job advertisement, *Evening Standard*, 1 September 1998)

tears of a clown see MOTLEY CREW

teeth see ARMED TO THE TEETH

tell me about it An exclamation that means the opposite of what it appears to, as its true sense is 'I know all about it'. It is a modern expression, which has largely replaced the earlier 'You're telling me!', current from the 1920s in the USA, and a decade later in the UK.

tell the truth see TRUTH TO TELL

telling see THAT WOULD BE TELLING

tender mercies This expression has been used ironically right from the start, for it comes from a biblical passage (Proverbs 12:10) which says, 'A righteous man regardeth the life of his beast: but the tender mercies of the wicked are cruel.'

'Tracing the original owner, I found that the wood was from a timber outbuilding, and has been left to the tender mercies of the council or the local pyromaniac.' (*Do It Yourself* magazine, 1992)

terminate with extreme prejudice see EXTREME PREJUDICE

it goes with the territory This is a modern expression, indicating something that is an unavoidable part of a situation, particularly when it is not strictly part of a job but nevertheless has to be done.

'Dealing with the guest who is in a delicate business situation or just a very bad mood all goes with the territory.' (*Caterer & Hotelkeeper*, 1991)

test of time Although this is recorded from the early nineteenth century, it does not seem to have become a cliché until the early twentieth. It can be used either to indicate something TRIED AND TESTED, or of lasting popularity.

'A standard technique that has stood the test of time is to analyse all paper work crossing your desk over a period of say a month.' (Andrew Leigh, *Twenty Ways to Manage Better*, 1992)

'The owner of Stonegate Teddy Bears, Kevin Scott said: "They are an early twentieth-century phenomenon which has stood the test of time and which are now as popular as ever." ' (*Yorkshire Life*, 1992)

thankful for small mercies An expression that developed towards the end of the nineteenth century, echoing the language of the Bible and religion, but which is generally used ironically, or at least with an element of self-mockery.

'After an absence of so many years, this kissing among men seems an odd thing, but one ought to be thankful for small mercies: at least it is only two kisses and not three, as is the Russian custom.' (*Guardian*, 20 December 1989)

'Not for them the comfortable life; they might get ideas above their station, which was to devote themselves to hard labour and be grateful for small mercies.' (Barry Turner, *And the Policeman Smiled*, 1991)

that was then, this is now A vogue cliché meaning things have changed. Although the form is new, the idea is not. It is found in the Latin tag *tempora mutantur, et nos mutamur in illis* ('times change and we change with them'), attributed to the Emperor Lothar I (795–855).

'The last time I went to Manzi's for a date . . . was seven years ago . . . and this celebrated family-run place on the outskirts of Chinatown was still buzzing. That was then. "Good God, is it still open?" said someone when I mentioned I was going.' (*Evening Standard*, 15 September 1998)

that would be telling This belongs with WAIT AND SEE and A LITTLE BIRD TOLD ME, all clichés used to convey superior knowledge and to infuriate the person on the receiving end. It is currently a catch-phrase associated with the film critic Barry Norman. In the form 'that's telling' it goes back to the eighteenth century.

that'll do nicely A well established expression which was given an extra resonance when it was used in saturation advertising for American Express credit cards in the 1970s and became a catch-phrase.

'I still had the suit on . . . so I got a "that'll do nicely" sort of smile and the up-from-under look which tells you that there are advantages to private medicine.' (Mike Ripley, *Angel Touch*, 1991)

that's a fact see FACT OF THE MATTER

that's a good question Used either as a filler while thinking, or as a way of wriggling out of answering the question, this is a cliché of the middle of the twentieth century, often now used as a conscious cliché.

'It is a good question, and I will come back to it, as well as considering Daly's own more recent attempts at word empowerment.' (Deborah Cameron, *Feminism and Linguistic Theory*, 1992)

'I think that's a very good question, I think though that that has been looked at very very thoroughly by the County Council, and certainly there are only a very limited number of options available around York which would actually meet the needs of York.' (Public County Council planning meeting, recorded on 18 November 1993)

that's all folks Famous from the 1930s as the sign-off slogan of the Looney Tunes Cartoons featuring such characters as Bugs Bunny and Daffy Duck, this has been taken up both as a general catch-phrase and as a way of ending programmes such as television news, often in the variant 'that's all for now'.

that's no lady, that's my wife see LADY WIFE

thereby hangs a tale This not very impressive pun on tail/tale, used to indicate that more information could be forthcoming, was revived in the nineteenth century as a quotation cliché. Shakespeare used it in four of his plays, and judging from the characters to whom he gives it, it was a cliché in his day.

there'll (or **they'll**) **be dancing in the streets tonight** see DANCING IN THE STREETS

there's no place like home see HOME SWEET HOME

(come) thick and fast A term from the early eighteenth century, this is an alternative to Burns's FAST AND FURIOUS.

'The rewards soon followed as league championship titles came thick and fast with five titles in the Thirties.' (*Evening Standard*, 10 September 1998)

thin end of the wedge If you want to split a log, you drive the thin end of a wedge, which will go in easily, into the wood, and then hammer it in down to its full thickness, causing the log to split. This image began to be used in the nineteenth century for something that seems minor at first, but which can lead to something much more serious.

'Railway bills were utilitarian but this was a different matter, the thin end of a wedge that placed aesthetic and sentimental considerations above the rights of property.' (*New Scientist*, 1991)

thing see CLOSE THING

a (or **the**) **... thing** Originally a very informal usage, this use of 'thing' to mean a specific activity or situation is rapidly spreading to more general use. It is sometimes found humorously in the form 'thang', in imitation of the Southern USA pronunciation.

'A coterie of academics is advising Tony Blair. Lucy Hodges looks at who helps him with the vision thing.' (*Independent Education*, 23 July 1998)

'This is a pure 15 thing and a 15-year-old boy at that.' (*Evening Standard*, 28 August 1998)

'I would say it's an educational thing. But I think the boundaries are drawn much clearer in working-class districts.' (*Independent*, 9 September 1998)

think the unthinkable A current cliché of political reform, although the idea has been floating around for some time. In 1962 Herman Kahn published a book called *Thinking the Unthinkable*, and two years later the American politician J. William Fulbright made a speech about the USA having better relations with the USSR, saying, 'We must dare to think "unthinkable" thoughts.'

'Time to think the unthinkable and take control.' (Headline, *Evening Standard*, 28 August 1998)

'It is, in other words, time for the Government to think the unthinkable ... It is time for a Novelist Laureate.' (*Independent*, 7 November 1998)

think twice A neat way of saying 'reconsider', this did not become a cliché until the late nineteenth century. In 1963 Bob Dylan gave it a new twist with his song 'Don't Think Twice, it's All Right'.

'Window locks are an essential deterrent to the opportunist; while they will be prepared to break a small area of glass and reach in to open the catch, they will think twice about smashing a whole pane – as it's very noisy and dangerous.' (*Adkin. Moving in Oxfordshire*, 1992)

... is the thinking man's or woman's ... A formula phrase, usually used to make a witty point. The most famous example, probably the source of the expression as a cliché, is the comment attributed to writer Frank Muir (1920–98) that the British broadcaster Joan Bakewell is 'the thinking man's crumpet'.

'I was the oldest ingenue in town, and shaping up real good as the thinking man's Baby Jane Hudson.' (*Guardian*, 5 September 1998)

things aren't what they used to be see DUMBING DOWN

third time lucky A proverb from the first part of the nineteenth century, this reflects what would nowadays be called the LEARNING CURVE.

'Coventry manager Gordon Strachan first tried to sign the 26-year-old defender two years ago . . . Last season, when he made another inquiry, Palace wanted £3m. But he made it third time lucky after striking a deal with Terry Venables.' (*Daily Mail*, 27 August 1998)

this could be the beginning of a beautiful friendship see BEGINNING OF A BEAUTIFUL FRIENDSHIP

thorn in the flesh (or **side**) This expression for a continuous source of irritation is from the Bible. It is found in Judges 2:3, where God tells the Israelites not to ally themselves to the people of their new land for 'they shall become as thorns in your sides'. The expression is picked up by St Paul in his second Epistle to the Corinthians (12:7) where he says, 'there was given me a thorn in the flesh, the messenger of Satan to buffet me'. The version with 'flesh' is the more popular in the UK, that with 'side' in the USA. 'Thorn in my Side' was the title of a hit song for Eurythmics in 1986.

'However, despite attempts to curb the spending power of various councils by rate-capping, local authority finances remained a thorn in the flesh of the government.' (Peter Hardy, *A Right Approach to Economics?*, 1991)

those were the days The elderly must have been reminiscing about the good old days since TIME IMMEMORIAL, but this particular expression is not recorded until the early twentieth century. Its use has been reinforced by the success of a song with that title, written by Gene Raskin and sung by Mary Hopkin, in 1968.

'The game was excellent – the only problem being we just managed to draw 3-3 – ahh well those were the days (NOT!).' (Leeds United e-mail list)

those who live by see LIVE BY

thousand cuts see DEATH BY A THOUSAND CUTS

thread see HANG IN THE BALANCE

in the throes of 'Throes' were originally intense or violent pains, such as those of birth and death (and the term 'death throes' is still used). 'In the throes of' started to be used figuratively at the end of the seventeenth century.

'The restaurant trade is currently in the throes of a colossal bull market.' (*Independent*, 8 September 1998)

through the mangle see PUT THROUGH THE MANGLE

through your paces see PUT THROUGH YOUR PACES

throw down the gauntlet see PICK UP THE GAUNTLET

throw out the baby with the bathwater A bringing together of two extremes of value: the useless in the dirty bathwater and the cherished in the baby, to conjure up a vivid picture of domestic tragedy. This expression for discarding the good with the bad came into use in the later nineteenth century, and may have been borrowed from an earlier German proverb.

'We are throwing out the baby with the bath water in this country if, in an attempt to have a standardised and demanding curriculum, we leave no room for teachers to exercise a little judgement and imagination.' (*Independent*, 3 December 1998)

throw the book at The book here is that containing the laws, or more generally the rule book, and 'throw' reflects the element of indiscriminate accusation suggested by the expression. It has been in use since the 1930s. Compare BY THE BOOK.

'Once the police have arrested you, or so it seemed to us, they will throw the book at you in order to make something stick.' (Linford Christie and Tony Ward, *Linford Christie: An Autobiography*, 1990)

tide see SWIM AGAINST THE TIDE

tidings of joy An expression based on the message of the angels to the shepherd in the Christmas story, 'Behold, I bring you good tidings of great joy, which shall be to all people. For unto you is born this day in the city of David a Saviour, which is Christ the Lord' (Luke 2:10–11), and reinforced by the chorus ('Tidings of comfort and joy') of a popular Christmas carol, *God Rest You Merry Gentlemen*. Its archaic nature means that it is rarely used other than ironically.

'There's something exciting about going back to your roots. So when I received word from the Ottershaw School Old Boys' Society about last Sunday's reunion . . . I anticipated tidings of joy.' (*Independent*, 24 September 1998)

tiger economy A useful way to describe those Asian economies that grew rapidly. Until the 1998 crashes it seemed journalists were unable to discuss Far Eastern economics without using it.

'Not only does his vision look tarnished given the collapse of the "tiger economies"; now the iron fist in the glove has been revealed, at the merest whiff of discontent caused by economic crisis.' (*Independent*, 23 September 1998)

tighten your belt This term for economizing is only recorded from the twentieth century, despite the fact that people must have been tightening their belts to ease the pangs of hunger for very much longer.

'However if the company has not managed to turn the corner by then, it will be forced to tighten its belt further as money shortages begin to affect day-to-day business.' (*Computergram International*)

till the fat lady sings see AIN'T OVER TILL THE FAT LADY SINGS

the . . . that time forgot A formula phrase, popular with journalists, based on the title of the 1924 science fiction novel *The Land that Time Forgot* by Edgar Rice Burroughs.

'Those with no stomach for sentimentality should leave this page now and turn instead to Sean O'Hagan's report on Hothouse Flowers and the hippies of Dublin (the City That Time Forgot).' (*The Face*, 1990)

time immemorial, **time out of mind** Strictly speaking, 'time immemorial' is any time before 1199, this being the date set in 1275 as the time before which no one could remember, and therefore no legal cases could deal with events before that date.'Time out of mind', recorded from the fifteenth century, is just the plain English version of the same thing. Since the eighteenth century at least, 'time immemorial' has been used in much the same way as the MISTS OF TIME, and both expressions are now often used vaguely to mean little more than in the past.

'Peaceful, mellow and noble, in the shade of a great sycamore, it is the sort of house that feels as though it has been there from time immemorial.' (Candida Lycett Green, *The Perfect English Country House*, 1991)

'From time immemorial it was a commonly held belief in Gaelic Scotland that where a disease occurred there would be found growing in the locality of its prevalence a plant which would cure that disease.' (J. M. Mullin and R. J. Pankhurst, *Flora of the Outer Hebrides*, 1991)

time is ripe The image here is of a situation gradually developing like a ripening fruit, until the moment when it is ready for action to be taken. It became common in the nineteenth century, probably from Shakespeare's 'When the time is ripe . . . I'll steal to Glendower and Lord Mortimer' (*I Henry IV*, I.iii).

'When an addition is made to the system of state-provided services, it is only made because there is a general opinion that the time is ripe for it and that such provision is "only right".' (Enoch Powell, *Reflections of a Statesman*, 1991)

tiny tot The journalistic cliché *par excellence* – even the origin of the word 'tot' is not known. 'Tot' for a child is first recorded in the eighteenth century and appears to be the same word as 'tot' for a small drink (found 100 years later), the common idea being limited size. The inevitable pairing with 'tiny' is a twentieth-century development.

'The thoughts and feelings of that poor mother, giving over that tiny tot to a complete stranger, still haunt me today.' (Barry Turner, *And the Policeman Smiled*, 1991)

'It overturned after hitting a car, shattering the incubator which was keeping tiny tot Victoria Elliot alive.' (*Daily Mirror*, 1992)

tip of the iceberg This is based on the well known fact that only a small proportion of an iceberg shows above the water, the rest lurking below ready to cause a disaster of titanic proportions. The expression has only been recorded from the second half of the twentieth century.

'Many . . . will have to lower their expectations and will find themselves underemployed, in jobs for which they are over-qualified. This, however, is just the tip of the iceberg. Statisticians . . . presented evidence . . . that the growth in graduate jobs has lagged well behind the expansion of student numbers.' (*Independent*, 24 September 1998)

tired and emotional This euphemism for 'drunk' was memorably used in the mid-1960s to describe the then Foreign Secretary George Brown in the satirical magazine *Private Eye*. It subsequently became its standard term for such a state, before spreading to more general use.

'The panel sat mesmerized until it slowly began to dawn that the applicant appeared to be suffering from the old Fleet Street problem of being tired and emotional.' (Chris Horrie and Peter Chippindale, *DISASTER! the Rise and Fall of News On Sunday*, 1988)

Titanic see DECKCHAIRS ON THE *TITANIC*

to a T The history of this expression for 'exactly', 'to perfection', is obscure. It is first recorded in the late seventeenth century, and it has been suggested that it is a shortening of the early seventeenth-century 'to a tittle', referring to doing something thoroughly, down to the smallest part (see JOT OR TITTLE). This would convince, were it not for the fact that many early uses involve something 'fitting to a T', which suggests the carpenter's T-square, linking the expression to FAIR AND SQUARE. Perhaps even if 'tittle' is the true origin, users identified it with the more obvious T-square.

to a turn see DONE TO A TURN

toe the line This expression comes from the starting line, marked in chalk, for a race. If you do not toe this line then you break the rules and step OUT OF LINE. It is a twentieth-century metaphor, to a large extent replacing the nineteenth-century 'toe the mark' (as in 'on your marks, get set, go') which came from exactly the same source.

'Calami's acting career began in 1938 when, favoured by the Fascist authorities who ensured that cinema promoted the party line, she took role after role in . . . heroic costume dramas . . . Small wonder then that the exposed breasts of this perfectly line-toeing actress caused a scandal.' (*Independent*, 23 September 1998)

tomorrow belongs to . . . One of the most memorable scenes from the 1972 film *Cabaret*, set in Germany during the rise of Nazism, was the perfect example of Aryan boyhood innocently singing the Nazi song 'Tomorrow Belongs to Me'. The song was written for *Cabaret*, but so convincing was this scene, that in an interview a few years ago the writers, John Kander and Fred Ebb, said they had overheard people reminiscing about having heard it in Germany in their childhood. From this song a formula phrase has developed.

'If he has the secret of putting bums back on pews – as his detractors certainly have not – then tomorrow's C of E may well belong to him.' (*Independent*, 17 September 1998)

tomorrow is another day Two lines stand out from the end of the 1939 film *Gone With the Wind*; Rhett Butler's weary 'FRANKLY, MY DEAR, I DON'T GIVE A DAMN', and Scarlett O'Hara's 'After all, tomorrow is another day', as she resolved to fight on. Although the expression was by no means original to Margaret Mitchell's book, it is now firmly tied to it in most people's minds.

' "Well, thanks a lot, Hercules. I must say, you've been a great help so far. I think I've had about as much as I can take for now." He paused, then sighed dramatically. "Still, tomorrow's another day." And with that, he got up and, head down, shuffled his way over to the exit.' (Timothy Boggs, *Hercules – The Eye of the Ram*, 1997)

too big for his boots This expression suggests someone whose idea of their own importance has outgrown their real size. The expression dates from the late nineteenth century, the similar 'too big for his britches' being half a century older. A similar image is found in being 'big' or 'swollen headed'.

'Buzz said, "The girls trust Adam, but he's getting too big for his boots – ordering everyone around." ' (S. Conran, *Crimson*, 1992)

too far see BRIDGE TOO FAR

too little too late A self-explanatory set phrase that is not recorded before the 1990s.

'Investors have criticised last week's fiscal package and interest rate cut as too little too late and voted with their feet for most of the week by selling out of the market.' (*Daily Telegraph*, 10 April 1992)

too numerous to mention A cliché from the nineteenth century, this is often used as a filler by public speakers, or as a lazy excuse by others for not doing research.

'To the many others, too numerous to mention, who have assisted in keeping my body and mind functioning throughout the year, a very happy 1993 to you all.' (*Today*, 1992)

'The ways in which the caterer is affected by the law are too numerous to mention.' (A. Pannett, *Principles of Hotel and Catering Law*, 1992)

top brass This was originally an American expression and comes from a disrespect-ful allusion to the gold braid worn on officers' hats (known as 'scrambled eggs' in the UK). Such people became known as 'brass hats' and then, from the late nineteenth century, they became 'big brass'. 'Top brass' is found from the middle of the twentieth, after which the expression rapidly spread to bosses in general.

'But do UEFA give a toss for these people? Of course not. What appealed to their top brass was the chance of an all-expenses paid jolly to a high-tone location at a great time of year.' (*Evening Standard*, 28 August 1998)

touch and go A nineteenth-century expression which seems originally to refer to something a bit closer than a near miss, to encounters in which vehicles touch each other in a glancing blow but do not actually crash. It is still used in much the same sense in aviation, where 'touch and go' describes a manoeuvre in which a plane touches down and then immediately takes off.

'A posse of American financial backers was rounded up and rode in – although it was touch and go at the time – to save the day.' (*Independent*, 8 October 1998)

touchy-feely A recent coinage, usually derogatory, applied to the sort of person who tries to express sensitivity or affection through physical contact, or to describe such an attitude to life.

'Too often emotional intelligence is seen as a touchy-feely kind of affair, as a saner, more feminine, version of the hard, macho ability to retain information.' (*Independent*, 30 September 1998)

'I think I had my own vision watching Sarah's touchy-feely conflation of therapy, counselling, healing, comparative religion and sexual assault.' (*Evening Standard*, 7 October 1998)

tough act to follow see HARD ACT TO FOLLOW

tough get going see GOING GETS TOUGH

tough love A recent coinage of the counselling industry, this is a more positive way of saying CRUEL TO BE KIND.

'Only "tough love" is helpful, loving the sufferer but allowing him or her to take the full consequences of all actions caused by the disease.' (Robert Lefever, *How to Combat Alcoholism and Addiction*, 1988)

(in for a or **give someone a) tough time** 'Tough' has been used to mean 'difficult to do' since the early seventeenth century, but this expression does not seem to have become common until the twentieth century. It is often used in an exaggerated or ironic manner.

'The judges are in for a tough time; they will be facing 36 different sausages, 44 breads, cakes and pastries, 61 preserves and condiments, not to mention fabulous ice-creams and cheeses.' (*You* magazine, 20 September 1998)

tower of strength As early as the fourteenth century people were being described as towers for their strength (compare PILLAR OF . . .). 'Tower of strength' – simply an old-fashioned way of saying 'strong tower' – was well established by the sixteenth century when it was used both in the Book of Common Prayer (1549), 'O lord . . . Be unto them a tower of strength', and by Shakespeare. Despite this, commentators credit Tennyson's 1853 *Ode on the Death of the Duke of Wellington* with establishing the expression as a cliché for someone who is a great support: 'O fallen at length, that tower of strength/Which stood four-square to all the winds that blew.'

'But today, fortified by her experiences, feeling six feet high and a tower of strength, Miss Fogerty led the entire school into morning assembly and faced a host of questioning eyes with unaccustomed composure and authority.' (Miss Read, *The World of Thrush Green*, 1990)

track record Those who bet on horses like to know how the animal has performed in the past on any particular track – what its track record is. This was transferred to people's achievements about the middle of the twentieth century. It is currently very popular business jargon, where it often seems to mean nothing more than 'experience'.

'A successful track record in business process analysis and re-design – gained from an accounting, consulting or business analysis background – would be ideal.' (Advertisement, *Independent*, 7 September 1998)

tracks see STOP YOU IN YOUR TRACKS

tragedy waiting to happen see ACCIDENT WAITING TO HAPPEN

transports of delight 'Transports', for keen emotional feelings, has been in use since the middle of the seventeenth century, but the *OED* has no record of 'transports of delight', although it does have a 'transports of joy' from 1715. This suggests that the expression may not have become a cliché until the twentieth century. It was certainly well enough established by 1960 for Flanders and Swann to use it as the title of a song about London buses, and the expression now lives a double life as a straightforward cliché and a punning one used by travel writers.

a . . . you will want to treasure A cliché of advertising, often used by those trying to evoke such set phrases as 'treasured memories' and 'treasured possessions', but rarely convincingly.

'Tomorrow we give every reader the chance to own Part 1 of our two-part tribute – Diana, the People's Pictures. This is a magazine you will want to treasure, and it comes only with the *Sun*.' (*Sun*, 20 August 1998)

trials and tribulations This vaguely biblical expression, with no known source, probably dates from the late nineteenth century, and is about the only time you will find 'tribulations' used in normal speech.

'Women walking their children to and from school will talk of the trials and tribulations of married life as part of their everyday conversation.' (Janet Mattinson and Christopher Clulow, *Marriage Inside Out*, 1989)

trickle down A cliché of right-wing economics, this theory that things that benefit the well-off will eventually benefit the poor is a creation of 1930s America.

'Conservatives are less concerned about equality and more concerned with generating production and income, believing that the benefits will "trickle down" through society to benefit all.' (Peter Hardy, *A Right Approach to Economics?*, 1991)

tried and tested A redundant pairing, as the two halves mean exactly the same, this is a modern development.

'Yet it is easy for pioneer users and IT investors to remain with the tried and tested applications and miss out on the cutting edge opportunities just around the corner.' (*Caterer & Hotelkeeper*, 1991)

trousers down see CATCH WITH YOUR PANTS DOWN

in the truest sense of the word One of those clichés designed to puzzle those who like to consider the literal sense of what is said, this has been current since the later nineteenth century. It evolved from earlier, philosophical uses of 'truest sense', where the expression had some meaning.

'It has taken some time but it is beginning to look as if Surrey have finally got it together in the truest sense of the word.' (*Independent*, 1 September 1998)

truth see ECONOMICAL WITH THE TRUTH

truth is out there This is a catch-phrase from the television series *The X Files*, which has been enthusiastically adopted by journalists and caption writers.

'The truth is out there – in your manager's X-file.' (Headline to a piece on personnel files, *Independent*, 26 August 1998)

truth is stranger than fiction see STRANGE BUT TRUE

truth, the whole truth and nothing but the truth This expression from the oath taken in court, much used in dramatic scenes on television and in film, has now been adopted for more general use. The *OED* first records it outside a legal sense in 1931 in the extraordinary line, 'The truth, the whole truth, and no cray-fishing, so help me God' (V. Palmer, *Separate Lives*).

'It doesn't matter whether your family have mined coal here for a hundred years, there's cheaper stuff around. The market is the only thing that defines the truth, the whole truth and nothing but the truth.' (*Independent*, 15 October 1998)

truth to tell (or **to tell the truth**) These have been used for emphasis or as fillers since the mid-fourteenth century. The opposite of this usage is when people correct themselves with 'No, I tell a lie.'

'Truth be told, I had been reading Conan Doyle novels for a year and jokingly thought I would apply the great Holmes' principles to the Lord Lucan case.' (*Daily Mail*, 10 July 1998)

it is a truth universally acknowledged that The opening words of Jane Austen's novel *Pride and Prejudice* (1813) – 'It is a truth universally acknowledged, that a single man in possession of a good fortune, must be in want of a wife' – were once elected the most instantly recognizable opening of any English novel. In recent years they have come to be used as a journalistic formula phrase.

'It is a truth universally acknowledged that a single man in possession of a large fortune must be a yuppie.' (*Independent*, 11 November 1995)

'It is a truth universally acknowledged that a single woman in possession of an interesting past must be in want of a chat show.' (*Independent*, 7 October 1998)

try this at home SEE DON'T TRY THIS AT HOME

tug of love This image, of two parents fighting over a child as if in a tug of war, is a vivid one, if over-used. It is not recorded in this sense until 1973, although there was a 1907 comedy by I. Zangwill called *The Tug of Love*. Mainly a journalistic phrase, the story is likely to involve TINY TOTS.

'Headline's big hype of the year, a "tug of love" story about an ex-drug addicted, illiterate black woman's fight to retrieve her son, adopted by a white family.' (Grant Uden, *Bookseller*, 1993)

turn back the tide SEE HOLD BACK THE TIDE

turn in your grave SEE SPINNING IN YOUR GRAVE

turn tail The image here is of an animal, many of which use their tails as warning signals when in flight, running away. The animal comparison makes the implied cowardice all the more stinging. The expression has been used since the sixteenth century.

'She wanted to turn tail and run and keep on running away from him, away from what she might discover, away from what could only break her heart, yet she knew that was impossible.' (Jennifer Taylor, *Destined to Love*, 1992)

turn up trumps SEE COME UP TRUMPS

(you can't) turn the clock back (or **turn back the clock**) In use since the middle of the nineteenth century, this expression is nearly always, but not invariably, negative, and is usually a nostalgic longing for the way things were.

'England has turned back the clock and chosen veteran Essex spinner Peter Such for this winter's Ashes battle.' (*Evening Standard*, 1 September 1998)

turn the corner A rather puzzling expression, mostly used of financial recovery, but also of things like illness. It dates from the nineteenth century, and is usually described as coming from the idea of turning into a new path or direction. However, this does not really match the way the expression is used, and since it can also mean to pass round the corner of a race-course, perhaps it comes from the idea of approaching the HOME STRETCH, and having the end in sight.

'The report by Germany's five leading economic research institutes said their more optimistic autumn predictions had been confounded because of east Germany's failure to turn the corner.' (*Daily Telegraph*, 14 April 1992)

turn the tables on This expression probably came from the medieval use of the word 'table' to mean a game, and refers to the turning round of a board such as a chessboard when the players change over pieces. The expression has been in use since the sixteenth century.

'Low inflation turns the tables on endowment mortgages.' (Headline, *Independent*, 9 September 1998)

twice as natural SEE LARGE AS LIFE

two bricks short of a load SEE BRICKS SHORT OF A LOAD

... U like The Spud-U-Like chain of takeaway shops has given rise to a formula phrase of the 'policy-U-like' kind, popular with satirists, and very similar to the ... R US formula.

U-turn This image of a car turning round and going back the way it came has been a popular cliché since the 1980s. It is nowadays almost invariably used of any change in government policy.

'Less than forty hectic hours later, Mrs Thatcher, who had once proudly proclaimed herself a "lady not for turning", had made the most dramatic U-turn of her whole political career.' (*Parliamentary Affairs*, 1991)

ugly customer A clichéd way, since the beginning of the nineteenth century, of describing someone who looks likely to cause trouble or be difficult to deal with. This use of 'ugly' probably developed from its earlier use to describe things such as unpleasant weather.

ugly duckling This comes from the Hans Andersen story of the cygnet hatched with a brood of ducklings; it was a social outcast because it was so ugly and ungainly, but it finally turned into a beautiful swan. This story was translated into English in the mid-nineteenth century and was established by the 1880s as a term for an apparently unpromising child (and later a project) but who had hidden talents or virtues.

'Less than glamorous, perhaps, but with lighter regulation and the prospect of consolidation on a regional level, the independent radio business is no longer the ugly duckling of the media world.' (*Independent*, 9 October 1998)

ultimatum SEE DELIVER AN ULTIMATUM

umbrage SEE TAKE UMBRAGE

unacceptable face of capitalism In 1973 the Prime Minister Edward Heath said of payments made to a politician by Lonrho, 'It is the unpleasant and unacceptable face of capitalism, but one should not suggest that the whole of British industry consists of practices of this kind.' The expression rapidly caught on, and is now also used as a formula phrase.

'In architects like Richard Seifert, they found their mid-twentieth-century Christopher Wren. His Centrepoint, once attacked as the unacceptable face of capitalist development, is now a listed building.' (*Evening Standard*, 28 August 1998)

'Welcome to the Hotel Boka: the unacceptable face of London's lucrative tourist trade.' (*Evening Standard*, 15 September 1998)

unaccustomed as I am to public speaking This has been a clichéd way of opening a speech since at least the middle of the nineteenth century. Nowadays it is usually used jokingly or as a conscious cliché.

'The evening event was thoroughly enjoyable with several awards being made, whilst Graham Crowe delivered one of his "unaccustomed as I am to making short speeches".' (*Environmental Issues*)

unalloyed delight, **pleasure** or **joy** These are clichés of the nineteenth century for pure, unmixed pleasure. The image here is of a precious metal in its purest form, unadulterated with anything baser. 'Unalloyed' is actually first recorded, in the mid-seventeenth century, in this figurative sense, nearly 100 years before the literal sense is found.

'But the mood changed abruptly to unalloyed delight during President Menem's speech when he took up Mr Naveiro's challenge and made a promise that the book paper import duties would not after all be raised.' (*Bookseller*, 1993)

'Bearing in mind the Opposition's unalloyed joy at the thought of an increase in national insurance contributions for people who earn more than that, is it time that the Opposition came clean on their plans for the self-employed . . . ?' (*Hansard Extracts 1991–1992*)

unavoidable delays An invaluable excuse for businesses, giving them a set phrase that avoids any need to explain what has happened. When used by public transport providers, the expression has became almost a joke.

'But, in the finest traditions of BR, the service was inevitably subject to a series of unavoidable delays.' (*Guardian*, 20 December 1989)

unbowed see BLOODY BUT UNBOWED

uncrowned king (or **queen**) Originally used, from the beginning of the twentieth century, for someone who had the sort of power a ruler traditionally had, by the 1930s it had come to indicate anyone who was pre-eminent in their field. It is particularly common in the fields of sport and entertainment.

'In his first season at Upton Park, he became the uncrowned King of the East End, scoring 28 goals in his first season and setting up an unrivalled scoring partnership with Tony Cottee.' (Stuart Cosgrove, *Hampden Babylon*, 1991)

under a bushel see HIDE YOUR LIGHT UNDER A BUSHEL

under a cloud An old expression for 'in disgrace', 'suspected' or 'out of favour', going back to the fifteenth century, and qualifying as a cliché from at least the eighteenth. It uses an image which contrasts all the positive associations of sunshine with the effects of being overshadowed by cloud (see TAKE UMBRAGE for a similar image). In modern times it has been popular with cartoonists, who have enjoyed drawing people literally under their own little cloud.

'She hadn't changed much over the years, her skin was still blooming and her hair was fine and curly; she looked little more than the girl she had been when she had left Swansea under a cloud two years previously.' (Iris Gower, *The Oyster Catchers*, 1992)

united we stand The sentiment that in unity is strength goes back to the ancient world, but the first recorded use of the proverb to which this refers is in 1768 in John Dickinson's *Liberty Song*: 'Then join Hand in Hand, brave Americans all, – By uniting we stand, by dividing we fall.'

'The two Richmond adult and tertiary colleges . . . are to "speak with a single voice" on matters of curriculum and good housekeeping. Well, united they stand, divided they fall.' (*Independent Education*, 23 July 1998)

university of life A similar concept to LIVE AND LEARN, and a cliché since the early twentieth century, this implies that the knowledge gained in the REAL WORLD is of equal (or superior) value to mere book learning.

'Candidates under 25 are supposed to have a minimum of 5 O levels and 2 A levels; for those aged 25 and over the university of life is enough.' (*Management Today*, 1991)

unkindest cut In Shakespeare's *Julius Caesar* (III.ii) Mark Antony shows the Roman crowd the cloak Caesar was wearing when assassinated, and pointing to where Brutus struck, says how much Caesar loved him, adding, 'This was the most unkindest cut of all.' 'Unkindest' here originally meant 'unnatural', but is always used in the sense 'most unkind', 'cruelest'. Even in the middle of the nineteenth century the expression was being used jokingly, and nowadays is often found with reference to vasectomies or neutering animals.

'They can be treated in the short term with an anti-male hormone injection from the vet and this will see them safely through difficult periods without the need for the unkindest cut.' (*Dogs Today*, 1992)

'But his unkindest cut at Elizabeth was to call her heartless; she had only too much heart for her comfort.' (Robert Liddell, *Elizabeth and Ivy*, 1986)

unmitigated disaster A modern set phrase, the word 'unmitigated' only rarely being found linked with any other term.

'Almost all of us have at some point in our lives embarked on a love affair that now seems like an unmitigated disaster. We look back on it with the kind of "How could I have done that?" incredulity that President Clinton must now view his liaison with Monica Lewinsky.' (*Daily Mail*, 27 August 1998)

unsung hero This picks up the language of classical epic – Virgil, for instance opens the *Aeneid* with 'of arms and the man I sing' – and classes the person referred to as undeservedly missing from the list of great heroes. 'Unsung' has been used in this way since Milton, but the most famous line containing it is Scott's in *The Lay of the Last Minstrel* (1805) where he writes of the wretch going to his grave 'Unwept, unhonoured, and unsung'.

' "Never has the saying 'a prophet is without honour in his own land' been more true than in the case of Thomas Crapper," asserts Wallace Reyburn in his lively, informative eulogy to the unsung hero who invented the modern WC cistern.' (*She* magazine, 1989)

unthinkable see THINK THE UNTHINKABLE

untimely end Recorded from the sixteenth century, and a cliché from the early nineteenth – a magazine article from 1812 says 'He sold forged notes . . . which led to his untimely end' – this expression for an early death is now getting rather dated.

'Although the original tree that sheltered Charles met an untimely end at the hands of over-zealous patriots, who hacked away branches and roots for souvenirs, you can still see a direct descendant of that famous oak, itself now nearly three hundred years old.' (*Northamptonshire Rose of the Shires*)

unvarnished truth Something made of wood that is unvarnished is still rough, without embellishments, and this is the image behind the expression. The first recorded use in any sense of 'unvarnished' is Shakespeare's 'I will a round, unvarnish'd tale deliver,/Of my whole course of love' (*Othello*, I.iii), and we probably owe our use of the word to mean 'plain', 'direct', to this. The linking of truth to unvarnished was established by the nineteenth century.

unwritten law In a literal sense there is a distinction between the written Parliamentary laws of Britain, and the traditional unwritten law that is the basis of common law. In this sense the expression was in use in the Middle Ages. It was transferred to mean generally accepted conventions and concepts in the seventeenth century.

'She had always accepted the unwritten law of the pop jungle – all publicity is good publicity – and no matter what the excuses, she needed the headlines as much as their writers needed her.' (Sasha Stone, *Kylie Minogue: The Superstar Next Door*, 1989)

up and coming This expression originally developed in the USA in the late nineteenth century with the sense 'energetic', 'active', the wording reflecting the behaviour of the person. However, that sense of energy had been transferred to mean someone promising, beginning to show success, presumably through their efforts, by the 1920s.

'Luciano Pavarotti took a night off from his sell-out performances of Tosca at Covent Garden last month to appear at a Masterclass for four up and coming young singers.' (*Accountancy*, 1992)

up north A clichéd expression used in England by southern journalists, intended to be read in a funny accent, to evoke the language and attitudes of working-class northerners.

'But young working-class Brits don't want to hang around with mum, dad and . . . half a dozen aunts from up North and sip wine all night like they do in Italy. And who can blame them?' (*Guardian*, 17 October 1998)

up to scratch In nineteenth-century boxing matches a scratch would be made in the centre of the boxing ring before the start of a fight. When a fighter was knocked down he was given a thirty-second count and then had to make his own way to the scratch if the fight was to go on. If he could not do this, he was not up to scratch and had lost the match. The expression was being used figuratively by the middle of the century. 'Scratch' was also used for the starting line on a race-course. Because of the handicapping system, some horses would be given a 'head start' and be placed in front of the scratch. Those with a better record would have to 'start from scratch', giving us two other clichés.

'I sensed that they approved of him whole-heartedly, and that by comparison I was no longer the blue-eyed boy of the family: I did not come up to scratch.' (James Kirkup, *A Poet Could Not But Be Gay*, 1991)

up (or **full**) **to the gills** The gills have been used jokingly of human throats since the sixteenth century. The *OED* lists a polychrome collection of phrases describing people's gills: rosy if in good health, white, blue or yellow about the gills for illness (but strangely not the now common green for feeling sick), and red for anger. However, to be full or up to the gills for having eaten a large amount, or drunk too much (compare DRINK LIKE A FISH – current from the seventeenth century) is missing from this list, which suggests it is a twentieth-century innovation.

up to your ears or **arse** see COMING OUT OF YOUR EARS

up your sleeve see ACE UP YOUR SLEEVE

user-friendly This expression, coined in the late 1970s to describe computer systems that are designed to be easy to use, rapidly spread to cover other services, and has spawned a new combining form, with -friendly tacked on to all sorts of other words.

'Frankly what this small, select band got up to with its slow, user-unfriendly computer links was of very little interest or importance to anyone but itself.' (*Independent*, 7 September 1998)

'The council is currently implementing a 10-year cemeteries development programme to make Peterborough's graveyards more user-friendly.' (*Peterborough Citizen*, quoted in *Private Eye*, 18 September 1998)

'Tam Dalyell's claim that Gus was made a minister as his reward for making Scottish Television devolution-friendly during the referendum may not be as paranoid or outlandish as it seems.' (*Private Eye*, 4 September 1998)

(round up the) usual suspects In the 1942 film *Casablanca* Louis, the world-weary, collaborating French police chief, says: 'Major Strasser has been shot. Round up the usual suspects' (see further at BEGINNING OF A BEAUTIFUL FRIENDSHIP). A 1995 film *The Usual Suspects* led to increased use of the expression.

'*Embarrassing Problems* by Dr Margaret Stearn covers everything from bad breath to sex headaches. All the usual suspects are there: piles, sticking out ears . . . and hair in places you'd rather it wasn't.' (*You* magazine, 20 September 1998)

vale of tears Although this is not actually found in the Bible, there are similar uses, such as 'Yea though I walk through the valley of the shadow of death, I will fear no evil' (Psalm 23), and the expression probably picks up on biblical language. 'This sorrowful vale' is found in the fifteenth century (and 'weeping dale', using good Anglo-Saxon equivalents of what were imported French words, is even earlier). 'This vale of tears' was a cliché by the seventeenth century.

'After all, she told herself in extenuation, this was the first thing she had ever done to please herself – but, said a small voice . . . they hadn't asked to come into this vale of tears.' (Jean Bow, *Jane's Journey*, 1991)

valiant effort An emotionally charged cliché from the mid-twentieth century, this often, but not invariably, carries a presupposition of failure.

'Then, realizing she was on the verge of helpless tears, she made a valiant effort to pull herself together.' (*Winter Challenge*, 1993)

values See FAMILY VALUES; VICTORIAN VALUES

vaulting ambition In Shakespeare's *Macbeth* (I.vii) Macbeth is hesitating about murdering his king and kinsman Duncan. He compares Duncan's saintliness with his own motives for murder: 'I have no spur/To prick the sides of my intent, but only/Vaulting ambition, which o'erleaps itself,/And falls on the other.' From this we get the expression 'vaulting ambition' for excessive ambition.

velvet glove See IRON FIST

vengeance See WITH A VENGEANCE

verb. sap. See WORD TO THE WISE

vested interest 'Vested' originally meant dressed, particularly of priests in their *vestments*. Special clothing or uniforms are worn to show that you have a right to be what you claim to be, that you have been *invested* in a certain rank. By the eighteenth century 'vested' had come to mean 'established', definitely assigned to something or someone. By the early nineteenth century 'vested interest' had become a legal term meaning a right to property, and from there it was transferred to mean a personal involvement or stake in something.

'Other people such as immediate work colleagues or fellow team members also have a vested interest in how someone is performing.' (Andrew Leigh, *Twenty Ways to Manage Better*, 1992)

vexed question This is a literal translation of a Latin term *vexata quaestio*, where the 'vexed' part has the meaning 'troublesome, difficult', a vexed question being something that needs debate, a MOOT POINT. It has been in use in this sense since the seventeenth century, but now modern use tends to be influenced by the more usual sense of vexed as irritated or angry.

vicarage tea party Despite the fact that they spend so much of the time dealing with the problems of the REAL WORLD, in popular culture vicars still have a reputation for unworldliness and innocence. This expression (along with the associated catch-phrase 'more tea, vicar?') has been in use as a comparative standard of innocence since at least the 1950s, usually in the format 'X [something new] makes Y [something with a reputation] look like a vicarage tea party'. An alternative form is 'makes Y look like a choirboy'.

'. . . the publisher's promise of a book that "will make President Clinton look like a choirboy".' (*Independent*, 18 September 1998)

vicious (or **virtuous**) **circle** In logic a circular argument is one in which each element depends on another, rather than consisting of a straight line of reasoning. A vicious circle is a circular argument that uses faulty logic, and the expression is recorded in this sense from the late eighteenth century. By the 1830s it was being used in the modern sense of a series of linked events which act upon each other to make a situation worse. A virtuous circle, a favourite of management gurus, dates only from the 1950s, and is the opposite: a cycle of events that reinforces benefits.

'There is the beginning of a virtuous circle where product enhancement leads to better circulation which brings increased revenue and provides funds for further product enhancement.' (*Evening Standard*, 10 September 1998)

victim of circumstances A useful get-out cliché, excusing the person referred to from responsibility, in the same way as UNAVOIDABLE DELAYS and CIRCUMSTANCES BEYOND OUR CONTROL. It was obviously well established when Kenneth Grahame used it in *The Wind in the Willows* (1908) of Toad's escape from jail in disguise: 'Toad was delighted with the suggestion. It would enable him to leave the prison in some style, and with his reputation for being a desperate and dangerous fellow untarnished; and he readily helped the gaoler's daughter to make her aunt appear as much as possible the victim of circumstances over which she had no control.'

Victorian values An expression much used by politicians in the 1980s, those on the right using it to suggest order, free enterprise, self-restraint and other old-fashioned values; those on the left pointing out that the Victorian age was one of gross inequality, poverty, squalor and widespread child prostitution. The expression got mixed in with various political scandals of the time and became associated with that Victorian vice, hypocrisy, and is now generally used mockingly.

'I suspect what he means, although he daren't say it (remembering the "Back to Basics" and "Victorian Values" fiascos) is "less divorce" and "bring back the nuclear family".' (*Independent*, 17 September 1998)

'For all his talk of modernisation, Blair's actions reveal a man who wants to propel us back to the nineteenth century as quickly as possible. If Margaret Thatcher hadn't already bagged the phrase, he might well describe his aim as a return to Victorian values.' (*Guardian*, 1 April 1998)

video nasty An expression from the 1980s, originally used for a gratuitously violent or pornographic video film, but now used generally for anything unpleasant.

'Jones, reeling from a £20,000 fine and suspended six-month ban imposed by the FA for his part in a video nasty about soccer dirty tricks, has to pick himself up at Middlesbrough.' (*Today*, 1992)

virtuous circle see VICIOUS CIRCLE

vision of beauty A more grandiose, but no less sentimental version of PRETTY AS A PICTURE. Sir Walter Scott was using 'beautiful vision' by 1823 and Benjamin Jowett, in his 1871 translation of Plato's *Republic* has: 'Yes, and the most ridiculous thing of all will be the sight of women naked in the palaestra, exercising with the men, especially when they are no longer young; they certainly will not be a vision of beauty, any more than the enthusiastic old men who in spite of wrinkles and ugliness continue to frequent the gymnasia.'

'Abuelo Freitas stood to attention as Lina came out, a vision of beauty in a froth of lace and tulle and fresh flowers.' (Jenny Ashe, *Sweet Deceiver*, 1993)

voice see SPEAK WITH ONE VOICE

Vorsprung durch Technik Literally meaning 'advantage through technology', this is the MISSION STATEMENT of the German car manufacturers Audi, which is written up over the factory gates. It was used heavily in advertising campaigns from 1982 and came to be used to symbolize the modern Germany.

'I once translated a research article from the German for the engineering department. I understood the original perfectly, but was then clueless on rereading my English translation; it was saturated in technical expressions I had to look up in a specialist dictionary. "*Vorsprung durch* gibberish" as they say in Germany.' (*Independent Education*, 23 July 1998)

'In Germany, sausages and Sachertorte combined with a commitment to Vorsprung durch Technik has made the most prosperous nation also the weightiest.' (*Independent*, 5 September 1998)

vote with your feet An expression that dates only from the 1960s, it used to mean showing approval or disapproval by your presence or absence, but can now be transferred to any action.

'Investors have criticised last week's fiscal package and interest rate cut as too little too late and voted with their feet for most of the week by selling out of the market.' (*Daily Telegraph*, 10 April 1992)

wages of sin 'The wages of sin is death' comes from the Bible (Romans 6:23). The peculiar grammar is because 'wages' was originally a singular noun, but because it ends in 's' has come to be treated as plural. Perhaps because of the uncomfortable grammar, the whole quotation is rarely used now, but merely alluded to. This expression is often used ironically.

'Wages of Sin: Teachers in central Russia will be receiving their monthly salaries in vodka because the government coffers are empty.' (*Independent*, 24 September 1998)

wailing and gnashing of teeth see OUTER DARKNESS

wait and see Although it had already been in use for many years, this expression became a catch-phrase in 1910 when the Liberal Prime Minister H. H. Asquith used it repeatedly in the House of Commons when asked when he was going to reintroduce a rejected budget. This won him the nickname 'Old Wait and See', and explains the provocative or coy associations this still has as a tag.

wait for dead men's shoes see DEAD MEN'S SHOES

walk a lonely road This cliché, and others in a similar vein, are stalwarts of the MAN'S GOTTA DO WHAT A MAN'S GOTTA DO school of literature and film. The influence of these expressions does, however, spread wider – to Bob Dylan's Zen-like 'How many roads must a man walk down/Before you can call him a man?' ('Blowin' in the Wind', 1962) and to clichés like 'a long, hard, road' (see under GO DOWN A ROAD). 'Plough a lonely furrow' has been used in the same sense since the nineteenth century.

'To be alone was nothing new for Storm. In one way or another he had walked a lonely road for most of his life. And sometimes it was easier to live with his inner loneliness . . . than to exist in a human anthill such as the Centre.' (Andre Norton, *The Beast Master*, 1959)

walk tall This American expression for being proud and self-confident, a companion to your HEAD HELD HIGH, received a boost in use when it was the title of a successful film in 1973. It is particularly used by sports journalists. A less common alternative is to 'stand proud'.

'And Britain can walk tall today after their first encounters with the might of the mainland.' (*Independent*, 17 September 1998)

'We get funny looks on the street a lot – the "toy boy" and "mutton dressed as lamb" thing – but we stand proud.' (*You* magazine, 20 September 1998)

walking wounded This is a military term to distinguish those who can get themselves off the battlefield from those who are 'stretcher cases'. Both these terms, first recorded from the First World War, have been used figuratively in the second half of the twentieth century; the first to mean survivors, the second to indicate someone or something probably past hope.

'The old contract between the sexes was written into every single social arrangement we had . . . To rewrite it is to cause social disruption on an almost unimaginable scale. So, no wonder there are so many walking wounded.' (*Independent*, 7 November 1998)

wall see BACK TO THE WALL

war of words A set phrase for an argument, either spoken or written. It is first recorded from Pope's 1725 translation of the *Odyssey*: 'O insolence of youth! Whose tongue affords/Such railing eloquence and war of words', but is now largely journalistic.

'Frank Dobson was locked in a war of words last night after claiming that NHS waiting lists had fallen by a record 54,000 in three months.' (*Daily Mail*, 27 August 1998)

warm (the cockles of) your heart The cockles of people's hearts have been warmed since the seventeenth century, but no one is really sure why. There are various theories: that the heart is vaguely the same shape as a cockle shell; that the zoological name for a cockle is *cardium*, which comes, via Latin, from the Greek for 'heart'; and that the phrase refers to the Latin name for the heart's ventricles, *cochleae cordis* (literally snailshells of the heart). This last seems the most likely, as it would give an image of warmth that goes right down to the component parts of the heart, and could have started life as one of those academic puns of the sort that lies behind the elbow's funny bone being at the end of the humerus.

'Temperatures out on the ice can vary from zero to –40C – but watching the seals will soon warm your heart.' (*Today*, 1992)

warm welcome A set phrase since the eighteenth century, this exploits the old associations of warmth with positive emotions and cold – as in the early nineteenth-century 'cold shoulder' – with negative ones.

'If you have children, it will be sensible to tell them how lucky they are to have Granny coming to live with them, and they should be encouraged to give her a warm welcome.' (Eleanor Deeping, *Caring for Elderly Parents*, 1979)

warts and all This is the popular version of words supposed to have been used by Oliver Cromwell when the fashionable, and generally flattering, portraitist Peter Lely (1618–80) was painting him: 'Mr Lely, I desire you would use all your skill to paint my picture truly like me, and not flatter me at all; but remark all these roughnesses, pimples, warts, and everything as you see me; otherwise I will never pay a farthing for it.' Hence, the expression is used to mean 'as things really are' or 'despite its faults'.

'Labour retains a fatal mistrust in the only assured source of wealth which, warts and all, is the market economy.' (*Daily Telegraph*, 9 April 1992)

wash and go In 1989 a new shampoo called 'Wash and Go' was introduced with a heavy advertising campaign. It did not take long for the name to become first a catch-phrase and then a formula phrase.

'Cheques – just Cash & Go.' (Advertising leaflet, Barclays Bank, November 1998)

wash your hands of The New Testament tells how the Roman governor of Judaea, Pontius Pilate, offered to release Jesus, but when the crowd demanded the release of Barabbas instead, he 'washed his hands before the multitude, saying I am innocent of the blood of this just person' (Matthew 27:24). It has been used since the sixteenth century, and by the eighteenth was a cliché that could be used of trivial things without conscious reference to the original.

'And if you push me much harder, I'll wash my hands of the whole thing and tell the Committee I can't cope, and make it clear I want you out.' (Claire Rayner, *The Meddlers*, 1991)

washing my hair A polite fiction like the CHEQUE IS IN THE POST, sometimes found as a way of getting out of doing something, but more often now used as a conscious cliché.

'But when the PM sends his personal invitation you can scarcely say: "Sorry I'm washing my hair."' (*Punch*, 1992)

watch this space A cliché of advertising and journalism, originally a means of holding the reader's attention until the next issue, this is recorded from as early as 1917.

'All those who have been sticking religiously to their macrobiotic diet sheets while dreaming wistfully of soft boiled eggs and buttered soldiers can probably breathe again (but watch this space).' (*Accountancy*, 1993)

water under the bridge A twentieth-century expression used to indicate something is past and gone and things have moved on. In North America the water is more likely to have gone 'over the dam' than under the bridge. Although the expression is recent, the image of time and events flowing on like water is not, going back at least to the sixth-century BC Greek philosopher Heraclitus, who commented, 'You can't step twice into the same river.'

'In any case, oceans of water have passed under the bridge since what happened in 1970. The statute of limitation must have run out on the affair.' (*Daily Mail*, 27 August 1998)

Watergate see –GATE

watershed A watershed is literally the place on a mountain which divides two different river systems, water flowing off in more than one direction. Its transference to an increasingly popular substitute for 'turning point' may be due to its use by Longfellow in an 1878 poem called *Kéramos*: 'Midnight! The outpost of advancing day! . . . The watershed of Time, from which the streams of Yesterday and To-morrow take their way.' See further under DEFINING MOMENT.

'They disagree strongly about its consequences: was it a watershed in British industrial relations, as some Communist writers would have us believe, or did it barely change the course of TUC and trade union policy, as Gordon Phillips has argued?' (Keith Laybourn, *Britain on the Breadline*, 1990)

watery grave A set phrase, the poetic 'watery' rather than the prosaic 'wet' is probably due to 'watery grave' appearing in Shakespeare's *Pericles*.

'Moves are now being made to lift the aircraft from its watery grave and preserve it locally.' (*FlyPast*, 1992)

on the same (or **different**) **wavelength** To pick up a radio broadcast, you have to 'tune in' to the same wavelength. To be on the same wavelength as someone therefore means to be able to understand them, to 'pick up the signals' they are sending you. The figurative use dates from the early days of radio in the 1920s.

'It was the first time they had met, but they were on the same wavelength. They discussed religion. Each has subsequently told me how much he likes the other.' (*Independent*, 22 September 1998)

way forward A modern political cliché used to create an atmosphere of up-beat positiveness, without being too specific.

'Sinn Fein is committed to exclusively peaceful and democratic means to achieve a way forward . . . Inclusive and honest dialogue is the only way forward in this country.' (Gerry Adams, quoted in the *Independent*, 2 September 1998)

we are not amused A catch-phrase cliché derived from a story that Queen Victoria had made the comment either when an equerry told an improper story within her hearing, or in response to catching someone doing an imitation of her. Victoria denied ever having said it.

'Victoria would not be amused.' (Headline, *Independent*, 26 November 1998)

weaker sex (or **vessel**) see FAIR SEX

wealth beyond the dreams of avarice see DREAMS OF AVARICE

weather the storm This expression for coming safely through a difficult time, like a ship surviving a storm, has been in use since the sixteenth century, and was a cliché by the early nineteenth.

'The Chancellor defied the global economic gloom by insisting . . . that Britain was in a strong position to weather the storm.' (*Independent*, 4 November 1998)

wedded bliss A set phrase since the nineteenth century, this expression for the joys of marriage can still be found used straight, but is more often now used ironically.

'The pressures of wedded bliss excluded Sadie as effectively from the life of her former friend as if they had been on different continents.' (Edward Chisnall, *Bell in the Tree. The Glasgow Story*, 1989)

wedge see THIN END OF THE WEDGE

weigh in the balance In the Old Testament Book of Daniel, chapter 5, Daniel interpreted the word 'tekel' in the WRITING ON THE WALL as 'Thou art weighed in the balances and art found wanting', with the consequence that Belshazzar and his kingdom will be destroyed. The expression that comes from this has been a cliché since the nineteenth century.

'At a subsequent mass meeting, John Templeton, secretary of the STA, referred to these "two great cases" (Neill's and Morrison & Gibb) and said that women workers in these firms had been "weighed in the balance and not found wanting".' (Sian Reynolds, *Britannica's Typesetters*, 1989)

well and living in see ALIVE AND WELL

well and truly A set phrase, each half of which merely repeats the other, this expression for 'thoroughly' is often a filler. It has been a cliché since the nineteenth century.

'The image of . . . the endowment mortgage has been well and truly tarnished, and now another sparring partner, the PEP mortgage, is also down in the popularity stakes.' (*Independent* 9 September 1998)

wend your way An elaborate archaism of the nineteenth century, used to replace the simple 'go'. 'Wend' was the standard Anglo-Saxon word for 'go' in the sense of travel, and had all but died out by the end of the Middle Ages except in dialect and a few technical senses, although Shakespeare does use it three times. It was revived by Sir Walter Scott and similar writers of medieval romances at the beginning of the nineteenth century, and this particular phrase stuck in the language thereafter.

'When construction, or rather demolition began, thousands of people had to wend their way through the mud and debris.' (Mark Almond, *The Rise and Fall of Nicolae and Elena Ceausescu*, 1992)

wet behind the ears This term for naiveté or inexperience uses an image of an animal so new-born that it has not even had time to dry out thoroughly. It is first recorded in the early twentieth century.

'Mr Toshikikaifu, Japan's prime minister, may still be a little wet behind the ears but, not for the first time, he has confounded his more experienced rivals.' (*The Economist*, 1990)

wet blanket The *OED*'s definition of this as 'a person or thing that throws a damper over anything, as a wet blanket smothers a fire' admirably sums up both the origin of this expression and its associated ideas. It has been in use since the early nineteenth century.

' "But I haven't done anything – except be an absolute misery," she added honestly as she realised for perhaps the first time what a wet blanket she had been.' (Emma Richmond, *A Stranger's Trust*, 1991)

wet your whistle Chaucer, describing the Miller's wife getting tipsy in *The Reeve's Tale*, says 'So was her jolly whistle well y-wet', showing that the idea of using 'whistle', for the source of the sound, the throat, is by no means new; nor wetting it for having a drink. The alliterative phrase was so popular that by the mid-eighteenth century there was even a slang expression 'whistle-drunk' to mean exceedingly drunk, full UP TO THE GILLS.

what a (or **hell of a**) **way to run a railroad/railway** A catch-phrase from North America, expressing general disgust at mismanagement, which probably originated in the late nineteenth or early twentieth century. It must have been well enough known to be instantly recognized when it was used in a famous cartoon in the 1930s showing a signalman looking out of his box at two trains about to collide and saying, 'Tch-tch – what a way to run a railroad!' Compare BACK TO THE DRAWING BOARD.

what it takes A modern cliché found used of personal qualities and abilities, and also popular with sports journalists writing about teams.

'The "great men" theory (i.e. that people are born with leadership qualities or traits, and either do or do not "have what it takes" to be leaders) has been challenged by writers of the human relations school.' (*Organisational Analysis*, 1990)

'After a summer of speculation at Old Trafford about the future of the Manchester United striker, manager Alex Ferguson insists the Welsh warrior still has what it takes to lead his side.' (*Daily Mirror*, 1992)

what's . . . got to do with it? A formula phrase based on the 1984 Tina Turner hit song 'What's Love Got to Do with It?' (written by Terry Britten and Graham Lyle).

'It's simple: if you're a female athlete who wants to make a splash (and make as much as the men), strip off or dress up and pout for Britain. It worked for our most famous Olympic swimmer, and it may work for professional golfers. What's sport got to do with it?' (*Independent*, 13 August 1998)

what's the damage? see DAMAGE

what's up, Doc? A catch-phrase cliché from Warner Brothers Bugs Bunny cartoons, which was first used in 1936. It was probably coined by Tex Avery, who was the chief writer of the cartoons, combining the already established catch-phrase 'What's up?' and the slang use of 'Doc' as a term of address. The expression was given further currency when it was used as the title of a successful film in 1972.

when all is said and done An expression dating from the sixteenth century, and a cliché by the nineteenth, this is usually a mere filler, an alternative to IN THE FINAL ANALYSIS or AT THE END OF THE DAY.

'She was, when all is said and done, no more than the necessary brood mare of reasonable pedigree required to continue the Windsor line.' (*Evening Standard*, 28 August 1998)

when in Rome, do as the Romans do When, in the fourth century, St Augustine wrote to St Ambrose to ask which Church rite he should follow, St Ambrose replied 'When in Rome do as the Romans do' (*Si fueris Romae, Romano vivito more*); in other words, Augustine was advised to follow the local practice. It is often shortened to 'When in Rome . . .'.

'Gazza knows that when in Rome, do as the Romans – so he got into the spirit with some impressive hand waving and high passion during a training match.' (*Daily Mirror*, 1992)

'Sometimes all one can do is remember "when in Rome –" and bear in mind some dos and don'ts.' (*She*, 1989)

when push comes to shove see PUSH COMES TO SHOVE

when the chips are down see CHIPS ARE DOWN

when the going gets tough see GOING GETS TOUGH

where angels fear to tread see FOOLS RUSH IN

where eagles dare see EAGLE HAS LANDED

where it hurts see HIT WHERE IT HURTS

where no man has gone before see BOLDLY GO WHERE NO MAN HAS GONE BEFORE

whimper see NOT WITH A BANG BUT A WHIMPER

whirlwind romance A journalistic cliché from the mid-twentieth century for a fast-moving affair, in which the lovers feel swept off their feet by the force of their passion.

'Said a source close to Paula, who is reported to be expecting their first baby in December: "They had a whirlwind romance and just wanted to get together straight away." ' (*Daily Mirror*, 1992)

whistle-blower see BLOW THE WHISTLE

whistles see BELLS AND WHISTLES

white Christmas This comes from the immensely successful song written by Irving Berlin in 1942. While heavy snow at Christmas is common in many parts of the USA, where the song was written, it is rare in the UK. However, such is the force of the song, Hollywood images and the traditional Christmas card scene, that the idea is firmly fixed that snow and Christmas go together, a cause of great disappointment for many children.

'While many children were hoping for a white Christmas, more than 500,000 families were packing their suitcases and heading for the sun.' (*Today*, 1992)

whiter than white This is one of those expressions that 'everyone knows', perhaps under the influence of all those 'Persil washes whiter' washing powder advertisements. In fact the phrase is not modern: Shakespeare has the lines, 'Who sees his true-love in her naked bed/Teaching the sheets a whiter hue than white' (*Venus and Adonis*). The expression is not recorded again until it appears in one of the *OED*'s own definitions, where 'exceeding-white' is defined, in 1924, as 'exceeding or surpassing white, "whiter than white" '. Many of the clichés in this book are only to be found in the text of the *OED* in the definitions of other words, but they would not have been used by the lexicographers if they were not already commonly used, well known terms.

'These are the new improved, biological, whiter than white heroes.' (Stewart Lamont, *In Good Faith*, 1989)

'I mean, we all bend the rules to our own advantage from time to time. I mean, nobody pretends they're whiter than white.' (Adult education seminar, recorded on 3 February 1994)

whole hog see GO THE WHOLE HOG

Who's afraid of . . . 'Who's Afraid of the Big Bad Wolf?' is the title of a popular song written by Frank E. Churchill and Ann Ronell in 1933, and used on the sound track of *The Three Little Pigs* cartoon, and later recorded by Duke Ellington. In 1962 Edward Albee wrote a play he called *Who's Afraid of Virginia Woolf?* which was made into a successful film starring Elizabeth Taylor and Richard Burton in 1966. From this it developed into a formula phrase, much used in headlines, where a person has the reputation of being fierce, powerful or difficult.

wild about see ALL THE RAGE

wild and woolly *Tales of the Wild and Woolly West*, the title of a book by Adair Welcker published in 1891, introduced this expression to the general public. Welcker's publisher provided a note saying, 'Woolly . . . seems to refer to the uncivilized – untamed-hair-outside, wool-still-in-the-sheepskin-coat – condition of the Western Pioneers.'

'They provide unity, and help to give the planting coherence and shape, without which herbs tend to get out of hand, and look wild and woolly, especially towards the end of the season.' (Ann Bonar, *Herbs*, 1989)

wild horses wouldn't drag (or **draw**) **. . .** This alludes to the Barbarian custom of punishing people by having them dragged along by wild horses. In the late eleventh-century French poem *The Song of Roland* the traitor Ganelon is executed in this way. In English literature the punishment is first referred to in the mid-thirteenth century, when deserving to be drawn by wild horses is one of the insults hurled between the comically quarrelling Owl and the Nightingale in the poem of that name. In the nineteenth century this was turned into the expression 'wild horses wouldn't draw . . .' with the more modern 'drag' probably being substituted in the twentieth century.

'In times past, successive teams of wild horses would have failed to drag him across the threshold.' (*Daily Mail*, 27 August 1998)

wild men of . . . Just as football has its HARD MEN, so fields such as rock and roll have their wild men, people who exemplify the SEX AND DRUGS AND ROCK AND ROLL lifestyle that goes with the job.

'Following the revelations in last week's Daily Mirror that former wild men of rock, Aerosmith, now no longer do anything more dangerous than eat sushi and play with their children, Bizzerk has found out that other rock stars are calming down their act too.' (*Sounds*, 1990)

wild oats This expression is found from the middle of the sixteenth century, and is summed up in a quote of 1576: 'That wilful and unruly age, which lacketh ripeness and discretion, and (as we say) hath not sowed all their wild oates.' Modern use, while still sometimes referring to youthful excesses in general, often refers to young men's casual sexual relationships. The expression comes from the idea of sowing wild oats, a problem weed of cornfields, rather than those that bear useful grain.

'As with most young men who had succeeded in sowing casual wild oats, it was a case of get away as fast as you can before they start getting ideas.' (Ray Pickernell, *Yanto's Summer*, 1988)

wild surmise 'Stout Cortez . . . and all his men/Look'd at each other with a wild surmise –/Silent, upon a peak in Darien', wrote John Keats in his poem *On First Looking into Chapman's Homer* (1817), describing the reaction of the first Europeans to see the Pacific Ocean after crossing Central America. The expression is now so integrated into the language that it has lost all connection with the poem.

'Even the wild surmise occurred to me that Leslie might have lost his memory; but commonsense reasserted itself, and I realised that this could not have been the fate of all his men.' (Irene Young, *Enigma Variations*, 1990)

win brownie points see BROWNIE POINTS

win hands down Although a guess might place this as an image from poker, it in fact comes from horse racing. A jockey who can see he is well ahead of the field will relax his hold on the reins and let his hands drop, allowing the horse to ease up. The expression has been used for 'win easily' since the middle of the nineteenth century.

'If, for example, you compared real, unground coffee beans with instant coffee by simply pouring boiling water over both, of course the instant would win hands down.' (*Gardener's World*, 1991)

win your daily bread see DAILY BREAD

win–win see NO WIN

wind of change In a speech made in Cape Town in 1960 the British Prime Minister Harold Macmillan (Lord Stockton) said: 'The wind of change is blowing through this continent, and, whether we like it or not, this growth of national consciousness is a political fact.' This popularized the expression, and it has now spread from politics to change in other fields.

'The wind of change is starting to blow through the business, as Internet book shops start to work wonders on the backlists.' (*Independent*, 5 September 1998)

winning streak 'Winning streak', like ON A ROLL, comes from gambling, and is a particularly common cliché of sports writing. 'Streak' has been used to describe a period of both good and bad luck since the first half of the nineteenth century.

'It was Charlton who stopped a winning streak at the end of last season which cost Leicester automatic promotion.' (*Belfast Telegraph*)

in his wisdom In the seventeenth and eighteenth centuries it was common for writers on moral subjects, echoing the Prayer Book, to write of things ordained by 'God in his wisdom'. In the nineteenth century the expression began to be used of people, with increasing irony, so that today it is used to imply the exact opposite of its apparent meaning.

'His research was aided by several files from Express Newspapers. Its new proprietor, Lord Hollick, in his wisdom, had decided to dispense with a great chunk of the cuttings library. The Lucan files were rescued and passed to George.' (*Daily Mail*, 10 July 1998)

wisely but too well SEE NOT WISELY BUT TOO WELL

wish list An expression for things you would like or want to happen, which came into use in about the early 1970s, and is rapidly becoming a cliché.

'Meanwhile we shouldn't make welfare reforms, shouldn't have tuition fees and so on. Liz, naturally, agrees. She wants higher rates of income tax kicking in at "over 20,000 or so", thus raising the revenue we need to fund health and education . . . Such wish lists do not make an economic strategy.' (*Independent*, 29 September 1998)

witching hour This is an adaptation of Shakespeare's 'Now is the very witching time of night,/When churchyards yawn . . .' (*Hamlet*, III.ii), an allusion to the fact that witches and ghosts are thought most likely to be active and powerful at midnight. It was an established cliché in the form 'witching hour' by the middle of the nineteenth century. In the 1980s the expression took on a special sense in stock market jargon as a time when accounts had to be settled.

'It was the witching hour of midnight back home, but the England nightmare had only just begun.' (*Liverpool Daily Post and Echo*)

with a little help from my friends SEE LITTLE HELP FROM MY FRIENDS

with a vengeance An expression from the seventeenth century which originally meant 'with a curse' or more physical sign of disapproval, then came to be used to mean 'extremely', 'very much', and nowadays is often no more than an empty phrase used for emphasis.

'Disco is back. With a vengeance. All over London people are digging out their platform shoes, boob tubes and flares.' (*Evening Standard*, 1 September 1998)

with dirty faces SEE ANGELS WITH DIRTY FACES

with head held high SEE HEAD HELD HIGH

with knobs (or **bells**) **on** Although the *OED* does not record 'with knobs on' until 1930, Eric Partridge dates it to the late nineteenth century, as he does 'with bells on' which the *OED* ignores. The idea behind the expressions is that of lavish embellishment. 'With knobs on' is particularly associated with schoolchildren trading insults, used to mean 'and the same to you', in which case it is often in the form 'with brass knobs on' as if referring to some ornate Victorian bedstead.

'There are horror movies and there are Japanese horror movies and without being remotely racist it is a proven fact that in the Land of the Rising Sun they like their severed limbs, blood and gore with knobs on.' (*Today*, 1992)

'Vodka and tonic is IT. With bells on.' (*Independent*, 8 September 1998)

with might and main SEE MIGHT AND MAIN

with the best will in the world SEE BEST WILL IN THE WORLD

without fear of contradiction Often a mere filler that makes the user sound pompous, if it has any function it is to raise in the hearer the very fears that it seeks to dispel.

'Labour's greatest ever achievement, without fear of any contradiction, the greatest achievement of the Labour movement was the introduction of the NHS which still remains to a large extent, the envy of the world.' (Labour Club public meeting, recorded, 3 July 1993)

without let or hindrance A set phrase, each half of which means the same as the other, 'let', here, being the old word for prevention, which is also the source of the 'let' in tennis, called when the net hinders the passage of the ball. The expression, a cliché since the mid-nineteenth century, has been familiar to generations of passport holders in the statement at the beginning of the document: 'Her Britannic Majesty's Secretary of State requests and requires . . . all those whom it may concern to allow the bearer to pass freely without let or hindrance . . .'

'It should flow easily, though not too swiftly, through the manholes, without let or hindrance.' (George Collard, *DIY Home Surveying*, 1990)

'What I am going to miss is the opportunity to pontificate in peace, without let or hindrance, as Punch has let me do for eight years.' (*Punch*, 1992)

without more (or **further**) **ado** 'Ado' is an archaic word for 'work', 'bother', obsolete except in these set phrases, which have been in use since the fourteenth century.

'One day, one of the mares cut her leg, and as it required stitching she was separated from the other horses and shut in a stable without more ado.' (Garda Langley, *Understanding Horses*, 1989)

'Ranulf returned with Sir James and a small convoy of cavalry and, without further ado, Corbett saddled a horse and rode back with them to the castle.' (P. C. Doherty, *Crown in Darkness*, 1991)

without reservation see CONDEMN WITHOUT RESERVATION

wolf from the door see KEEP THE WOLF FROM THE DOOR

women and children first This clichéd cry, the heroic equivalent of 'ladies first' (see LADY WIFE), got its associations of chivalry and the manly STIFF UPPER LIP after the wreck of the *Birkenhead* in 1852. One of the first iron ships commissioned by the navy, the *Birkenhead* was a troop-ship sailing to South Africa. She struck a rock off the Cape of Good Hope (now known as the Birkenhead Rock) and went down with 487 officers and men in shark-infested waters. The wreck became famous, the subject of many paintings and poems, because of the unusual discipline shown by the troops in evacuating the ship, ensuring that the women and children were put in the lifeboats first and saved.

won the battle but lost the war This saying acts as a substitute for a PYRRHIC VICTORY. It appears to be modern, and perhaps reflects the decline in Classical studies, that it has been necessary to express this ancient idea directly rather than allusively.

won't lie down see DEAD BUT WON'T LIE DOWN

wood for the trees see BIG PICTURE

woods see NECK OF THE WOODS

come out of the woodwork The image here is of some nasty vermin appearing from the decent obscurity of the hidden corners of a house. The expression, which is not recorded before the 1960s, has an opposite, to 'crawl back into the woodwork'.

'No doubt the anti-political correctness lobby will be swarming out of the woodwork as I write.' (*Independent*, 28 August 1998)

word to the wise This is the English translation of the Latin proverb, used by Plautus, *verbum sapienti sat est* ('a word is enough for a sensible man'), itself a cliché in the shortened form '*verb. sap.*'. It is used as a warning to someone that they are about to run into trouble, and has been used in English in various forms since the thirteenth century. In the 1590s Ben Jonson showed it was already well understood as a warning or even threat, in his play *The Case is Altered*: 'Go to, a word to the wise; away, fly, vanish.'

to have your work cut out for you This expression for a difficult job at first sight looks self-contradictory – how can you have a job still to do if it has already been cut out for you? However, 'to cut out work' for someone has been used to mean to plan or prepare work for them since the early seventeenth century. The image is probably from tailoring when, in the days before sewing machines, once the work was cut out there remained the long hard grind of putting it all together.

'This month *Stuff*'s food and drink man had his work cut out for him. After testing 29 bottles of Scottish malt whisky . . . he still had to whittle down his favourites.' (*Stuff*, October 1998)

I work hard and I play hard A typical businessman's boast to give him a LIVE FAST, DIE YOUNG image, this is often a coded way of saying that the speaker likes to get drunk noisily and regularly.

'Let me tell you something. Tad Friendly works hard – and plays hard . . . But nothing compares to the sheer rocket-fuelled rush of the *deal*.' (*Evening Standard*, 10 September 1998)

worked a charm This, like its companion, 'worked like magic' (often just shortened to 'magic!' meaning 'excellent'), implies that something went really well, as if the people involved were bewitched. The expression dates back to the nineteenth century, but 'magic!' as an exclamation did not become prominent until the 1970s.

'It worked a charm, they were so enthusiastic and great, it reminded me of why I'd got into theatre.' (*You* magazine, 20 September 1998)

a world away This set phrase for something very distant, has as a companion cliché 'worlds apart'. 'Worlds' has been used for emphasis, in the sense of 'infinitely', 'a great deal', since the sixteenth century, but as clichés these seem to be from the twentieth century.

'The bells of the local Catholic church . . . rang at 10 minutes past three, and the population stopped what they were doing and observed a minute's silence. But Ulster and the Troubles were a world away and when the last solemn bell had rung, Ardmore returned to its easy everyday rhythm.' (*Independent*, 5 September 1998)

world class An expression adopted by politicians and the like from the world of sport, intended to be vaguely uplifting but imprecise, implying, but not stating, that whatever it is is of as good a quality as any in the world. 'World beating' is used in the same way. Compare BEST . . . IN THE WORLD.

'The deputy Prime Minister, John Prescott, promised "world-class government for a world-class city" yesterday when he published the Government's Bill to create a mayor and assembly for London.' (*Independent*, 4 December 1998)

do the world of good A set phrase, a cliché from the nineteenth century, using 'world' in the emphatic sense discussed at A WORLD AWAY.

'The Mall is doing the North-west the world of good. It's given councillors, businessmen and town centre managers the kick up the pants that they've deserved for years.' (*Independent*, 2 September 1998)

worm turns This is a shortened version of the proverb found variously as 'tread on a worm and it will turn' or 'even a worm will turn'. It has been used in English since at least the sixteenth century, but is now usually found in the shortened form to indicate someone who has been pushed too far and strikes back.

worms see CAN OF WORMS

worse than his bite see BARK WORSE THAN HIS BITE

worst of times see BEST OF TIMES

worth his salt The idea behind this expression goes back to Roman times, when the soldiers, just as today, were given their food and equipment as part of their wages. There was a special ration of that essential item salt, and at some point this was converted to a cash payment, a *salarium* ('money for salt'), which is the basis of our word 'salary'. As interest in and knowledge of philology grew in the nineteenth century some wit saw the connection and substituted 'salt' for salary, and a cliché was born.

'No businessman worth his salt would even consider taking over the club.' (*Daily Mail*, 27 August 1998)

worth the candle see GAME IS NOT WORTH THE CANDLE

he would, wouldn't he Although the expression was well established at the time, these words took on a new meaning, full of innuendo, in 1963, during the scandalous trial of Stephen Ward, charged with living off immoral earnings. Mandy Rice-Davies had supplied a list of men she had had relationships with, which included the name of Lord Astor. When asked in court, 'Do you know Lord Astor has made a statement to the police saying that these allegations of yours are absolutely untrue?' she replied 'He would, wouldn't he?' This was greeted with shocked delight at a time when such informal language in court came as a surprise, as did the offhand assumption that a Lord would lie, and the expression has been used in similar contexts ever since.

'Certainly Mr Clinton is making macho noises, but with his domestic situation he would, wouldn't he?' (*Evening Standard*, 7 October 1988)

would you believe (it)? An older, companion cliché to BELIEVE IT OR NOT, this has been in use since the eighteenth century and serves much the same role as a filler or as an expression of exasperation.

'The London marathon approaches, would you believe, and one of those who'll be taking part is Clive Guthrie from Bicester.' (Fox FM News)

wrack and ruin see RACK AND RUIN

wreak havoc 'Wreak' is an archaic term related to 'wreck' and the (w)rack of RACK AND RUIN. It has been used to mean to inflict (or do) something in vengeance since the end of the Middle Ages, but did not become common in this sense until the nineteenth century. The combination of the two words, used as an alternative to 'cause chaos', seems to date only from the twentieth century.

'Thousands of British holidaymakers were fleeing their resorts today as Hurricane Georges threatened to wreak havoc in Florida.' (*Evening Standard*, 24 September 1998)

the writing on the wall This is an allusion to the same passage in the book of Daniel that gives us WEIGHED IN THE BALANCE. King Belshazzar has profaned the sacred vessels of the Temple of Jerusalem by using them for his feast, and as a warning of the consequences of this impiety a hand appears and writes the words 'mene, mene, tekel, upharsin', on the wall, words which Daniel is called on to interpret. The scene is sometimes alluded to as the 'handwriting on the wall', and is the inspiration behind Edward Fitzgerald's much-quoted lines, 'The moving finger writes; and having writ,/Moves on' (*Rubáiyát of Omar Khayyám*, 1859).

'The writing's on the wall for offensive advertising posters.' (Headline, *Independent*, 23 September 1998)

'All hail the market. It is the moving finger which writes on the wall, and if you don't follow its dictates, then screw you.' (*Independent*, 15 October 1998)

wrong kind of snow An excuse once offered by British Rail when they found that their snow-clearing equipment could not clear the tracks, this has stuck in the national consciousness as the ultimate unconvincing or outrageous excuse. The train services have learnt nothing from it, for they have not dropped their 'the wrong kind of . . .' formula (rapidly turning into a formula phrase); Virgin trains recently excused opaque train windows as 'due to the wrong kind of dirt'.

'The PR geniuses who gave us "the wrong kind of snow" are in greater demand than ever in the privatised railway as worsening performance gave rise to the need for ever-more creative explanations.' (*Private Eye*, 18 September 1998)

'Following the pioneering work by British Rail (remember the wrong kind of snow) some of our most prominent captains of industry are churning out world-beating [excuses] faster than you can say: "The dog ate my homework, Sir."' (*Independent*, 27 July 1998)

wrong side of the bed There is an ancient superstition, going back to Roman times, that to get out of bed on the left hand side, or with the left foot first, is unlucky. However, to get out on the right side, or backwards, if done without premeditation, is lucky. Allusions to these beliefs are recorded in English from the sixteenth century, but as a cliché for being grumpy this dates from the nineteenth century.

X marks the spot A cliché from the earliest days of newspaper photography where the scene of the crime would be shown with an X to mark where the deed was done. It goes back even further in romantic accounts of such things as pirate treasure maps. The expression was being used jokingly by the 1920s, and now can be found as a formula phrase.

'Jack Schofield on how MIT's networking system is throwing open the windows. X marks the future.' (*Guardian*, 23 November 1989)

yawning gap (or **gulf**) The idea of a chasm being like the earth yawning goes back in English as far as King Alfred's translation of Orosius in the ninth century, and 'yawning gulf' is found in this sense in Edmund Spenser's *Faerie Queen* (1590). 'Yawning' was being used figuratively by the end of the eighteenth century, but these set phrases seem to date only from the twentieth century.

'A yawning gap exists in the supposed overlap of services between the home help and the nurse, which needs to be filled by a small army of "hands-on" carers.' (E. Murphy, *After the Asylums*, 1991)

years of age/years young The first is an unnecessarily long-winded way of stating someone's age, where just 'years' or 'years old' would do just as well. The second is a condescendingly facetious way of saying someone is old but fit and was a cliché by the 1960s.

'She had taken that step; and now she, at only 36 years of age, had to bring up her children alone, and help them in their turn to make that large and difficult step.' (Loranne S. Dorman and Clive L. Rawlins, *Leonard Cohen: Prophet of the Heart*, 1990)

'Our 84 years young Vice-President had the honour of being presented to Her Majesty The Queen.' (*Medau News*, 1985)

yesterday's men This was used as an election slogan by Labour to describe the Conservative Party, in the 1970s British general election (Labour lost). The Labour Party campaign featured grotesque caricatures of the leaders of the Conservatives over the slogan, and caused such an outcry that it had to be withdrawn; but the phrase lived on, used of anyone whose career was over. A possible inspiration for the slogan was a 1965 song written and performed by Chris Andrew called 'Yesterday Man'.

'Just five years ago, John Travolta was yesterday's man. The fame he'd won with *Saturday Night Fever* had long disappeared.' (*You* magazine, 20 September 1998)

you always hurt the one you love see HURT THE ONE YOU LOVE

you don't get many of those to the pound A highly colloquial and vulgar cliché of sexual innuendo, used to comment on a woman's large breasts. Finding dating evidence for this sort of expression is always difficult. It was certainly in use by the 1960s, but is unlikely to have been in use before the twentieth century.

you, me and the bedpost see BETWEEN YOU AND ME

young feller me lad A conscious cliché evoking the world of the Edwardian adventurer or the clubland hero, this is now used jokingly as encouragement or to create a STIFF UPPER LIP atmosphere.

your call A slangy expression for 'the decision is yours', 'it is up to you', this comes from the term used when bidding in the card game of bridge.

'Two years of adventure might give you the taste for more. Or you could just walk away and do something else. It's your call.' (Recruitment advertisement for the Royal Navy, August 1998)

you're history see HISTORY

you're telling me! see TELL ME ABOUT IT

your own see COME OF AGE

your own thing see DO YOUR OWN THING

Zeitgeist see MOOD OF THE MOMENT

zero hour Originally a military expression, dating from the First World War, for the time when soldiers were to go into action, this is now widely used to mean the time when something happens or must be ready.

'Similarly any prerecorded voices, sound effects and incidental music needed to be prepared and in the hands of the Grams Operator, in order of cueing, before zero hour on the big day.' (J. Bentham, *Doctor Who: The Early Years*, 1986)

PENGUIN ONLINE

READ MORE IN PENGUIN

In every corner of the world, on every subject under the sun, Penguin represents quality and variety – the very best in publishing today.

For complete information about books available from Penguin – including Puffins, Penguin Classics and Arkana – and how to order them, write to us at the appropriate address below. Please note that for copyright reasons the selection of books varies from country to country.

In the United Kingdom: Please write to *Dept. EP, Penguin Books Ltd, Bath Road, Harmondsworth, West Drayton, Middlesex UB7 0DA*

In the United States: Please write to *Consumer Services, Penguin Putnam Inc., 405 Murray Hill Parkway, East Rutherford, New Jersey 07073-2136.* VISA and MasterCard holders call 1-800-631-8571 to order Penguin titles

In Canada: Please write to *Penguin Books Canada Ltd, 10 Alcorn Avenue, Suite 300, Toronto, Ontario M4V 3B2*

In Australia: Please write to *Penguin Books Australia Ltd, 487 Maroondah Highway, Ringwood, Victoria 3134*

In New Zealand: Please write to *Penguin Books (NZ) Ltd, Private Bag 102902, North Shore Mail Centre, Auckland 10*

In India: Please write to *Penguin Books India Pvt Ltd, 11 Community Centre, Panchsheel Park, New Delhi 110017*

In the Netherlands: Please write to *Penguin Books Netherlands bv, Postbus 3507, NL-1001 AH Amsterdam*

In Germany: Please write to *Penguin Books Deutschland GmbH, Metzlerstrasse 26, 60594 Frankfurt am Main*

In Spain: Please write to *Penguin Books S. A., Bravo Murillo 19, 1°B, 28015 Madrid*

In Italy: Please write to *Penguin Italia s.r.l., Via Vittorio Emanuele 45/a, 20094 Corsico, Milano*

In France: Please write to *Penguin France, 12, Rue Prosper Ferradou, 31700 Blagnac*

In Japan: Please write to *Penguin Books Japan Ltd, Iidabashi KM-Bldg, 2-23-9 Koraku, Bunkyo-Ku, Tokyo 112-0004*

In South Africa: Please write to *Penguin Books South Africa (Pty) Ltd, P.O. Box 751093, Gardenview, 2047 Johannesburg*

READ MORE IN PENGUIN

POPULAR SCIENCE

How the Mind Works Steven Pinker

'Presented with extraordinary lucidity, cogency and panache ...
Powerful and gripping ... To have read [the book] is to have consulted
a first draft of the structural plan of the human psyche ... a glittering
tour de force' *Spectator*. 'Witty, lucid and ultimately enthralling'
Observer

At Home in the Universe Stuart Kauffman

Stuart Kauffman brilliantly weaves together the excitement of
intellectual discovery and a fertile mix of insights to give the general
reader a fascinating look at this new science – the science of complexity
– and at the forces for order that lie at the edge of chaos. 'Kauffman
shares his discovery with us, with lucidity, wit and cogent argument,
and we see his vision ... He is a pioneer' Roger Lewin

Stephen Hawking: A Life in Science
Michael White and John Gribbin

'A gripping account of a physicist whose speculations could prove as
revolutionary as those of Albert Einstein ... Its combination of
erudition, warmth, robustness and wit is entirely appropriate to their
subject' *New Statesman & Society*. 'Well-nigh unputdownable' *The
Times Educational Supplement*

Voyage of the *Beagle* Charles Darwin

The five-year voyage of the *Beagle* set in motion the intellectual
currents that culminated in the publication of *The Origin of Species*.
His journal, reprinted here in a shortened version, is vivid and
immediate, showing us a naturalist making patient observations,
above all in geology. The editors have provided an excellent
introduction and notes for this edition, which also contains maps and
appendices.

READ MORE IN PENGUIN

POPULAR SCIENCE

In Search of Nature Edward O. Wilson

A collection of essays of 'elegance, lucidity and breadth' *Independent*. 'A graceful, eloquent, playful and wise introduction to many of the subjects he has studied during his long and distinguished career in science' *The New York Times*

Clone Gina Kolata

'A thoughtful, engaging, interpretive and intelligent account ... I highly recommend it to all those with an interest in ... the new developments in cloning' *New Scientist*. 'Superb but unsettling' J. G. Ballard, *Sunday Times*

The Feminization of Nature Deborah Cadbury

Scientists around the world are uncovering alarming facts. There is strong evidence that sperm counts have fallen dramatically. Testicular and prostate cancer are on the increase. Different species are showing signs of 'feminization' or even 'changing sex'. 'Grips you from page one ... it reads like a Michael Crichton thriller' John Gribbin

Richard Feynman: A Life in Science John Gribbin and Mary Gribbin

'Richard Feynman (1918–88) was to the second half of the century what Einstein was to the first: the perfect example of scientific genius' *Independent*. 'One of the most influential and best-loved physicists of his generation ... This biography is both compelling and highly readable' *Mail on Sunday*

T. rex and the Crater of Doom Walter Alvarez

Walter Alvarez unfolds the quest for the answer to one of science's greatest mysteries – the cataclysmic impact on Earth which brought about the extinction of the dinosaurs. 'A scientific detective story par excellence, told with charm and candour' Niles Eldredge

READ MORE IN PENGUIN

PHILOSOPHY

Brainchildren Daniel C. Dennett

Philosophy of mind has been profoundly affected by this century's scientific advances, and thinking about thinking – how and why the mind works, its very existence – can seem baffling. Here eminent philosopher and cognitive scientist Daniel C. Dennett has provided an eloquent guide through some of the mental and moral mazes.

Language, Truth and Logic A. J. Ayer

The classic text which founded logical positivism and modern British philosophy, *Language, Truth and Logic* swept away the cobwebs and revitalized British philosophy.

The Penguin Dictionary of Philosophy Edited by Thomas Mautner

This dictionary encompasses all aspects of Western philosophy from 600 BC to the present day. With contributions from over a hundred leading philosophers, this dictionary will prove the ideal reference for any student or teacher of philosophy as well as for all those with a general interest in the subject.

Labyrinths of Reason William Poundstone

'The world and what is in it, even what people say to you, will not seem the same after plunging into *Labyrinths of Reason* ... holds up the deepest philosophical questions for scrutiny in a way that irresistibly sweeps readers on' *New Scientist*

Metaphysics as a Guide to Morals Iris Murdoch

'This is philosophy dragged from the cloister, dusted down and made freshly relevant to suffering and egoism, death and religious ecstasy ... and how we feel compassion for others' *Guardian*

Philosophy Football Mark Perryman

The amazing tale of a make-believe team, *Philosophy Football* is the story of what might have happened to the world's greatest thinkers if their brains had been in their boots instead of their heads ...

READ MORE IN PENGUIN

LITERARY CRITICISM

The Penguin History of Literature

Published in ten volumes, *The Penguin History of Literature* is a superb critical survey of the English and American literature covering fourteen centuries, from the Anglo-Saxons to the present, and written by some of the most distinguished academics in their fields.

New Bearings in English Poetry F. R. Leavis

'*New Bearings in English Poetry* was the first intelligent account of the work of Eliot, Pound and Gerard Manley Hopkins to appear in English and it significantly altered critical awareness . . . Leavis gave to literary criticism a thoroughness and respectability that has never since been equalled' Peter Ackroyd, *Spectator*. 'The most influential literary critic of modern times' *Financial Times*

The Uses of Literacy Richard Hoggart

Mass literacy has opened new worlds to new readers. How far has it also been exploited to debase standards and behaviour? 'A vivid inside view of working-class culture and one of the most influential books of the post-war era' *Observer*

Epistemology of the Closet Eve Kosofsky Sedgwick

Through her brilliant interpretation of the readings of Henry James, Melville, Nietzsche, Proust and Oscar Wilde, Eve Kosofsky Sedgwick shows how questions of sexual definition are at the heart of every form of representation in this century. 'A signal event in the history of late-twentieth-century gay studies' Wayne Koestenbaum

Dangerous Pilgrimages Malcolm Bradbury

'This capacious book tracks Henry James from New England to Rye; Evelyn Waugh to a Hollywood as grotesque as he expected; Gertrude Stein to Spain to be mistaken for a bishop; Oscar Wilde to a rickety stage in Leadsville, Colorado . . . The textbook on the the transatlantic theme' *Guardian*

READ MORE IN PENGUIN

LITERARY CRITICISM

The Practice of Writing David Lodge

This lively collection examines the work of authors ranging from the two Amises to Nabokov and Pinter; the links between private lives and published works; and the different techniques required in novels, stage plays and screenplays. 'These essays, so easy in manner, so well-built and informative, offer a fine blend of creative writing and criticism' *Sunday Times*

A Lover's Discourse Roland Barthes

'May be the most detailed, painstaking anatomy of desire we are ever likely to see or need again ... The book is an ecstatic celebration of love and language ... readers interested in either or both ... will enjoy savouring its rich and dark delights' *Washington Post*

The New Pelican Guide to English Literature Edited by Boris Ford

The indispensable critical guide to English and American literature in nine volumes, erudite yet accessible. From the ages of Chaucer and Shakespeare, via Georgian satirists and Victorian social critics, to the leading writers of the twentieth century, all literary life is here.

The Structure of Complex Words William Empson

'Twentieth-century England's greatest critic after T. S. Eliot, but whereas Eliot was the high priest, Empson was the *enfant terrible* ... *The Structure of Complex Words* is one of the linguistic masterpieces of the epoch, finding in the feel and tone of our speech whole sedimented social histories' *Guardian*

Vamps and Tramps Camille Paglia

'Paglia is a genuinely unconventional thinker ... Taken as a whole, the book gives an exceptionally interesting perspective on the last thirty years of intellectual life in America, and is, in its wacky way, a celebration of passion and the pursuit of truth' *Sunday Telegraph*

READ MORE IN PENGUIN

LANGUAGE/LINGUISTICS

Language Play David Crystal

We all use language to communicate information, but it is language play which is truly central to our lives. Full of puns, groan-worthy gags and witty repartee, this book restores the fun to the study of language. It also demonstrates why all these things are essential elements of what makes us human.

Swearing Geoffrey Hughes

'A deliciously filthy trawl among taboo words across the ages and the globe' *Observer*. 'Erudite and entertaining' Penelope Lively, *Daily Telegraph*

The Language Instinct Stephen Pinker

'Dazzling . . . Pinker's big idea is that language is an instinct, as innate to us as flying is to geese . . . Words can hardly do justice to the superlative range and liveliness of Pinker's investigations' *Independent*. 'He does for language what David Attenborough does for animals, explaining difficult scientific concepts so easily that they are indeed absorbed as a transparent stream of words' John Gribbin

Mother Tongue Bill Bryson

'A delightful, amusing and provoking survey, a joyful celebration of our wonderful language, which is packed with curiosities and enlightenment on every page' *Sunday Express*. 'A gold mine of language-anecdote. A surprise on every page . . . enthralling' *Observer*

Longman Guide to English Usage
Sidney Greenbaum and Janet Whitcut

Containing 5000 entries compiled by leading authorities on modern English, this invaluable reference work clarifies every kind of usage problem, giving expert advice on points of grammar, meaning, style, spelling, pronunciation and punctuation.

READ MORE IN PENGUIN

The Penguin Dictionary of the Third Reich
James Taylor and Warren Shaw

This dictionary provides a full background to the rise of Nazism and the role of Germany in the Second World War. Among the areas covered are the major figures from Nazi politics, arts and industry, the German Resistance, the politics of race and the Nuremberg trials.

The Penguin Biographical Dictionary of Women

This stimulating, informative and entirely new Penguin dictionary of women from all over the world, through the ages, contains over 1,600 clear and concise biographies on major figures from politicians, saints and scientists to poets, film stars and writers.

Roget's Thesaurus of English Words and Phrases
Edited by Betty Kirkpatrick

This new edition of Roget's classic work, now brought up to date for the nineties, will increase anyone's command of the English language. Fully cross-referenced, it includes synonyms of every kind (formal or colloquial, idiomatic and figurative) for almost 900 headings. It is a must for writers and utterly fascinating for any English speaker.

The Penguin Dictionary of International Relations
Graham Evans and Jeffrey Newnham

International relations have undergone a revolution since the end of the Cold War. This new world disorder is fully reflected in this new Penguin dictionary, which is extensively cross-referenced with a select bibliography to aid further study.

The Penguin Guide to Synonyms and Related Words
S. I. Hayakawa

'More helpful than a thesaurus, more humane than a dictionary, the *Guide to Synonyms and Related Words* maps linguistic boundaries with precision, sensitivity to nuance and, on occasion, dry wit' *The Times Literary Supplement*

READ MORE IN PENGUIN

REFERENCE

The Penguin Dictionary of Troublesome Words Bill Bryson

Why should you avoid discussing the *weather conditions*? Can a married woman be celibate? Why is it eccentric to talk about the aroma of a cowshed? A straightforward guide to the pitfalls and hotly disputed issues in standard written English.

Swearing Geoffrey Hughes

'A deliciously filthy trawl among taboo words across the ages and the globe' Valentine Cunningham, *Observer*, Books of the Year. 'Erudite and entertaining' Penelope Lively, *Daily Telegraph*, Books of the Year.

Medicines: A Guide for Everybody Peter Parish

Now in its seventh edition and completely revised and updated, this bestselling guide is written in ordinary language for the ordinary reader yet will prove indispensable to anyone involved in health care: nurses, pharmacists, opticians, social workers and doctors.

Media Law Geoffrey Robertson QC and Andrew Nichol

Crisp and authoritative surveys explain the up-to-date position on defamation, obscenity, official secrecy, copyright and confidentiality, contempt of court, the protection of privacy and much more.

The Penguin Careers Guide
Anna Alston and Anne Daniel; Consultant Editor: Ruth Miller

As the concept of a 'job for life' wanes, this guide encourages you to think broadly about occupational areas as well as describing day-to-day work and detailing the latest developments and qualifications such as NVQs. Special features include possibilities for working part-time and job-sharing, returning to work after a break and an assessment of the current position of women.

READ MORE IN PENGUIN

DICTIONARIES

Abbreviations
Ancient History
Archaeology
Architecture
Art and Artists
Astronomy
Biographical Dictionary of
  Women
Biology
Botany
Building
Business
Challenging Words
Chemistry
Civil Engineering
Classical Mythology
Computers
Contemporary American History
Curious and Interesting Geometry
Curious and Interesting Numbers
Curious and Interesting Words
Design and Designers
Economics
Eighteenth-Century History
Electronics
English and European History
English Idioms
Foreign Terms and Phrases
French
Geography
Geology
German
Historical Slang
Human Geography
Information Technology

International Finance
International Relations
Literary Terms and Literary
  Theory
Mathematics
Modern History 1789–1945
Modern Quotations
Music
Musical Performers
Nineteenth-Century World
  History
Philosophy
Physical Geography
Physics
Politics
Proverbs
Psychology
Quotations
Quotations from Shakespeare
Religions
Rhyming Dictionary
Russian
Saints
Science
Sociology
Spanish
Surnames
Symbols
Synonyms and Antonyms
Telecommunications
Theatre
The Third Reich
Third World Terms
Troublesome Words
Twentieth-Century History
Twentieth-Century Quotations